EXPLORING THE NEW TESTAMENT

Exploring
the
New Testament

Ralph Earle, Th.D., editor

Harvey J. S. Blaney, S.T.M.

Carl Hanson, Th.D.

BEACON HILL PRESS OF KANSAS CITY
Kansas City, Mo.

ISBN: 0-8341-0006-1

Printed in the United States of America

30   29   28   27   26   25   24   23

PREFACE

The present volume has been prepared as a text for the required course in New Testament survey for lower division students in college. Hence the editor and his associated writers have not incorporated a discussion of critical questions. In line with this policy, footnotes have been kept to a minimum. It was felt that such materials more properly belonged to the field of New Testament introduction, which is taught at the upper division and graduate levels.

Since this is primarily a book for study rather than devotional use, the American Standard Edition of the Revised Version has been used as the basic text. Quotations from other versions are so indicated. While the King James Version still reigns supreme for devotional reading of the Bible, conservative teachers in colleges and Bible schools have long used the American Revised Version as the textbook in their classes. It is universally recognized as a more literal, accurate translation of the original languages.

The Pauline Epistles have been treated in their probable chronological order, and the same has been done with the General Epistles. It was felt that the Epistles cannot be understood properly except as they are placed in their historical setting.

The preparation of this volume has been truly a team effort in which the work of each writer was open to study and suggestion by the others. However, the pilot writing of various chapters was assigned specifically as follows: Dr. Blaney, Chapters I, VII, XI—XII, XV—XVI; Dr. Earle, Chapters III, VIII—X, XIII—XIV; and Dr. Hanson, Chapters II, IV—VI. The entire final manuscript was read and approved by each member of the writing group.

This book is sent forth with the prayer that it may help many to find "a straight course in the word of truth" (II Tim. 2:15). It has been the desire of the writers to make the picture of Christ in the pages of the New Testament more clear to the readers.

RALPH EARLE, *Nazarene Theological Seminary, editor*
HARVEY J. S. BLANEY, *Eastern Nazarene College*
CARL HANSON, *Northwest Nazarene College*

ACKNOWLEDGMENTS

We should like to express appreciation to the following publishers for permission to quote from the books indicated:

The Westminster Press: *Our English Bible in the Making,* by George G. May

Harper and Brothers: *The Apostolic Fathers,* by Edgar Goodspeed

Abingdon Press: *The Interpreter's Bible*

Wm. B. Eerdmans: *The New Testament,* by Merrill C. Tenney

Fleming H. Revell: *The Corinthian Letters of Paul,* by G. Campbell Morgan

TABLE OF CONTENTS

ABBREVIATIONS

A.R.V.—American Revised Version (1901)

K.J.V.—King James Version (1611)

R.S.V.—Revised Standard Version (1946)

R.V.—A.R.V. + R.S.V.

LXX—Septuagint
ca.—about
c.—chapter
cc.—chapters
v.—verse
vv.—verses

CHAPTER I

WHY STUDY THE NEW TESTAMENT?

THE WORD OF GOD

The Bible is the unique and sufficient revelation of God to man, although there are other sources of divine knowledge (Rom. 1:19-20). The Church has not always agreed as to what books should be included in the canon of the Scriptures. The Catholic church includes the Apocrypha besides the sixty-six books in the Protestant Bible. No originals are preserved, and scholars are still laboring diligently to ascertain as accurately as possible what the originals contained. It is encouraging to know that the changes brought about by the latest scholarship are of a minor nature, and we can be confident that the New Testament as we have it is essentially the same as the originals.

All Biblical documents available today are either copies or translations. Copies often suffer by the carelessness of the copyist, and translations suffer from the difficulty of reproducing exact thoughts from one language to another. One's idea of the inspiration of the Scriptures must be such as to include the Bible as it is available to him. A theory of inspiration which can be applied only to the originals puts God in the rather awkward position of inspiring a Book which He has withheld from man except in imperfect forms. The amount of imperfection, then, becomes a matter of very grave concern. The perfection of the Scriptures must be seen in the message which they convey rather than in the form in which they are cast.

The Bible may be considered the Word of God in the same way that Jesus is the Son of God, called by John the Word. Jesus is the Word of God incarnate in human nature; the Bible is the Word of God incarnate in human literature. The recognition of certain human limitations in Jesus, such as becoming hungry and weary (John 4:6), learning things as a growing boy (Luke 2:52), and lacking complete intuitive knowledge in some situations (John 11:34), does not detract from His claim to deity. The Incarnation means that He who was truly God became also truly man. And therein lies the glory of Jesus as

9

the Saviour of the world. A saviour who does not demonstrate both of these natures in real form is not the Saviour portrayed in the New Testament. When He walked the shores of Galilee and the hills of Judea, He lived under the same conditions and limitations as other men of His day. He was not a privileged person, living by His power to work miracles. When He hung on the cross, He had to endure all the sufferings of any man thus killed, though He was also God. The crowd was unable to distinguish Him from a common thief.

In like manner the Scriptures demonstrate both the human and the divine elements. They are the Word of God, but they are clothed in human form. Rather than being just so many words and books of truth which God gave to man in finished form, they are literature which has emerged from the very matrix of human life and experience. They were conceived of God and brought forth from the lives of men of old in the form of literature of various kinds. There are history, law, poetry, prophecy, Gospel, Epistle, and Apocalypse. These make up the various parts of the human vehicle in which the eternal Word of God is incarnate.

There have been men of every age who have been unable to distinguish the Bible from other literature. But, as with those who failed to recognize Jesus as the Son of God, not the Word but the unbelievers have suffered. They have burned the Book as well as crucified the Christ. But men's hammers have broken while God's anvil still stands.

There may be some advantage in comparing the Bible with other literature and in showing it to be superior, but one might question whether the comparison can be sustained at every point. Such superiority could have much the same effect as showing Jesus to have been a superman. The divine element is not enhanced by elevating the human element above its true status. True merit is found in the proper recognition of both the divine and the human.

There is history in the Bible—human history. But it is history plus God—the history of the affairs of men and of God's dealings with those men. There is law, and God is the Lawmaker. There is prophecy, but the prophets gave forth the "Thus saith the Lord." There are Gospels, but only because of Him who gave the gospel. There is Apocalypse, but the forces are spiritual as well as material, and God determines the outcome.

The Christology of the Church through the centuries has swung back and forth from the emphasis upon Christ's deity at the expense of His humanity to the opposite emphasis upon His humanity at the expense of His deity. Somewhat of the same can be observed concerning the Bible. Those who comprehend only the fact that it is a divinely inspired Book may overargue the case. A discrepancy in figures or narratives is either ignored, or denied, on the grounds that we do not have all the facts. On the other hand, those who recognize only the human element of the Bible easily become absorbed in its history and literature, and by secular standards honor it where it stands and crucify it where, in their judgment, it fails. The first, by an unreasoned faith, and the second, by a faithless rationalism, fail to see the Bible for what it is—the Word of God incarnate in human literature. When viewed in this way, its glory rests not only in the fact that God has spoken, but that His word has been given a human form.

What do we mean by the inspiration of the Scriptures? Wiley defines it as follows:

> By inspiration we mean the actuating energy of the Holy Spirit through which holy men were qualified to receive religious truth, and to communicate it to others without error.[1]

BIBLE STUDY

Bible study begins with Bible reading. To say that a Christian will automatically love to read and study the Bible is an over-exaggerated statement. He will desire to know the truths it contains—but some people just do not like to read. It is also true that some who otherwise read prolifically do very little Bible reading. Even in college classes it is easier to get students to read books about the Bible than to read the Bible.

One reason for this may well be the format of the average Bible. Two columns, fine print, very thin paper, and a flexible cover make the average Bible so different from most other books that it does not fit the pattern of reading that people have developed. These same features are found in newspapers

[1] H. Orton Wiley, *Christian Theology* (Kansas City: Beacon Hill Press, 1941), I, 169.

and periodicals, which are of temporary interest, and in encyclopedias and reference works. But the Bible is of permanent value and use and is much more than a reference book. It is a Book to be read and reread and studied. The continued use of a limp-cover volume, with fine print and with pages which tend to cling to each other, is not conducive to long periods of study. A study Bible should be one with reasonably large print, a hard cover, and paper sufficiently heavy so that one can write comments on it.

Another reason for the general lack of Bible reading may be the chapter and verse divisions. They are helpful for reference, but they make the Bible appear as a book of proverbs, or a string of beautiful beads, or, when one reads it, like a corrugated road over which one is traveling. Those divisions were not in the minds of the authors when they wrote. The chapter divisions were made early in the thirteenth century and the verse divisions in the sixteenth century. The habit of good people reading the Bible by starting almost anywhere and stopping anywhere is unfortunate. It is true that many a gem of truth can be found in a verse of scripture, and that in the books of Proverbs and Psalms and in some of Jesus' teachings the whole body of material is phrased in short, concise expressions. But for the historical and prophetic books and the Epistles each verse and statement must be considered in the light of the entire context. One might say that reading one or two disconnected verses from the Bible is worth more than reading several pages of anything else. But that is condemning the Good Book with faint praise. It should be a source of great concern that the Bible is often read less intelligently than other books.

But after we have excused all of our bad habits connected with the use of the Bible, it is finally one's own responsibility to find ways of becoming more and better acquainted with this Book of books. Let us not equivocate before any advancement, even in the form of new editions and translations of the Scriptures, if they help to make the Word of God more easily accessible and more readily understood.

REASONS FOR READING THE BIBLE

First, the life of the Christian must be Bible-centered. His authority and standard for living is the Bible, correctly understood. Second, the Bible is God's message to man, and it still speaks to our day. Because it goes to the very center of life and speaks to the inner nature of man, it is continually contemporary. Third, the Bible reveals Christ as the Saviour of the world. To neglect the Word is to be ignorant of the Christ. Fourth, the Bible speaks directly to the individual. By it one is checked on his attitudes and behavior. It makes its appeal to the moral and volitional nature of man. Fifth, it should be read because of the elevated place it holds as the greatest religious literary writing of the world. To neglect it is to neglect—and therefore fail to understand—the Christian religion.

How to Read the Bible

First, the Bible should be read systematically. Random selections may prove profitable for devotions and pleasure, but each separate book must be read through if one is to understand the meaning of the author. Second, it should be read thoughtfully. While some truths lie in plain view, the choicest gems lie hidden beneath the surface. Surface truths make surface Christians. Third, it should be read prayerfully. The help of the Holy Spirit is essential to profitable Bible reading. Fourth, it should be read recreationally; that is, as good literature for the pure enjoyment of reading it—this library of masterpieces. Fifth, it should be read devotionally. Linger over it; soak it up; let it speak to you; store it up in your heart and mind. Let it throw its light upon the problems and tasks of life, and it will help you to see things from God's point of view and keep you steady in the midst of the rush and pressures of life.

How to Study the Bible

The proof-text method has its merits—the method of gathering verses or portions of verses which seem to bear upon a subject. This, however, can very easily become the bane of Bible study, because many passages when taken in context have a very different meaning from what they have when taken by themselves. Each book of this library should be studied as a unit. One should seek to find the purpose of the author for writing and the general pattern of what he is saying. Only then can one properly understand what specific passages mean. One must generalize before he can particu-

larize. One is ready to begin his interpretation of a book of
the Bible only after he is able to put into a few sentences
the central thesis of the author.

Another important factor in Bible study is to recognize
first of all the different types of literature which comprise it.
Prose must be recognized as prose and poetry as poetry and
each studied as becomes its style of expression. History and
drama must be recognized for what they are and be interpreted accordingly. Symbolism must be distinguished from
factual statement, lest the Bible be made to say things never
meant by either God or the writers.

G. Campbell Morgan[2] gives the fundamental processes of
Bible study under the two headings of activity and results.
First, survey, which means reading, and results in impression.
Second, condense, which means thinking, and results in outline.
Third, expand, which means work, and results in analysis.
Fourth, dissect, which means sweat, and results in knowledge.

Our plea is for a more intelligent approach to Bible study.
Science and literature and history must be studied diligently
and under guidance in order to be mastered. Why should the
Bible be treated less seriously? Why should anyone think that
his own intuitive insight is sufficient to learn its secrets or that
his own short lifetime is sufficient to fathom its truths? Why
should it be thought that the last few minutes before turning
off one's light at the close of the day is the best time for reading
the Bible? One should bring to it the best possible helps and
methods of study, an earnestness of mind, and a reverent attitude of reliance upon the Spirit of God for illumination. The
results will fully reward the effort.

A WORD TO COLLEGE STUDENTS

Some type of course in religion is standard in the lower
division curriculum of most colleges today. In Christian colleges a survey course in both the Old and New Testaments is
required. And for those who choose either to major or to
minor in Biblical literature the courses are graduated from
these general courses up to the specialized exegesis of particular books with the aid (in New Testament) of the original
Greek.

[2] "How to Study and How to Teach the Bible," *The System Bible
Study* (Chicago: The System Bible Company, 1922), pp. 696-700.

Every college student should be as well informed on the Bible as possible, and while in school he should choose some of his electives from the courses in Biblical literature. They will provide him with valuable material in his church and Sunday-school work in later years.

Let us emphasize the fact that primary attention should be given to the reading of the Bible itself. What someone else has said about it becomes important only after one has read the Bible for himself. All Bible study should be done with the Scriptures open for constant reference. Reading and re-reading are necessary to any proper understanding of what the Bible says. The study of the present volume is by no means intended to be a substitute for reading the Book of books.

One's Bible study in college should be done with a view to continued study afterward. Certain principles of study should be gained along with an incentive to learn more and more of the Word of God as revealed in its holy pages. Unless some such motivation has been gained, one can count his study of the Bible in college as worth the *A* or the *D* which he received—and little more.

One excellent product of Bible study in college is the acquaintance one gains with different books and authors. This acquaintance with the names of authors who have been well recommended or whose works have been found personally profitable is a wonderful aid in choosing books and in building up one's own library. The brief bibliography included in this volume is offered as reliable, although very far from exhaustive.

The suggestions offered here are particularly important for the student who plans on entering the ministry or some other branch of active Christian service. If one plans to attend a seminary after graduation from college, he will, of course, do most of his specialized work in Biblical literature and theology there. Some will choose to major in religion in college. Whatever the case, one's chief concern should be to know the Scriptures better. A minister without an avid yearning for the Word of God, and without knowing how to study it fruitfully and interpret it sanely, is like a physician with no interest in his medical books. It is safe to say that our generation is in need of a well-educated, Bible-centered, God-anointed ministry and a reverent, well-informed laity. The educational institutions of evangelical churches maintain this as one of their goals—"that the man of God may be complete, furnished completely unto every good work" (II Tim. 3:17).

CHAPTER II

THE WORLD INTO WHICH THE NEW TESTAMENT CAME

A. The Jews in Palestine Until a.d. 70

I. Independence Won and Lost

1. From the Return to the Revolt (538-168 b.c.)

The fall and destruction of Jerusalem (586 b.c.) was followed by the return from Babylonian exile after Cyrus issued his famous decree (539). After some initial discouragements, those who returned from exile, inspired by the preaching of Haggai and Zechariah, rebuilt the Temple, which was dedicated in 516 or 515 b.c.

The silence is broken next by the preaching of Malachi, and the reforms of Ezra (458?) and Nehemiah (445 or 444). Little definite information is available for the period between Nehemiah and the Greek period, which begins with the conquests of Alexander the Great, the son and successor of Philip of Macedon and brilliant pupil of Aristotle.

After a rapid succession of victories Alexander became master of the eastern Mediterranean area; crushing the residue of the army of Darius III at Gaugamela, he moved on to India. However, he did not live to execute his plan to unite the world into one great brotherhood with a predominantly Greek culture.

Following Alexander's death (323 b.c.) civil war broke out among his generals for the control of the empire. Seleucus regained control of Babylon and established the Seleucid dynasty, the headquarters of which were subsequently moved to Syria. A little later Ptolemy I Lagos founded in Egypt the other dynasty that figures prominently in Jewish affairs in this period. Eventually Egypt gained control of Palestine (*ca.* 301 b.c.), which it held for slightly more than a century. Control then passed from the "king of the south" to the "king of the north"—the Seleucid dynasty.

Shortly after Syria annexed Palestine (*ca.* 200 b.c.) Antiochus IV, called Epiphanes, became king. As a result of Jewish unrest and the frustration of his plans by Rome, he added to the insult of Temple looting the massacre of many of the

17

citizens of Jerusalem, the selling into slavery of her women and children, and the burning of the city. However, his fury was not satisfied; so he decided to root out the cause of Jewish opposition to his policies. He would outlaw Judaism and force Hellenism on the Jews. Accordingly he commanded all offerings and sacrifices to Jehovah to cease. Sabbath observance was prohibited, and death was the penalty for the mere possession of the Torah or the performance of circumcision. The Temple at Jerusalem was defiled and made a shrine of the Olympian Zeus, to whom a small altar was erected on the top of the altar of burnt offering. This was called "the abomination that maketh desolate" in Daniel (11:31; 12:11) and I Maccabees (1:54). Ten days later (December 25, 168 B.C.) on the altar a sacrifice of swine prefaced the smearing of unclean blood in the Temple, while soldiers committed indecent acts in the sacred enclosure. Heathen altars were erected in various places throughout the land on which the Jews were commanded to sacrifice swine.

The Jewish reaction was mixed. Evidently some welcomed the change and others complied through fear. The Hasidim ("holy or pious ones") at first offered only passive resistance and continued to obey the Mosaic law secretly, risking their lives lest they violate even the most insignificant dietary regulation. Many died as martyrs. Others decided to contend for their faith with swords and spears.

2. The Maccabean Revolt (168-142 B.C.)

The first open opposition to the agents of Antiochus occurred at Modin (or Modein), northeast of the Beth-horons near the edge of the coastal plain. At this peaceful village Appelles, the king's officer, appeared with promises of royal favor to Mattathias, a retired, aged priest, on condition that he would sacrifice a pig on the altar to the gods of Greece. Mattathias refused to comply. When a degenerate Jew stepped forward to carry out the king's command, Mattathias killed the Jew and then the king's officer.

Together with his five sons Mattathias fled to the hills. Faithful Jews rallied to his standard. The Hasidim, who by principle opposed the use of such human devices as military arms or diplomatic maneuvers and preferred to rely entirely on divine aid, were now by the pressure of circumstances driven to adopt these human devices. After about a thousand of their number had been massacred on the Sabbath, they decided that defensive warfare on the Sabbath was justifiable. Nor was their campaign confined exclusively to military issues. They would suddenly spring from their mountain retreats of northern Judea and destroy all evidences of apostasy and heathenism that they could find, both personal and impersonal (I Macc. 2:19-48).

On his deathbed, Mattathias selected his son Judas Maccabeus[1] as his successor. The record of Judas' exploits against almost insurmountable odds makes fascinating reading. By his heroic example he inspired his followers to acts of bravery —bravery encouraged, too, by the fact that many of these men were fighting for principle, for the faith of their fathers, and for their very lives. With an uncanny skill he manipulated his relatively small forces so that the rough terrain of the region near Jerusalem was always to his advantage. By surprise tactics and by anticipating the moves of his foes he was able to win victories against overwhelming odds.

After decisively defeating Lysias, Judas gained control of the Temple. Exactly three years after its desecration, the smoke of sacrifice rose to Jehovah from a newly constructed altar in a recleansed Temple. This event is celebrated in the annual Feast of Lights or Feast of Dedication (John 10:22).

After several significant victories in which Judas consolidated his gains, the Hasidim, who saw that Judas and his followers were now fighting for political goals, deserted. Fighting against impossible odds, Judas fell and his army suffered a disastrous defeat at Elasa in 161 B.C. So died the greatest military genius Judaism ever produced.

Jonathan, who succeeded his brother Judas, was a commander without an army and without adequate popular support. Operating as a freebooter, he consolidated his power and waited for his opportunity, which came as a result of civil war in Syria. By clever strategy Jonathan gained concessions from all contenders until in addition to the high priesthood he was civil and military commander of Judea and parts of Samaria, and his brother Simon was military commander of the region between the Lebanons and Egypt.

---

[1] Maccabeus is usually interpreted to mean "hammerer." It is from this nickname that the five brothers are commonly known as the Maccabees.

Succumbing to the treachery of Trypho, one of the Syrian contenders, Jonathan was captured and later killed. Simon, the remaining son of Mattathias, was enthusiastically elected as leader (143 B.C.), but the cause of the Jews appeared hopeless. However, by demanding complete independence of Demetrius II, another contender for the Syrian throne, Simon scored a victory for the Jews. The surrender of the Acra (May, 142 B.C.), a fortress on a hill south of the Temple which had been garrisoned with Syrian soldiers, was a happy event celebrated annually until well into the Christian era. Jews began to date their documents according to the year of Simon.

3. The Hasmonean Dynasty (142-63 B.C.)

The only political independence enjoyed by the Jews from the Babylonian captivity until recent times (1948) belongs to this period which came to such an unhappy end. In 141 B.C. by popular vote the grateful Jews acclaimed Simon as military commander, civil governor, and high priest, the offices being hereditary until a faithful prophet should appear who would direct otherwise. Simon's career was cut short when he fell into the hands of his treacherous son-in-law, Ptolemy, the governor of Jericho, who killed Simon and two of his sons (135 B.C.).

A third son, John Hyrcanus, escaped and became high priest. After initial reverses he took advantage of the struggle for the Syrian throne to enlarge his domains. After victories in Transjordan he subdued the Samaritans, destroying their temple at Mount Gerizim. Then he forced the Idumaeans to accept circumcision or deportation. Ironically, from these subjugated Idumaeans came the rulers who succeeded the Hasmoneans. The most powerful, most capable, and most hated of the Jewish kings, Herod the Great, was an Idumaean. During the latter part of Hyrcanus' thirty-one-year reign, Judea enjoyed the peak of her prosperity. However, the emergence of the two great religious sects of Judaism, the Pharisees and Sadducees, is probably the most significant event in his reign.

After the brief reign of Aristobulus I, the oldest son of Hyrcanus, Alexander Janneus, or Jonathan, became high priest and king. This cruel, ambitious warrior attempted to complete the conquest that his father had begun, but almost lost the kingdom in the attempt. In a civil war his opponents enlisted the aid of Syria, and Janneus was saved only by the last-minute desertion of some of his former Jewish foes from the Syrian ranks and their enlistment in his own. In the wake of his victory Janneus introduced the Roman cross on the Judean hills by crucifying 800 of the leaders of the revolt. As a result of successful campaigns near the close of his career he left to his widow, Alexandra, a domain that, with the possible exception of the coastal cities, extended from the Mediterranean Sea to the desert and from the Lebanon Mountains to Egypt.

Because of her wise policies and the aid of Rome in curbing the ambition of Tigranes of Armenia, Alexandra (76-67) was able to control the domains she inherited.

The Pharisees, who had been suppressed during the latter part of Hyrcanus' reign and during the reigns of his successors, now enjoyed royal patronage. Scribes were added to the local Jerusalem council, which was given more authority, and her Pharisaic brother, Simon Ben Shetach, became her adviser. Thus the Pharisees of later days could look back on Alexandra's reign as the golden age of Pharisaism.

Alexandra's fatal illness provided the opportunity for Aristobulus, her ambitious second son, to defeat Hyrcanus, the legitimate heir to the high priesthood and throne, and seize these prizes for himself. Hyrcanus, who was permitted to retire to private life, would probably have faded out of the political picture had it not been for Antipater, the Idumaean. The wily Antipater, father of Herod the Great, succeeded in inducing Hyrcanus to enlist the aid of the Nabatean king, Aretas. At this juncture Aristobulus was saved from certain defeat only by the action of Scaurus, the Roman legate, who ordered Aretas home.

When Pompey arrived in Damascus early in 63 B.C. he was met by three delegations of Jews. In addition to groups favoring each of the brothers was the Pharisaic delegation, which requested that the rule should revert to the high priest and senate. Eventually Pompey sided with Hyrcanus. After Pompey had taken Aristobulus prisoner, the remaining resistance was crushed when the wall of the Temple was breached on the Day of Atonement (October), 63 B.C. Out of curiosity, Pompey entered the holy of holies and was amazed to find there no visible object of worship. He then ordered the cleansing of the Temple and the continuance of its services, which had not been interrupted even during the siege.

Aristobulus and his sons were taken to Rome to embellish Pompey's triumph. Many other Jews, taken to Rome at this time as slaves, after gaining their freedom became the nucleus of a flourishing colony. All non-Jewish cities taken by the Hasmoneans, including towns in Transjordan, harbors on the Mediterranean coast, and such cities as Samaria and Scythopolis, were removed from Jewish control and restrictions. Hyrcanus, who was made high priest and ethnarch of Judea, was accountable to the governor of Syria. The political independence of the Jews was at an end.

II. Under the Roman Eagle

1. Herod the Great (37-4 B.C.)

The name Herod at once brings to our minds the name of One whose name is above every name, for it was "in the days of Herod the king" that "Jesus was born in Bethlehem of Judaea" (Matt. 2:1). Even apart from the connection of Herod's name with the central event in the world's history—the Incarnation—Herod's character and life are of interest.

Because he considered correctly that loyalty to Rome's interests was loyalty to Herod's also, his fidelity to Rome never wavered. In the fluctuating fortunes that attended the civil strife at Rome it was not easy to forecast the outcome. Whenever Herod found that he had been championing a losing contender he quickly offered his services and loyalty to the victor and was always rewarded for doing so.

The Roman senate conferred upon Herod the title "king of the Jews" but he was a king without a kingdom. Because the limited Roman reinforcements sent to aid Herod had responded to bribes offered by Antigonus, Herod's effective control of Palestine did not begin until three years later (37 B.C.).

Herod married Mariamne, granddaughter of Hyrcanus II, who was of the royal Hasmonean line. Dismissing his first wife, Doris, and her son, Antipater, Herod lavished his passionate affection on Mariamne. But at last after she learned of his two jealous plots to have her killed in case he failed to return from dangerous missions, and after she knew that Herod had engineered the deaths of her brother and grandfather, Mariamne became coldly reproachful. Salome, Herod's sister, who hated Mariamne because the latter's contempt for "the Idumaean woman" was thinly veiled, had on a previous occasion charged Mariamne with adultery. Now she bribed Herod's cupbearer to say that Mariamne had attempted to poison the king. Herod had Mariamne executed (29 B.C.), an act which soon plunged him into melancholy.

Herod was a great builder and promoter of Graeco-Roman civilization. He beautified Samaria, renamed it Sebaste in honor of Augustus (Greek, *Sebastos*), and erected in it a beautiful temple to the divine Augustus. To facilitate and encourage the celebration of games in Augustus' honor he built stadia, hippodromes, amphitheaters, and theaters. In Jerusalem he built, besides a theater, a royal palace and the Tower of Antonia, which overlooked the Temple area. One of his greater achievements was the building of a city on the site of Strato's Tower which he named Caesarea in honor of Caesar. Using heavy stones to create a breakwater, Herod constructed a splendid harbor. He was twelve years in building the city which became the capital of the procurators and was then the most important city of Judea. In addition to these projects he erected citadels at strategic points and built and named other cities in honor of his friends and relatives.

By far the greatest achievement of Herod's reign from an architectural standpoint was his rebuilding of the Temple. Although opposed by suspicious subjects who thought he was using treachery to get the old Temple destroyed, Herod took precautions to allay their fears, even training priests to do the work of masons and carpenters, so that only consecrated people would set foot on the holy ground. The main building, begun in 20 B.C., was completed in about eighteen months but the outer courts were not completed until A.D. 62-64—just a few years before the Temple was destroyed in A.D. 70. Herod's Temple of white marble, much of it overlaid with gold, surpassed in beauty and grandeur Solomon's Temple as much as Solomon's Temple exceeded that of Zerubbabel. His architectural taste and accomplishments and ability to keep the peace endeared Herod to Augustus.

His own family life, especially after the death of Mariamne, deteriorated increasingly. Living with nine wives and even the families of their offspring under the roof of the palace was difficult enough for Herod. But his sister Salome con-

tinued to feed his suspicions with fabrication and fact until
Herod was led to kill three of his sons, the last of them, Antipater, only five days before he himself died.

2. Herod's Successors

a. *Archelaus* (4 B.C.—A.D. 6). According to the terms of
Herod's last will three of his sons were to share the kingdom.
Antipas and Philip were given domains with the title of eth-
narch; to Archelaus went the control of Judea, Samaria, and
Idumea with the title of king.

Crushing by force a riot during the Passover season, Archelaus hastened to Rome for confirmation of his title as king.
In spite of vigorous opposition to his appointment by an em-
bassy from Jerusalem, Augustus confirmed his territorial domain but gave him only the title of ethnarch until he should
prove himself worthy of the title king. This incident seems
to be the background of Luke 19:12.

Archelaus succeeded in scandalizing his subjects by ar-
bitrarily removing and appointing the high priests and by
marrying a widow, Glaphyra, who had three sons by a previous
marriage—an act which was forbidden by Mosaic law. A
reckless despot, he was thoroughly hated by his subjects, a
delegation of whom complained to Augustus and succeeded in
securing his ouster and exile to Vienna in Gaul (A.D. 6). The
fears of Joseph and Mary which led them to settle out of the
domains of Archelaus were thus not without foundation
(Matt. 2:22).

b. *Herod Antipas* (4 B.C.—A.D. 39). Antipas had been appointed tetrarch of Galilee and Perea in the terms of Herod's
last will. The southern boundary of the region known as Galilee extended from the end of Mount Carmel to a point on the
Jordan River just north of Scythopolis. The Jordan River
formed its eastern border together with the Lake of Galilee.
Perea was east of the Jordan.

Sepphoris, only an hour's walk from Nazareth, Antipas
rebuilt and made his capital. Doubtless Jesus watched this
project, which was begun about A.D. 6. He also rebuilt Tiberias
(A.D. 26-27) on the heights above the southwest shore of the
Sea of Galilee. This city with its Greek organization, stadium,
and colonnaded streets became a Hellenistic center and displaced Sepphoris as Herod Antipas' capital.

Antipas, it will be remembered, married his brother Philip's wife, Herodias, which brought him into conflict with John the Baptist, whom he imprisoned and later reluctantly beheaded at the instigation of Herodias (Mark 6:14-29). Hearing of the deeds of Jesus, Herod Antipas was afraid that John the Baptist, whom he had beheaded, was raised from the dead. Herod was then afraid of Jesus and sought to kill Him. Because Herod was so sly, crafty, and vindictive, Jesus referred to him as "that fox" (Luke 13:32). Since he was by religion a Jew, he was present at Jerusalem for the Feast of the Passover when Pilate sent Jesus to him for trial (Luke 23:7). He was finally exiled in A.D. 39.

c. *Herod Philip* (4 B.C.—A.D. 34). On the west his territory was bounded by the upper part of the Jordan River and the Lebanon Mountains. From Mount Hermon on the north his domain reached to the Yarmuk River on the south, while the eastern frontiers stretched out into the desert (cf. Luke 3:1).

A just, efficient, and peace-loving ruler, he succeeded in preserving the *Pax Romana* in a previously turbulent district. With a Herodian fondness for building he erected his beautiful capital city near the site of Panias, the ancient shrine of Pan, and in honor of the emperor named it Caesarea Philippi. Near here Peter made his great confession (Matt. 16:16). Evidently early in his reign he rebuilt Bethsaida (Matt. 11:21), which he renamed Julias in honor of the daughter of Augustus. When the hatred and fear of Antipas and the anger of the Pharisees imperiled Jesus' life, it was to the realm of Philip that He retreated.

3. *The First Procurators of Judea* (A.D. 6-41)

Beginning with the deposition of Archelaus, Augustus acceded to the wishes of the people in Judea and gave them Roman rulers instead of the Herods. The Jews evidently thought that the Romans would not be as anxious to force Hellenism on them as were the half-Jewish Idumaeans. These Roman rulers of Judea were called procurators. They were directly responsible to the emperor.

The first procurator who figures to any extent in the New Testament story is Pontius Pilate, the fifth in the series (A.D. 26-36). Of him we know comparatively little outside of what is said in the New Testament. Since it was Josephus' purpose to show that the procurators drove normally peaceful Jewish subjects to rebellion, his account is probably focused on the less desirable incidents in Pilate's regime. However, Pilate is revealed as one who gave offense needlessly to the Jews either out of ignorance or out of disdain for their prejudices.

Luke's statement (13:1) indicates that the Jews were restive under Pilate's control. Finally the fanatical outburst of some Samaritans led to Pilate's recall and dismissal.

4. King Herod Agrippa I (A.D. 37-44)

The life story of this grandson of Herod the Great reads more like a romantic novel than actual history. Educated in Rome, he was constantly in financial trouble in his youth. Banished by Tiberius in his middle age, he was dissuaded from suicide only by the pleas of his wife. Later an incautious remark to Gaius reported to Tiberius left him in chains in Rome.

What looked like the end for Agrippa, however, turned out to be a blessing in disguise, for one of Gaius' first official acts as emperor was to reward his friend who had suffered this punishment because of loyalty to him. In place of the iron chains with which Agrippa had been bound, Gaius gave him a golden chain of equal weight and made him king of the combined tetrarchies of Philip and Lysanias. To this domain Agrippa soon was able to add that of Herod Antipas, even though at an earlier time the latter had befriended him while he was in need.

In A.D. 41 Agrippa I became the ruler of the province of Judea (which included Samaria and Idumea). Whereas his grandfather had been hated, Agrippa was very popular, being careful not to offend the religious scruples of his subjects. Feigning great piety, one of his first official acts was to present to the Temple the golden chain that Gaius had given him. The people were happy to have a Hasmonean ruler—his grandmother was Mariamne—on the throne of David. Courting the favor of the Jews, he killed James and laid violent hands on other Christians. He arrested Peter, intending to have him executed after Passover; but God delivered the apostle from prison (Acts 12:1-10).

When Agrippa I died after a sudden illness (Acts 12:20-23), the rule of Judea—now standing for all of Palestine, which had once more been reduced to one political unit—reverted to the procurators.

5. The Later Procurators and the Revolt of the Jews (A.D. 44-70)

In this period Judea had seven procurators. The first one mentioned in the New Testament was Felix, who ruled from 51 to 58. By marrying three princesses, one of whom was Drusilla, daughter of Agrippa I and sister of Agrippa II (Acts 24:24), he fell into disfavor with the Jews. By his use of force in suppressing the Zealots he made them martyrs in the eyes of the people and contributed to the rise of the Sicarii, or Assassins, and to the uniting of patriots and religious fanatics in a common aim to fight Rome secretly and openly until victory was theirs. His avarice and lack of principle are evidenced by his treatment of Paul (Acts 24:26).

Festus (58-62), who succeeded Felix (Acts 24:27), was an honest and efficient administrator, but he was unable to stem the mounting unrest. He is of special interest because of his contact with Paul (Acts 25 and 26).

The situation deteriorated under Albinus (62-64), who promoted lawlessness that he might profit thereby. The sins that Albinus committed in secret his successor flaunted openly. Florus plundered entire cities. Imprisoning indiscriminately friends and foes of Rome, he freed all who were willing to pay an adequate bribe. It was in his administration that war against Rome erupted (A.D. 66).

The most capable of Nero's commanders, Vespasian, was placed in charge of a Roman army of about 60,000 men. In A.D. 67 and 68 Vespasian reduced nearly all of Palestine except Jerusalem and its environs, which he wisely let alone so that the three factions there could destroy one another. After Nero's death Vespasian was acclaimed as emperor and he placed Titus in charge of the operations in Palestine.

After a siege of four months the gates of the city were burned and the next day the Temple courts were the scene of battle. During the melee a soldier hurled a torch into the building and the Temple that Titus had ordered preserved burned. A month later all of the ruined city was in Roman hands.

Besides the destruction of the beautiful Temple and the complete ruin of the national and religious capital of the Jews, the defeat had other implications. The Zealot cause was destroyed. The offering of sacrifices ceased and with it the high priestly Sadducean party. Judaism henceforth was a continuation of Pharisaism. The powers of the Sanhedrin that were left were absorbed by the rabbinic schools at Jamnia and Tiberias on the shores of the Mediterranean Sea and the Lake of Galilee respectively. The school at Jamnia was noted for its fixing of the limits of the canon of the Old Testament in a council held in A.D. 90.

B. JEWISH LIFE IN THE TIME OF JESUS

1. The Scribes

Since the essence of Judaism was the observance of the law, it was necessary that the law be not only known but understood and applied to the changing life situations. This rendered necessary the services of the scribes, the first of whom was Ezra (Ezra 7:10 f.).

Called lawyers (Luke 11:45) and doctors of the law (Luke 5:17) in the New Testament, the scribes were Biblical scholars, exegetes, and theologians, as well as copyists of the Scriptures. It was their task to preserve and transmit orally the interpretations of the law exactly as they had received them and to deduce the exact applications of the law for every circumstance that might arise. The body of traditions and rules which they received, or originated, and transmitted—called "the tradition of the elders" (Matt. 15:2)—was regarded as authoritative and became the chief pillar of Pharisaism. Under their influence, all originality, and with it the spirit of prophecy, was stifled. Under their influence, too, knowledge of the law came to be thought of as not merely a means to piety but piety itself.

Although the scribes were laymen—and unless they were wealthy earned their living at a trade—they were supposed to render their instructional services free. By the time of Christ the scribes, most of whom were Pharisees, constituted an organized guild with representatives in every community. As teachers they exacted more honor from their pupils than the pupils were to accord their parents—which honor the scribes loved. It was they who molded the religious life of the Jews.

II. *Religious and Political Groups*

1. *The Pharisees*

The most significant Jewish religious group in the time of Christ was the Pharisees, who first appear as the *Haberim* or "neighbors" in the reign of Hyrcanus. They were the most zealous participants in a reform introduced by that ruler which had as its object the proper separation of the tithes and the strict observance of the Torah. These descendants of the Hasidim, or pious ones, who supported Judas with arms until religious freedom was won, had in the time of Christ abstracted themselves from politics as far as they could.

Since God had foreseen the needs of His people and met these needs in the law, it was their task to render explicit what was implicit in the law. This idea, coupled with new customs which required the sanction of divine law, led to false and artificial methods of exegesis. Popular religious practices and regulations for which the Scriptures made no provision were also justified by the fiction that, in addition to the Pentateuch, God gave to Moses a body of laws which was transmitted orally through official channels without change to their own day. This was a fiction created to justify popular religious practices and regulations for which the Scriptures made no provision. The Pharisees were marked by peculiarities of dress and practice by which they separated themselves from the less religious, and gained for themselves their name, which means "the separated ones."

However, the Pharisees did keep the Torah alive, brought it to the people, and kept it in contact with the problems of life. Their influence on the life of the people was probably beneficial, as the appeal to be holy was held up as an ideal. However, the mixture of ritual and ethical tended to weaken the force of the moral requirements. Even the Pharisees admitted seven types of their number, most of which were sinful. Not all of them, however, are to be classed as hypocrites. Probably the best piety of the day was represented in Pharisaic circles.

The Pharisees, who as a rule did not belong to the aristocratic or politically favored class, lived in hope of the Kingdom. The expectation of the Messiah's coming—when this expectation was found—was associated with the kingdom of

God, which the Pharisees usually thought of as a literal, temporal reign of God on this earth in which they (the pious) would exercise authority.

2. The Sadducees

These theological opponents of the Pharisees are thought to have acquired their name from Zadok, the high priest invested by Solomon, whose descendants functioned as high priests until the time of Antiochus Epiphanes. The Sadducees rejected the oral tradition and all new developments in doctrine, including the resurrection and the elaborate angelology and demonology that the Pharisees borrowed from the Persians. Since the Sadducees accepted the Torah, which mentions angels, it was probably this theoretical development that they rejected instead of the existence of angels and spirits (Acts 23:8). As interpreters the Sadducees were the forerunners of modern scientific methods of exegesis. Since they were usually well situated the hope of the Kingdom was not stressed.

3. The Herodians

While the Sadducees had definite theological convictions and were not mere opportunists, the Herodians were primarily a political party which favored the Herodian regime. Their union with the Pharisees in the Gospels was cemented only by their common hatred of Jesus.

4. The Samaritans

While the Jews repudiated any connection with the group, Judaism in the time of Jesus cannot be understood without some knowledge of the Samaritans. In New Testament times the word "Samaritan" (e.g., Luke 10:33) designated one who was an inhabitant of the district of Samaria and a person of mixed race and religion.

In 722 B.C., Sargon took captive many Israelites, and shortly afterwards he introduced idolatrous colonists into the region of Samaria. Later, at the request of these colonists he sent an Israelite priest, who was unable to persuade the people to give up their idolatry which they were attempting to combine with Jehovah worship (II Kings 17:24-33). This dual worship was continued until after the downfall of Judah in 586 (II Kings 17:34-41). In the meantime later Assyrian monarchs had continued the process of populating Samaria with heathen colonists (Ezra 4:2, 9-10). These intermarried with the Israelites until the inhabitants were a mixture in race and religion. After the more skilled and ambitious classes of the Southern Kingdom had been deported to Babylon (597 and 586), intermarriage between those who were left in the land and the heathen who migrated into the now defenseless region was common.

In his reform movement Nehemiah drove away one of the grandsons of the high priest, Eliashib, who had married a daughter of Sanballat, the Horonite. It is probable that Sanballat was the founder of the rival temple at Mount Gerizim, where Antiochus Epiphanes later erected an altar to "Jupiter the Defender of Strangers" (II Macc. 6:2). Still later Hyrcanus destroyed the temple (Josephus, *Ant.*, VIII.9.1) but the worshipers continued to offer their sacrifices on the top of the hill on which the temple had been located (John 4:20).

Although they had a vital Messianic hope (John 4:25), in most doctrinal points the Samaritans were in essential agreement with the Sadducees. For Scripture they accepted only the Pentateuch. In the time of Christ the earlier contempt of the Jews for the Samaritans was unabated. Likewise persisted the resentment of the Samaritans against this pride of race and grace (John 4:9; Luke 9:52 f.).

5. *The Amme ha-arets*

This term means literally "the masses" and its singular denotes the "people of the land." This group, constituting those ignorant of the rabbinic refinements of the law, was considered to be lacking in piety by the Pharisees, who held its members in contempt (John 7:49). Since Jesus and His disciples did not conform to Pharisaic practice in ablutions and Sabbath observance, the Pharisees considered them as members of this class. Probably the greater portion of Christ's wider following was recruited from the ranks of this despised group.

III. *The Synagogue*

Perhaps originating during the Exile, the synagogue became the vital center of Judaism. By the beginning of the Christian era it was required that a synagogue be established wherever ten adult male Jewish attendants could be found.

The worshipers always sat facing toward Jerusalem, but the scribes and Pharisees who occupied the "chief seats" faced the congregation. At the end of the room in front of the congregation was the chest in which the Scriptures were kept and before it a curtain, in front of which a lamp burned continuously.

Formal services were conducted every Sabbath morning and on feast days. The Shema (Deut. 6:4-9; 11:13-21; Num. 15:37-41), recited in unison, was followed by a number of benedictions. Next, prayers and responses preceded the reading of portions selected from the law and the prophets in Hebrew, together with a free translation into Aramaic. This was followed by a discourse from someone chosen by the synagogue ruler (Acts 13:15). A priestly benediction or prayer brought the service to a close. Informal services were conducted on Mondays and Thursdays for the convenience of country people who came to town on business on those days. Informal services were also conducted on Sabbath afternoons.

However, the most important function of the synagogue was instruction in the law provided by ordained rabbis or scribes. This educational function of the synagogue was one of the most powerful influences in preserving the Jewish way of life, especially in the Diaspora.

The synagogue was controlled by a group of elders who in Palestine exercised civil as well as religious authority in the community. A "ruler" (Mark 5:22) had charge of the regular services and the building. An attendant (Luke 4:20) had charge of the scrolls, the care of the building, and other routine matters. Other officials had charge of the collection and distribution of alms.

IV. The Temple and Priesthood

The entire Temple enclosure was in the shape of a trapezoid approximately twelve hundred feet from north to south, the northern boundary of about one thousand feet being slightly longer than the southern border. Bounded on the east by the Valley of Kidron and on the west by the Tyropoeon Valley, it occupied the eastern heights of the city. Entrance to the enclosure was gained by two gates on the south and four on the west. On all sides the court was surrounded with colonnades or cloisters, the most beautiful group of which at the southern end of the enclosure was called the royal porch. This portico contained 162 white pillars, each of which was a monolith about forty feet in height. These were arranged in four rows. Solomon's porch (Acts 3:5), on the eastern side of the area, received its name from the fact that it was considered a remnant of Solomon's Temple. These porches served as places for religious discussion and instruction. This part of the Temple area was intended to carry out the ideal of Isaiah (56:6-7) and was called the Court of the Gentiles.

A wall excluded the Gentile from closer approach to the inner shrine, which was located near the northwest corner of this court. The Beautiful Gate (Acts 3:10) gave access to the Court of the Women, beyond which the women could not enter. To the west of this was the Court of Israel, which any adult male Israelite who was ritually purified might enter. Beyond this was the Court of the Priests, containing the altar of burnt offering and the huge laver.

Entrance to the Temple proper was gained through a porch on the east end. The first room of the Temple, called the holy place, was about thirty feet in width and sixty feet in length. On the north side of this room stood the table for the Bread of the Presence, while the south side was graced with the presence of the seven-branched lampstand, and in between them the altar of incense was situated. While ritually consecrated priests had continual access to the holy place, only the high priest had access to the most holy place and his approach could be made only one day in the year and then with definite restrictions (Heb. 9:7). The veil which separated the two parts of the Temple symbolized the limited access to the divine presence afforded by Judaism (Heb. 9:8). The inner shrine of Herod's Temple, like that of its predecessor, was bare, the ark having been lost in 586 B.C.

Worship in the Temple was conducted by the priests who offered the morning and evening sacrifices daily. At each of these daily sacrifices an unblemished yearling lamb was offered, together with a "meat offering" and a "drink offering." These offerings were accompanied by the burning of incense and vocal and instrumental music furnished by the priests and Levites. Sacrifices for individuals seeking to fulfill the Mosaic law were being offered continually throughout the day.

Since the support of the Temple itself came from other sources, chief of which was the annual half-shekel tax, and since the Jews of the Diaspora as well as those of Palestine made these contributions, a huge revenue was continually flowing into the priestly treasury. Moreover, because a select few of the priests were able to seize the larger share of these funds, these few became very rich. In the first century of our era because Herod, and after him the Roman officials, had deposed and created high priests at will and these high priestly families had intermarried, there developed an elite group who controlled the enormous wealth of the Temple as well as a great deal of political power. Thus we have not only to do with a high priest but also with a circle known as "chief priests," some of whom were ex-high priests or belonged to the families or to related families that as a rule supplied the high priests. It was this wealthy group that helped to engineer the death of Jesus and the persecution of the Early Church.

V. *Economic and Social Conditions*

In Palestine in Jesus' day the masses were extremely poor. Most of the people depended on the soil for a living, and the lack of tillable land, fertility, and dependability of rainfall kept them in economic destitution. In addition to this Herod's building operations, taxes levied by Rome, and religious revenues for the Temple, priesthood, and synagogue all conspired to keep the people poor. Many were driven to lives of shame and occupations which caused them to be despised by the scribes and Pharisees.

Grapes, sheep, fruit, and grain were raised for home use and export. Fishing was another source of food and income. Slaves were used by owners of large estates, but slavery was on the decrease. Since most farms and industries were small, hired labor was not much in demand. The average wage was one denarius, or about twenty cents, a day; its purchasing power, however, was much more. Not many of the Jews in Palestine engaged in commerce, since the scribes had drawn up rigid laws regulating contact with foreigners. Exports were chiefly agricultural products, salt, and fish. Imports consisted mainly of luxury items.

Towns (not villages) were walled and entrance was gained by the city gate, inside of which people gathered for trade and social intercourse. No doubt much of Jesus' teaching was given in the public squares of the villages He visited. Large cities had imposing buildings, but peasants lived in closely spaced flat-roofed houses of sun-dried mud or stone. In contrast to these poorly furnished, windowless, one-room houses were the homes of the wealthy. Here one might pass through an outer court (Matt. 26:71) to a vestibule, where a door led to an inner court which was sometimes used by several families. The various rooms were reached from this inner court, the most secluded being reserved for the women. A large guest room was built on the roof with an outside stairway. It was in such a room as this that Jesus and the disciples ate the Last Supper. Furniture varied from the expensive tables, chairs, couches, and lamps owned by the rich to the barest necessities used by the poor. For them sometimes mats or rugs served as beds, a stone or low stool as a table, and the floor as a seat. Generally, sanitary arrangements were nonexistent, and water was carried from a spring or cistern through the narrow streets. In towns the only public building, if any, was the synagogue.

Jewish fathers were required to teach their sons a trade. Manual labor was respected. Jesus was a carpenter (Mark 6:3) and Paul a tentmaker (Acts 18:3). Usually even the rabbis worked at a trade.

Rigidly fixed customs governed betrothal and marriage. Betrothal involved solemn ceremonies and could be broken only by divorce (Matt. 1:19). The friend of the bridegroom drew up the terms of a betrothal, which were supposed to be agreeable to the bride as well as her parents. The betrothal ritual consisted of a public ceremony in which the bride was given a piece of money, together with a written statement of promises made by her future husband and of the amount to be paid to the bride's father. At the time of the wedding the groom—in Judea accompanied by the groomsmen—brought the bride from her home to his. After a brief ritual and benediction the festivities, including a marriage feast, concluded the ceremony.

Although divorce and infidelity were not as common among the Jews as among the heathen, the woman was still regarded as the husband's property, and girls were not given the same educational opportunities as the boys. A joyous celebration attended the birth of a boy but disappointed silence the birth of a girl. Forty days after the birth of a boy or eighty days after the birth of a girl the mother was required to bring a stipulated offering for her purification. On the eighth day the male child was circumcised and named. Since the Jews had no surnames the name of the father, occupation, or city followed the given name to provide identification (e.g., Joseph of Arimathaea).

In Palestine, Aramaic was the language commonly spoken by the Jews. It was closely related to the Hebrew in which most of the Old Testament was composed and which was still spoken by the rabbis and used in part of the synagogue service. Although Latin was the official language of the Roman government, Greek was the tongue usually employed by the Gentiles and was more or less familiar to the Palestinian Jews.

VI. The Clash of Cultures

Palestine in the days of Christ contained many non-Jewish inhabitants; and even among the Jews, particularly those of the higher social classes, Hellenistic culture had long been making inroads. The main center of Greek culture, however, was in the Decapolis (Matt. 4:25; Mark 5:20; 7:31), which, as its name implies, was originally a confederation of ten cities. These Hellenistic cities which had been subdued by Alexander Janneus were freed from Jewish domination by Pompey (63 B.C.). Widely separated geographically, their league seems to have been for the purpose of defending their interests and culture against the Semites, particularly the Jews. All but one of their cities, Scythopolis—said by Josephus to be the greatest—were in Transjordan. The tetrarchy of Herod Philip, which included part of this general area, was mainly non-Jewish in population and culture.

Largely because of the influence of Herod the Great and his sons, Greek culture flourished also in western Palestine. Herod the Great built at Strato's Tower a great city and the only important seaport of Palestine. Here on an eminence he erected a temple containing a colossus of Caesar and one of Rome. In addition to the emperor cult about a dozen other heathen cults were found at Caesarea. A similar situation prevailed at Samaria, which Herod the Great rebuilt and renamed Sebaste (Augustus). Remains of a large temple erected in Caesar's honor are still to be seen. His son Philip erected a temple to Caesar near Banias (or Panias). At Scythopolis, a city about eighteen miles east of Nazareth and probably in Jesus' lifetime eclipsing Jerusalem in population and splendor, a huge temple of Bacchus crowned the hilltop. Emperor worship and pagan cults were probably to be found at Tiberias, which Antipas erected to honor that emperor. Bethsaida Julias (Mark 6:45), rebuilt by Philip and named in honor of Julia, the daughter of Augustus, was likewise probably a seat of Hellenistic culture.

In addition to these dominantly non-Jewish centers and cities, on the coast and maritime plain, which were also Hellenistic in culture, there were many foreigners situated in Jewish centers in Palestine—soldiers, traders, government officials, and others.

Besides heathen temples, the Greek festivals, games, hippodromes, theaters, baths, language, and many other things called the attention of the Jew to the hated Gentile influence. This conflict with Greek culture goes far towards explaining the strictness of the Pharisees in their ritualism and the resentment of the Zealots and their predecessors which erupted frequently in revolt. These Jews felt that the Roman rule which fostered this heathen culture was a threat against their existence.

C. The Graeco-Roman World

I. Religion

1. Greek Polytheism

Some of the gods of the Greek pantheon are mentioned or suggested by the New Testament. The hill on which Paul spoke to the assembled philosophers (Acts 17:19) was named for Ares, the Greek equivalent for the Roman god Mars. Ephesus was the center of Artemis worship (Acts 19:23 ff.). Her image, which was believed to have fallen from heaven, was housed in a temple that was regarded as one of the seven wonders of the ancient world. Apollo inspired poets, prophets, and seers. At Delphi a temple was erected over a cavern whose vapors were believed to be the breath of Apollo. A priestess inhaling these vapors would fall into a trance and her incoherent words would be recorded and interpreted by the priests who were present. Because Delphi was formerly known as Pytho, the name of Pythian-Apollo was attached to the shrine and the spirit of inspiration was known as the Python. Thus the slave-girl that Paul encountered at Philippi who was making profit for her masters by fortunetelling had a "python spirit" (Acts 16:16, Gk.).

By New Testament times polytheism had lost much of its appeal and power. Philosophers had shown how ridiculous were the actions of the gods as represented by Homer. In order to retain their faith in the traditional gods, many interpreted the Homeric poems allegorically. Others abandoned their ancestral faith. Because of migration the gods of one area were imported to another locality and naturalized there. Greek gods were identified with Roman gods who fulfilled the same functions. From the idea of a Zeus or Jupiter who was able to control the other gods it was only another step to monotheism. This step some of the philosophers had already made before Paul preached his message on Mars' Hill pleading for his audience to do likewise (Acts 17:22 ff.).

2. The Mystery Cults

The extreme religiousness observed by Paul in the vicinity of Athens (Acts 17:22) is attested by Pausanias, who a little over a century later wrote his *Description of Greece*. With the discovery of the individual came a deepening of the sense of sin and a desire for fellowship and union with the divine. The average man was no longer satisfied with gods whose conduct was selfish and sensual. He wanted a god who was sympathetic with his lot and who would answer his prayers. Not satisfied with the certain prospects of a gloomy future in the shadows of Hades, he wanted some means of assurance that beyond the grave an eternal life of bliss would be his. Thus for many the so-called mystery cults displaced or overshadowed the older polytheism.

Only a bare indication of some of the common features of these mystery cults is possible here. The cults are based on myths which explain the annual cycle of life and death in the plant world in terms of the death or imprisonment of a god or goddess (the spirit of vegetation) and the subsequent release or resurrection of this deity. The ritual of the cults includes mourning because of the imprisonment or death of the vegetation god and rejoicing over his liberation or resuscitation. In many of the cults the god won his victory and consequent immortality through his own struggles and suffering in an existence like ours. The secret of his victory which he left behind he revealed to the initiate. The term mystery (from the Greek *mysterion*) meant, not something vague or unexplainable, but a secret which, unknown to an outsider, might be known fully by the initiate. Usually there was a rite of purification connected with the initiation ceremony. The initiate was convinced that by this rite his sins had been washed away and that he had been regenerated—born again for eternity.

Salvation was by means of mystical union with deity without the necessity of a moral quality of life which was fitted for a blissful eternal existence. By union with the god in his death and resurrection the worshiper was assured of immortality. Salvation was effected magically and mechanically by means of ritual.

3. The Religion of Rome

At Rome the old polytheism and impersonal state religion alike had lost their appeal before the inroads of these popular mystery cults. When imperial efforts to revive the old state religion failed, the emperors used another means to make loyalty to Rome a matter of religion. Augustus instituted the worship of Julius Caesar and decreed that the *genius* of the living emperor should be worshiped. Nero and Domitian decreed that they should be worshiped during their lifetime. The demand for emperor worship was pressed with great zeal by priests of the cult, especially in the provinces. The emperor cult was strong in the region of Asia, to churches of which the Revelation of John was originally addressed, and especially powerful in Pergamum ("where Satan dwelleth"—2:13), and is referred to as the second beast (Rev. 13:11 ff.) which compels the worship of the first beast, the Roman Empire. The temptation to burn a little incense and sprinkle a few drops of wine on an altar in front of the emperor's image must have been great to the early Christians, who could by this means escape economic boycott (Rev. 13:17) as well as other forms of persecution and possible martyrdom.

4. Magic

Magicians of New Testament times used their black art in support of pagan religions. Bar-Jesus, or Elymas, the magician, attempted by the use of magic to keep Sergius Paulus from accepting Christ (Acts 13:6-12). The emperor cult employed magic to deceive the people so that they would worship the beast (Rev. 13:11-15). At Ephesus, center of the worship of Artemis, magic was also widely practiced (Acts 19:18-19). Simon, the magician, interpreted the work of the apostles in connection with the outpouring of the Holy Spirit as a display of magic—whose secret he wanted to buy (Acts 8:9-24). In two instances in Acts the magicians are stated to be Jews (13:6; 19:13-14).

II. The Intellectual World

1. The Greek Language

It was once thought that the Greek of the New Testament, which is somewhat different from that of the classical writers, was a special "Holy Ghost language." However, an abundance of nonliterary materials including letters, contracts, receipts, and the like written on broken pieces of earthenware or papyrus, and inscriptions such as epitaphs on tombstones testify that the Greek of our New Testament was the language commonly spoken throughout the Roman Empire. This fact is an argument in favor of modern versions designed to express the truths of the New Testament in the language spoken and understood by the people of our day.

The Greek language was carried throughout the eastern Mediterranean world by the conquests of Alexander the Great. Thus the way was prepared for the rapid spread of Christianity.

2. Greek Philosophy

a. *Socrates and Plato.* Some earlier philosophers had pointed to the absurdity of polytheism and had asserted the possibility of personal immortality. Socrates (469-399 B.C.) and Plato (427-347) established belief in a supreme Intelligence on a rational basis and showed that belief in personal immortality was intellectually respectable. The most direct contribution of Plato to our understanding of the New Testament, however, is his theory of ideas. He held that every physical object of a given class derives its reality from a perfect idea or pattern in the invisible world. The real world is the invisible and spiritual order. This line of thinking is especially evident in Hebrews (8:1-5; 10:1; 12:22-23).

The dualism which Plato shared with the Persians reappeared in the Gnostic movement. Such dualism formed the basis for denying that the divine Christ had a real body and suffered a real death. Either His body was a phantom or the Christ must be distinguished from the man Jesus on whom the Christ descended at baptism and from whom He departed before Jesus' death. This teaching is attacked in First John and repudiated in the prologue of John's Gospel. The idea of a Demiurge, or inferior deity who created the physical world, the Gnostics also shared with Plato. The dualism which located evil in matter gave rise to contradictory tendencies in life. In some instances it resulted in an extreme asceticism which denied legitimate sense pleasures while in other instances it issued in a libertinism in which it was held that sins of the flesh were unable to contaminate the spirit (II Pet. 2; Jude; Rev. 2:14-15; 20:23; I John 3).

b. *The Epicureans.* Among the philosophers that Paul encountered at Athens were the Epicureans (Acts 17:18), whose teachings were widely accepted in the Hellenistic world. For Epicurus pleasure was the supreme good; so whatever produced physical pain or mental disquiet was evil.

c. *The Stoics.* The other and more important group of philosophers that Paul met at Athens was the Stoics (Acts 17:18). The Stoics held that virtue is knowledge and that, since reason is the essential and divine part of man, the life of virtue is the life of reason. Since emotions and desires interfere with the exercise of reason, they are diseases of the soul and should be suppressed or eradicated. A virtuous man has so suppressed the emotions that neither prosperity nor adversity causes him to give way to them. One should follow always his conscience, which guided by reason will show him his duty.

III. *The Jews of the Dispersion*

1. *The Causes and Extent of the Dispersion*

The extent of the dispersion in the time of Christ can be inferred from Luke's record of the Jews from other lands present at the first Christian Pentecost (Acts 2:5-11). Probably no single factor was more significant in preparing the world for the advent of Christ than the Jews outside the borders of Palestine. Luke's account suggests that, while the resided elsewhere, Jerusalem remained their capital and Palestine their fatherland. Their fidelity to their ancestral religion was exhibited in pilgrimages to Jerusalem in times of the great festivals and in their payment of the annual half-shekel temple-tax.

The Dispersion (*diaspora*) began with the deportation of some of the Israelites to Assyria by Tiglah-pileser III in 732 B.C. (II Kings 15:29). Other deportations of Israel followed, including that of 722 or 721 B.C., when Israel ceased to exist as a nation. The fate of the so-called "ten lost tribes" is not indicated in extant secular or sacred records. Even though Paul speaks of the twelve tribes as being contemporary (Acts 26:7), most of them probably lost their religious and racial identity.

Although both Israel and Judah suffered extensive deportations during the Assyrian period, the real Jewish Diaspora begins with Nebuchadnezzar's victory in 597. Other deportations followed in 586 and 581, in which Jews were removed likewise to Babylon. Although according to Jeremiah's records the total number was not great, the deportees represented the flower of Jewish ability and ambition. Many of these chose to remain in Babylon, where their businesses and homes were established, rather than return to reclaim the ruined cities and lands overgrown with brush and weeds.

In Egypt the Diaspora began when Jehoahaz, and probably others, were brought there by Necho. Soon after this colonies of Jews were to be found at Tahpanhes and Pathros (Jer. 44:1). Jeremiah himself was forced by some of the Jews to accompany them in their flight to Tahpanhes in the Nile Delta (Jeremiah 43).

In the period after Alexander the Great inducements were offered the Jews which led many of them to settle in Syria and Asia Minor—more than were left in Palestine. Many Jews were found at Ephesus. Synogagues in Antioch and Iconium in Asia Minor, as well as in Thessalonica, Corinth, and Athens to the west, testify to the presence of Jews. Later Ptolemy (62 B.C.) brought many captives to Rome. They became the nucleus of a strong Jewish colony that was later accorded many privileges.

However, the most important group for the background of the Christian movement was at Alexandria. As a reward for their assistance against the Egyptians, Alexander established a colony of the Jews in a special part of the city where they could be free from pagan defilement. As a result of the continuation of this policy by the Ptolemies, over a million Jews were to be found in Alexandria—a number much larger than the population of Palestine.

2. *The Septuagint*

Since the Jews of Alexandria needed a Greek Bible that they could read, not only to keep them from losing out to the disintegrating influence of Hellenism but also to get the Gentiles to appreciate and embrace their religion, the Septuagint was produced. It was called the Septuagint (abbreviated LXX) because according to a legendary account it was produced by seventy-two scholars in seventy-two days at the request of Ptolemy Philadelphus. Actually, the translation probably began in his reign (*ca.* 250 B.C.), the Pentateuch being the first part which was translated. By the time the prologue to Ecclesiasticus was written (132 B.C.) probably all of the Old Testament had been rendered in Greek. This was the Bible of Jesus and the apostles. It was the most important tool in the hands of the first missionaries, for Greek was understood throughout the Roman Empire.

3. *Proselytes and God-Fearers*

Among those who were attracted by the lofty messages of Israel were Gentile proselytes who attained full membership in the Jewish church and accepted all of the rites of Judaism. Others, however, accepted the monotheism, morality, and Messianic belief of Judaism but not its ritualism. It was especially among these so-called "god-fearers" that Christianity made many converts (Acts 10:2; 13:16, 26, 43, 50; 16:15).

IV. *The Roman Empire*

At the time of Augustus (Octavian) the Roman world embraced all the territory from the Euphrates River to the Atlantic Ocean and from the Danube River and the southern borders of Scotland to the Sahara Desert. This meant that the entire Mediterranean world was under one roof. In fact, the Romans could call the Mediterranean Sea "Our Sea."

The Roman peace not only provided an ideal atmosphere for the reception of a gospel of peace but also aided the missionaries in their labors and travels. Thus Paul could travel from Palestine to Syria and thence through Asia Minor to Greece and even to Rome without any of the inconveniences and delays experienced today in traveling from one country to another. Often Paul was protected by Roman officials. Excellent roads connected all parts of the empire.

D. "WHEN THE FULNESS OF THE TIME CAME" (Gal. 4:4)

The Jews had given the world a monotheism. Because Israel's God was a supremely moral Person, the Jewish faith was ethical to the core, even though at times an elaborate ritualism had obscured this fact. The hope of a better day in which God would rule the world had prepared the Jewish people to receive the Messiah and His message, although perversions of this hope led to a failure of most of His contemporaries to understand the spiritual nature of His kingdom.

Through the Diaspora and its synagogue services many pious Gentiles had been drawn to appreciate the monotheism, morality, and Messianic hope of Judaism. These "god-fearers" furnished a fertile and cultivated field in which the early missionaries sowed the gospel seed. Besides preparing a people for the gospel message, the synagogue taught the Early Church to worship and suggested to it primitive forms of organization. From the Greek Septuagint, bequeathed to the Church by the Diaspora, early missionaries derived texts proving that Jesus was the Messiah. The task of presenting the gospel was made much easier because the Church had a written translation in a language spoken throughout the Graeco-Roman world.

Greek philosophy had discontinued the older polytheism and prepared the way for monotheism. The rise of individualism had made men conscious of their strivings and hopes, suffering and desire. The mystery religions of Greece and the Orient had nourished a longing for redemption and personal immortality, but because of their inability to purify man's ethical and spiritual nature they were unable to satisfy the desires they fed. Philosophers like Philo had pointed to the necessity of a Mediator between the Creator and the universe and between God and man.

Both heart and head were thus prepared for the advent of Christ and the universal gospel. Because the gospel was designed to meet the deepest need of each individual it had a universal appeal. Thus it was that "when the fulness of the time came, God sent forth his Son . . . " (Gal. 4:4).

CHAPTER III

THE NEW TESTAMENT TRANSMITTED AND TRANSLATED

The first generation Christians had no New Testament to read—they wrote it! The "Bible" of the Apostolic Church was our Old Testament, written originally in Hebrew and Aramaic but translated into Greek about two hundred years before Christ. Since the common people among the Jews, as well as all the Gentiles, did not read Hebrew in Jesus' day, it was this Greek translation which was used by the Early Church. This is called the Septuagint, because of the tradition that some seventy Jewish scholars translated the Pentateuch into Greek in Alexandria, Egypt, at about 250 B.C. Probably the rest of the Old Testament was translated into Greek between 250 and 150 B.C.

I. The Writing of the New Testament

It is commonly held by conservative scholars that all of the New Testament, with the possible exception of James and Galatians, was written in the second half of the first century, A.D. 50-100. It is also generally agreed that it was all written originally in Greek, although there are some who believe that the Gospels and Acts were first composed in Aramaic.

1. Paul's Travel Letters

It is possible that the Epistle of James was written about A.D. 45 and the Epistle to the Galatians about A.D. 48. But it is more generally believed that the first book of the New Testament to appear was Paul's First Epistle to the Thessalonians. This was written from Corinth probably in A.D. 50 or 51, during Paul's stay of a year and a half there on his second missionary journey. A short time afterward, and from the same place, Paul wrote his Second Epistle to the Thessalonians.

It is very instructive to notice the nature of these first books of the New Testament. They were not theological treatises. Rather they were missionary letters sent to newly founded churches to deal with definite needs and problems in those congregations. In other words, the inspired literature

of Christianity was not written by some armchair philosopher
or mystic in the seclusion of a cloistered cell. It was composed
in the heat of battle. The new Christian sect was being persecuted by the Jews. The latter either opposed the Christians
openly or else sought to lead them captives in the bondage
of Judaism. Then, too, the Gnostics were claiming a superior
gnosis, or knowledge, and Gnosticism was threatening to convert Christianity into a false philosophy. Last, but not least,
the new converts in the Gentile world were surrounded by
the seductive atmosphere of heathen morals. It was to combat
these dangerous influences that Paul wrote letters to his missionary churches.

During his third missionary journey Paul wrote two letters to the Corinthian church. The first was written from
Ephesus, about A.D. 55. The second was written shortly after
from somewhere in Macedonia. Galatians was perhaps written
at about the same time, though exactly where or when we
do not know. Romans was written from Corinth when Paul
decided to return to Jerusalem, about A.D. 56.

2. The Prison Epistles

After Paul's three great missionary journeys he spent two
years in prison at Caesarea, headquarters of the Roman government in Judea. This was followed by two years as an
imperial prisoner at Rome. During this period—probably to
be dated A.D. 59-61—Paul wrote his so-called Prison Epistles:
Philemon, Colossians, Ephesians, and Philippians. In these
he gives us the cream of his thinking under the inspiration
of the Spirit. Here he had plenty of time for meditation and
prayer. Out of the richness of his fellowship with Christ
"in the heavenlies" he has shared with us some of the most
profound and precious truths in all of Holy Writ. We would
be much poorer today if Paul had not spent those years in
prison.

3. The Pastoral Epistles

The last of Paul's letters are called the Pastoral Epistles.
In chronological order they are I Timothy, Titus, and II Tim-
othy. The last was written shortly before Paul's death under
Nero, which probably took place in the winter of A.D. 67-68
(Nero died in 68). If so, Paul's final Epistle was written in
the fall of A.D. 67. For he asked Timothy to bring the cloak

he had left at Troas and urged him to come before the cold winter set in (II Tim. 4:13, 21).

4. The General Epistles and Hebrews

Tradition asserts that Peter likewise died under Nero. So probably II Peter was written at about the same time as II Timothy. That would mean that I Peter, Jude, and perhaps James, were written just previous to this, while I Timothy and Titus were being written. The Epistle to the Hebrews was also presumably written at this time, about A.D. 66.

5. The Synoptic Gospels and Acts

The first Gospel was written by Mark at Rome. Although nearly a generation had gone by since Jesus' crucifixion in A.D. 30, the story of His life, death, and resurrection had up to this time circulated in oral form. But now those who had been eyewitnesses of these things were fast dying off. It was of utmost importance that the record be written down while it could be corroborated by living witnesses.

Soon after this the other two Synoptic Gospels, Matthew and Luke, were written. They incorporate more of the teachings of Jesus than does Mark. Luke tells us (Luke 1:1-4) that he consulted with eyewitnesses in preparation for giving us an authentic account of Jesus' ministry. He followed it with Acts, a history of the Early Church.

6. The Johannine Literature

Soon after Paul's death, then, which occurred about A.D. 65 or 67, the bulk of the New Testament had been written. There remained only one group, but a very important one— the Johannine Writings.

Five books are traditionally ascribed to John: the Fourth Gospel, three Epistles of John, and Revelation. Only the last, Revelation or the Apocalypse (from the Greek apocalypsis, meaning "revelation"), carries the name of the writer. But the Church across the centuries has attributed all five to John the Apostle, the son of Zebedee. It is generally held by conservatives that these Johannine books were written in the last decade of the first century, perhaps around A.D. 95.

II. THE FORMATION OF THE CANON

The term canon comes from the Greek word kanon. Originally it meant a rod, next a measuring rule, and then a rule or standard. By the canon of the New Testament we mean the authoritative list of Christian writings accepted by the Church as having been divinely inspired. There are twenty-seven books in the New Testament canon. Other early Christian writings are called noncanonical.

1. The Beginnings of a Canon

a. *The Collecting of the Books.* The first step in the formation of a canon would be the collecting of the books that had been written. Probably the first collection consisted of Paul's Epistles. Professor Goodspeed thinks that the appearance of Acts caused some admirer of Paul to launch the important project of gathering together the letters of the great apostle.[1] We can imagine someone at Colossae, for instance, starting with the letter to the church in that city, as well as the personal note to Philemon, in whose house the church met. Not far away, at Ephesus, he would find another Epistle. Crossing over to Europe he would pick up one at Philippi, two at Thessalonica, and two at Corinth. Going on to Rome, he would find a very important one there. Back in Asia Minor, he would secure the letter written to the churches of the province of Galatia. At Ephesus he would also have found the two letters to Timothy, and at Crete the one to Titus. Thus he would have thirteen Epistles of Paul.

The collection of the four Gospels could not be made, of course, until after John's Gospel was written at the end of the first century. But such a collection was probably made in the first quarter of the second century. Ephesus would be the most likely place for the assembling of these Gospels, since John's, the last, was written there. It is also possible that Asia Minor was the place where the rest of the New Testament books were first collected.

b. *The First Bound Volumes.* Each of the books of the New Testament was probably written on a papyrus roll, or scroll. Until very recently scholars had assumed that these circulated on separate rolls for the first three hundred years. That is because our first bound volumes of the Greek Bible are from the fourth century. But about twenty-five years ago an important discovery was made which changed this opinion. Scholars found many leaves of a bound papyrus volume of

[1] Edgar J. Goodspeed, *New Chapters in New Testament Study* (New York: Macmillan Co., 1937), pp. 62-63.

Paul's Epistles and also of another volume containing the four Gospels. Both of these come from the third century. It seems apparent that the New Testament circulated in the third century—and also probably late in the second—in four volumes. The Gospels comprised one, Paul's Epistles a second, the General Epistles a third, and Revelation a fourth. Acts was sometimes placed with the Gospels and sometimes with the General Epistles. It is closely connected with the latter in our earliest Greek manuscripts. That is why the General Epistles follow Acts in the Westcott and Hort Greek Testament.

2. Reasons for the Formation of a Canon

At first the Church did not feel any necessity for deciding which Christian writings should be accepted as authoritative. But soon situations arose which pointed up the need for differentiating between those books which were held to be divinely inspired and those which were not. Thus gradually there appeared the concept of a New Testament canon.

a. *Marcion's Canon.* About the middle of the second century there lived in Rome a man named Marcion. Apparently he accepted the teaching of the Gnostics that all matter is evil and all spirit is good. This led him to reject the Old Testament with its story of creation and to hold that the God of the Old Testament was not the true Supreme Being. Furthermore, of the New Testament writings he accepted only Luke's Gospel and ten Epistles of Paul (excluding the Pastorals). And since the first two chapters of Luke describe the human birth of Jesus he removed them from the Gospel.

Because Marcion was a very influential man, the Church was faced with the need of meeting his limited canon with a correct and more complete one. Scholars are generally agreed that his action was one of the first factors which caused Christian leaders to give attention to the matter of an orthodox canon.

b. *Use of Apocryphal Books.* Even within orthodox Christianity there was a difference of opinion about some books. The church of Alexandria, Egypt, was consistently generous in its attitude toward the matter of canonicity. Such apocryphal books as Clement's First Epistle to the Corinthians, the Didache, the Epistle of Barnabas, and the Shepherd of

Hermas were widely accepted and used in the Eastern churches as sacred scripture. In fact the last two of these are found at the end of the great fourth century manuscript, Sinaiticus, while First Clement is found at the end of Alexandrinus (fifth century), one of the three oldest existing manuscripts of the Greek New Testament. (The other fourth century manuscript, Vaticanus, is broken off in the last part.)

It was bad enough to have such leading scholars as Clement of Alexandria (*ca.* 195) and Origen (*ca.* 220) quoting some of these books as holy scripture. But the problem really became acute when heretical writers began to use certain apocryphal books in support of their objectionable ideas. It can easily be seen that the Church had to decide which books were to be accepted as authoritative for determining theology and which were to be excluded. This process of canonization continued through the second, third, and fourth centuries.

c. Edict of Diocletian. In 303 the Emperor Diocletian decreed that all the sacred writings of the Christians were to be burned. That raised the question: For what books should one risk his life? Christians had to decide whether it was wise to become a martyr for possessing a copy of the Shepherd of Hermas, for instance, if that book was not really included in holy scripture. So persecution had its part in hastening the formation of a New Testament canon.

3. Tests of Canonicity

Dr. Thiessen has given a good summary of the factors involved in determining whether a book should be accepted or rejected as sacred scripture. He lists four tests of canonicity,[2] which we shall note briefly (with some adaptation).

a. Apostolicity. The first question asked was probably this: Was the book written by an apostle, or at least under the close influence of an apostle? With reference to the Gospels, Matthew and John would be acceptable as written by the apostles themselves. Mark's Gospel was connected with Peter, and Luke's with Paul in Early Church tradition. It seems probable that this test was applied to each of the twenty-seven books of our New Testament.

[2] Henry C. Thiessen, *Introduction to the New Testament* (Grand Rapids: Wm. B. Eerdmans Publishing Co., 1943), p. 10.

b. Contents. Were the contents of the book of unquestionably high spiritual character? It is likely that the apocryphal books were eliminated one by one on the basis of this question. Anyone today may read these noncanonical Christian writings[3] and thus check for himself the judgment of the Early Church, guided by the Holy Spirit. In most cases the contrast between the canonical and apocryphal books is so striking as to leave little room for question.

c. Universality. Was the book received u n i v e r s a l l y throughout the Church? Some apocryphal books accepted in the East were thus eliminated because rejected in the West. Such disputed books as Hebrews were fully canonized because all sections of the Church finally accepted them.

d. Inspiration. The ultimate test, of course, was inspiration. Only those books were allowed in the canon which gave adequate evidence of having been divinely inspired. Surely the Holy Spirit guided the Early Church in its selection of those very books which He had inspired men to write.

4. History of the Canon

The early second century writers, such as Ignatius and Polycarp, quote freely from many of the New Testament books. Justin Martyr (*ca.* 150) refers to fourteen of our twenty-seven books. At the close of that century Irenaeus, Clement of Alexandria, and Tertullian show a knowledge of practically the entire New Testament. The Muratorian Canon (*ca.* 200) omits four books—Hebrews, James, I Peter, and II Peter.

In the third century Origen classified the books of the New Testament into two categories: acknowledged and disputed. In the second group he placed James, II Peter, II and III John, and Jude. He was followed in this by Eusebius, who wrote the first great *Church History* (A.D. 326). Hebrews and Revelation were also disputed at this time, the former in the West and the latter in the East.

Finally, at the end of the fourth century, the Council of Carthage (A.D. 397) officially settled the extent of the New Testament canon, adopting exactly our twenty-seven books. All others were placed outside the canon and their use in the churches was banned.

[3]See, for instance, M. R. James, *The Apocryphal New Testament* (Oxford: Clarendon Press, 1924).

III. THE TRANSMISSION OF THE TEXT

1. *The Necessity for Textual Criticism*

a. The Missing Autographs. The one basic and all-important fact which meets us at the very outset of our study of the text is this: all the original copies—called autographs—of the books of the New Testament have been lost. If we had them there would be no science of textual criticism. But since all we have is manuscripts containing texts that have been copied and recopied, it is necessary to compare them carefully in order to recover, as nearly as possible, the exact text of the original.

The fact is that no two manuscripts of the Greek New Testament agree exactly. This may at first seem somewhat disconcerting. But a little thought will show that it was inevitable. The New Testament was copied by hand for fourteen centuries, until the beginning of printing about 1455. (These hand-written copies are called "manuscripts.") Humanly speaking it is simply impossible for a person to copy such a long manuscript as the New Testament without making mistakes.

However, we are not beginning to face up to the real problem involved until we take a glimpse at one of those early manuscripts. We look in vain for chapter or verse divisions. But, far worse, there are no punctuation marks to indicate where sentences begin or end. But that is not the worst. There is no separation between words! Letter after letter, line after line, column after column, the text runs on for the length of the whole book. In the case of Luke's Gospel or Acts this would mean a scroll about thirty feet long, with no indication whatsoever of chapter, verse, sentence, or word divisions. What that would mean can scarcely be imagined by us today. Let me repeat: WHATTHATWOULDMEANCANSCARCEL YBEIMAGINEDBYUSTODAY. We can certainly be thankful for the mechanical devices which make for easy reading and quick reference in the use of our Bibles now. But for centuries the scribes did it, as we would say, the hard way.

b. Writing Materials. Not only are all the autograph copies of New Testament books lost, but there is practically no possibility that they will ever be found. This is due to the fact that they were probably all written on papyrus, although A. T. Robertson thinks that some of the longer books may have been written on parchment rolls.[4]

Papyrus, which gives us our word paper, was made from the plant by that name, a water reed that grew in marshes and on the banks of rivers. The inner bark of the plant was cut into strips. These were laid flat in a vertical position. Then another layer, with the papyrus running horizontally, was laid on top. Between was a kind of paste or glue. The two layers were pressed firmly together. Then the top surface was rubbed to make it smooth. Several of these pieces would be glued together to form a roll.

While this material was used until paper replaced it in the eighth and ninth centuries, yet one can easily imagine how brittle it was. Papyrus rolls would wear out very rapidly. This would be especially true of the longer ones, which would require considerable handling. For instance, if one wished to check a passage in the middle of Luke's Gospel he would have to unroll with his right hand and roll with his left until some fifteen feet had been handled in this manner. It is not surprising that most of the Early Church fathers quote the New Testament more freely than accurately. The task of looking up a passage in Acts, for instance, was a very different one then from what it is now with our bound volumes, easily turned pages, chapter and verse divisions, and a concordance to tell us just where to find the text we are looking for. We have very little excuse today for being too careless to check passages in the Bible.

Not only were these papyrus rolls very brittle, but they were also very perishable from dampness. That is the reason that almost all extant papyrus documents have been found in Egypt. In the southern part of that country, in the Fayum district, the climate is so constantly dry that thousands of papyrus letters and miscellanea have been recovered from the sands.

In III John 13 there is a reference to "ink and pen." The former was made out of charcoal, gum, and water. The Greek word John uses simply means "black." The pen of that day was a reed, whittled to a sharp point at the end.

[4] A. T. Robertson, *Studies in the Text of the New Testament* (New York: George H. Doran Co., 1926), p. 21.

The loss of all the autographs, as well as practically all the manuscripts of the second, third, and fourth centuries, may be due partly also to persecution. Even in our day there has occurred the burning of Bibles where true Christians are being persecuted for their faith.

2. Manuscripts of the Greek New Testament

There are extant some four thousand Greek manuscripts of the New Testament, in whole or in part. These may be divided into three main classes: papyri, uncials, and minuscules.

a. *Papyri.* Most of the important papyrus manuscripts of parts of the New Testament have come to light since 1930. So this phase of textual criticism is decidedly new.

Papyrus was apparently used for New Testament books almost entirely during the first three centuries. Our earliest vellum manuscripts are from the fourth century.

There are some fifty-three papyrus fragments of the New Testament now known. The most important are the Chester Beatty papyri. Mr. Beatty was an Englishman who in the winter of 1930-31 had the good fortune to secure possession of some ancient papyrus sheets from Egypt. When they were examined by scholars they were found to contain considerable portions of the Gospels and Paul's Epistles. Further study revealed the fact that they came from three original bound volumes. There were thirty leaves of a codex—technical name for a bound book—which originally contained the four Gospels and Acts. Eighty-six leaves—thirty of which are in this country at the University of Michigan—were found which belonged to a codex of Paul's Epistles. Since the volume had some one hundred leaves altogether, we have the larger part of it extant. The third codex contained Revelation. Ten leaves—out of an original thirty-two—are extant.

The special value of these Chester Beatty papyri is that they all come from the third century. They thus constitute the earliest witness of any extent to the text of the New Testament.

b. *Uncials.* The word "uncial" literally means "inch-high." These manuscripts are so called because they contain a text written in large, square letters. The material is vellum. They date from the fourth to the tenth centuries.

THE NEW TESTAMENT TRANSMITTED AND TRANSLATED 55

There are about two hundred uncials now extant. The two oldest, Vaticanus and Sinaiticus, come from the fourth century. The latter was purchased from the Russian government by the British Museum in 1933 for about $500,000.00, the highest price ever paid for a book.

c. *Minuscules*. Of the minuscule manuscripts there are over 2,400 known to scholars. Since these come from the late Middle Ages (ninth to fifteenth centuries) they are much less valuable than the uncials.

The minuscules are also called "cursives" because written in a running script, with letters often joined together. They are thus less cumbersome than the uncials.

One sometimes hears it said that there are "thousands of variant readings in the Greek manuscripts of the New Testament." Technically this is true. But actually the vast bulk of these variants is of no importance, the differences being only matters of spelling or grammatical form. The really significant variations amount to only "a thousandth part of the entire text," according to Hort,[5] and none of them adversely affect matters of doctrine. Since we have some 4,000 manuscripts of the Greek New Testament, in whole or in part, we need not feel any uneasiness about possessing a substantially reliable text which approximates very closely the exact original.

IV. THE ENGLISH NEW TESTAMENT

In the second century the New Testament was translated into Latin and Syriac, and soon after into various languages of the then known world. But we cannot take time to discuss them. We should note, however, before taking up the English versions, that the official Bible of the Roman Catholic church has been for many centuries and still is the Latin Vulgate. This was *the* Bible of the Middle Ages.

1. *Wycliffe's New Testament* (1382)

The first complete Bible in English was put out by John Wycliffe (whose name is spelled a dozen different ways!). The New Testament appeared around 1382 and the whole Bible about two years later.

The Wycliffe Bible was translated from the Latin Vulgate, not from the original Hebrew and Greek. But it performed

[5] B. F. Westcott and F. J. A. Hort, *The New Testament in the Original Greek* (New York: Harper and Brothers, 1882), II, 2.

a tremendous service by placing the Word of God in the hands of the people. Of course all copies had to be made by hand. So they were few and very expensive. But there are today about 170 copies still in existence.

Archbishop Arundel castigated Wycliffe as "that wretched and pestilent fellow of damnable memory, son of the old serpent, and the very herald and child of anti-christ, . . . who crowned his wickedness by translating the Scriptures into the mother tongue."[6] The archbishop also forbade anyone to read Wycliffe's Bible, on penalty of imprisonment. Strangely, Wycliffe was allowed to die a natural death. But later (1428) his bones were dug up and burned, and the ashes cast into the river Swift.

2. *Tyndale's New Testament* (1525)

The most important single individual in the history of the English New Testament was William Tyndale. He translated from the original Greek and published the first printed English New Testament, in 1525 or 1526. More than any other person he influenced the language of the King James Version.

It has been estimated that one third of the King James Version of the New Testament is worded as Tyndale had it, and that even in the remaining two thirds the general literary structure set by Tyndale has been retained. Some scholars have said that ninety per cent of Tyndale is reproduced in the King James Version of the New Testament.[7]

Tyndale was not allowed to do his work in England; so he moved to the Continent. But even there he was hounded from city to city, his life and writings often in danger. The head of the opposition was the Bishop of London, who ordered all copies of Tyndale's New Testament to be burned.

But fortunately Tyndale had a friend named Packington, who was a merchant in London. He agreed to buy up all the copies he could find—they were being concealed in bales of merchandise shipped into England—and turn them over to the angry bishop, who paid him well for them. This money he then turned over to Tyndale, who was thus enabled to put out a second, more accurate printing of his New Testament. But the picture of the Bishop of London burning copies of

[6] George Gordon May, *Our English Bible in the Making* (Philadelphia: Westminster Press, 1952), p. 26.
[7] *Ibid.*

Tyndale's New Testament at St. Paul's Cross is one of the sad spectacles of church history. Of course these bonfires only made the people more eager to see the work for themselves, and soon thousands of copies were secretly reaching the hands of enthusiastic readers.

We are not surprised to learn that Tyndale died a martyr's death. Very treacherously a supposed friend of his, to whom he had just loaned some money, caught him in a trap. After suffering in prison for nearly a year and a half, Tyndale was strangled and burned in 1536. His dying words were, "Lord, open the King of England's eyes."

3. Coverdale's Bible (1535)

The first complete printed English Bible was that put out by Miles Coverdale. He had friends in important positions and so escaped martyrdom.

Coverdale used Tyndale's New Testament (slightly revised) and parts of the Old Testament which Tyndale had managed to translate before his untimely death. But some of the phrases which Coverdale introduced are still retained today in our latest versions.

4. "Matthew's Bible" (1537)

This translation was put out by John Rogers, who assumed the pen name Thomas Matthew. The New Testament was Tyndale's, as well as considerable sections of the Old Testament. One of the strange ironies of history is that this Bible, two-thirds of which came from Tyndale, was licensed by the king only one year after Tyndale was burned to death for doing exactly that work of translating. It is also a strange coincidence that John Rogers himself died a martyr's death, in the reign of the Catholic Queen Mary. Men perished, but the work went on.

5. The Great Bible (1539)

This version is of special interest because it was the first authorized English Bible. The title page—beginning with the second edition of 1540—carried these words: "This is the Byble apoynted to the use of the churches."

It was given the name "Great Bible" because its pages measured 16½ by 11 inches. These impressive volumes were placed in the churches, chained to a reading desk. So eager were the people to hear the Bible read that they gathered around to listen to the Word of God instead of the sermons of the priests—much to the annoyance of the latter!

6. The Geneva Bible (1560)

During the reign of "Bloody Mary" many Protestants fled from England to Geneva, Switzerland. There they occupied their time very profitably by making a new translation entirely from the original Hebrew and Greek. It was a monumental piece of work and very well done, and immediately it became the popular Bible with the common people of England and Scotland. The Pilgrims and Puritans brought it to America, where they long continued to use it in preference to the King James Version, which had recently appeared.

7. The Bishops' Bible (1568)

The bishops of the Church of England were not at all pleased with the Geneva Bible, which was too Puritan to suit them. So they put out their own version. It was largely a reprint of the Great Bible of 1539. But its language was rather stilted and it never became popular with the common people.

8. The Rheims New Testament (1582)

In an effort to win England back to the papacy the Catholics put out an English translation of the New Testament at Rheims (France) in 1582. The Old Testament was published at Douai, in 1609. The extreme Latinized nature of this work can be seen at many points. In Phil. 2:7 where the King James reads, "made himself of no reputation," and the American Standard Version more literally renders it, "emptied himself," the Rheims New Testament has, "he exinanited himself." Obviously such a translation would not do much to enlighten the common people as to the meaning of the Word of God.

9. The King James Version (1611)

In 1604, King James I of England authorized a new translation of the Bible to be made. He appointed fifty-four to do the work, although only forty-seven names are listed in the records that have come down to us. They worked in six companies, two each at Westminster, Oxford, and Cambridge. The project was formally activated in 1607 and completed in 1611.

The King James Version was specifically a revision of the Bishops' Bible, which was to be "as little altered as the truth of the original will permit." This fact is responsible for some of the less satisfactory features in King James Version. But the new version was such a marked improvement over the Bishops' Bible that it finally replaced it. However, our use of "forgive us our trespasses," instead of "our debts," in saying the Lord's Prayer goes back to the earlier version, which has been retained in the ritual of many churches.

In spite of its defects the King James Version is a majestic translation and has been the favorite Bible of the English-speaking world for three hundred years. It is so deeply intrenched in both literature and life that to be ignorant of its language is to be illiterate in a very true sense. No one can read intelligently the literature of the last three centuries unless he knows his English Bible. While Shakespeare, of course, quoted from an earlier version, most of the writers since his day have used the King James Version.

10. John Wesley's New Testament (1755)

John Wesley believed passionately in honest scholarship. During the years of his mature ministry his Greek New Testament was his constant companion. The inevitable result was that he became increasingly aware of the defects of the King James Version. So he finally made his own translation of the New Testament. He first put it out with his "Explanatory Notes on the New Testament." But finally he published the text alone in several pocket editions for his Methodists to use.

In Wesley's translation of the New Testament there are over 12,000 changes from the King James Version. In his preface he stated that the latter version could be improved in three ways: better text, better sense, better English. That is what he set out to do.

11. The English Revised New Testament (1881)

Since the King James Version was made in 1611 hundreds of old Greek manuscripts have come to light. That fact alone demanded that a revision should be made. Consequently, in 1870 the Convocation of Canterbury ordered such a revision. After ten and a half years of arduous labor, for which the translators received no remuneration, the New Testament appeared in 1881. This was the same year in which the monumental Westcott and Hort Greek New Testament was published.

The revision was very carefully done, with twenty-seven scholars doing the translating, and the whole group checking the entire manuscript. But this version has not supplanted the King James, in spite of its recognized greater accuracy. One of the main reasons is that its language is too stilted, due to the effort to translate the Greek as literally as possible. It has been characterized as "strong in Greek, but weak in English." It does not have the smoothly flowing style of the King James.

12. The American Standard Version (1901)

American scholars were invited to advise with the British committee of translators. When the English Revised Version was published the preferences of the American committee were printed in an appendix. The Americans agreed not to put out a separate version for fourteen years after the entire Bible was published in England in 1885.

In 1901, therefore, the American Standard Edition of the Revised Version appeared, incorporating the preferred readings of the American group. This version has never become popular with the common people. However, because it is a more accurate translation of a better Greek text than is the King James Version, it has been widely used for study purposes. Most scholars agree that it is the best study Bible in the English language.

13. Modern Speech Translations

The twentieth century has witnessed the appearance of many private translations of the New Testament. The two outstanding British ones are those by Weymouth and Moffatt. The former is especially beautiful in its diction. The latter is very pointedly British in vocabulary and style. For the American reader Goodspeed's *American Translation* is often very helpful. Verkuyl's "Berkeley Version" is also good. All of these may be used beneficially.

14. The Revised Standard Version (1946)

Because the American Standard Version, though excellent for study purposes, was not acceptable for private devotional use and for reading in public worship services, a new translation was finally undertaken. The International Council of Religious Education in 1929 appointed the American Standard Bible Committee to study the matter of the text.

In 1937 the Council voted to have the text revised. It was to be a revision of the American Standard Version "in the direction of the simple, classic English style of the King James Version," in order to make it more acceptable for use in worship services. The New Testament was completed and published in 1946.

The Revised Standard Version is based on an older Greek text than was the King James. The latter was translated from the so-called Textus Receptus, which was practically the same as that of Erasmus, who published the first printed Greek Testament in 1516. For this task he had only a handful of Greek manuscripts—some eight of them for different parts of the New Testament. Not one of them was older than the tenth century.

Today the picture is a very different one. We have 4,000 manuscripts of the Greek New Testament, in whole or in part. A number of them come from the sixth and fifth centuries, two great ones from the fourth century, and now some on papyrus from the third century.

The Revised Standard Version is also written in the English of our day. There are some two hundred words in the King James Version which have changed their meaning since 1611. In a few cases a word has exactly the opposite meaning from what it had three hundred years ago. For instance, "he who now letteth will let" (II Thess. 2:7) does not mean "he who allows," but "he who hinders or restrains."

The work of translation has been going on for many centuries and will continue until Jesus comes. Meanwhile let us apply ourselves to the earnest study of God's Word, using any and every means which will help us to understand it more fully.

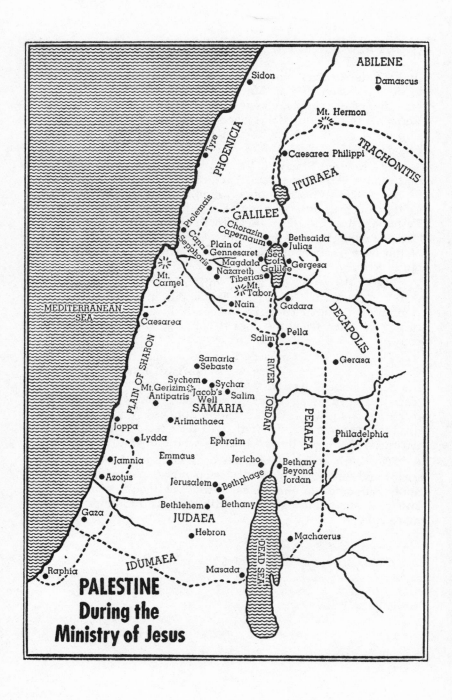

PALESTINE
During the
Ministry of Jesus

CHAPTER IV
THE MESSIAH-KING
(MATTHEW)

A. INTRODUCTION TO THE SYNOPTIC GOSPELS

I. The Importance of the Gospels

The event that called into being a Church with its need for a New Testament was unique. God had spoken in a Son whose life was the light of men. The advent of that incomparable life into the world of man through the Incarnation was an event in eternity. It was fitting therefore that the literature that recorded the birth, life, teachings, death, and resurrection of our Lord should be a new type of literature. This the Gospels were; for while both Epistle and Apocalypse had their counterpart in earlier Jewish literature, the Gospels were a new departure.

The term gospel means "the good news." The four Gospels are the primary sources for most of our knowledge of the events of Jesus' saving life and death. They are therefore records of supreme worth to the entire race of sinful men. Since they are so valuable it is important that we have a knowledge of their origin and validity. Fortunately, since our Gospels are true, they will bear investigation. We do not need to defend the record but rather to understand it.

II. Origin of the Synoptic Gospels

1. Introduction

That the Master Teacher had no stenographer present to take down His teachings as He uttered them may come to many as a surprise. Fortunately for us, such a record was not made. A record made in this manner would have involved much repetition, and material of only local and temporary relevance would have been included.

Many factors delayed the production of the Gospels. As long as Jesus, the Fountain of their inspiration, was with them there was no need to write, and the Twelve found it difficult to believe that He would not be with them always. After His death they expected Him to return soon, and so there was no incentive for writing a record of His life. As long as early Christianity was confining its efforts within the boundaries of Palestine, little need was felt for a written gospel. Moreover, there was a Palestinian aversion to the writing of other books in addition to the Old Testament, which was regarded as sufficient. Collections of Old Testament prooftexts were considered adequate for a record of Christ's life. The vivid account of the eyewitness was preferred to the more impersonal written record. Emphasis was placed on the inner life of the Spirit instead of the written letter of the word. In addition to this the high cost of writing materials made the possession of written documents difficult or impossible for poor Galilean peasants. Finally, the art of writing was not common; and the apostles were not literary men by preparation or calling. They had been commissioned to preach and evangelize, not to write.

Anyone who examines carefully a harmony of the Gospels in which similar or identical material is printed in parallel columns will see at once that Matthew, Mark, and Luke present a common outline of the life of Christ. In addition to this he will see many statements in two or more of the Gospels that are almost alike and some that are identical. Because these books view the life of Christ from a common point of view they are called the Synoptic Gospels.

In contrast to these similarities there are equally striking differences. This gives rise to the so-called "Synoptic problem." In brief the problem is this: What account of the origin of the first three Gospels best explains their similarities and differences?

Had the Gospels been written down as the events occurred and the teachings were given there would have been no problem. But, as we have noted, the Gospels were not at first written down. Moreover, the original manuscripts were anonymous.

2. Light from Luke's Preface (1:1-4)

Fortunately, one of our Gospel writers has told us something about Gospel origins. Luke's preface contains the oldest and most significant testimony regarding the production of written gospels.

Forasmuch as many have taken in hand to draw up a narrative concerning those matters which have been fulfilled among us, even as they delivered them unto us, who from the beginning were eyewitnesses and ministers of the word, it seemed good to me also, having traced the course of all things accurately from the first, to write unto thee in order, most excellent Theophilus; that thou mightest know the certainty concerning the things wherein thou wast instructed (Luke 1:1-4).

Luke's statement reveals that already there were in existence several more or less complete narratives of the life of Christ. Gospel writing was already a common practice (1:1). These little gospels were based on an authentic oral tradition founded on the reports of those who from the first had been eyewitnesses commissioned to proclaim the good news of the Kingdom. Although he had access to information from one or more of the apostles, Luke belonged to the second generation of believers. While he modestly places himself in the same category with earlier gospel writers, Luke hints that previous gospels were lacking in accuracy, completeness, or order.

Luke lived in a day in which research was not uncommon and he claims to have done careful research (1:3). He aimed to produce a more adequate record in which facts derived from various sources were stated in order with superior accuracy. Having the advantage of writing with the entire scope of Christ's life in view, Luke's Gospel records the earthly life and ministry of Jesus.

Luke wrote for a very practical purpose. His letter is addressed to Theophilus, who may have been an official who by hearsay evidence had been misinformed about Christianity. In this case Luke wrote that an official might hear the truth about Christianity and see for himself that it was not a subversive sect. On the other hand, Theophilus may have been a wealthy patron, a convert who previously had received oral instruction. In this case the Gospel was written that a new Christian, by a more complete written record of the things he had received orally, might have his faith confirmed.

It should be noted also that the Gospels were written in an age in which writers were uninhibited by footnotes and copyright laws. Wholesale borrowing of form as well as content was universally practiced. The gospel materials were regarded as common property of the Church and considerable freedom in the treatment of sources was not considered irreverent.

3. The Earliest Testimony About the Origin of Mark and Matthew

Since the titles of the books form no part of the original text, our information must come from other sources. Later writers all seem to be indebted to Papias for their data, since they add nothing to Papias' statements about the origin of these Gospels except that which they might have inferred, correctly or incorrectly, from his words. Since, then, statements of later writers are of value mainly as corroborating what Papias said, we should give primary attention to his testimony.

    a. Papias' Testimony About the Origin of Mark. Concerning Mark, Papias (*ca.* A.D. 140) said:

> The Elder said this also: Mark had been the interpreter of Peter, and wrote down accurately, though not in order, everything that he remembered that had been said or done by the Lord. For he neither heard the Lord nor followed him, but afterward, as I said, attended Peter, who adapted his instructions to the needs of his hearers, but had no design of giving a connected account of the Lord's oracles. So then Mark made no mistake in thus writing some things as he remembered them; for he made it his one concern not to omit anything that he had heard, or to make any false statement in them.[1]

There is reason to believe that Papias' statement is essentially correct and that Mark's Gospel, in at least its main outlines and the major portion of its content, is derived from Peter's preaching. Corroborating Papias' testimony is the rough style of Mark which matches that of Peter's addresses recorded in Acts and that of his Epistles. In addition to the tradition that links Peter with Rome is that which connects Mark and his Gospel with Rome. We are safe in concluding, then, that after having served many times as Peter's interpreter, rendering Peter's Aramaic discourses into Greek for the crowds at Rome, Mark wrote down, as the Holy Spirit assisted him, what he remembered of Peter's preaching in the Gospel that bears his name. The obscurity and relative

---

[1] Eusebius, *Church History*, III, 39; Goodspeed's translation, *The Apostolic Fathers* (New York: Harper and Brothers, 1950), p. 266.

unimportance of Mark, as indicated by our records, would have left no motive for advancing his name as the author of the Gospel unless he was in some way connected with its production.

b. *Papias' Testimony About the Origin of Matthew*. Concerning Matthew, Papias writes: "So Matthew composed the Sayings in the Aramaic language, and everyone translated them as well as he could."[2]

Some think that the phrase *ta logia*, translated here as "the Sayings," refers to a collection of proof-texts compiled by Matthew to prove that Jesus was the Messiah. More commonly it is thought that the phrase refers to discourse material, particularly sayings of Jesus drawn up by Matthew. The phrase could scarcely have included narrative material to the extent that it is found in the first Gospel. Moreover, Papias says that the *logia* was written in a Semitic language, and it is generally agreed that our Greek Matthew is not a translation Gospel.

4. *Mark, One of the Sources of Matthew and Luke*

When the Synoptic Gospels are compared carefully with the aid of a reliable harmony, several very interesting facts are revealed. Matthew and Luke travel their separate ways until Mark joins the company with his account of the preaching of the Baptist. From this point on Matthew and Luke as a rule agree with each other and with Mark both in their general historical framework and in the order of events included within the various periods. With a few slight exceptions, Matthew and Luke have taken between them the entire Gospel of Mark, which furnishes the historical framework of the Synoptic Gospels. This is remarkable since so small a proportion of Jesus' life and ministry is actually recorded and since John does not share much of this material or order with the first three Gospels.

Equally striking is the lack of agreement of Matthew and Luke in their placing of the events and teachings which they share with each other but not with Mark. An example of this may be seen in Luke's reproduction in smaller, scattered segments of much of the material found in Matthew's version of the Sermon on the Mount.

[2] *Ibid.*

It is obvious that in material shared by all three Gospels, Mark resembles each of the other two in order and in content much more closely than Matthew and Luke resemble each other. Indeed Matthew and Luke never agree in order against Mark in the content of portions common to all three. They agree against Mark only infrequently in a brief phrase or in an omission. The evidence indicates that Matthew and Mark must have derived their outline from a common source, that Luke and Mark likewise secured their outline from a common source, and that Mark or a document almost identical with Mark is the middle term between Matthew and Luke.

This conclusion is supported by the fact that in content shared by the three even the details are given in almost the same order. Over 90 per cent of Mark's content is reproduced by Matthew in language almost the same as that of Mark and over half of Mark's content is reproduced by Luke in the same manner. These identical words include unimportant and unusual terms and even quotations from the Old Testament that depart from both the Septuagint and Hebrew text. Furthermore, even parenthetic material and transitional statements which formed no part of the original discourse are sometimes given in almost identical language.

Both Matthew and Luke have many important inclusions. The most significant is the so-called Perean ministry of Jesus recorded in Luke 9:51—19:10, which contains a great deal of unparalleled material. Matthew's peculiar material is all discourse except for the infancy account, the story of the guards at the sepulcher, and some small additions.

With respect to Mark the story is different. Over 96 per cent of Mark is reproduced by Matthew or Luke or both. According to Dana's reckoning, Mark's peculiar material totals only about twenty-six verses.[3] The omission of these verses by Matthew and Luke can be explained without difficulty.

Departures from Mark's style by Matthew and Luke are likewise evidence of Mark's priority. In spite of the greater length of the other Synoptists they usually shorten Mark's narrative, using fewer words to describe the same incident. Mark is more vivid as well as more detailed, which also argues for its priority.

[3] H. E. Dana, *New Testament Criticism* (Fort Worth: World Co., 1924), p. 162.

5. "Q," the Other Source Shared by Matthew and Luke

Matthew and Luke share about two hundred verses of material that is not found in Mark. In addition to the similarity of the contents and usually of order of these materials in Matthew and Luke, there is often identical wording, extending in some instances to rare words. All these factors point to either the dependence of the one on the other or their use of a common source. The former alternative does not seem likely here, so that the majority of scholars prefer to postulate a source which they call Q, the abbreviation for the German word meaning "source." The existence of this source cannot be proved.

III. The Validity of the Gospel Record

Behind these written sources was the oral tradition originating from eyewitnesses whose retentive Oriental memory and purpose to tell the truth served to keep the record accurate. Even the enemies of the Early Church, who would have pounced eagerly on any misstatements of fact, helped to guard the record from error.

Perhaps all of this discussion of sources leaves the beginner a little bewildered. But the investigation should have left faith on a firmer foundation of fact than when we started our study. For we have not followed "cunningly devised fables" (II Pet. 1:16), but have records based on the evidence from eyewitnesses. Our written sources carry us to within a few years of Jesus' ministry, and these written sources were based on the statements of those who had been with Jesus and heard Him as He taught the crowds, and witnessed the miracles that He had performed. Far above and beyond all this, we have the inspiration of the Holy Spirit guiding the writers of the Gospels.

B. INTRODUCTION TO MATTHEW

I. Position

Although Matthew was not the first book of the New Testament to be written, its position did not come about by chance. For two reasons, at least, its position is appropriate.

In the first place, Matthew forms the connecting link between the old covenant and the new. It shows how Jesus built on the foundation of the permanent element in the Old, which He emancipated from the choking weeds of tradition and reinterpreted in terms of the divine purpose. It discloses how Jesus fulfilled the Messianic expectations of the old covenant and came as the true, spiritual Messiah of the Jews. It reveals the Messiah's purpose to set up a spiritual and universal Kingdom by beginning with a nucleus of His own people who were responsive to His claims. It manifests the reasons that the Jews failed to recognize and respond to their opportunity and the cause of their consequent rejection.

In the second place, Matthew's value and usefulness to the Church won for it the position at the beginning of the fourfold gospel. This position and popularity which it had from the first it never lost. It is to Matthew that Christians usually turn for accounts of the Beatitudes, Sermon on the Mount, Lord's Prayer, and other items. Like a great and beautiful cathedral, Matthew still towers to the glory of God and His beloved Son. It is, as Renan observed, the "most important book in the world."

II. Origin, Place, and Date

1. Origin

The first Gospel, like the other Synoptic accounts, is anonymous in the oldest manuscripts, the titles having been added when the four Gospels were published as a unit. The oldest tradition to which appeal is sometimes made in support of Matthean authorship is, in that tradition, connected with a Semitic original—probably the *logia* mentioned by Papias— and is not brought into contact with the Greek Gospel that we now possess. Papias' statement about the *logia*, which seems to be the source of this line of tradition, probably does not refer to our Gospel in its present form, but to one of its sources. But the Church has traditionally held that the author of our first Gospel was Matthew the publican, one of the twelve apostles.

2. Place and Date

The Jewish and Gentile elements in the book would possess a peculiar appeal for a community in which both groups were found. This situation is especially true of Antioch in Syria, which for other reasons also, is often linked with the origin of Matthew.

Since the writer evidently used Mark as one of his sources, the book would be dated sometime later than Mark. It could be dated in the sixties or seventies.

III. Purpose

The twofold reason for the position of Matthew at the beginning of the New Testament affords an insight into the purpose for which the Gospel was written and a suggestion concerning some of the special features of the book.

On the one hand, it established Jesus' position as the Jewish Messiah, whose coming had been long expected. Matthew proved that Jesus was "the Son of David" (1:1; 21:9) and the rightful "king of the Jews" (2:2; 27:37). Matthew reports that Jesus often called himself the "Son of man"— the heavenly being of the apocalypses. Moreover, He is "the Son of God" (16:16). Israel should accept her Messianic King.

On the other hand, the growing Church of Matthew's day was faced with definite needs which that writer hoped to supply. The reason for Israel's rejection of her Messiah and the Church's Lord was needed for apologetic and polemic purposes. Stories about Jesus would be required in the Church's ministry of teaching and preaching. Rules regarding retaliation, oaths, divorce, and the treatment of offenders were needed, as well as a definition of the relation of the Christian to the law. The Church had devotional needs. The followers of the Way required to be shown how they were to differ from the Jews and heathen in their fundamental attitudes. Antinomianism and other heresies had to be met. To supply these needs the Holy Spirit inspired the writing of the Gospel of Matthew, embodying in addition to most of Mark's content the fullest statement of Jesus' ethical teachings.

IV. Characteristics

1. Style

Matthew's style and vocabulary are midway between Mark's roughness of style and limited vocabulary and Luke's smoother style and richer vocabulary. Lacking in the vivid descriptive details in which Mark abounds, Matthew's balanced sentences, stanzas, and closing refrains are adapted to the presentation of Jesus' sayings in a continuous statement.

2. A Jewish Gospel

Besides its manifest interest in the Jews, revealed in the fact that Jesus is the Jewish Messiah and that His mission was first of all to the Jews, other features give the first Gospel a Jewish stamp. There are over sixty references to the Old Testament, including many recurrences of the phrase "that it might be fulfilled" or a similar formula. The genealogy with which the book begins traces Jesus' ancestry through Israel's great warrior-king, David, to the patriarch Abraham. The genealogy is somewhat artificially divided into three groups, each containing the double of seven generations. This preference for certain numbers, especially three, five, and seven, Matthew shares with Judaism. Jewish also are such expressions as the "holy city" and "holy place" and "city of the great King," employed only by Matthew as synonyms for Jerusalem.

3. The Gospel of the King and the Kingdom

Seven times Jesus is called the Son of David. The genealogy represents Jesus as a Descendant from David's line. The question of the Magi addressed to the startled ears of Herod the Great was, "Where is he that is born King of the Jews?" (2:2.) His triumphal entry is pictured as that of a peaceful King (21:5, 7). Asked by Pilate if He were King of the Jews (27:11), He did not deny the charge. The trilingual inscription above His head on the cross read, "This is Jesus the King of the Jews" (27:37). When He returns in glory He will sit on His glorious throne (25:31).

The phrase "the kingdom of heaven," employed only by Matthew, is found thirty-three times, often when the other Synoptic Gospels use "kingdom of God." This alternate formula Matthew employs six times. Twelve parables begin with the expression "the kingdom of heaven is like . . . " The spiritual and ethical nature of the Kingdom is expressed in the Sermon on the Mount.

4. The Didactic Gospel

Matthew contains the fullest account of Jesus' ethical teaching, the largest single block of which is found in the so-called Sermon on the Mount. Each major section of Matthew's Gospel, except the Passion narrative, is constructed around a lengthy discourse. The material in each discourse is arranged topically. Comparison with parallel accounts indicates that Matthew has grouped much of his material for the benefit of his readers. The parables of chapter 13 and eschatological discourse of chapters 24 and 25 show how the Evangelist put the story into a form that would suit the memory of teachers and hearers. The arrangement of the material into groups of three, five, and seven would facilitate memorization. There are some indications that the Gospel was composed with the needs of teachers especially in mind. At least, the Gospel presents an orderly arrangement of the priceless teaching of the Master Teacher, whose words are the basis of life here and hereafter.

5. The Gospel of the Church

Matthew alone of all the Gospels mentions the church. This he does three times in two passages (16:18; 18:17). In the latter passage the church is probably a local congregation; in the former it is the Church universal.

6. An Ecumenical Gospel

While in some ways Matthew is more Jewish than the other Gospels, in other ways it is anti-Jewish and anticipates the Gentile mission. The visit of the Magi (2:1 ff.) is often regarded as symbolic of the Gentile ingathering. Together with Luke, Matthew records the healing of the Gentile centurion's servant (8:5 ff.) and the admission of some of the Gentiles to the Kingdom from which part of the Jews are excluded (8:11 f.; 21:43). The Great Commission (28:18-20) embraces the evangelizing, baptizing, and teaching of all nations.

C. CONTENTS

I. Beginning (cc. 1—4)

1. The Genealogy of Jesus (1:1-17)

a. *Matthew's Record.* "The book of the genealogy of Jesus Christ, the son of David, the son of Abraham (1:1)." These words were originally intended for the genealogy only, or for the first two chapters of the Gospel. But they also form an excellent statement of the purpose for which the entire book was written.

The word Christ is from the Greek *Christos,* which translates the Hebrew and the Aramaic terms that are transliterated into the English word Messiah. The word Messiah, which originally designated only an "anointed one" and so anyone anointed with holy oil, came in the pre-Christian period to mean one especially empowered by God's Spirit to bring deliverance to Israel and to establish the Kingdom. The word translated "genealogy" means "beginning." Hence we have here the origin of the Messiah, the son of David, and so heir to the throne; the son of Abraham, and so heir to the promise.

Since the Jews attached great importance to genealogical lists, it was only natural for Matthew to begin with a list containing the names of many of Jesus' ancestors. It was an argument needed to satisfy the Jewish mind that Jesus was the son of David and could be the Messiah. Probably for the writer it was a concession to the prejudice of his readers. For him Jesus' messiahship rested, no doubt, as it does for us, on His spiritual claims. At least, Jesus never depended on any Davidic blood for His authority; and Matthew is tracing Jesus' legal genealogy, for He had no human father (1:18 ff.).

Another concession to Jewish thinking is found in Matthew's artificial arrangement of the genealogy. In this arrangement, although there are three sets of fourteen generations, only forty-one names appear, David's being counted twice and the Captivity serving as one point of division. There are also several omissions, which, however, do not make the record false but only incomplete—"begat" implying only direct line of descent and not necessarily paternity.

An unusual feature is the inclusion of the names of several women in the list, three of whom were of doubtful morality (Tamar, Rahab, and Uriah's wife), and one of whom was a foreigner (Ruth). This displays God's amazing grace.

b. *Matthew's Genealogy Compared with Luke's* (Luke 3:23-34). Probably the first major difference one notes between the accounts is that, while Matthew begins with Abraham and ends with Jesus, Luke begins with Jesus and works back through Adam to God. Thus, whereas Matthew only hints at a universalism by his inclusion of women in his list, Luke asserts a universalism which almost eclipses the original purpose of these genealogical tables. The fact that Jesus is the son of David is subordinated to the fact that He is the Son of God. This may reflect a waning interest in the genealogical proof of Jesus' messiahship, or it may be due to the fact that Luke was writing for Gentiles.

A comparison of the lists will reveal several differences in the names included. Several solutions have been proposed for this problem, but all that succeed in reconciling the differences are complicated, and scholars do not agree that any one solution is adequate. While two or three of the hypotheses advanced would harmonize most of the differences, our knowledge of the facts is so meager that dogmatism is unjustifiable. We should remember, however, that, as Wesley says, the difficulties "rather affect the Jewish tables than the credit of the evangelists."[4]

The theory that Matthew gives the legal genealogy through Joseph and Luke gives the actual genealogy through Mary has in its favor the fact that Matthew's selection of incidents in the birth and infancy narratives is presented throughout from Joseph's point of view while the selection in Luke reflects Mary's standpoint. There is almost no duplication between Matthew and Luke in this section apart from the genealogies.

2. The Birth of Jesus (1:18-25)

This wonderful incident is told with the beautiful simplicity and delicacy native to the soil of truth. After Mary had been betrothed to Joseph but before their marriage "she was found with child . . . " (1:18). Unfaithfulness after betrothal was considered adultery. Hence, since Joseph was a law-observing Jew, only two alternatives appeared to be open to him. He might bring Mary before the court and expose her to the shame of a public trial, or he might hand her a certificate of divorce in the presence of two witnesses.

After he had resolved to take the latter course of action, the angel of the Lord in a dream revealed that Mary had not been untrue after all, for that which was conceived in her was "of the Holy Spirit" (1:20). Therefore Joseph was not to fear to take Mary as his wife. The son that she would bear should be called Jesus or "Saviour"; for He would save the people from their sins.

[4] John Wesley, *Explanatory Notes on the New Testament* (London: Epworth Press, 1941), p. 15.

3. The Visit of the Magi (2:1-12)

The next scene is that of the Magi, priestly astrologers from Persia, appearing before Herod and inquiring concerning the whereabouts of one who has been born king of the Jews. Claiming to be prophets and mediators between Deity and man, the Magi generally were known for their incantations. Hence the Greeks began to apply the name magician to all who practiced Oriental methods of enchantment (Acts 13:6; 8:9). Beyond the data implicit in their name and the meager statement of Matthew, we know nothing about them. The inference that they were three kings has no basis.

As astrologers they had studied the stars, which they believed could be the counterparts or angels of great men. The appearance of a new brilliant star told them that a great king had been born. Perhaps they were familiar with the "star out of Jacob" prophecy (Num. 24:17), for there were still many Jews in Persia. At least they seem to have journeyed in the direction of the star until they were certain that the ruler would come from Palestine. They presumed that a ruler would be born in a palace.

Their appearance at the palace, however, produced consternation. Herod—suspicious and insanely jealous of his office, and therefore cruel—was not the rightful heir; and here was a claimant who was born a king. Was not this a threat to the continuation of his dynasty? The priests and other ecclesiastical leaders, probably included at least in the "all Jerusalem" of verse three, were alarmed. Was it because the appearance of a legitimate heir to the throne might plunge the nation into civil war, with the consequent loss of the religious liberty it now enjoyed and the forfeiture of the special privileges that accrued to these hierarchs under the Roman rule? Or was it fear of some such act of cruelty on the part of Herod as his Slaughter of the Innocents?

When Herod inquired of the proper authorities where the Messiah was to be born, they cited the beautiful prophecy of Mic. 5:2, which indicated Bethlehem of Judea. So Herod sent the Magi with instructions that after they had found the young prince they were to bring him word, so that he too might come and worship the babe.

Once out of Herod's presence, they again saw the star, which now guided them to the young Christ child. Verses nine and ten suggest that these travelers may have had to journey by faith much of the way. God's accommodation to their superstition is a reminder that all of God's disclosures to us involve condescension on His part, inasmuch as there are always error, prejudice, and ignorance on ours that limit the revelation. It also reminds us that God reveals himself to those who sincerely want to know the truth.

The contrast between the attitudes of Herod and the Magi affords an interesting study. Herod, in whom selfishness, suspicion, jealousy, moroseness, and cruelty had so blocked the channels of devotion that worship of another was impossible; the Magi, foreigners who although they possessed only star light found no sacrifice too great and no gift too costly to express their devotion to One that their value-sensitive consciousness told them was worthy of their highest devotion. Their offering will always breathe "the sense of wonder and thanksgiving that through the birth of this Child, and his subsequent life, death, and resurrection, the world has been redeemed."[5]

4. The Flight to Egypt and the Fulfillment of Prophecy (2:13-23)

The Magi, having been warned in a dream not to return to Herod, departed by a different route. Another dream warned Joseph to flee with the Babe to Egypt, which he did in order that an ancient prophecy might be fulfilled.

5. The Work of John the Baptist (c. 3)

a. The Ministry of John the Baptist (3:1-12). All three Synoptic Gospels indicate that the main emphasis of John's message was on repentance. He wanted the Jews to repent of their sins, that they might be ready to receive the Kingdom through accepting Jesus as their Messiah. This the rulers refused to do.

Matthew and Luke agree in quoting John's declaration that the Coming One would baptize "in the Holy Spirit and in fire" (v. 11; Luke 3:16). Fire is a cleansing, purifying agency. The baptism with the Holy Spirit purifies the inner nature of the believer, destroying the carnal mind.

[5] S. Johnson, Interpreter's Bible (IB), VII, 256.

b. The Baptism of Jesus (3:13-17). This passage gives us the first clear view of the Trinity in the Bible. As Jesus came up out of the Jordan, the Spirit of God descended upon Him in the form of a dove, while the Father's voice from heaven said, "This is my beloved Son" (v. 17). Here we find Father, Son, and Holy Spirit meeting in this wonderful event of Jesus' baptism. Here also we have a definite affirmation of the deity of Jesus.

6. The Temptation of Jesus (4:1-11)

In Matthew and Luke three specific temptations of Jesus are listed, although not in the same order. While the complete significance of these tests of Jesus' moral strength can never be fathomed, underneath there was the suggestion that Jesus was not God's beloved Son and that His sense of special relationship and mission were only figments of His imagination. "If thou art the Son of God . . . " the satanic voice suggested subtly. These are the types of temptation that often confront those Jesus came to save.

a. The First Temptation (4:1-4). The devil took advantage of Jesus' hunger to suggest that if He were God's Son He should not be hungering in the desert. If He were really divine, let Him use His miraculous power to satisfy His personal needs. Had He succumbed to the siren voice He would have disqualified himself as the Pioneer or Trail Blazer of our salvation, for we cannot satisfy our physical needs by performing miracles.

This scene is in decided contrast to that in the Garden of Eden, where Adam and Eve succumbed to the devil's temptation. They were surrounded by plenty; He was fasting alone in the wilderness. They had everything in their favor; it seemed that everything was stacked against Him. Yet He was Conqueror, and through Him we can conquer.

Since Jesus was probably laying plans for His program, there was, no doubt, the suggestion that He give primary attention to men's physical and economic needs. By giving attention to physical needs He could acquire a following that would enable Him to establish the Kingdom. In fact the temptation may have had its basis in a popular expectation that the Messiah would do no less than Moses, who had given Israel bread from heaven (John 6:30 ff.).

To Jesus, keenly aware of the poverty and suffering He daily encountered, the temptation represented not merely a single drama but a continual struggle in the depths of His sensitive soul. Often He was forced to tear himself away from the suffering who sought physical healing, so that He could minister to deeper needs. For, while man needs bread, he cannot "live by bread alone." Bread is only a means, and physical values mock the soul's deepest need.

b. *The Second Temptation* (4:5-7). "If thou art the Son of God, cast thyself down: for it is written . . . " (4:6). This time the devil quoted scripture (Ps. 91:11 f.), but only in part and out of context, as many of his helpers have done since. If God had given Him a special call, surely He would furnish miraculous signs by which all would recognize that He was the Messiah. Perhaps He needed a physical sign to reassure himself of His divine sonship and commission.

A Jewish tradition, if then current, may have afforded the basis of the tempter's suggestion. "When King Messiah is revealed, he comes and stands upon the roof of the Holy Place: then will he announce to the Israelites and say, Ye poor, the time of your redemption is come."[6] The Messiah by casting himself down from the pinnacle of the Temple would give the sign for the people to revolt against their enemies and those of God.

Even if this Messianic tradition were not then current, there was still the temptation to use spectacular means to convince the sign-seekers. Constantly He was confronted by those who sought the spectacular sign. Even at the Crucifixion the sign-seekers were present to taunt and to jeer (27:39 ff.). But the spectacular, then as now, was powerless to effect spiritual transformation. Even thermo-nuclear energy cannot change character.

Jesus repudiated a course of action that would lead men to expect divine intervention with miracles of power not governed by ethical considerations. For Jesus there was an economy of the miraculous. While God might occasionally intervene with a miracle to save a person from a predicament, this was not to be expected. To expect such intervention, to

---

[6]*Pesikta Rabba*, 162 a, quoted by William Manson, *The Gospel of Luke* (New York: Harper and Brothers, 1930), p. 38.

insist on a spectacular display of God's power, was to tempt Him or put Him to the test.

c. *The Third Temptation* (4:8-10). After Jesus had met the second temptation with another quotation from Deuteronomy, the devil entered a third solicitation to evil. He promised Jesus all the kingdoms of the world in exchange for Jesus' worship. The temptation no doubt was not put as bluntly as that, but then, as now, it was concealed in the lie that the end justifies the means. Achieve success by short cuts and compromise. Bow to the wishes of the people and be acclaimed a political messiah. Make a deal with the Parthians, who were anxious to help "liberate" the Jews from the Roman yoke.

In the invitation, as construed by the Jews of His day, to ask God for the nations as His Messianic inheritance, Jesus recognized a surrender to the methods and aims of Satan. Revolt and bloodshed was not the method of God, who commands men to love their enemies and to conquer evildoers by applying the philosophy of the second mile (5:39 ff.). Again Jesus met and defeated the devil with appropriate words from Deuteronomy. The use Jesus made of scripture in this time of testing indicates the value of having one's mind saturated with the Bible.

7. *Jesus Begins His Ministry in Galilee* (4:12-25)

Matthew finds in Jesus' removal to Capernaum a fulfillment of prophecy (4:12-16; cf. Isa. 9:1-2). The time of the beginning of Jesus' ministry is fixed as after John's arrest (4:12). His message is summarized: "Repent ye; for the kingdom of heaven is at hand" (4:17).

After the call of the four fishermen, Matthew tells of Jesus' itinerant ministry of teaching, preaching, and healing in Galilee with the consequent spread of His fame and a great influx of candidates for His healing touch.

II. The First Great Discourse: the Sermon on the Mount
(cc. 5—7)

In this period of Jesus' initial popularity Matthew places the great body of teaching popularly called the Sermon on the Mount. Luke gives a shorter version.

1. The Beatitudes and Statements on Salt and Light (5: 3-16)

The discourse begins with a series of nine beatitudes which describe those who are truly happy or fortunate and indicate rewards appropriate to each virtue.

a. *The First Beatitude:* "Blessed are the poor in spirit" (5:3). Luke has, "Blessed are ye poor" (6:20), but at that time the poor, who were the spiritual offspring of the pious of the later psalms, were those that in their need cast themselves wholly on God (Luke 4:18; Isa. 61:1). The first step toward God is a confession of our own spiritual bankruptcy. An attitude of self-sufficiency keeps us from receiving God's blessings.

The word "blessed" may be translated "happy." But its primary reference is to divine blessedness.

b. *The Second Beatitude:* "How happy are those who mourn . . . " (5:4, author's translation). Congratulations in that you mourn your loss—in that you are bereaved. We think otherwise. Yet we must admit that comfort comes only to the mourner, as rest is experienced only by the weary. In life peace comes after the discords have been resolved. Blessed are those who mourn because of a sensitivity to sin in self and society, for they shall be comforted.

c. *The Third Beatitude:* "Happy are the meek, for they shall inherit the earth" (5:5, author's translation). How paradoxical! Meekness for us is sometimes associated with littleness or spinelessness. In the New Testament, however, it signifies one who is "mild," "gentle," "humble-minded." It is a word that pictures strength, poise, and self-control. Jesus and Moses are both described as meek. The term describes those who are more concerned with the progress of the Kingdom than with personal prestige. Those who persevere to the end in submissive endurance will inherit, possess as a gift, that for which the self-assertive strive in vain.

It is probable, however, that the promise means something more than the mere possession of real estate. Ps. 37:11, on which the promise is based, is probably Messianic. In that case it may mean the restored earth of the Messianic Age and all the good things that accompany that age.

Some hold that all the beatitudes are Messianic. The Kingdom promised is God's, but the rule is exercised through

His Messiah. The Messiah was to bring comfort (Isa. 61:2; Luke 2:25), and some rabbis even called the Messiah "the Comforter."

d. *The Fourth Beatitude* (5:6). A lack of intense desire is often the reason for barrenness or shallowness in one's Christian experience. The one who hungers and thirsts after righteousness is assured that he will be filled. One application of this could be to the hunger for holiness, which will result in being filled with the Holy Spirit. The word "filled" probably has the primary meaning "satisfied."

e. *The Fifth Beatitude* (5:7). That the merciful shall obtain mercy is scarcely a paradox. Christ indicates that to be merciful as God is merciful is life's highest ideal (Luke 6:36). For Micah, mercy is the heart of religion (6:8). The word employed by Micah, the translation of which Matthew (9:13) quotes from Hosea, is *chesed*. The Revised Standard Version usually renders this word by "steadfast love." It is a term which embraces love plus loyalty, the kind of love that should bless every marriage. It implies an ability to share vicariously the experiences of others because of a profound appreciation of them as persons. Only those who extend this kind of intelligent good will are capable of receiving it.

f. *The Sixth Beatitude* (5:8). The way to see God here and hereafter is to have a pure heart. Sin clouds the vision so that one cannot see God. Only those whose hearts have been cleansed from all sin can have full fellowship with God. Rejection of holiness means rejection of heaven.

g. *The Seventh Beatitude* (5:9). The peacemakers who are here pronounced as blessed are not those who merely refrain from making or becoming involved in trouble. Instead they become actively involved, promoting good will where ill will and strife had existed. Their reward is to be called "sons of God," which reduced to English idiom means "God-like."

h. *The Eighth and Ninth Beatitudes* (5:10-12). A blessing is pronounced on those who are persecuted for righteousness' sake. If righteousness in verse 10 means the triumph of God's cause as embodied in His Messiah, verses 10 and 11 mean about the same thing. It may be that the former verse states the general principle and the latter applies this to the lives of

Jesus' disciples. The disciples, now hunted down, reproached, slandered, are the true heirs of the realm and lords of the coming age.

i. *Salt and Light* (5: 13-16). If the disciples possess the qualities, indicated in the Beatitudes, they will exert a saltlike, preservative influence on society. But if they lose these qualities they will be worthless. Their Christian influence cannot be hidden. The very fact that they are Christians places them in a place of eminence. Fear should not cause Christians to hide the light of their witness under a bushel. Their light is to be available for others, so that men from their lives might see what God is like and be led to glorify the Father who is in heaven.

2. *Jesus' Relation to the Law* (5: 17-20)

Christ came to fulfill the law and the prophets, or Old Testament system, by bringing all that was provisional and imperfect in that system to ideal realization. In this fulfillment all that was temporary or imperfect in the old drops away, and the perfect, essential, and abiding elements are retained in Christianity.

By realizing perfectly in His own life the ideal to which the Old Testament pointed, Christ fulfilled the law and the prophets. In His teaching, Jesus fulfilled the law by lifting out of the Old Testament universal principles of goodness and righteousness. Sin and righteousness He traced to their source in spirit and motive. By giving His life, Jesus established the new covenant that made it possible for all who obey Him to enjoy an inner disposition that conforms to God's will (cf. Jer. 31: 31-34; Heb. 8: 7-13; 10: 1-18).

Since all in the old system that was permanent and of eternal validity is preserved in the new, it follows that the Old Testament system as such has no longer control over the Christian (see Gal. 3: 23 ff.; Rom. 10: 4). The Christian is under the higher law of liberty (Jas. 1: 25), which is summed up in one word, "love." For he that loves fulfills the law (Gal. 5: 14; Matt. 22: 36-40; I John 4: 7; I Tim. 1: 5). Thus the Old Testament system passes away like the blossom which precedes the fruit, and the new system replaces the old (Heb. 8: 13).

3. The Theme of the Sermon (5:21-48)

This section may be considered as a discourse on the text recorded in 5:20—"Except your righteousness shall exceed." Six points of contrast are presented between the Pharisaic ethics taught by a majority of the scribes and the moral code advocated by Jesus.

a. Murder (5:21-26). The law pronounced the death sentence on the murderer. Jesus says that under His law anger and angry and insulting words make one guilty before God and liable to divine judgment (5:21-22). The anger and intention that have led up to the act are more serious than the act, for without the bad temper the act would never have been committed. Therefore the one who is angry with, and expresses contempt for, his brother is liable to divine judgment in its severest form—the Gehenna of fire.[7]

In the following verses (5:23-24) Jesus indicates that even the most sacred acts of worship are of no value unless first one is in right relationship with his fellow man. Parallels to the next two verses are found in a different connection in Luke (12:57-59).

b. Adultery (5:27-28). Jesus next traces adultery to the entertainment of impure desires. Just as anger is the root of murder, impurity is the root of adultery. So he who deliberately looks on a woman *in order to* lust has already become guilty in the sight of God. No sacrifice is too great to preserve one's purity (5:29-30).

c. Divorce (5:31-32). Even marriages legally permitted may really be only adulterous unions. For whoever gives his wife a certificate of divorce, a practice which Moses permitted, except for unchastity—either marital or premarital—makes her an adulteress and her new mate an adulterer.

Jesus is not legislating. He is against the whole system that treated woman as a piece of property. He is against the

---

[7] The word Gehenna is the Greek writing of the Hebrew "Ge-Hinnom" or "Valley of Hinnom," also called Topheth (Jer. 7:31). Originally the scene of Moloch worship, it had been defiled by Josiah (II Kings 23:10). After this, bodies of executed criminals were thrown into the valley, which became a sort of city dump, the continually burning fires of which symbolized the punishment to be meted out to sinners after the last judgment or in the period between death and the judgment (cf. Isa. 31:9; 66:24; Enoch 54:1-2; 56:3 f.; II Baruch 59:10; 85:13).

lax view of the followers of Hillel, who permitted divorce for
any reason the husband might advance. He is against the idea
that marriage is an experiment to be dissolved if it does not
work. He taught that marriage was of such a spiritual and
sacramental character that no legal form or judicial act could
dissolve it. By forbidding divorce and remarriage He would
leave the door open to reconciliation and reunion.

d. *Swearing* (5:33-37). Next Jesus attacks swearing. The
Jews considered oaths to be binding only if the name of God
was used. In this case the perjury would be a personal affront
to God; but in cases in which His name was not used, God
was not concerned. So the scribes calculated just which for-
mulas involved the use of God's name and so were binding
(Matt. 23:16-19). But Christ declared that the expressions
they used in pretending that they were making valid oaths
did involve God (23:17-22) and so all oaths were binding
(5:33-35). Even to swear by one's head is to involve God,
who alone can control the color of one's hair (5:36). The
whole system of oaths, Jesus held, stems from the fact that
men often lie unless compelled to tell the truth. His followers
should so reverence the truth that a bare statement would be
sufficient (5:37). Jesus' words again are not legislation and
do not prevent the Christian from taking the oath when the
law of the land requires this. Even Jesus seems to have admitted the oath of the high priest (26:63 f.).

e. *Retaliation* (5:38-42). Jesus now turns to the law of
retaliation. The so called *lex talionis,* which was found in the
Old Testament in three passages (Exod. 21:23-25; Lev. 24:17-
21; Deut. 19:16-21), is as old as Hammurabi's Code. The law
had set limits on retaliation. It said in effect: Injure the other
fellow exactly as much as but no more than he has injured
you. But Christ said that the very principle of retaliation was
wrong. He said: If someone deliberately injures you, do not
use the same kind of weapons against him. Overcome his
evil by doing good.

f. *Love for Enemies* (5:43-48). Finally, Jesus contrasts
His ethics with the scribal code concerning one's attitude
toward his enemies. The scribes had appended to the Old
Testament law. "You shall love your neighbor," (Lev. 19:18)
the words "and hate your enemy," which are not in the Old

Testament. One difficulty for the Jews is that they made the word "neighbor" too narrow. Even the words of Lev. 19:18 quoted here indicate that for the writer "neighbor" meant fellow Israelites.

Jesus included in the category of neighbor the enemy and the persecutor. These are to be loved even while they are persecuting us. We are to exercise the desire to give help —intelligent good will—towards even those who are wronging us. To do less is to act like the worldlings, and there is no excitement in a life on that level! "To return evil for good is the devil's way: to return good for good is man's: to return good for evil is God's."[8]

The reward for loving our enemies is that we shall be like our Father[9] in heaven, who gives sun and rain to the just and unjust without distinction. There is no higher ideal than the command and promise, "Ye therefore shall be perfect, as your heavenly Father is perfect" (5:48). The word perfect normally denotes the attainment of a certain goal, and is relative to that goal. Here perfection is defined in terms of the ethical teaching Jesus has just given. Since the immediate context has to do with love, we may also say that Jesus is talking about being made perfect in love.

4. Three Acts of Righteousness (6:1-18)

From ethics, man's relation with his fellows, the sermon now turns to religious practice. Christ contrasts His standard with the practice of the hypocrites. Righteousness is not a mask of piety on the outside to conceal a wicked, selfish life, but an inward disposition that shines forth in genuine goodness.

Verses 2-18 constitute a sermon with three points based on the text in verse one. "Take heed that ye do not your righteousness before men, to be seen of them." To the second section (on prayer) Matthew has added an appendix containing the disciples' prayer and a comment on the necessity of forgiveness. Apart from these appendixes the sections are symmetrical, each containing two refrains depicting the reward the hypocrites receive and the source of the reward of the true

[8] A. M. Hunter, *A Pattern for Life* (Philadelphia: Westminster Press, 1953), p. 58.

[9] The phrase "son of" often means "possessing the character of."

disciple. In each case the cardinal sin is hypocrisy and the cardinal virtue is sincerity. If your acts of worship are for men's approval, God does not regard them; the attention of men is your reward. You might as well write, "Paid in full."

When you give alms (vv. 2-4) you are not to sound a trumpet to call the attention of others. Acts of mercy are to be done as secretly as possible.

Likewise when you pray (vv. 5-15) do not, as the hypocrites, purposely get caught at the busiest street corner at the hour of prayer. Do not seek a large audience of men so that you can display your oratory. Moreover, "do not pray by idle rote like pagans, for they suppose they will be heard the more they say; you must not copy them" (6: 7-8a, Moffatt). Do not utter mere words that you do not mean and repeat empty phrases, as if the words of prayer were expected to have some magic effect. A practical point for us in this connection is the avoidance of the excessive use of the divine names in prayer. The etiquette of prayer also demands that we be alert and refrain from doing all the talking. Prayer is not merely asking; it is communion.

The beautiful prayer often called the "Lord's Prayer" (6: 9-13), but really a pattern prayer for the disciples, is given in both Matthew and Luke. Matthew's version with its full liturgical clauses is the universal favorite.[10] A careful analysis of the prayer with the implications of the various words and phrases is beyond the scope of this text, but such a study with the aid of a good commentary is rewarding. One notes that the prayer begins with an address to our Father. Prayer is a corporate act. We are all part of the body of Christ. The term "Father" suggests authority as well as care and provision for the child. "In heaven" speaks of a God whose love and power and holiness we cannot fathom.

There are seven petitions, which number in Jewish symbolism denotes completeness. The contents of the petitions broadly interpreted are quite inclusive of God's interests as well as our own. The first three petitions concern God. We are to pray that His name be reverenced, that His kingdom come, and that His will be performed on earth as it is in heaven. The next four concern our own needs, physical and

[10]The liturgical ending is not found in the oldest MSS.

spiritual. The implications of verse 12 are expanded in verses 14 and 15. If one is unforgiving he has no claim on God's forgiveness.

Fasting, the third illustration of righteousness (6: 16-18), is not to be for the purpose of impressing others with one's piety. One is not to smear ashes on his face and wear a strained, "pious" look as the hypocrites of that day did to hear men say, "There goes a holy man."

5. *The Outworkings of True Righteousness in Devotion and Trust* (6: 19-34)

a. *Seek Enduring Values* (6: 19-21; cf. Luke 12: 33 f.). Life is motivated by the things we value. Values are thus a true index of character. They indicate the factors that influence our choices, the forces that motivate our actions. If we desire to be Godlike, we must elevate to supreme place the values that God reckons as supreme. This beautiful little paragraph contains at once a warning against the materialism that marked the rich man of Luke 12 as a fool and an exhortation to seek first God's kingdom. If our hierarchy of values is right, everything in the system will fall into its proper place. The profound observation indicates that treasures are like a magnet drawing the heart. Will it be earthward or heavenward? If you want to be drawn heavenward, invest all you are and have in the currency of heaven. "For where your treasure is . . . "

b. *The Single Motive* (6: 22-24; cf. Luke 11: 34-36). "The single eye" is a metaphor denoting either generosity as opposed to the "evil eye" (which is used in proverbs for miserliness) or singleness of aim. A healthy ("sound") eye gives clear—not double—vision and a man has physical illumination. The diseased eye leaves a man in physical darkness. Therefore keep the eye of your soul clear and undistorted, that you may see the will of God. If you attempt to focus the eye of your soul on earthly and heavenly values at the same time, you will become spiritually blind.

Slaves might legally belong to two masters but could scarcely be slaves to both. At least a slave could not hold both in equal regard. Neither can a man maintain a state of unstable equilibrium in his devotion to spiritual and material values. He cannot continue serving as a slave to God and gold.

c. *Be Not Anxious but Trustful* (6: 25-34; cf. Luke 12: 22-31). This is another very beautiful passage preserved in essentially the same form in Matthew and Luke. To most of us, with our constant struggle for existence, it sounds as unreal as Utopia. An ideal, we say, perhaps possible if we were not constantly forced to face the first-of-the-month bills. But things were not exactly Utopia in first century Palestine either. Wrapped up in this message we should find the secret of tranquillity.

Jesus did not say, "Quit working and trust God to supply your needs." He, the Carpenter, who rejected as a solicitation of Satan the suggestion that He supply His own needs by miraculous means, would not counsel His followers to take this course of action. Nor did He say, "Take no thought" (6: 25, K.J.V.), but, "Do not be anxious," or, "Do not be distracted by cares." He does not command us to cease planning. Often He advises careful planning for the future. He tells us to surrender the worry and nervous anxiety that do not make us more efficient as workers or as witnesses. This counsel remains the best prescription for ulcers and nervous disorders.

Jesus asks His followers: If God gives life, which is the greater gift, will He not provide for its sustenance food and raiment, which are the lesser gifts? If God provides for the birds, who have nothing stored up for the future, will He not care for you, who are of infinitely more value to Him? If He clothes the grass of the field, which is only an instrumental value, living but for a day, with regal splendor that eclipses Solomon's, will He not much more clothe His own who do have the intelligence and capacity to plan and work and who live, not just for a brief span, but forever?

Being distracted by cares will not add half a step to one's span of life (6: 27).[11] The heathen seek food, drink, and clothing—material values—"and your heavenly Father knoweth that ye have need of all these things" (6: 32). The best way to overcome worry about our own needs is to fill our minds with

[11] This is perhaps to be preferred to "stature," for Luke (12: 26) calls the adding of a cubit (about eighteen inches) a small thing, but the addition of that much to a man's height could scarcely be so termed.

concern about the victory of God's cause. If we seek God's kingdom first—make it our paramount concern—God will add all the other things as well. Each day brings its own allotment of cares, and one should not add to today's worries those that belong to tomorrow.

In the last section of this chapter Jesus has been insisting, as He does elsewhere, that all of life is sacramental; all is invested with religious significance. Religion is not something added to the rest of life like another room to a building, nor is it to be relegated to only one room of life reserved for the sacred. There is no part of life that is unrelated to God.

6. *The Outworking of True Righteousness in Our Treatment of Others* (7:1-6, 12; cf. Luke 6:37-38, 41-42).

a. *Judge Not* (7:1-5). Jesus first warns His disciples against censorious judgment of others. This does not mean that we are to dispense with our law courts, nor yet that we are to cease attempting to evaluate other people. No one who was not a judge of men would long survive in a place of leadership involving the delegation of responsibility to others. All of us need to be judges of others in order that we may make our closest friendships with those whose lives prove of greatest stimulation to our own maximum development as persons.

There is, however, a type of judgment that is always wrong. That is the tendency to suspect the worst about others, especially those with whom we differ, and so to weight the scales of our judgment against them. Judgment is always to be tempered with mercy, remembering that we do not have all the facts nor understand all of the causes of a brother's action. Even if serious lapses are beyond question, it is not often necessary to spread the evil news. We can become parties to malicious gossip not only with our mouths but with our ears as well.

Judgment without mercy is not only wrong; it is dangerous. For with the same quality of judgment that we judge we shall be judged. The spirit with which we judge is automatically passing sentence on us. None of us lives so flawlessly that he can afford to be judged without mercy.

Jesus tells us that we are not to go about with a magnifying glass looking for flaws in our neighbor's life while we have to stretch to see over our own enormous faults. We see not

only what is outside of us, but what we are ourselves we bring
to each situation. How easy therefore it is for us to discover
in others even a trace of that evil which looms so large in
ourselves and yet to be totally oblivious to our own faults!
It is like offering to help another remove a splinter from his
eye while we have a sawlog in our own!

b. *Do Not Profane the Holy* (7:6). Yet we must not be
undiscriminating. We are not to cast our supreme values indiscriminately to the unappreciative. The deep things of the
Kingdom, the mystical experiences that are almost too sacred
to be told at all, are not to be flung carelessly before men de-
void of appreciation for spiritual things. The values that the
man of the street most needs to bring him to an appreciation
for the richest experiences of divine revelation and grace are
those incarnate in the life of the Christian who daily reflects
the love of Christ.

c. *The Golden Rule* (7:12; cf. Luke 6:31). The negative
form of this is given by Hillel, a great rabbi: " 'What is hate-
ful to thee, do not to thy neighbor: this is the whole Torah,
all else is interpretation' "[12] But Jesus was the first one to
give the principle positive form, so that it becomes not merely
a matter of prudence but a way of active benevolence.

7. *Prayer Answered Because God Is Our Father* (7:7-11;
cf. Luke 11:9-13)

This section stands out of connection in Matthew, yet in
three figures of speech it affirms the fact that if we persevere
God will answer our prayers. As dependent children we ask
sometimes not even articulately for what we think we need.
If we ask sincerely, God answers by supplying our real needs.
If we seek persistently for life's hidden gold, we will find it
at the end of a consecrated quest. For life's greatest values
come only after the expenditure of sweat, toil, tears, and
frustrating experiences. But treasure will be ours if we persevere. If life's doors are bolted at midnight, they will open
to the knocking of our battered knuckles. All this because
God is our Father. He does not mock us by offering us values
that are counterfeit. The deep desires for soul rest and com-

---

[12] Johnson, IB, VII, 329, cf. Tobit 4:15—"Do that to no man which
thou hatest" (K.J.V.). Cf. also Hunter, *op. cit.*, p. 86, for similar statements of Confucius and the Stoics.

munion and an abundant spiritual life are not illusions to
torture our thirsty souls but values that may be ours. The God
that created the desires provided also for their fulfillment,
for He is our Father.

8. *Three Warnings* (7:13-23)

The first warning about the narrow gate is treated in
Luke (13:23 ff.). The second warning relates to false teachers,
who were as abundant then as now. A religious teacher is
known by his character, not mere profession, just as a tree
by its fruit. The mere addition of good works does not make
a man good any more than tying grapes on a thistle will change
the nature of that thorny plant. A radical inner change effected by God's grace is necessary before a bad man can become good. It is well to remember, however, that even after
the tree is made good the fruit does not mature overnight.

The third warning is also treated in Luke (6:46; 13:26 f.)
where the version is different. Neither profession, orthodoxy
(calling Jesus "Lord"), preaching in His name, nor the performance of miracles in Jesus' name are a passport to heaven.
In fact, it is implied that one can do all this and be lost. The
basic test is "he that doeth the will of my Father" (7:21). He
does not say he who is emotional, or demonstrative, or prays
eloquent prayers, or makes a high profession. It is not enough
to be merely sentimental about God's will. The irreducible
minimum standard for entrance into and continuance in the
Kingdom is doing the will of God.

9. *Conclusion: The Two Builders* (7:24-29; cf. Luke 6:47-49)

There are some minor points of difference between the
two accounts. Luke represents the builders as building in
the same location with the difference that the wise builder
dug deeply and built the house well. In Matthew, however,
part of the point seems to be that the builders did not choose
the same location.

The wise man built his house on a rock—probably not in
the path of the oncoming floods. One who took the precaution
to build on a good foundation should have had the good sense,
energy, and patience to build well, and Luke affirms that
he did so. The life that the builder and house symbolize was
built on obedience to Jesus' commands. Because of its structure, location, and, most of all, foundation, this house did not

fall when the storms came. The storms signify the tests of life and perhaps the supreme test at the Judgment.

The foolish builder, on the other hand, built on the alluvial soil in a wadi or gulch that was dry most of the year. Little effort was needed in clearing away a place on which to build. We imagine that he built of shoddy material—perhaps telling himself, as many of us do, that this was only his temporary quarters; he would not live here always. Laying his foundation on the sands, he was preparing for trouble, for the storm was certain to come, bringing the raging torrent. When it struck the house the foundation was quickly undermined, and the adobe walls soon crumbled "and great was the fall of it."

III. The Narrative Resumed: a Ministry of Miracles[13]
(8:1—9:34)

1. Events of This Period Covered in Chapters on Mark or Luke (8:1—9:26)

In this section Matthew includes the cleansing of a leper (8:1-4), the healing of a centurion's servant (8:5-13), and of Peter's mother-in-law and others (8:14-17). Next the nature of discipleship is discussed (8:18-22), the calming of a storm (8:23-27), and the restoration of two Gerasene demoniacs (8:28-34) are described. Following this are recorded the healing of a paralytic (9:1-8), the call of Matthew (9:9-13), the discussion about fasting (9:14-17), and the raising of Jairus' daughter and healing of the woman with a hemorrhage (9:18-26).

2. Two Additional Miracles of Healing (9:27-34)

The description of the healing of two blind men (9:27-31) is much like that recorded in Matt. 20:29 ff. and parallels. The two blind men persistently followed Jesus, crying out to Him in terms that showed that they recognized Him as the Messiah. When, in response to Jesus' question, they declared their faith that Jesus was able to heal them, He touched their eyes, saying, "According to your faith be it done unto you" (9:29). When their sight was restored, Jesus gave them a stern command to keep the matter quiet. Instead they spread His fame throughout that area.

[13]The largest body of teaching in this section is the isolated paragraph about fasting (9:14-17).

After this, Matthew tells of the healing of a dumb demoniac (9:32-34), which caused the crowds to marvel and the Pharisees to assert that Jesus was able to cast out demons because He was in league with their prince.

IV. The Second Discourse: Special Instructions (9:35—11:1)

1. The Sending of the Twelve (9:35—10:16)

This is discussed in chapter five. The essential additions here are the well-known words of 9:37-38 and the difficult statements of 10:5-6. In these verses of chapter 10 Jesus forbids the disciples to work among the Samaritans and Gentiles. These instructions do not, however, indicate a permanent policy of Jesus nor reflect His fundamental attitude. The disciples were as yet unfitted because of their exclusivism to transmit the gospel to the Gentiles, and the Jewish people should have been better prepared than the Gentiles to be the first recipients of Jesus' message. The message and miracles, to be given without pay, are defined in verses seven and eight.

2. Face Persecution Fearlessly (10:17—11:1)

Much of the material in the first paragraph is almost word for word the same as that found in the eschatological discourse in Mark (13:9-13) where it is discussed. The next paragraphs are treated in their Lukan context (Luke 12:2-9, 51-53; 14:26-27). The discourse ends with a pronouncement of blessing on those who receive the disciples, and the well-known saying about the "cup of cold water."

V. The Narrative Resumed: Jesus Rejected (11:2—12:50; cf. Luke 7:18-35)

1. John the Baptizer's Relation to the New Order (11:2-19)

The report of Jesus' miracles reached the ears of John the Baptizer, who was languishing in prison, so that he sent a delegation to Jesus to inquire whether He was the Messiah. Jesus' reply to their question was to cite His miracles (Luke 7:21) of healing and raising the dead and the preaching of the gospel to the poor. These miracles were all signs of the Messianic age (Isa. 29:18 f.; 35:5 f.; 61:1 f.) and so constituted an indirect affirmation by Jesus that He was the Messiah.

The meaning of the beatitude in verse six is not clear. It may contain a veiled hint that He and His work are not to be ignored. Possibly it is a guarded appeal for faith in himself as a Person, or it may refer to His scandalizing of those who

expected a political and military Messiah to deal a deathblow
to the tyranny of Rome and Herod.

After the delegation had left, Jesus praised John warmly,
saying that he was a prophet and more than a prophet; he
was the forerunner of the Messiah. He was the greatest of
men, "yet he that is least in the kingdom of heaven is greater
than he" (11:11, K.J.V.). This verse proves that Jesus thought
of the Kingdom as in some sense already present. The enig-
matic statement does not exclude John from eternal life, but
it does indicate that John came before the Kingdom appeared
as a historical movement. He stood on the threshold of the
new order but did not enter, perhaps because of his moral
sternness, which kept him from appreciating fully Christ's
gracious spirit and stamped him as belonging to the old order.
At least, those who are the least in the Kingdom enjoy greater
privileges and blessings than he.

In the concluding part of this section Jesus identified John
as the Elijah of Mal. 4:5 who was to come before the day of
the Lord. Then He compared the generation then living to
a group of spoiled children, who when invited by another group
to join them in a game of "weddings" refused. To humor these
un-co-operative children, the second group proposed a game
of "funerals" and was again met with a petulant refusal. Jesus says this represents the attitude of His contemporaries,
for John came as an ascetic and he was charged with being
demon-possessed. Jesus then entered fully into the social life
of His day and was rejected as a glutton and a drunkard. And
this foolish display of childish behavior is taking place while
its actors face the supreme crisis of history—the advent of
the Son of Man and the offer of the Kingdom.

The final verse of the section may mean in Matthew's
version that Jesus' course of action is justified by its outcome.
In Luke's slightly different version (7:35) the meaning may
be that "wisdom is justified as against her children"; that is,
against the Pharisees, who considered themselves children of
wisdom. Or it may mean that wisdom is justified by those
who accept Jesus' message and who are thus her true children.

2. *Contrast Between the "Wise" and the "Babes"* (11:20-30)

a. *Woes on the Cities of Galilee* (11:20-24; cf. Luke 10:13-
15). The condemnation of these cities is that they had been

unresponsive to great light. The principle is suggested that severity of judgment will correspond to the amount or intensity of available light refused.

b. *Jesus' Solemn Self-disclosure* (11:25-30; cf. Luke 10:21 f.). Here Jesus thanks God that the revelation is given to "babes." The statement is found in Luke, where it is Jesus' joyous outburst occasioned by the return of the seventy and refers primarily to them. Jesus then declares that He, God's Son, is the only avenue by which man may know the Father.

The section ends with a beautiful invitation for those who labor and are heavy laden to come to Him for rest. Originally the words embraced those laboring under a religion of legalism with its heavy burdens imposed by the scribes. The appeal to take His yoke meant in the terminology of the Jews to take His message as the rule of life. All are to learn of Christ, not only His words, but also His life. Instinctively we feel that the words "labor and are heavy laden" are directed to us.

3. *Opposition and Rejection Illustrated* (12:1-50)

a. *Two Sabbath Controversies* (12:1-14). Several items in this section are treated in part in chapter five. Among these are the controversies over plucking grain on the Sabbath (12:1-8) and the healing of the man with a withered hand on the Sabbath (12:9-14).

In connection with the former incident, Matthew adds Jesus' words which show that the priests who in the discharge of their duties profane the Sabbath are considered guiltless. The idea is that in case of so-called conflict of duties the greater overrides the lesser. The Temple in this case is greater than the Sabbath and takes precedence over the Sabbath law. But Jesus affirms that He is greater than the Temple, and therefore much more His program takes precedence over the Sabbath law. With that Jesus said, "If ye had known what this meaneth, I desire mercy, and not sacrifice, ye would not have condemned the guiltless" (12:7).

b. *The Healing of the Multitudes by Jesus* (12:15-21). This, too, is discussed in the chapter on Mark. Matthew declares that this was to fulfill Isa. 42:1-4, which he quotes here.

c. *The Unpardonable Sin* (12:22-37). The healing of a
blind and dumb demoniac led people to question if Jesus were
not the Messiah. The Pharisees desperately attempted to sup-
press what they thought might erupt into a widespread movement. Hence their desperate charge: Jesus is in collusion
with the demons; that is how He casts them out.

Jesus was not ignorant of their reasonings. He then gave
the classic statements about the instability of the divided
kingdom and the divided city or house, showing the illogical
position of His scribal opponents. Jesus followed this by a
query that if answered would imply that their sons also cast
out demons by the same means. He continued: "But if I by
the Spirit of God cast out demons, then is the kingdom of
God come upon you" (12:28). This verse is interesting in
that it refutes the idea that Jesus thought of the Kingdom
as something entirely future.

Jesus then affirmed that one could not remain neutral
toward Him. This affirmation is followed by a text which is
often used to prove that God's patience is soon exhausted.
But the best exegetes find that the sin here depicted is the
determined and malignant opposing of God and goodness. The
only Spirit capable of casting out demons is the Holy Spirit,
and to call Him evil is to subvert all moral and spiritual values;
it is to identify God with the devil. Deliberately to ascribe
deeds of pure goodness to the devil is to place oneself in the
category of those who call evil good and good evil because
of a settled preference for evil. The sin is thus not a single
act but a malignant attitude. The sin is no less dangerous because it does not represent an abitrary deadline drawn by God.
The sin draws the line in our lives until it is practically impossible for one who has arrived at this state to repent and
believe and so receive God's forgiveness. We can be thankful,
though, that God's love and concern for the wayward are
unchanging. He can never be other than what He has always
been—Holy Love.

The section closes with an indication that evil words are
symptomatic of an evil heart. Since unguarded speech is thus
an index to what lies beneath the surface, there is nothing we
say that is without moral significance. The words in verses
36 and 37 are not so much a warning to guard our words—
although of course our speech should be such as befits fol-

lowers of Christ—as it is a warning to look deeper and watch our hearts—our secret thoughts, imaginations, affections, motivations. The reason the scribes were speaking evil was that they could not speak good, for they were speaking out of the abundance of their evil hearts.

d. *Against Seeking for Signs* (12:38-42; cf. Luke 11:29-32). In response to a request from some scribes and Pharisees for a sign, Jesus said that seeking for a sign marked them as the products of an evil generation. The sign of Jonah alone would be given. The men of Nineveh who repented at Jonah's preaching and the Queen of the South who came to hear Solomon's wisdom will in unison condemn this generation because they have rejected the preaching and the wisdom of One greater than Jonah and Solomon.

e. *The Example of the Empty House* (12:43-45; cf. Luke 11:24-26). This might also be called "the return of the expelled demon," for that is the subject discussed under the figure of a house that has been cleaned and arranged. The house from which one demon has been expelled becomes in the end the abode of the original inhabitant plus seven demons more evil than the first. This illustrates the danger of the ritually clean but empty Judaism of Jesus' day. It is a warning to us that life cannot remain a vacuum. Unless we fill it with good thoughts and deeds, with prayer and worship, our lives, too, may be again filled with evil more completely than at the first.

f. *Jesus' True Relatives* (12:46-50). This paragraph, found also in Mark and Luke, brings to a close this section which is mainly occupied with examples of opposition to and rejection of Jesus.

VI. *Third Discourse: Parables of the Kingdom* (c. 13)

1. *Introduction*

a. *Definition and Characteristics of Parables.* A parable in its simplest form is "a metaphor or simile drawn from nature or common life, arresting the hearer by its vividness or strangeness, and leaving the mind in sufficient doubt about its precise application to tease it into active thought."[14] Parables are usually comparisons by which something that is

[14] C. H. Dodd, *The Parables of the Kingdom* (London: Nisbet and Co., Ltd., 1936), p. 16.

known is used to describe that which is less well known; they are often employed to teach moral and religious truth.

Although Jesus made use of parables and gave the term parable immortality, parables had been employed at an earlier date by others, having been used in the Old Testament and subsequently by Jewish rabbis. For Jesus a parable was a picture of the visible and well-known used to illustrate, reveal, and explain the unseen and less well-known. He used the activities of everyday life to illustrate principles that are true in the life of the spirit. Jesus' parables have about them the freshness and realism of life. A keen observer of life, His characters and their actions are drawn from life. Underlying His use of parables is His conviction that there is an essential unity between the natural and the supernatural. Therefore He could say that the kingdom of Heaven is like a process of nature or an experience in the normal life of man.

It is unnecessary to point out the distinction between parables and myths, fables, and proverbs. In fact, the distinction between parables and proverbs is often a very fine line. One distinction, however, should be made. The true parable is not an allegory. The parable has only one main point of comparison to which all else is subordinated. The details contribute to the picture but do not detract from its unity by intruding independent lessons of their own. An allegory, on the other hand, contains a comparison in which each detail carries its own special meaning.

b. *Principles of Interpretation.* In the last paragraph it is suggested that the details of the true parable are subordinate to the main picture or point of comparison. This fact is often forgotten by interpreters who treat the parables as allegories. It is true that some of the comparisons that are termed parables are allegorized in the Gospels. But this does not give us liberty to allegorize them all. The classical illustration of allegorizing the parables is found in Augustine's treatment of the Parable of the Good Samaritan. The "certain man" is Adam; Jerusalem is the city of peace from which Adam fell. Jericho is our human mortality toward which he goes. The thieves are the devil and his angels who strip from Adam his immortality.[15] The absurdity of such interpretation should re-

---

[15] Bowie, IB, VII, 173.

mind us that the details of a parable are subordinate to its one main lesson.

A second principle of interpretation is the fact that, since the parables were originally addressed to simple people, the main lesson must have been easily grasped. Therefore any lesson derived by means of clever exegetical tricks is almost certainly not the one intended.

A third principle for the interpretation of parables is the need of a knowledge of the historical context. In order to understand the parables as Jesus' hearers understood them, we need to place ourselves back in first century Palestine. This means that we need to become so familiar with the thought and life of the times that we can imagine the impact of the parable on one of Jesus' hearers who was hearing it for the first time.

Finally, in parables that expressly define the Kingdom the truths that are taught oppose and correct first century ideas. In interpreting any parable of this class one is to ask what Jewish belief this parable destroys or corrects. It is the new element of teaching in these parables that is to be sought.

2. The Reception of the Message (13:1-23)

a. The Parable of the Soils (13:1-9, 18-23). Jesus is pictured as teaching from a boat the great crowds assembled on the beach. The first "parable" is the one usually known as the "parable" of the sower. The interpretation given (13:18-23) stamps it as possessing an allegorical element. This parable indicates that, just as the productivity of the seed is determined by the quality and preparation of the soils, the fruitfulness of the gospel message will depend upon the attitude and moral and spiritual depth of the hearers. The harvest or lack of harvest resulting from the same gospel message is dependent upon the reception accorded to it. The parable answers the question that often arises: Why is it that so few who hear the gospel message are completely and permanently transformed by it?

In the interpretation the seed is the Word. Just as the seed that falls on the beaten path has no chance to germinate before the birds eat it, the gospel message is snatched away from the hardhearted and spiritually insensitive before it has a chance to germinate and take root. The shallow soil represents those who live superficial lives. They are the sentimentalists whose attachment to religion is almost entirely a matter of emotional response. They are apt to be demonstrative when they respond to the message, but there is no depth to their lives. The bedrock of unyieldedness lies too close to the surface, so that the gospel plant will in times of testing soon dry up. The other two types of hearers are described in such terms as to render fuller explanation superfluous.

b. *The Reason Jesus Spoke in Parables* (13:10-17). On the surface in Mark's account (4:10-12), Jesus seems to say that He uses parables to conceal the truth from the people. It may be that later in His ministry Jesus found it necessary to speak in figures to prevent His enemies from bringing about His death prematurely by means of political charges or otherwise. However, to believe that Jesus deliberately withheld saving truth from people is to attribute malice to Him, and this is not compatible with His character as it is portrayed consistently in the New Testament.

Matthew reports Jesus' statement of the principle that, while receptivity to spiritual truth will bring an increasing awareness of spiritual values, an unreceptive attitude to truth will take away even the limited ability to know and appreciate spiritual values that one now possesses (13:12-13). The quotation from Isaiah (6:9-10; cf. Matt. 13:14-15) indicates that, as the people of Isaiah's day would be unreceptive to his message because of their materialism and worldliness, even so the people of Jesus' day were unresponsive to the divine message for the same reason. We are to understand probably that the unspiritual scribes and Pharisees had limited their ability to understand the truth by their previous attitude, so that what might have been truth to them became darkness to their hardened, evil minds. Hence the parables intended to convey light or spiritual truth became in practical effect the means by which the haters of truth found themselves in ever-increasing darkness. Matthew preserves the fullest statement here and his words inform us that it was *because* of men's obtuseness that Christ used parables. The parables were intended to be like illustrations—windows to let in the light.

3. Two "Parables" of Judgment (13:24-30, 36-43, 47-50)

    a. The Parable of the Tares (13:24-30, 36-43). This so-called "parable" is really an allegory, as its interpretation reveals (13:36-43). The allegory explains the appearance of evil in the society of professed believers and how, at the end, the Kingdom is to be purged of all evil.

    Although the Son of Man sowed the field with certified, weed-free seed noxious weeds soon appear. How is this to be explained? The devil has sown the evil seed while men slept. The presence of evil and the causes of sin in the Kingdom are thus explained.

    What is then to be done? Are not the weeds to be pulled up? Not yet, says Jesus. We must take care lest, while we are pulling out the weeds of evil, we root up the wheat also. Besides this, it may be added, the weeds indicated here are not easily distinguished from the wheat until both are mature.

    In its proper time and by approved agencies the separation will be effected. The separation will take place at the harvesttime—at the end of the age—when the duly constituted reapers—the angels—will be sent to "gather out of the kingdom" and burn "all things that cause stumbling, and them that do iniquity" (13:41). This judgment, with its destruction of evil and rewarding of the righteous, will be supervised by the Son of Man, who sowed the good seed.

    The allegory suggests several truths: the reason for the presence of evil among the professed followers of Christ; the proper scope of missionary activity—"the field is the world" (13:38)—and the Great Judgment with its final separation of the evil from the righteous and the fixed destinies of both. In addition there is the teaching that it is impossible to purge the Christian society of all evil.

    b. The Parable of the Dragnet (13:47-50). Just as a seine, because of its size, traps all kinds of fish, the gospel net will attract people of all kinds, some who are worthy and some who are unworthy. And just as the time for the sorting comes at the end of the fishing when the net with its contents is drawn ashore, the time for the judging of those taken by the gospel net and the removal of the bad is at the end of the age. The punishment of the evil is described in the same terms as in verse 42.

Both "parables" contain a new element of teaching which originally may have constituted their main point. Judgment, which in the apocalyptic thinking of Jesus' day was placed at the beginning, is now relegated to the end of the period of the Kingdom's development and growth. There was to be no violent overthrow of evil by supernatural means prior to the inauguration of the Kingdom. It was not to come with observable signs (Luke 7:20-21), for it was a spiritual realm within their midst disclosed only to those who by the experience of the new birth were able to appreciate spiritual things (John 3:1-3). The Kingdom was to develop through regular stages of growth by means of a power inherent in the gospel seed (Mark 4:26-29) until it reached maturity.

4. *Two Parables of the Growth of the Kingdom* (13:31-33)

a. *The Mustard Seed* (13:31-32). This parable indicates extensive development of the Kingdom from small, unpromising beginnings to a size disproportionate to these humble beginnings. The parable is a corrective of the idea that the Kingdom descends from heaven fully developed, as the apocalyptists taught. It is also a source of encouragement that from meager beginnings God brings enormous increase. Starting with twelve peasants God launched a program destined to reach around the world, embrace millions of people, and prevail against the forces of evil.

b. *The Leaven* (13:33). This parable indicates the power of the gospel to permeate and transform society. Jesus shows His boldness and originality by adopting a term that the rabbis employed as a symbol for evil, and using it here to describe the transforming influence of the Kingdom. The power of the gospel to transform and elevate society is seen in countless ways in the culture that is ours. The increase and spread of the leaven throughout the three measures of meal indicates quiet, unobtrusive growth instead of a mighty empire emerging suddenly, fully developed.

5. *Two Parables on the Joy of the Kingdom* (13:44-46)

a. *The Hidden Treasure.* The parables of the hidden treasure and the pearl stress the fact that because of the Kingdom's great value any apparent sacrifice is made joyously to gain it. In the parable of the treasure-trove the find was a sheer accident. The man stumbled on the find. He had nothing to lose in selling all that he had to purchase the field, for it was apparent that here was wealth that far surpassed his meager possessions.

b. *The Pearl.* In the case of the pearl merchant there was a systematic quest for valuable pearls. He discovered one that he recognized as of supreme value. Staking all that he had on his estimate of value, he sold all to purchase the pearl. He represents those who in their quest for truth and goodness come at the end of their quest upon the gospel pearl, which they appraise correctly as worth their all and whose appraisal leads them to joyous action. Or it could refer to Christ giving His all to purchase salvation for us.

6. *The Parable of the Scribes of the Kingdom* (13: 51-52)

In this parable Jesus indicates how the scribe of the Kingdom is to differ from the scribes of the Pharisees and Sadducees. Unlike the Jewish scribes, he is to be able to give out fresh insights and not to be restricted to the stale interpretations of tradition.

VII. *The Narrative Resumed: a Universal Church* (14:1— 17:27)

1. *Jesus' Visit to Gentile Territory* (14:1—15:20)

The effect of the news of Jesus' activities on Herod after the latter had murdered John the Baptizer are noted in connection with the Gospel of Mark. Here, too, the result of Herod's guilty fears and of Jesus' miracles on His movements are indicated. Matthew follows Mark in recording after the account of the death of John the feeding of the 5,000 and the terror of the disciples when Jesus walked to them on the water. Matthew adds the account of Peter's unsuccessful attempt to duplicate this miracle of Jesus (14:28-33). Likewise, along with Mark, Matthew after noting the healings at Gennesaret treats the controversy of Jesus with the Pharisees over the nature of defilement. Thus Jesus rejects Pharisaic ideas of separation and opens the way for His mission to the Gentiles, which in connection with the political developments forms a temporary retreat from the region of Herod Antipas.

2. *Jesus in Retirement Ministers to the Gentiles* (15:21-39)

Here Matthew's account follows the Marcan version with slight differences. In Matthew the cure of the Syrophoenician

woman's daughter was immediate but Jesus' reluctance to help
is heightened. In the Decapolis, Jesus carried on an extensive
healing ministry, at the conclusion of which He fed the 4,000.

3. *Jesus Rejects the Teaching of the Pharisees and Sadducees*
   (16: 1-12)

In Mark's account Pharisees—here coupled with Sadducees—come seeking a sign from heaven. Jesus offered to
these sign-seekers only the sign of Jonah and warned the
disciples to beware of the teaching of the Pharisees and Sadducees.

4. *The First Two Predictions of the Passion* (16: 13—17: 23)

Again Matthew follows Mark's order exactly in reporting
the Great Confession, Jesus' first prediction of His passion,
Jesus' statement of the conditions of discipleship, the Transfiguration, Jesus' interpretation of Elijah's coming, the healing
of the epileptic boy, and the second prediction of the Passion.

Although most of this material is given also in Mark, the
statement about the power of "faith as a grain of mustard
seed" is found only here (17: 20). A far more significant passage contains Jesus' statement to Peter, "Upon this rock I will
build my church" (16: 18). On the rock of a faith like Peter's,
which embodies a belief in Christ's messiahship stemming
directly from divine revelation, Christ will build His Church,
which death itself cannot destroy. Peter is to receive the
"keys of the kingdom," a phrase indicating that Peter has
now become an accredited teacher in the things of the Kingdom, so that whatever judgments he makes on earth because
they are true will be valid in heaven. Probably this does
not indicate a personal prerogative conferred on Peter so much
as an authority delegated by Jesus to Peter as the representative of and spokesman for the Twelve and through the
apostles to the primitive Church.

5. *Paying the Temple Tax* (17: 24-27)

Jesus here seems to argue that He and His followers stand
in such a close relationship to God, in whose honor the Temple
tax was paid, that He and the Twelve should be exempt from
the tax, just as the close relatives of a reigning monarch were
free from such obligations. Yet, lest the liberty of Christ and
His disciples become an occasion of offense, that freedom
should be renounced and the tax paid.

VIII. Fourth Discourse: Problems of the Christian Community (c. 18)

1. About the "Little Ones" (18:1-14)

The dispute about greatness and Jesus' teaching on the subject are recorded by Mark (9:33-37), who also relates Jesus' teaching on causing a little one to be tempted and on the necessity of rigid self-discipline (9:42-48).

The parable of the lost sheep, found in Luke in another connection, is used here to illustrate the loving care of the Heavenly Father for "one of these little ones" and to teach us that, since this is God's attitude, we should not despise them.

2. About Discipline (18:15-20)

In dealing with an offender every possible means should be used to win him over and restore him to the fellowship. The first overture is to be made by the injured party in private. If he fails in this he is to take two or three with him to make another attempt to win back the erring brother. As a last resort, after the church, too, has made a vain appeal, the man is to be excommunicated. The paragraph concludes with statements about the absolute validity of the church's decisions, the prayer power of a united church, and the assertion that the living Christ is present "where two or three are gathered together in my name" (18:20).

3. About Forgiving Others (18:21-35)

Peter, thinking that he was suggesting an absolute limit, asked Jesus if he should forgive an offending brother as many as seven times. But if Peter's suggestion of seven times implied completeness, Jesus' reply, "Seventy times seven," meant without limit. To clinch the teaching, Jesus gave the parable of the unforgiving servant. This servant, whose king and creditor forgave his debt of about ten million dollars, would not extend the time for his fellow servant to repay him twenty dollars, but cast him into prison. When the report of the servant's cruel act reached his master, the master was very angry and delivered him to the torturers until he should pay all of his debt. "So shall also my heavenly Father do unto you, if ye forgive not every one his brother from your hearts" (18:35).

IX. The Narrative Resumed: on the Way to Jerusalem (19:1—23:39)

1. On Marriage, Divorce, Eunuchs, and Children (19:1-15)

Each of these subjects is considered in its Marcan context except for the unique section on eunuchs. Jesus indicates that besides those who are physically not capable of marriage there are those whose devotion to the Kingdom is such that they voluntarily forego marriage.

2. On Riches and Rewards for Renunciation (19:16—20:16)

The turning away of the rich young man and the saying about the "needle's eye" which the incident provoked are discussed in connection with Mark's record of these events. The incident served to call to Peter's mind and lips the sacrifice he and his companions had made to follow Jesus. To this Jesus replied that the Twelve would share with Him in His future rule, receive a hundredfold in this life "with persecutions" (Mark 10:30), and in the age to come eternal life.

Perhaps Jesus had sensed in Peter's attitude a note of selfishness or of complacency, as if his sacrifice had earned merit before God and entitled him to salvation. In the Parable of the Laborers in the Vineyard, Jesus taught that those who attempt to drive a hard bargain with God will be the losers. The workers who toiled through the heat of the day have been identified by some with the Pharisees, and the workers who began working at the eleventh hour as the "people of the land" and other outcasts. This is in keeping with the main point of the parable, which is directed against the legalistic righteousness of the Pharisees and their idea that one could acquire merit so that salvation would be God's payment of a debt. They had misunderstood God's character, for He is a God of grace.

3. A Prediction, Request, and Healing (20:17-34)

The third prediction of Jesus' passion and the selfish request of (the mother of) James and John are developed in connection with Mark's account. In Matthew two blind men who urgently request Jesus to restore their sight are healed. Mark's account mentions only one blind beggar, Bartimaeus, perhaps the more prominent of the two. The apparent discrepancy as to the location of the healing (cf. Matt. 20:29 with Mark 10:46 and Luke 18:35) may be explained by supposing that the cure was effected after Jesus had left old Jericho but before He had arrived at the new Jericho constructed by Herod the Great.

4. *From the Triumphal Entry to the Parable of the Wicked Tenants* (c. 21)

Nearly everything in this chapter is found in almost the same order in Mark (11:1—12:12). Both Gospels describe the Triumphal Entry, cleansing of the Temple, cursing of the fig tree, question about authority, and the Parable of the Wicked Tenants. Between the last two items Matthew includes the Parable of the Two Sons. In this parable the son who disobeyed his father's command and refused to work but afterward repented obviously represents the tax collectors and harlots who "are preceding you into the kingdom of God" (21:3, Gk.). The other son who professed obedience but failed to carry out his promise represents the decadent religious leaders who were opposing Jesus and His program.

5. *The Parable of the Marriage Feast* (22:1-14; cf. Luke 14:16-24)

Guests invited to a marriage feast given by a king in honor of his son scorn the invitation or mistreat and kill the messengers. In anger the king dispatches troops who kill the murderers and burn their city. Since those first invited are unworthy, servants are sent to invite all they can find on the highways. At last the hall is filled with guests. But one of them is found who has no wedding garment. The attendants are instructed to "bind him hand and foot, and cast him into the outer darkness; there shall be the weeping and the gnashing of teeth" (22:13).

This parable indicates that the Jews who rejected Jesus would be excluded, while the Gentiles would be invited to the blessings of the Kingdom. It also indicates that one cannot be a guest at the Master's table without the requisite robe of righteousness. The guest without the proper attire illustrates the fact that, while the call is to the many, salvation is for the few because it is only the few who give serious heed to the **divine will.**

6. Other Questions Discussed and the Seven Woes (22:15—23:39)

The questions about tribute, the resurrection, the great commandment, and David's son are discussed in this order in connection with Mark 12:13-37. The twenty-third chapter of Matthew is devoted almost entirely to a castigation of the scribes and Pharisees. They "preach, but do not practice" (23:3, R.S.V.), and are heartless in demanding rigid adherence to the added restrictions of their oral law (v. 4). They love ostentation and the praise of men, making a display of their religiousness (vv. 5-7). In contrast to this spirit, the true disciple is to be governed by a passion for service and not to seek for mere titles of honor (vv. 8-12).

In seven devastating woes Matthew summarizes Jesus' denunciation of the "scribes and Pharisees, hypocrites!" It is from this passage that the term "Pharisee" has in the minds of many become so inseparably linked with hypocrisy. Not all the Pharisees were hypocrites, but hypocrisy was sufficiently common among them for the denunciations of Jesus to be merited.

Instead of using their teaching power to help men into the Kingdom, they used the key to lock them out while they themselves refused to enter (23:13). Their missionaries left their converts in a worse condition than they were originally (23:15). They used deceit to avoid the obligation of the solemn oath (23:16-22). Meticulous in tithing garden herbs, they had neglected the great principles of justice, mercy, and faith (or fidelity; loyalty to truth, principles, friends), which were dear to God's heart. They were as foolish as a man who strains out a gnat and then swallows a camel (23:23-24)! Cleansing the outside of the cup and the hands in order to protect themselves from ritual defilement, they were totally oblivious to the real moral and spiritual defilement that infected their minds and hearts (23:25-26). Their righteousness was as external as a whitewashed tomb which was beautiful on the outside but, to one sharing Jewish ideas, full of defilement within. Likewise inwardly they were filled with hypocrisy and iniquity (23:27-28). By their hypocritical honoring of the prophets they were priding themselves that they were more righteous than their fathers who had slain the prophets.

Yet in their hearts there was that same rebellion and hatred of the truth that had led their fathers to kill the prophets. One day it would erupt into a venomous display of hatred, cruelty, and murder, so that this generation could be said to be guilty of all the innocent blood shed from Abel to Zechariah (23:29-36).

In the concluding verses Jesus' lament over Jerusalem is recorded, as well as His expression of a desire often felt to gather her children under His protecting care as a hen gathers her brood from the threat of a hawk. " . . . and ye would not' Behold your house is left unto you desolate" (23:37 f.).

X. Fifth Discourse: Eschatology (cc. 24—25)

1. The Apocalyptic Discourse (24:1-36)
The teaching recorded in this section is discussed in connection with Mark 13.

2. Teaching on Preparedness (24:37—25:13)
    a. The Need for Watchfulness and Fidelity (24:37-51). Everything will be continuing on a "business as usual" basis when Christ comes, with the result that many will be totally unprepared for His coming. When He comes the prepared will be accepted and taken, while the uprepared will be left to their doom. We are to keep awake, and not to be like the man who sleeps on guard while the thief comes and steals the valuables. We should be faithful in the appointed task, lest the Master, appearing at an unexpected hour, find us shirking our task and we be punished.
    b. The Parable of the Ten Virgins (25:1-13). The maidens await the return of the bridegroom, who has gone to bring his bride from her father's house to the new home. This was the high point of a festive occasion. The point of the parable is the need of prudence and foresight in preparing for unexpected emergencies such as the delay indicated in this parable. The difference is not one of watchfulness—they all slumbered and slept. The difference lies in the fact that the stupid had brought no reserves to the occasion while the wise had prepared themselves for just such an emergency. The immediate reference of the parable is to the need for adequate reserves that will enable the Christian to stand in spite of the delay of Christ's return. Although His coming is certain, the time of its occurrence is uncertain; so there is need for constant pre-

paredness. But the parable teaches the wider lesson of the need for adequate reserves so that one can face all of life's emergencies victoriously. There is a suggestion here of the necessity of being filled with the Holy Spirit (typified by oil).

3. The Parable of the Talents (25:14-30)

A similar parable in Luke (19:12-27) was given to suggest that the Kingdom would not appear immediately (Luke 19:11). The point here is that men should invest wisely all that they are given in the work of the Kingdom and that those who do so will be commended and receive a greater responsibility. The failure to invest what one has will result in his condemnation and the loss of the capital originally entrusted to him. The one-talent man is condemned, not because of his little capacity, but because of his inaction. Regarding his master as being difficult to please, the one-talent man had refrained from making any investment, lest he make the wrong investment and be punished. This suggests the truth that men are often prevented from making a full consecration to God because of fear arising from a mistaken idea as to what God is like. He is not to be compared to a hard man. The parable also suggests that if a capacity is not used it is lost.

4. The Sheep and the Goats (25:31-46)

When Christ returns in glory He will separate men as a shepherd separates the sheep from the goats. The basis of the separation will be, not profession, but action. "Inasmuch as ye did it [or 'did it not'] unto one of these my brethren, even these least, ye did it [or 'did it not'] unto me" (cf. 25:40, 45). Each group registers genuine surprise. Let him that thinketh he standeth beware.

XI. Narrative Resumed: Last Scenes and Death (cc. 26—27)

These are discussed in connection with Mark 14:1—15:47. Matthew's unique contributions are: Jesus' words after Peter's use of the sword in Gethsemane (26:52-54); an account of the death of Judas (27:3-10; cf. Acts 1:18-20); the record of Pilate's vain attempt to cleanse his hands of Jesus' blood (27:24-25); an additional statement of mockery directed by the Jewish religious leaders at Jesus as He hung on the cross

(27:43); the account of the earthquake and the raising of many of the bodies of the saints (27:51b-53); and the story of the guard at the tomb (27:62-66).

XII. The Resurrection (c. 28)

1. The Women Find an Empty Tomb but a Risen Lord (28:1-10)

Matthew adds the account of the supernatural means by which the stone was rolled back and the effect of this phenomenon on the guards. He also recounts the appearance of Jesus to the faithful women who had come to anoint His body but became heralds of the good tidings that Jesus had risen from the dead.

2. The Report of the Guards and the Appearance to the Eleven (28:11-20)

When the chief priests heard the news of Jesus' resurrection they bribed the guards to say that while they were asleep the disciples had stolen the body. This was the account that was current in Jewish circles.

In Galilee at a prearranged meeting place Jesus appeared to the eleven disciples with a solemn charge to them. In this parting charge, appropriately called the Great Commission, the disciples are told: "All authority hath been given unto me in heaven and on earth. Go ye therefore, and make disciples of all the nations, baptizing them into the name of the Father and of the Son and of the Holy Spirit: teaching them to observe all things whatsoever I commanded you: and lo, I am with you always, even unto the end of the world" (28:18-20). With this ringing, climactic appeal the Gospel ends, but its challenge will remain until the end of the age.

CHAPTER V

THE CONQUEROR-SERVANT
(MARK)

A. INTRODUCTION

I. The Origin of the Book

The Gospel is anonymous and contains but little data about the writer's interests or possible identity. Fortunately, testimony of early Christians has been preserved which indicates the belief of responsible members of the Church of the second century. The earliest testimony is that of Papias (ca. A.D. 140), whose statement about Mark has been presented in the previous chapter. Also preserved is a statement from Irenaeus in his writing *Against Heresies* (A.D. 174-89). Irenaeus wrote:

> Matthew published his Gospel among the Hebrews in their own language, while Peter and Paul were preaching and founding the church in Rome. After their death, Mark, the disciple and interpreter of Peter, also transmitted to us in writing those things which Peter had preached; and Luke, an attendant of Paul, recorded in a book the gospel which Paul had declared. Afterward John published his Gospel while staying in Ephesus in Asia.[1]

Eusebius also reports that Clement of Alexandria[2] (ca. A.D. 190-210) and Origen[3] (died ca. A.D. 254) connected the origin of the Gospel with Peter and Mark. Internal evidence from the standpoint of style also corroborates this conclusion.

Not much is known about this Mark, who was almost certainly intended to be John Mark, Peter's companion in "Babylon" at the time of the writing of his First Epistle (5:13). If so he was the son of Mary, an early Christian of comfortable circumstances, who owned a house and kept servants. Christians were meeting at their home at the time of Peter's release from prison (Acts 12:12-17). His first name was John, by which he is designated in Acts 13:5, 13. Mark was his surname (Acts 12:12, 25; 15:37). A cousin of Barnabas

---

[1] Irenaeus, *Adv. Haer*, III.
[2] Eusebius, *Church History*, II, 15.
[3] *Ibid.*, VI, 26.

(Col. 4:10), he accompanied the great missionary pair to Antioch in Syria (Acts 12:25) and then on their first tour as far as Perga (Acts 13:5-13). His defection and return to Jerusalem led Paul to oppose taking him on a second proposed tour. So strenuous became the argument that Barnabas and Paul separated (Acts 15:36-41). About ten years later, however, Mark was in Rome with Paul and joined the apostle in sending greetings (Col. 4:10, Philemon 24). Still later Paul wrote a brief commendation regarding the young man who at first had failed (II Tim. 4:11).

II. Date and Place

The passage quoted from Irenaeus probably means that Mark was not written until after the death of Peter and Paul, although other early writers place it during Peter's lifetime. Perhaps a date in the sixties would be acceptable, although an earlier dating is not excluded. The tradition that Mark's Gospel originated at Rome is early and almost unanimous.

III. Characteristics of Mark's Gospel

The Gospel of breathless action, Mark has a style of urgency and haste. Events cascade toward the climax. The Greek term *euthus* or *eutheos*, translated by "forthwith," "immediately," "straightway," and so forth, is used over forty times in Mark—half the total number of times in the New Testament —whereas Luke's much longer account employs the term only eight times. On the first full page of Mark's Gospel in Nestle's Greek text (1:10-22), Mark employs the formula *kai euthus* ("and straightway") five times and the simple *kai* ("and") twenty times. This Gospel reflects the personality of Peter in that "like him it is quick in movement, active, impulsive."[4]

In keeping with his stress on action, Mark has less of Jesus' teaching than the other Synoptic Gospels but proportionately more of His miracles. Of seventy parables and parabolic statements contained in the Gospels, Mark includes only eighteen; but of the thirty-five miracles, he records eighteen. Sparing in his use of the Old Testament, especially with reference to the fulfillment of prophecy, he explains Jewish customs and terms and does not once use the word "law,"

4 Ralph Earle, *The Story of the New Testament* (Kansas City, Mo.: Beacon Hill Press, 1941), p. 25.

although each of the other Gospels uses it several times. Several Latinisms (Latin words in Greek form) occur, corroborating slightly the strong tradition favoring Rome as the point of origin of the Gospel. The character of the Gospel, too, would appeal to the practical Roman mind.

The writer is a word-painter. From his pen flow in rapid succession a series of life pictures so graphically painted that they stand out in three-dimensional reality. Although not as long as Matthew or Luke, Mark alone preserves many minute details concerning the life of Jesus. Often these details are given in single words or brief phrases. It is Mary who recalls that John the Baptizer had said that he was not worthy to *stoop down* as a slave to untie the thongs of Jesus' sandals (1:7). After Jesus has come up out of the water at the time of His baptism, Mark snaps his verbal camera to catch the heavens in the act of being rent. Mark remembers to "unroof the roof" or break a hole in the mud or tile (Luke) roof, so that the paralytic can be brought into Jesus' presence (2:4). Again it is the second Gospel that tells us that while a great storm was in progress Jesus was in the stern of the boat asleep on the single "pillow," which was probably a wooden headrest (4:38). At the feeding of the five thousand Mark tells us that Jesus commanded the people to sit in companies or parties on the *green* grass. The term used by Mark for "ranks" means literally "flower beds" or "garden beds" and conveys the picture that the people with their colored clothing against the background of green grass looked like flower beds. These examples illustrate but do not exhaust Mark's vivid descriptions.

The vivid particulars reported by Mark often seem to reflect the memory of an eyewitness. This is true in scenes in which only Peter, James, and John were present with Jesus. The early martyrdom of James and the fact that John is responsible for another account leave only the Big Fisherman as the eyewitness. This conclusion is also supported by the silence of the Gospel on items that reflect credit on Peter and its superior record in places in which Peter alone was an eyewitness or alone was able to give a complete account of an event.

Mark's realism is revealed in many minute touches, constant care being used in details to make a scene definite and clear. Mark often furnishes particulars with regard to places, persons, numbers, times, and other items. He records the effect or impression made by Jesus' words and deeds on different individuals and groups, as for example the fear, astonishment, and amazement of the disciples (4:41; 6:51; 10:24, 26). Mark captures the *"eagerness, the impetuosity, the unrestrained insistence* of the people as they *thronged* and *pressed* him till they left him and those with him *scarce room to stand, or sit down, or even to eat"*[5] (2:2; 3:10, 20, 32; 4:1; 5:21, 31; 6:31, 33; 8:1). Other Gospels might present the subjective, mystical, and theological elements connected with Jesus' life and ministry, but Mark was interested in achievement, not theorizing.

The Gospel of historical fact, Mark contains little personal reflection and shuns literary devices which might have been used to show connections or link together parts of the narrative. Without any fanfare the writer proceeds at once to his subject—the public ministry of Jesus. The Master is presented as men had seen Him as He was mingling with different classes of people in Galilee and Judea, healing the sick, performing miracles, debating with the scribes and Pharisees, teaching the multitudes and the Twelve, facing the Cross, and conquering death. Without apology and without exaggeration Mark presents the record that he had received—a simple, factual report of selected scenes from the life of Jesus of Nazareth, whose mighty words and deeds attested that He was "the Son of God" (1:1). Jesus is presented "in the awe-inspiring grandeur of his human personality as a Man who was also the Incarnate, the wonder-working Son of God."[6]

B. CONTENTS

I. The Beginning of the Gospel (1:1-13)

1. The Title (1:1)

The Gospel of Mark begins with what is properly its title. The first verse should end with a period. It means: "Here begins . . . the gospel of Jesus Christ, the Son of God."[7] Al-

---

[5] S. D. F. Salmond, *St. Mark* (Edinburgh: Jack and Jack, n.d.), p. 35.

[6] F. W. Farrar, *The Messages of the Books* (New York: Macmillan Co., 1927), p. 57.

[7] Grant, *Interpreter's Bible* (New York: Abingdon-Cokesbury Press, 1951), VII, 647.

though the phrase "the Son of God" is not found in all of the early manuscripts, it aptly expresses the Marcan theology. The word gospel means not only the message from the lips of Christ but also the "good news whose content is Christ himself beginning with his human ministry."[8] Since among the Jews it was a common practice to refer to books by a significant word of the opening sentence, it was only natural that the word gospel should be selected for a shorter title. Later when it became necessary to distinguish the Gospels from each other, the phrase "according to" was added and the name of the writer or guarantor of the message completed the title. Thus we see how the word that describes the good news of God's offer of salvation made available through Jesus Christ became attached to the documents which are our primary sources for the life of Him who is the very incarnation of the gospel.

2. The Preparation for Jesus' Public Ministry (1:2-13)

a. *John the Baptist and His Work* (1:2-8). Mark's Gospel opens with two quotations,[9] by which the Evangelist relates the work of John the Baptizer to the Messiah. John was early identified with "Elijah," whose coming was to precede the establishment of the Messianic kingdom (9:11 ff.). Hence the announcement of the good news concerning Jesus, who was both Messiah and Son of God, begins with John's preaching in the desert.

John's appearance and message were as rugged and remote from the culture and religion of his day as were the wastes he inhabited. Dressed in rough garments of camel's hair gathered at the loins with a leather girdle, this rugged denizen of the desert presented a striking figure. His garments attested his self-identification with the prophets (II Kings 1:8; Zech. 13:4) and set him apart from the wealthy aristocrats of his day (Matt. 11:8) who were identified with a culture that demanded regeneration. Like Amos, another of God's spokesmen who heard the voice of Jehovah in the solitude of the wilderness, John came preaching judgment (Matt. 3:7-10; Luke 3:7-9). The crowds continued to come

[8] R. H. Strachan, "The Gospel in the New Testament," *Interpreter's Bible*, VII, 3.

[9] Verse 3 is from Isa. 40:3; verse 2 is from Mal. 3:1.

acknowledging their sinfulness by submitting to the rite of baptism. By this act they were virtually admitting their unfitness to enter the Messianic kingdom that John was preaching (Matt. 3:2) and their need of the cleansing promised to fit the elect people for the coming rule of God. In the Jewish thought, public confession was demanded as the normal complement of repentance, without which forgiveness was not possible.

b. *The Baptism of Jesus* (1:9-11). John's preaching included the announcement of a mightier One than he, the thong of whose sandals John was not worthy to stoop down and untie. He was to baptize with a greater baptism—one that effected a cleansing that water could only symbolize. The baptism with the Holy Spirit was to be a purging, purifying baptism, cleansing the heart from all sin.

Although Jesus' sinless life exempted Him from any need of confession of sin or baptism of repentance, He insisted (Matt. 3:13-15) on carrying out this rite, perhaps because in so doing He the more completely identified himself with the race of sinners that He came to save. It was in this act of identifying himself with us; that the voice from heaven acclaimed Him as "my beloved Son," and added, "In thee I am well pleased" (1:11). At this time the Spirit descended upon Him who was to baptize with the Holy Spirit (1:8). These manifestations to Jesus meant that God had sent Him to be His selected Representative, His Messiah.

c. *The Temptation of Jesus* (1:12-13). From the exaltation accompanying the Father's witness to the divine sonship and Messianic mission, Jesus was "immediately"—a term often used by Mark—cast out or driven into the lonely wilderness by the Spirit to be tempted by Satan. It was necessary—even inevitable—that One whose work embraced the establishing of God's kingdom should form definite plans as to what kind of kingdom He wished to establish and what measures He would employ to accomplish His goal. It was in relation to the fulfillment of His Messianic mission that Jesus was severely tempted by Satan.

Temptation need not mean defeat; it can result, as in the case of Jesus, in a clearer view of values, a firmer attachment to the higher values, and greater strength, which will permit one to overcome tests that are increasingly difficult. The aloneness of Jesus is graphically suggested by Mark—"in the wilderness . . . with the wild beasts." Temptation, even when it comes from the enticement of others, is a solitary affair to be fought alone—alone except for the fact that "in Christ" one is never alone. He has always at his disposal the virtue of One who was tempted in every respect as we, yet apart from sin (Heb. 4:15). At the conclusion of this period of testing—about forty days—the devil left Him and the angels ministered to Him. The temptations, which are listed in Matthew and Luke, are probably representative of those that confronted Jesus repeatedly throughout His career.

II. The Great Galilean Ministry (1:14—7:23)

1. The Beginning of His Ministry (1:14-39)

After the temptation which marks the close of the period of preparation, Jesus launched His program of establishing the Kingdom by "preaching the gospel of God" and announcing that "the time is fulfilled, and the kingdom of God is at hand: repent ye, and believe in the gospel" (1:14 f.).

When Jesus came preaching that "the kingdom of God is at hand," He was speaking on a subject that had great popular appeal. For many the idea of the Kingdom involved the sudden, cataclysmic overthrow of the existing order, including the Roman rule, and the setting up of a heavenly kingdom in which righteousness would prevail. For others the main idea was an overthrow of Rome by force if necessary and the elevation of the Jewish nation to a place of supremacy in world affairs.

For Jesus the Kingdom was something spiritual. One could see or enter it only by a spiritual birth. Before one could experience this birth he must repent—have a change of mind with respect to life's supreme values—and exercise faith—be willing to receive the Kingdom as a gift. The continued possession of the Kingdom is dependent upon the possession of such spiritual qualities as those which are listed in the Beatitudes.

The kingdom of God for Him signified spiritual, not territorial, sovereignty. The Kingdom came as God's will was done. It was the realm in which God exercised personal fatherly rule over His obedient, happy family. The Kingdom was one of righteousness in which man's will was aligned with God's. It was to be accepted as a gift because it was a Kingdom of grace accessible to all. Of incomparable value, the Kingdom was man's highest good, in exchange for which he should be willing joyously to part with all else. Present even when Jesus was ministering in Palestine, and subject to growth and development, its consummation is future and will take place when Jesus returns. His kingdom will never end because it is of an eternal quality.

The launching of the new program required the help of others to insure its continuance after the departure of the Founder. Jesus, well aware of this, selected two sturdy fishermen and challenged them with the summons, "Come ye after me, and I will make you to become fishers of men" (1:17). Their immediate response was matched by that of two other fishermen who likewise accepted Jesus' challenge.

Next we accompany Jesus through the activities of a busy day at Capernaum. Here His authoritative teaching in the synagogue was interrupted by a man with an unclean spirit, which Jesus cast out. The people, astonished not only at the ring of authority in His teaching but also by His command of the unclean spirits, were spreading His fame throughout the surrounding area.

After this He cured Simon's mother-in-law of an illness, the dominant symptom of which is described as "a fever." In the evening Jesus was thronged by the sick and demon-possessed, many of whom He restored. But He would not permit the demons to disclose His identity, for "they knew him" (1:34).

Although weary from the strain of the previous day's labor that must have extended well into the night, Jesus arose before dawn and retired to a lonely place to pray. No doubt He prayed for direction and for energy to fulfill the herculean task that He faced. It was difficult for One whose heart was constantly moved with compassion to leave a place where there was still so much need (1:37). Yet this was the very choice that He must make, for He felt an obligation to minister to the needs of those in the adjacent towns. There is also the hint that He considered the preaching of the gospel His supreme task (1:38).

2. Two Miracles of Healing (1:40—2:12)

a. *The Cleansing of the Leper* (1:40-45). Jesus' initial ministry in Galilee may be regarded as concluding with the effecting of two cures: the first bringing Him undesired fame as a Healer; and the second, conflict with the scribes. After a preaching tour throughout Galilee, in which Jesus cast out demons, a leper came pleading to be made clean. It was not the certification of cleanness that the man desired—the priests had authority for that—but the performance of a miracle that would cure the disease.

The leper indicated that he believed that Jesus could cleanse him if He desired to do so. The miracle is that He desired so earnestly to do so that He touched the untouchable —for the leper was ritually unclean—and thus brought ritual defilement upon himself. To aid the outcast whose malady had placed him outside the pale of respectable society and who probably felt he was rejected by God as well, Jesus had voluntarily, if temporarily, made himself an outcast. The immediate cure was accompanied by a dual charge sternly given. On the one hand, the cleansed leper was to comply with the Mosaic law which demanded that lepers present themselves to the priests for certification that the disease was cured and submit to the prescribed ritual, presenting the offering stipulated in this connection (Leviticus 14); on the other hand, he was to remain silent concerning the miracle Jesus had performed. The last half of the command was disobeyed, so that Jesus was besieged even more by those who desired to be healed.

b. *The Healing of the Paralytic* (2:1-12). The news soon spread that Jesus was back at home in Capernaum. The throngs crowded about Him until there was not even standing room about the door of the house. Four determined men had brought their paralytic friend to be healed but could not get through the crowd to Jesus; so they tore a hole in the mud or tile roof and let down the man on his pallet. When Jesus had seen the faith of these men He said to the paralytic, "Son, thy sins are forgiven" (2:5). But some of the scribes were "reasoning in their hearts" and finding fault: "He blasphemeth: who can forgive sins but one, even God?" (2:6b-7b.) Jesus thus far had not said anything that should have caused offense even to an orthodox Jew, but now that the issue had arisen He faced it squarely. Intimating that it was as easy for Him to forgive sins as to heal, Jesus said, "But in order that you [scribes] may know that the Son of Man has authority to forgive sins on earth . . . I say to you [the paralytic], Get up, take up your pallet, and go home" (2:10-11, Gk.). The man's immediate, spectacular recovery amazed them all.

We need not be bewildered by Jesus' miracles; His very personality is a miracle. It would be difficult for one who has experienced the new birth to conceive of a Christ who was not a Worker of Miracles. Surely the One who mediated creation would be able to control its functioning. Yet the miracle must be used only for moral ends, lest it degenerate into magic. And miracles must be few, for otherwise the cosmos would be changed into chaos and life would be impossible.

3. *Teaching in Galilee* (2:13—4:34)

a. *The Call of Levi* (2:13-17). Jesus, passing by a tollhouse, saw a tax collector and challenged him with a call to discipleship. Not only had Jesus now touched the untouchable; He had invited an outcast to be one of His inner circle of disciples. Levi, for that was the tax collector's name, in joyous gratitude evidently prepared a banquet in Jesus' honor and invited his old associates (Luke 5:29). The Pharisees would have but little association with men who were not as rigorous about ritual purity as they were. Hence their scribes were scandalized that Jesus was eating with tax collectors and sinners and was thus having closest fellowship with those that these religionists regarded as defiling. Jesus' reply to those who questioned His disciples regarding this breach of the Pharisaic manual is a brief and pointed statement of His program. "They that are whole have no need of a physician, but they that are sick: I came not to call the righteous, but sinners" (2:17).

b. *The Question of Fasting* (2:18-22). In the incident noted above, complaint was made to the disciples about the conduct of their Rabbi; here it is the failure of Jesus' disciples to join in a fast that was then in progress (2:18) that led to a complaint made against them to Jesus (cf. Matt. 9:14). It was a fast in which both John's disciples and the Pharisees were engaged; and Jesus could not very well by direct statement criticize the practice of fasting without alienating John's disciples, nor give general approval to the custom without bringing His own disciples under the charge of being not as religious as these other groups. His wise, parabolic answer suggested the reason that His disciples could not fast. He, the Bridegroom, was with them and it was fitting that they should rejoice and not fast. But the time would soon arrive when the Bridegroom would be taken away. Then in their sorrow fasting would be fitting. The joyous nature of the new religion would not tolerate its being placed in the old, brittle container (wineskin) of Judaism, lest the container burst and the gospel wine be lost. To attempt to make Christianity a new patch on the garment of Judaism was likewise a fruitless and foolish project. The unshrunken patch would pull away from the threadbare garment. The new religion is entirely incompatible with the old.

c. *Two Sabbath Controversies* (2: 23—3: 6). Two stories follow about Jesus in conflict with the Pharisees concerning Sabbath observance. In the former account (2: 23-28) the disciples on their way through the grain fields plucked and ate the kernels of grain after rubbing the heads in their hands. The Pharisaic objection was not that the disciples were dishonest, for the practice had the sanction of Mosaic law (Deut. 23: 25), but that they were violating the Sabbath. According to the Pharisaic definition of work they were breaking the fourth commandment in two particulars: plucking the grain was considered labor and rubbing it out in the hands was threshing! Jesus countered with a reference to David's eating of the sacred bread of the Presence, which could be eaten lawfully by the priests only. Jewish expositors, aware of the difficulty, excused David's act on the ground that his life was in danger, the teaching of the rabbis admitting the suspension of the law in such cases. Although Jesus' reply is related to regulations regarding food, whereas His disciples were charged with violations of the Sabbath law, His answer had a general relevancy. The Sabbath law, like other regulations of the Torah, was subordinate to human need. The law of human need was primary.

The same type of logic was used by Jesus in the second clash with the Pharisees concerning Sabbath observance

(3:1-6). His question put them on the defensive: "Is it lawful on the sabbath day to do good, or to do harm? to save a life, or to kill?" (3:4.) Sullen silence reigned. Mark alone notes one of the rare instances of Jesus' anger—not anger because His personal plans were opposed, but anger coupled with grief over the hardheartedness of the Pharisees who would allow men to suffer rather than change their dogma. We may be certain that even in His anger Jesus still desired only the good of all men, including the Pharisees who were attempting to prevent His healing touch. With burning resentment and sullen indignation the Pharisees slunk away to join their political foes in making plans to destroy Jesus.

d. *Reactions of Friends and Foes* (3:7-35). Jesus' fame had spread to regions beyond Galilee and Judea, bringing such crowds that He ordered a boat, so that He could escape being crushed by the mob. Retiring to the hills, He appointed the Twelve. When He returned the eager crowd was there again, so that Jesus and His disciples had not even time to eat. Friends thought He was insane, and scribes from Jerusalem accused Him of casting out demons by the prince of demons. His reply, which showed the absurdity of the charge, is followed by a statement about "an eternal sin." The chapter concludes with Jesus' description of His true relatives—"whosoever shall do the will of God" (3:35).

e. *Teaching in Parables* (4:1-34). This part of Mark ends with a section of parabolic teaching in which the Parable of the Soils is recorded and given an allegorical meaning and the purpose of parables is stated. Sayings on the responsibility of hearing precede the parable of the seed growing *automate* —"of itself." The central teaching of this parable, which is recorded only in Mark, seems to be that the Kingdom will certainly and inevitably come once the seed is sown. We do not create nor bring the Kingdom; ultimately that is God's province. We can but sow in faith and await the results. Yet there is probably truth in the suggestion that the parable indicates the growth of the Kingdom by regular stages. Judgment here, as in the parables of the Tares and Dragnet, does not take place before the beginning of the Kingdom but at the end of the period of its growth (v. 29). The section ends with the Parable of the Mustard Seed and the intimation that

Jesus used many more parables which He explained to His disciples.

4. Mighty Works Which Evoke Belief and Unbelief (4:35— 5:43)

a. *The Stilling of the Storm* (4:35-41). A word picture is painted of Jesus and His disciples caught in the fury of a great storm as they crossed the Lake of Galilee. Weary, asleep on the boat's lone cushion, Jesus, awakened by their alarmed cries, calmly rebuked the wind. When the wind had subsided He chided the disciples for their lack of faith. His command of the wind and the sea filled the disciples with awe.

b. *The Gerasene Demoniac* (5:1-20). When Jesus stepped from the boat on the east side of the lake in the country of the Gerasenes, or Gergesenes,[10] a man with an unclean spirit met Him, confessing His deity and worshiping Him. Dwelling among the tombs, the favorite abode of the demons according to the then current belief, constantly crying out and bruising himself on the rocks, unable to rest even at night, the man was in a pathetic condition. Although physical bonds could not restrain the maniacal strength of the man, Jesus fearlessly confronted him. After learning his name and granting the request of the demons, He cast out the unclean spirits, restoring the man to sanity and serenity. But the townspeople evidently feared sanity more than insanity; for when they saw the demoniac sitting there, "clothed and in his right mind . . . they were afraid" (5:15). Since the restoration of the demoniac had involved the destruction of a herd of swine, they begged Jesus to depart. How different the attitude of the restored man, who begged to be allowed to accompany Jesus! But Jesus told him to be a home missionary. This he was in a wide area, for Mark tells us that he witnessed "in Decapolis how great things Jesus had done for him" (5:20).

c. *Jairus' Daughter and the Woman with a Hemorrhage* (5:21-43). Jesus, urged to depart by the selfish, superstitious people of a village on the east shore, was welcomed by a waiting crowd when He returned to the other side (Luke 8:40). Here He was requested to heal the little daughter of Jairus,

[10] The name "Gadarenes" rests on inadequate MS evidence. A few valuable MSS read "Gergesenes." While the city of Gerasa was not near the lake, the "country" of Gerasa may have extended that far.

a ruler of the local synagogue, who lay at the point of death. While Jesus was on the way to minister to the girl who was desperately ill, a woman that for twelve years had had an incurable hemorrhage touched Jesus' garment and was healed. Jesus sensed the difference between the touch of faith and the jostling of the crowd, and, when He had secured a public confession from the woman, gave her a word of reassurance.

Not daunted by the report that the girl was dead, Jesus told the mourners—probably professional, in part at least—that the girl was only asleep. Ignoring their jeers, He put them outside while He took the parents and Peter, James, and John and "goeth in where the child was" (5:40). Taking the little girl by the hand and addressing her in her native tongue—Aramaic—He told her to arise. Immediately she arose and walked before the astonished crowd. Jesus charged them not to publish the miracle.

5. *Conclusion of the Main Phase of the Galilean Campaign* (6:1—7:23)

a. *The Rejection at Nazareth* (6:1-6). The rejection of Jesus by His townspeople, whose unbelief stands in vivid contrast to the faith of the woman who had touched only the fringe of His garment, is recorded next. Unable to deny His wisdom and power, the people of Nazareth were unwilling to admit that they came from God. This willful refusal to receive the evidence and to admit that God's presence and power were being manifested constituted the essence of their sin—the sin of unbelief. The startlingly bold statement that "he could there do no mighty work" (6:5) is to be coupled with the unbelief that made the Master marvel. Of interest is the fact that Jesus is referred to as "the carpenter" (6:3) and that four of His brothers are named and sisters are referred to as "here with us" (6:3).

b. *The Mission of the Twelve* (6:7-13). After this episode in Nazareth, Jesus continued His itinerant ministry and sent out the Twelve in pairs with instructions as to their procedure. They were to depend on God to supply their needs. Their mission not only provided training; it was beneficent in its results as well, for they cast out demons and healed the sick.

c. *The Death of John the Baptist* (6:14-29). Meanwhile, disturbing reports regarding the activities of Jesus had reached the ears of Herod Antipas, the tetrarch of Galilee and Perea. The vague statement in verse 14 may mean either that Herod heard about Jesus' ministry as it was being extended through the Twelve or that the reports of what the people were saying about Jesus had reached his ears. Herod's guilty conscience recalled his murder of John the Baptizer. The circumstances of John's murder at the instigation of Herodias, who had a grudge against John because he had publicly denounced her union with Antipas as adulterous, are given in gruesome detail. This is one of the incidents which is recorded most completely in Mark's Gospel.

Herod's fears apparently had their effect on the movements and ministry of Jesus. The violent death of a person was thought by the ancients to endow his soul with supernatural energy. Herod supposed that Jesus was either John revived or in league with John's supernatural powers. This would increase Herod's guilty fears and lead him to seek Jesus' life. Luke (13:32) indicates that at a later time some friendly Pharisees warned Jesus about Herod's desire to kill Him. From this time on, Jesus, when He could do so conveniently, avoided the territory of Antipas. Probably the popularity associated with the miraculous feedings of the multitudes on two different occasions was for Herod a source of increasing fear and desire to destroy Jesus. Manifestations of Jesus' popularity now precede periods of retirement to areas outside the·jurisdiction of Antipas.

d. *The Feeding of the Five Thousand* (6:30-44). When the Twelve had returned, Jesus invited them to a retreat from the incessant demands of the throngs. But the crowds, seeing Jesus' intention, came on foot before Jesus and His disciples could arrive by boat. Jesus' compassion on the hungry crowd led to the miraculous feeding of the five thousand. After this Jesus surprised the disciples by walking on the sea. On the return to Gennesaret, the people came flocking from the entire neighborhood, bringing their sick and begging to touch even the fringe of His garment, for all who touched it were healed.

e. *Nature of Real Defilement* (7:1-23; cf. Matt. 15:1-20). Faultfinding scribes from Jerusalem, apparently with the approval of the local Pharisees, complained that some of Jesus' disciples were not washing their hands properly before eating. The complaint did not involve sanitation but ritual purity. The Pharisees, in an attempt to make Israel a holy nation, separated from things defiling, were trying to force on *all the people* ritual requirements originally intended only for the *priests* when they ate holy food. Handwashing, originally an act of consecration, communion, and thanksgiving for food which was God's gift, had degenerated to a mere form. The Pharisees demanded that a certain minimum amount of water be poured twice over the hands, care being exercised that it be not poured too high on the wrist, lest it flow back and defile the hands. The word translated "diligently" means literally "with the fist" or with the inside of the fist but may be translated "up to the elbow" or "up to the wrist."

In answer to the charge that His disciples were not walking according to the tradition of the elders (Pharisaic oral tradition), Jesus quoted from the Septuagint of Isa. 29:13 and countered that the Pharisees and scribes were rejecting "the commandment of God" that they might "keep your tradition" (7:9), a "tradition of men" (7:8). Jesus illustrated His charge with the Pharisaic Corban rule by which if a son, even in a fit of anger, vowed that the support his parents had a right to expect of him was given to God his vow was valid and that which was devoted could not be used for the support of the parents. The scribes by their deceit had elevated mechanical rule and ecclesiastical law above the moral law. No wonder Jesus charged: "You have a fine way of rejecting the commandment of God in order to keep your tradition!" (7:9, R.S.V.)

After this Jesus called the people to Him and explained that real defilement did not concern the ritual impurity of food but the heart, from which spring evil thoughts, which in turn are the source of a black family of evils. Three of the specific evils named are sins of passion: fornications, adulteries, and lasciviousness. Three other sins are against the persons and property of others: murders, thefts, and covetings. The rest are sins of the mind and heart, except for wickedness, which is a general term for moral evil. It is a sobering thought that deceit, an evil eye ("a jealous, grudging disposition,"[11] or envy), and slander are not less sinful than the sins of passion and sins against which society has guarded by stringent legislation. It is also to be noted that pride or arrogance, which excludes God's grace, and foolishness, a perverse indifference that willfully confuses moral values and refuses spiritual values, bring the list to a close. These sins are heinous and serious because the attitude of mind from which they spring leaves no room for repentance and reform.

In this discourse, Jesus showed that real defilement is moral and spiritual and springs from twisted thinking out of an evil heart. Mark interprets Jesus' statements about food as implying that Jesus obliterated distinctions between the ritually clean and unclean. In so doing, Jesus struck at the base of the entire ceremonial system of Judaism.

III. Events from the Retirement to the Triumphal Entry (7: 24—10: 52)

1. Events Connected with the First Retirement to the North (7: 24—8: 26)

   a. The Faith of the Syrophoenician Woman (7: 24-30). Probably to avoid Antipas, and perhaps also because of the opposition that his controversy about the clean and unclean had stirred up, Jesus retired to the district of Tyre and Sidon. There He hoped to find rest and quiet. But "he could not be hid" (7: 24). A woman whose little daughter was possessed by an evil spirit begged Jesus to cast out the demon. Jesus replied that the children first should be fed, "for it is not right to take the children's bread and throw it to the dogs" (7: 27, R.S.V.). But with a ready wit the woman, sticking to her request, noted that even the house dogs got their share. She was willing to receive aid for her daughter even though it were just a crumb. Jesus then rewarded her faith by announcing that her daughter was restored.

This strange reluctance of Christ to respond to the cries of this Phoenician woman of Syria and His words that seem to class her as a dog are difficult to explain. The reluctance is even more obvious in Matthew, where her continued cries are the occasion for the disciples' requesting Jesus to send her away. His reply to them, "I was not sent but unto the lost sheep of the house of Israel" (Matt. 15: 24), seems strange in

[11] Buttrick, IB, VII, 753.

this setting. But of course the answer might lie in the question of priority. He is asked here to do for a stranger what He is unable to do for His own people. Then, too, Jesus came for rest and seclusion; and a miracle was not the best way to keep His presence unknown.

Christ may have wished to rebuke with gentle irony the prejudice of the Twelve against the Gentiles. The disciples in common with many of their countrymen probably thought of the Gentiles as "dogs." Again, Christ may have wished to test her faith, and probably gave her encouragement by tone or manner as well as by His selection of words. On this occasion He may have used Greek, since the woman probably spoke Greek. In that case perhaps the use of the diminutive, or word meaning "doggies" or "puppies," was significant. Instead of insinuating that her daughter was a vicious wild dog, Jesus used a term that might be used to designate a household pet. The woman was quick to see the implication of the term Jesus selected and with a flash of wit won Jesus' approval for her display of faith. By using persistence and brains she secured the help she desired for one she loved.

b. *The Healing of the Deaf Mute* (7:31-37). Soon after this Jesus moved on northward to the vicinity of Sidon, and from there He may have followed the highway over the Lebanon Mountains to the region of Damascus, which was once included in the Decapolis. The account indicates that Jesus avoided the territory of Herod Antipas. Somewhere in the Decapolis a deaf mute was brought to Jesus. A description is given of material means that Jesus used to encourage the man's faith. Jesus used precautions to prevent knowledge of the miracle from reaching the public and precipitating an avalanche of cure-seekers. However, His precautions failed to keep the matter quiet. Matthew indicates that at this time Jesus carried on an extensive healing ministry among the Gentiles who glorified Israel's God.

c. *The Feeding of the Four Thousand* (8:1-10). Matthew's account indicates that the praise and excitement attending the cures Jesus was performing caused a great crowd to assemble. Jesus was loath to send them home because, having been with Him for three days, they had nothing left to eat. So once again He performed a miracle to satisfy the hungry crowds. This time seven biscuits and several sardine-like fish, blessed by Jesus and distributed by His disciples, provided sufficient food for four thousand men besides women and children.

d. *The Disciples Warned Against the Pharisaic Leaven* (8: 11-21). When the Pharisees asked for a sign from heaven that they might test Him, Jesus refused, saying that no sign would be given to that generation. He then warned the Twelve to beware of the leaven of the Pharisees and of Herod, which after explanation they understood to refer to doctrine (Matt. 16: 12).

e. *The Healing of the Blind Man at Bethsaida* (8: 22-26). Once more material means are used. The fact that the cure was effected by stages may have been intended to cause the man to see that the cure was no performance of magic. It has been suggested also that the gradual restoration of the man's sight symbolizes the slowness of the disciples to believe. Jesus sent the man home, charging him not even to enter the village. He wanted no turbulent crowds but seclusion, so that He could teach the Twelve lessons that they had been so slow to learn.

2. *The Great Confession and the Cross* (8: 27-38)

On the way to the villages in the region of Caesarea Philippi, Jesus was asking His disciples who men were saying that He was. This leading question, which evoked various replies, Jesus used to open the way for a direct question to the Twelve: "But who say ye that I am?" (8: 29.) Peter immediately responded with the declaration called "The Great Confession," "Thou art the Christ" (8: 29). The disciples were then cautioned against revealing to anyone that He was the Messiah.

Peter had recognized Jesus' messiahship but had failed to see that its true nature was not political but spiritual— that the path to glory was not by military and political success but by suffering. So Peter began to rebuke Jesus for saying that He must suffer, be rejected, be killed, and rise from the dead. At this first prediction of the Passion, Peter evidently shared the attitude of the rest of the disciples. With a normal solicitude for what he considered the Master's welfare, he recoiled from the cross. Probably the force of the temptation to Christ is indicated by the severity of His reply,

"Get behind me, Satan! For you are not on the side of God, but of men" (8:33, R.S.V.).

Immediately after this incident the Twelve and the crowd were told that there was a cross for them, too, and for all those who would come after Jesus. The paradox of self-denial and cross-bearing is this: that one who loses himself in the interest of Christ and His kingdom will find himself—his true life. One lives only when he dies to selfish interests, and finds his true life only in a cause for which he is willing to die. To fling one's self with reckless abandon into the service of Christ and to confess Him before men is the only way to life here and hereafter. No material values, Jesus says, are of sufficient weight to balance the scales against the worth of a human self or personality. Hence one who barters his life for even a whole world of material values is the loser.

3. The Transfiguration (9:1-13)

Apparently six days after the Great Confession and the teaching connected with that occasion, Jesus selected three disciples to accompany him to the top of a high mountain—probably Mount Hermon. There, as He was praying (Luke 9:29), an inner radiance changed His appearance. Jesus was manifesting himself as the Son of God, as He now appears in heaven and will appear at the Second Advent. Then the lawgiver, Moses, the prototype of the Messiah (Deut. 18:15), and Elijah, the prophet and forerunner of the Messiah (Mal. 4:5), appeared, talking with Jesus about His approaching death (Luke 9:30-31). When the visitors were about to depart, Peter in fear and confusion proposed the building of three booths in honor of the three principal personalities who were present. Since Israel's Messianic hope then seemed to associate her triumph over her foes with the coming of all nations to worship at Jerusalem at the Feast of Booths (Zech. 14:16-19), perhaps Peter thought that the great day had dawned and that the guests from heaven—Moses and Elijah—were here to stay. According to rabbinic teaching another indication of the arrival of the Messianic age was the reappearance of the Shekinah, the symbol of the divine presence (Exod. 16:10; I Kings 8:10 f.). It is significant that the divine voice attesting that Jesus was God's beloved Son came out of such a cloud.

While the climax of the Transfiguration experience came with this divine announcement, the words "hear ye him" (9: 7) and the disappearance of Moses and Elijah so that the disciples "saw no one any more, save Jesus only" (9: 8) are also significant. Jesus is seen to be the climax and goal of the revelation. The law and the prophets, which are represented by Moses and Elijah respectively, fade out of the picture, since their function is fulfilled in Jesus, the Lawgiver and Prophet of the new age.

4. The Epileptic Boy (9: 14-29)

On the way down the mountain, Jesus gave the disciples strict orders to reveal to no one what they had seen until after His resurrection. When the disciples asked Him why the scribes taught that first Elijah must come, Jesus replied that Elijah had already come and men had done to him as they pleased. By this statement the disciples knew that Jesus was speaking about John the Baptizer.

When they had come to the rest of the disciples they found them in the midst of a throng, arguing with the scribes. Jesus discovered that the occasion of the argument was the failure of the disciples to restore to normality a boy who was subject to epileptic fits. Rebuking the crowd as representatives of a "faithless generation," He requested that the boy be brought. In the presence of Jesus the boy was seized again with an attack and the desperate father cried out, "If thou canst do anything, have compassion on us, and help us" (9: 22). Jesus' exclamation, "If thou canst" (9: 23), may be either an echo of amazement that His ability was called into question, or, with the emphasis on "thou," a reply to the father. Jesus' added statement that, to one who continues to believe, all things are possible is a challenge to every generation. The father then asserted his will to believe, but, realizing the impossibility of overcoming unaided the pressures of doubt and unbelief against which his anguished soul was struggling, he begged for Jesus to help his faltering faith. Jesus then rebuked the cause of the epilepsy and effected a permanent cure. When the disciples asked for an explanation of their failure Jesus replied that "this kind can come out by nothing, save by prayer" (9: 29). In view of His seemingly irresistible power, Jesus' answer implying that successful expulsion of evil spirits cannot be accomplished without prayer sounds strange from His lips. However, it should be remembered that for Jesus prayer was not the mere mouthing of words but was a life of personal communion with God. In this communion there was the contact with divine dynamic sufficient to deal with the powers of evil.

5. *Second Prediction of the Passion and Dispute About Greatness* (9:30-37)

Jesus and the disciples were still (7:24) traveling as secretly as possible because He was teaching the disciples a solemn lesson. The substance of that lesson was His approaching death and resurrection. It was essentially the same teaching that Jesus had given immediately after Peter's confession; but the disciples, still clinging to their ideas of a political Messiah, did not grasp what Jesus was saying. How often prejudice blinds us to the lessons that Jesus would teach us!

When they had arrived in Capernaum, Jesus asked what the subject of the conversation had been. An awkward silence followed this question, for they had been discussing who would be the greatest. This again was probably a reflection of their gross misconception of the nature of the Kingdom. Jesus' reply defined true greatness in terms of service and not in terms of superior position—a definition we are in danger of forgetting. He further intimated that there is no higher or nobler service than that which is rendered to boys and girls for His sake. Matthew's record here also adds something to our understanding of the situation. Unless the disciples were to turn about and adopt the humble attitude of a little child they could not even enter the Kingdom, much less be greatest in it.

6. *Concerning Followers and Offenses* (9:38-50)

Perhaps this teaching on the need for humility probed John's conscience on another point. He indicated that he had been involved in forbidding another to cast out demons in Jesus' name "because he was not following us" (9:38, Gk.). How often since that time has this narrow, sectarian spirit been displayed to the detriment of Christ's cause!

The teaching concerning offending the little ones who believe on Christ seems to be more closely connected with verses 33-37 than with the verses immediately preceding. However, the same selfish spirit that was rebuked in verses 33-37 was manifest also in the attitude of John and his group toward the man casting out demons. Selfish ambition and pride displayed by professing Christians in places of leadership in the church still constitute a stumbling block to many who are weak in the faith. There is danger of scandalizing, or driving away by a harsh and contemptuous attitude, those whose faith is faltering. We can use our faculties—hands, feet, and eyes— selfishly and thereby sin and cause others to sin. Better never to have been born than for this to happen. Better to have a huge millstone—the kind driven by a donkey—hanged about one's neck and to be drowned in the depth of the sea than to be a stumbling block to one of these babes in Christ. Throughout the passage the refrain recurs that the lesser values are to be sacrificed for the supreme value.

7. Concerning Divorce and Children (10:1-16)

Jesus left Capernaum and came to the region of Judea "and beyond the Jordan" (10:1), where He taught the crowds who were gathering. At this point the Pharisees presented a question designed to trap Jesus. "Is it lawful for a man to divorce his wife?" they asked (10:2, R.S.V.). Matthew's added words "for any cause" (19:3) suggest that these Pharisees found in a current debate in Judaism an occasion that they hoped to use to embarrass Jesus. According to Deut. 24:1 a man could write a bill of divorce for his wife if he found in her "the shameful thing." The school of Shammai interpreted this strictly as meaning infidelity alone. The school of Hillel, however, permitted divorce even for such minor faults as burning the bread. If Jesus adopted the strict interpretation of Shammai, He would offend the crowds who then as now favored easy divorce; if, on the other hand, He adopted the liberal view of Hillel, He could be charged with laxity.

Too wise for His questioners, Jesus asked what Moses had *commanded*. They replied that Moses had *permitted* a man to write a certificate of divorce and to put away his wife. Jesus responded that this was indeed a *concession*—a concession made because of the hardness of their hearts. Appealing to the creation account in Genesis (1:27; 2:24), He showed that from the first the divine ideal had embraced not only monogamy but a permanency of the marriage union. He lifted marriage from the plane of convenience and pleasure to the spiritual level of God's purpose. In so doing He criticized the Mosaic law, which, while it alleviated woman's lot by protecting her from being taken again by her former husband in case her second husband died or divorced her, made divorce easy and regarded the wife as chattel of the man. Jesus, on the other hand, in a social order in which the man had all the rights,[12] recognized in easy divorce a cruel and heartless treatment of woman. In stressing the permanent and holy character of the marriage union, Jesus became a champion of woman as a person endowed with the rights inherent in personality. It is evident that Jesus was not attempting to legislate on divorce but was setting forth principles which would raise the entire question of marriage and divorce above the plane of the sensual and earthly to the spiritual level of God's will. If more marriages were begun on this plane, fewer would end in the divorce court.

Immediately after the discussion of divorce, Jesus' attitude toward children is presented. So often divorce deprives the children of their rights to the security and affection afforded by an unbroken home. In the Gospel account people were bringing their children for Jesus to place His hands on in blessing. But the disciples thought that Jesus should be free to attend to more important things; so they rebuked the people severely for bringing the children to Jesus. When Jesus saw what was going on He was indignant and said: "Suffer the little children to come unto me; forbid them not: for to such belongeth the kingdom of God" (10:14). No one can enter the Kingdom, He declared, unless he receives it as a child. In other words, just as a child is dependent and receptive, so must be anyone who is to receive God's great gift—the Kingdom. Nothing can exclude one from salvation more quickly than pride and self-righteousness. The picture of the child resting his head on Jesus' strong arm (v. 16) reflects the attitude of receptivity and dependence upon the Son of God that should characterize us all.

8. The Rich Young Men (10:17-31)

As Jesus was starting on His way a young man (Matt. 19:20) of influence (Luke 18:18) came running and knelt be-

---

[12] This was true in Judaism. At Rome, where Mark was written, the women also exercised the right to divorce their husbands. Mark 10:12 reflects the situation in Rome, not Palestine.

fore Him asking what he should do to inherit eternal life. Jesus told him that he already knew the commandments and quoted the sixth, seventh, eighth, ninth, and fifth commandments, so that the man would not make any mistake as to which were intended; for to the Jew of that day "the commandments" would not be as definite as they are to us today. When the man observed that he had kept all of the commandments from his youth, Jesus told him that he lacked "one thing." He needed to dethrone the riches which were usurping the command of his life, so that God could be enthroned. Jesus made the advice personal and definite. For this young man to become a disciple would involve disposing of his riches, giving his wealth to the poor, and following Jesus. The young man went away sad, for, after facing the cost of discipleship, he considered the price too great. How many young men since his day have turned away likewise to their sorrow!

This incident led Jesus to observe that it was "easier for a camel to go through a needle's eye, than for a rich man to enter into the kingdom of God" (10:25). This is a characteristic use of Oriental hyperbole. After this, in reply to the question, "Then who can be saved?" (10:26), Jesus indicated that, while salvation was impossible on the human plane, all things are possible to God.

9 The Third Prediction of the Passion and a Selfish Request (10:32-45)

After Peter had mentioned the sacrifice that he and the rest of the Twelve had made, Jesus had assured them that they were being and would be well repaid. Then, on the way up to Jerusalem, Jesus a third time predicted His death and resurrection. Immediately after this, Zebedee's sons, James and John, came requesting positions of pre-eminence[13] in Christ's glory. Evidently they were either wanting places of honor at the Messianic banquet, or places of honor and authority in a political Messianic kingdom which they thought was about to appear. Jesus replied by asking them if they were able to drink the bitter cup that He was about to taste and be baptized with the baptism to which He was about to

---

[13] Note that in Matt. 20:20 it is the mother of James and John who makes the request. Probably the three came together to Jesus.

submit. In response to their proud rejoinder that they were able Jesus said that the rewards requested were not His to grant.

When the ten became aware of this selfish request they became indignant because they, too, wished preferment. In this tense situation Jesus patiently explained that true greatness was not exercised by those who "lord it over" others but by those who serve. The greatest is he who serves all the rest. "For the Son of man also came not to be ministered unto, but to minister, and to give his life a ransom for many" (10:45).

IV. From the Triumphal Entry to the Anointing in Simon's House (cc. 11—13)

1. The Triumphal Entry (11:1-11)

Immediately after the healing of blind Bartimaeus (10:46-52) the scene shifts to Bethphage and Bethany, as the Master and His disciples approach Jerusalem. Two of the disciples are dispatched to Bethphage (Matt. 21:1 f.) to obtain an unbroken colt, so that Jesus may ride it into the city and thus fulfill the prophecy of Zech. 9:9. The symbolism of a king riding on a donkey was well known to the Jews of Jesus' day. To them it meant that the rider was coming humbly and peaceably. How fitting a symbol for One who described himself as "meek and lowly in heart" (Matt. 11:29)! Jesus told the disciples where the colt would be found and what to say to anyone who objected to their taking the animal. With Jesus riding on the donkey and the people spreading their garments and leafy branches on the road, the procession moved forward shouting joyously, "Hosanna; Blessed is he that cometh in the name of the Lord: Blessed is the kingdom that cometh, the kingdom of our father David: Hosanna in the highest" (11:9 f.). Mark tells us only that Jesus went into the Temple, and "when he had looked round at everything, as it was already late, he went out to Bethany with the Twelve" (11:11, R.S.V.).

2. The Cursing of the Fig Tree and the Cleansing of the Temple (11:12-25)

a. *The Cursing of the Fig Tree* (11:12-14, 20-26). The next morning as Jesus was returning to Jerusalem He was hungry; so when He saw a fig tree in leaf He turned aside to see if He could find fruit on it. It has been thought that this account reflects on Jesus' intelligence, since Mark states that the season of figs had not yet come (11:13). While the main crop of figs does not ripen in the vicinity of Jerusalem until August, smaller figs begin to appear on the old wood as soon as the leaf buds are put forth—usually about the end of March. Most of these figs are shaken off by the gusts of wind and never reach maturity. Even these immature figs were eaten by the peasants. The few early figs that did ripen (in June) were especially prized for their delicacy. Thus Jesus was justified in expecting something to eat even though the time for mature fruit had not arrived. The lack of any fruit on the tree was proof of its barrenness. No doubt this suggested to Jesus the Jewish religion with its abundant green foliage of religious profession and barren performance in real righteousness. The cursing of the fig tree has always been regarded as an acted parable of the doom of the Jewish nation because its proud pretense was not matched by even the promise of the fruit of righteousness.

The next day Peter, amazed that the fig tree was already withered to the roots, called Jesus' attention to the fact. Jesus then used the incident as an occasion for setting forth the two conditions of effective prayer: faith towards God and forgiveness towards others.

b. *The Cleansing of the Temple* (11:15-19).[14] Worshipers coming to Jerusalem found it necessary to exchange Roman coins for Tyrian half-shekels, which Jewish law required for the payment of the annual head tax. Since this tax was due by Nisan first—just before Passover—about a week prior to that time the money-changers established their headquarters in the larger outer court of the Temple area, called the Court of the Gentiles or "the mountain of the house." In this area traders sold ritually perfect animals to the worshipers. Originally, no doubt, both operations were instituted for the convenience of pilgrims who often came from great distances. Later on it is probable that the traders fleeced the pilgrims

[14] Matthew places the cleansing at the time of the Triumphal Entry (Matt. 21:10-17). John places a cleansing at the beginning of Jesus' ministry (2:13-17). It seems clear that there were two cleansings, one near the beginning and the other near the end of Jesus' ministry.

with the consent of the priests who shared the unfair profits. The noise of the Orientals haggling over prices, and the sounds and smells that would emanate from the beasts, would not contribute to the sacred atmosphere of the place.

Small wonder, then, that Jesus was righteously indignant and drove out both buyers and sellers, upset the tables of the money-changers and the seats of those who sold pigeons (also used for sacrifice), and prevented people from making the "mountain of the house" into a short cut for secular traffic. The Court of the Gentiles was obviously not fulfilling its God-intended use while it was serving as an Oriental bazaar, cattle yard, and thoroughfare for secular traffic. Concerning its use Jesus gave instruction from Isa. 56: 7. The Court of the Gentiles should serve as "a house of prayer for all the nations," but buyer, seller, and pedestrian had all served to pervert its true function. They, by their actions, were despising the house of God as if it were a cave serving as a hide-out for robbers betweeen their acts of crime (11: 17; cf. Jer. 7: 11).

3. Jesus' Authority Challenged (11: 18-19, 27-33)

As a result of Jesus' action and teaching, the chief priests, scribes, and "principal men of the people" (Luke 19: 47) were enraged and sought to destroy Him, but because of Jesus' great popularity they were afraid to take action against Him openly. However, when He returned the next day they sought to discredit His teaching by challenging His right to teach. The questions which these representatives of the Sanhedrin asked Jesus: "By what authority doest thou these things? or who gave thee this authority to do these things?" (11: 28), were loaded questions. The Temple was controlled by the high priests—with some interference from Rome—and this delegation was certain that Jesus had no authority from these sources. They were sure, too, that He was no rabbi by official ordination—the laying on of hands or *semikhah* which gave one the authority to teach and to render valid decisions. By challenging Jesus' authority they expected Him to have recourse to one of three alternatives, the adoption of any of which would have been fatal to Him or His influence. If He claimed divine authority He could be convicted of blasphemy. The claim of being Son of David would make Him liable to a charge of treason against Rome. If He claimed no special authority, that would be proof that He was an impostor and so would discredit Him in the eyes of the people.

Two courses of action, however, were open to Jesus. He could have claimed the call of God for His prophetic behavior in cleansing the Temple, as Amos did when he was challenged for his messages of judgment (Amos 7:14 f.), or He could put His opponents on the defensive. In replying with a question He was following a custom often used in Jewish discussions. Asking His opponents whether John's baptism was "from heaven, or from men" (11:30), He placed them in a difficult place. If they answered, "From men," they would alienate the people who accepted John as a spokesman for God. If, on the other hand, they answered that his authority was from God, they would be admitting John's testimony to Jesus as the "Lamb of God" (John 1:29) and the "Son of God" (1:34). Thus they would also be forced to concede that His authority in a higher sense than John's was likewise from God. In pleading ignorance on so vital a religious question, these ecclesiastical leaders were forced to admit that they had no competence as teachers of Israel.

4. The Parable of the Wicked Tenants (12:1-12)

In this parable Jesus takes the offensive against His opponents. The background for this parable or allegory is found in Isaiah's "Parable of the Vineyard" (5:1-7), which likewise pictures the Jewish people as a vineyard of God. Jesus' allegory gives a philosophy of Jewish history reaching far into the past, involving the present conflict and pointing to a future judgment. In this allegory the absentee landlord is God; the vineyard planted, hedged, with its tower for the detection of marauders and shelter of vinedressers, and its trough for the winepress for the processing of the harvest, is Israel or Jerusalem, whose Owner has done everything possible to insure a satisfactory harvest; the tenants are the evil rulers of Judaism; the servants are the Old Testament prophets; the beloved son is Jesus, whose crucifixion is the murder of the heir; the destruction of these wicked tenants is the judgment on the Jewish nation; and the entrusting of the vineyard to others, probably the apostles, points to the Gentile mission. To this figure Jesus added a Messianic text (Ps. 118:22 f.) which, although changing the metaphor, completes the thought of the rejection of the wicked tenants. The stone which was rejected by the builders—these same wicked rulers—becomes the head of the corner. This, too, predicts the embarrassment of the Jewish hierarchy because God had elevated the One they had rejected.

Of course the wicked hierarchs could scarcely have failed to see that they with their murderous motives were the evil tenants whose intention included the killing of the son. Perhaps this was a last desperate attempt of Jesus to get them to see the blackness of the crime and to pass sentence on its perpetrators, so that they could not carry out their evil plot. But the rulers were too hardened in their opposition to truth to repent. Instead they would have arrested Him had it not been for their fear of the multitude.

5. *The Question of Tribute to Caesar* (12:13-17)

The question of whether or not it was lawful to pay tribute to Caesar was another burning issue. The Pharisees and Herodians, who with flattery handed the question to Jesus, hoped for a yes-or-no answer that would in either case spell out the end of Jesus' career. If He answered that it was lawful He would thereby offend many of the nationalists who were to be numbered among His followers, for they held that Rome had no God-given right to rule over them. The payment of the tax was not so much an economic hardship as a bitter reminder that they were under the Roman rule and even then nominally a part of an imperial province which was considered too unstable for senatorial control. But if Jesus answered that it was not lawful to pay the tax, He could be reported to Rome; and Rome was severe in its treatment of those guilty of treason.

The combination which was conspiring against Jesus is peculiar—Herodians and Pharisees. The only point they held in common was their hatred of Jesus: the Pharisees because He was disturbing the religious *status quo* and exposing their empty hypocrisy; the Herodians because these supporters of the Herodian family against the Maccabean line did not want the political situation changed—a situation from which they were able to derive special favors.

Again Jesus refused to be drawn into the trap. Instead He surprised His opponents into an admission that they were even then carrying Caesar's money and so were, especially as measured by the thinking of that day, admitting the sovereignty of Rome. For "sovereignty was coterminous with the rights of coinage and the validity of one's money."[15] Furthermore, the use of the Roman coin implied the acceptance of the benefits of a stable government. Jesus does not say that they should have accepted these benefits or what kind of government if any should exist. But He does indicate that the acceptance of these benefits of a government meant incurring an obligation to obey its laws. Those who taught that one could not be loyal to God and pay the tax to Rome had exactly reversed the real alternatives. One could not be loyal to God unless he honored his obligations. Let Caesar have back that which belonged to him—his demand was small anyway.[16] But above all else give God what belongs to Him. To God all owe a debt of reverence, duty, obedience, service, love, and worship. If they gave God His due they would not be burning with resentment over such slight provocations. This was the high road hidden to their eyes because they were trying to find a solution on too low a level. The fate of the Jews is a sad commentary on the fact that Jesus' advice went unheeded for too long by too many.

6. *The Question About the Resurrection* (12:18-27)

The Sadducees who denied the resurrection now came to Jesus with an extreme hypothetical case proving, they thought, that the doctrine of the resurrection was absurd. The Mosaic law stipulated that if a man lived on the same estate with his married brother who died childless leaving a widow, it was the duty of the surviving brother to take the widow as his wife. The first son of this union was to perpetuate the name, family, and inheritance of the deceased man.

In the hypothetical case advanced by the Sadducees seven brothers had all successively had the same woman as their wife, but she had borne no children to any of the seven. Whose wife would she be in the resurrection? Jesus in a question rebuked the experts on the Scripture, indicating that they were wrong because they knew neither "the scriptures, nor the power of God" (12:24).

Specifically the Sadducees were wrong because they were thinking on a crass, materialistic plane. Their dilemma would

[15] B. H. Branscomb, *The Gospel of Mark* (New York: Harper and Brothers, n.d.), p. 214.
[16] Only about twenty-five cents a person each year.

hold only in conditions similar to those existing in this life, in which death makes procreation necessary for the continuance of the race. In the resurrection men are equal to angels and cannot die (Luke 20:36) and do not marry (Mark 12:25). Even the Torah (Pentateuch), which they acknowledged as the only valid basis for doctrine, teaches the resurrection, for there God is represented as the God of the patriarchs (Exod. 3:6, 15). Hence, Jesus is founding His conviction on the truth that the purpose of God, who in redeeming love entered into fellowship with the patriarchs who responded in faith, is not to be limited to this life alone. God desires an eternal relation of fellowship based on His redemptive will. Hence, to the Sadducees, Jesus could say, "Ye do greatly err" (12:27).

7. The Great Commandment (12:28-34)

Since there were according to the rabbinic methods of calculation 613 commandments (of which 365 were prohibitions), there would arise occasions on which the commands might conflict. So it was necessary to know which command should be obeyed in case of conflict. The rabbis usually held that the weightier commands were those sanctioned by the heavier penalties. But Jesus, along with those of deeper ethical understanding, interpreted the greatest commands as those which included the rest.

So when the scribe, who had evidently come to admire Jesus for the understanding He displayed in dealing with difficult questions, approached Christ with the query, "Which commandment is first of all?" Jesus replied with a summation of the law. This was taken partly from the Shema, which constituted a portion of the daily prayers of the Jews. To this Jesus joined a statement found in Lev. 19:18, ". . . thou shalt love thy neighbor as thyself."

As a result of Jesus' joining or sanctioning the union of these two commandments they have become indissolubly fixed as the foci of the Christian religion. Love to God and to one's neighbor were joined not only in word but in deed by Jesus, whose life was a constant expression of this command.

Mark alone records the scribe's words of appreciation for Jesus' answer and his expression of agreement with the philosophy that to love God supremely and one's neighbor as oneself transcended by far the ceremonial aspects of religion.

Jesus' response, "Thou art not far from the kingdom of God," is intriguing.

8. Jesus Raises a Question and Makes Observations (12:35-44)

a. *David's Son* (12:35-37). While Jesus was teaching in the Temple, He asked how the scribes could say that the Messiah was David's son, since David in the Psalms calls Him "Lord." The answer, of course, is that Jesus was the eternal Son of God, though born of the seed of David.

b. *Woes Against the Pharisees and the Widow's Gift* (12:38-44). Jesus counseled His hearers to beware of the Pharisees whose religious ostentation was only a cloak to cover their moral wrongs. Perhaps it was the widow whose house the Pharisees devoured (12:40) who dropped two small copper coins into the Temple treasury. Jesus' comment on her gift shows that God puts more premium on the cost or sacrifice involved than He does on the size of the gift. He judges giving more by what is left than by the amount that is given.

9. The Apocalyptic Discourse (13:1-37)

a. *The Occasion* (13:1-4). As Jesus was leaving the Temple one of the disciples called His attention to the beauty of the stones and the building. Jesus replied that the Temple would be destroyed so completely that not one stone would be left upon another. As Jesus sat on the Mount of Olives facing the Temple the three of the inner circle (James, Peter, and John), along with Andrew, asked, "When shall these things be? and what shall be the sign when these things are all about to be accomplished?" (13:4.) The answer is to be found with difficulty in the paragraphs that follow.

All three of the Synoptic accounts give essentially the same data. However, Matthew's statement of the questions asked by the disciples is instructive. There the questions are: "When shall these things [i.e., the destruction of the Temple] be? and what shall be the sign of thy coming, and of the end of the world?" (24:3). This shows that in the confused apocalyptic thinking of the disciples the destruction of Jerusalem was lumped together with Christ's coming and the end of the age. There is some evidence that while Jesus in His reply kept these things separate, the disciples tended to relate all Jesus' statements to one idea-complex in which the Second Coming and end of the age are joined with the destruction of Jerusalem. This makes the task of understanding the discourse more difficult but not less interesting.

b. *"The Beginning of Travail"* (13:5-8). For the Jews this expression (v. 8) was a technical rabbinical formula for the disasters associated with the Messiah's advent that were to befall the nation. Here the expression may refer to the pangs attending the birth of the new order or the "regeneration" (cf. Matt. 19:28). It will be noted that the advent of false messiahs—three are mentioned in Acts (5:36, 37; 21:38) and many have arisen since, the most notable being Bar Cochba, who precipitated a revolt about A.D. 132—and wars, rumors of wars, famines, and earthquakes are but evidences of the beginning of these birth pains of the Kingdom.

c. *The Persecution of the Disciples* (13:9-13). Luke says that "before all this" the apostles will be persecuted because of their witness for Christ (Luke 21:12). They are to be delivered up to the "councils" and beaten in the "synagogues" (Mark 13:9). This passage probably refers primarily to the apostolic period. History indicates that during this period the Jews were especially malevolent toward the Christians.

When on trial for their lives the disciples are not to be anxious about their defense nor to give a premeditated and perhaps softened answer, for the Holy Spirit will speak through them. Families will be divided on account of the gospel, and people will deliver up their nearest relatives and friends to death. The presence of false prophets and wickedness will increase the disciples' peril. Salvation is for those only who in the face of all hazards persevere to the end, which will come only after the gospel has been preached as a witness to all nations (Matt. 24:14).

d. *Persecution in Judea* (13:14-23). The appearance of "the abomination of desolation" (13:14) is to be interpreted by the official reader as the sign for precipitate flight from Judea to the mountains. Unparalleled tribulation will prevail, so that except for the fact that the Lord had shortened it for the sake of His elect no human being would be spared. False messiahs and false prophets will arise and by signs and wonders will deceive many. This is an interesting passage. What does the expression "the abomination of desolation" mean? It is "the 'abomination' that drives God from His temple" (cf. Ezek.

8:10).[17] The formula is used in I Maccabees (1:54-59; 6:7) to refer to the erection of an altar to Zeus on the altar of burnt offering in the Temple area on which a pig was sacrificed in 168 B.C. In Daniel (9:27; 11:31; 12:11), from which the phrase in the Gospels is derived, it was evidently used to refer to the same thing. Here the reference is to a secondary fulfillment of Daniel's prophecy.

The differences in the Synoptic accounts should be noted. Mark says the desolating sacrilege will be "standing where he ought not" (13:14). Evidently the official reader was supposed to have the key: "Let him who reads aloud understand" (13:14, literal translation). Many feel that for Mark a vivid recollection of Caligula's order that his statue be set up in the Temple (A.D. 41)[18] suggested a similar attempt in the future.

For Luke, who does not use the exact expression, the cryptic sign is interpreted as the Roman armies surrounding Jerusalem. This is to be followed by the period of unparalleled distress mentioned by Matthew and Mark. The siege of Jerusalem is to result in its being "trodden down of the Gentiles, until the times of the Gentiles be fulfilled" (Luke 21:24).

As a matter of historical record, the inhabitants of Jerusalem did pass through a horrible experience.[19] The Christians having been warned by an oracle—perhaps this very passage—fled to Pella, east of the Jordan, where they were preserved.[20]

e. *The Second Coming of the Son of Man* (13:24-27). An indefinite statement indicates that sometime after the tribulation, which Luke at least identified with the siege of Jerusalem, celestial disturbances will produce distress, perplexity, and fear under which men will faint (Luke 21:25-26). The appearance of the Son of Man coming in clouds with great power and glory will cause all peoples to mourn. The angels with a loud trumpet blast will gather all His elect. His coming will be visible to all as the lightning that illumines the sky. So they were not to go after false messiahs who would appear in secret (Matt. 24:26-27; Luke 17:23 f.).

17 Grant, IB, VII, 860.
18 See Josephus, *Wars*, II.10.1-5.
19 See Josephus, *Wars*, Books V and VI.
20 See Eusebius, *Church History*, III, 5.3.

f. The Date of the Second Coming (13: 28-37). Jesus said that just as the appearance of new leaves on a fig tree indicates the approach of summer, completion of "these things" means that "he is nigh, even at the doors" (Mark 13: 29).

A problem is presented by the statement, "This generation shall not pass away, until all these things be accomplished" (13: 30). If "these things" involves the Second Coming, we are left with the alternatives (1) of adopting the doubtful expedient of making "generation" here mean "race," (2) of supposing that the record is seriously out of order, or (3) of attributing a mistake to Jesus. Probably we are safer to adopt the view that "these things" refers to the events connected with the destruction of Jerusalem and the downfall of the Jewish state in A.D. 70. There is a fourth alternative possible, namely, that the generation which would see the beginning of these signs would not pass away before the coming of Christ.

The date of the Second Coming itself no one knows—not even the Son. How much foolish and harmful speculation would be avoided if so-called prophetic scholars took Jesus seriously! If Jesus did not know, how much less the heathen designers of pyramids and modern designers of prophetic time-tables!

Since Jesus was a Prophet, even if He had known definitely the time of the Second Coming, He would not have disclosed it. To have done so would have been to subvert the very purpose of prophecy, which is ethical and practical. By leaving no signs that men could read like a calendar, He says, "Be prepared, for you do not know the time" (cf. 13: 33, 37, etc.). The uncertainty as to the time of His coming means that we are to be ever in readiness.

Again Jesus' purpose was to forewarn His disciples, so that when evil days arose they would be forearmed. Persecutions, seductions of false prophets and false messiahs, the destruction of the Jewish state and many of its institutions of religion, and many other perplexing signs were announced so that when these events took place they would not take the disciples by surprise and sweep them off their feet.

On the one hand, He says, "Be prepared, I may come at any time"; on the other hand, He exhorts His followers to work and fight for a long period, for His coming may be delayed. In the hysteria of these times we still need His wise counsel. Let us live each moment as if He were present; for He is! Let us prepare and plan as if we had eternity before us; for we have!

V. The Passion Narrative (cc. 14—16)

1. The Anointing and the Plot (14:1-11)

a. The Anointing in the House of Simon the Leper (14:3-9). Two days before the Passover, while Jesus was a Guest in the house of Simon the leper, a woman, identified by John as Mary of Bethany, came bringing a jar of pure nard, which she broke, pouring the contents on Jesus' head. To anoint the heads and beards of guests with perfumed oils was the custom among the wealthy at their fashionable dinners. But to those of the disciples who were mercenary the contrast with their frugal way of life was too great. They asked indignantly why the nard was wasted, since it might have been sold and the proceeds given to the poor.[21]

The ringleader in this clamor was Judas, whose concern was not for the poor but for his own profit. John tells us that he helped himself freely to the contents of the money box (John 12:6), which was in his custody, since he was the treasurer of the company. Against the beautiful deed performed by Mary in anointing Jesus beforehand for His burial, the sordid selfishness of Judas forms a black background. Her lavish display of love for her Lord is "a thing of beauty and a joy forever" wherever the gospel is preached.

b. Judas' Evil Bargain (14:1-2, 10-11). Judas, stung by Jesus' rebuke, made his way to the chief priests, who, together with the scribes, were already plotting to arrest Jesus by stealth and kill Him after the feast was over and the crowds, which would contain many enthusiastic followers, had left Jerusalem. When Judas arrived and offered to betray Jesus the chief priests were glad and promised him money. Judas then sought an opportunity to betray Jesus.

2. The Last Supper (14:12-25)

a. The Preparation (14:12-16). The Passover was a formal meal and required bitter herbs such as lettuce, chicory, and endives, a sauce (charosheth), water, wine, and unleav-

---

[21] The 300 denarii would be equal to about $60.00, but the purchasing power would be about four times that amount.

ened cakes, in addition to the lamb which must be brought
from the Temple and roasted. This was the task the disciples
were sent to perform. But first they must find the proper
place: a commodious upper room with an outside entrance.

Evidently Jesus and a disciple had agreed on a certain
sign that would be used to guide the disciples to his house in
order that they might prepare the Passover. The sign was to
be a man carrying a waterpot—a sufficiently uncommon thing
to be easily noticed, yet not so extraordinary that it would
attract undue attention. The man, who apparently received the
messengers graciously and had everything in readiness for
the occasion with the necessary table and carpets or couches,
must have been a disciple—John Mark's home is sometimes
suggested.

b. *Prediction of Betrayal* (14:17-21). While they were
eating, Jesus announced that one of them would betray Him.
One by one the sorrowful disciples asked, "Is it I?" Jesus
replied that it was one who was dipping bread in the same
dish with Him. Again how black Judas' picture is painted:
a traitor to One with whom he joined in the sacrament of
friendship at a common meal! And since this meal commemorated the escape from Egypt and the birth of the nation, it
should bind each loyal Jew to his fellow and to his God.
Better surely that one who had fallen so low had never been
born.

c. *The Institution of the Lord's Supper* (14:22-25). At
this time by means of the broken bread and the cup of wine
Jesus graphically portrayed the establishing of the covenant
which was to replace the old covenant made at Sinai.

The blood symbolized the outpoured life (see Lev. 17:11)
which was available as a means of covenant oneness with
God. When the old covenant was inaugurated, the blood was
applied to the people (Exod. 24:8; Heb. 9:19). Christ's blood
is the better blood of a new kind of covenant that realizes the
communion that the old covenant could only anticipate. According to sacrificial thought, it too must be applied personally to those it brought into covenant fellowship (see Heb.
9:13 f.).

The body of Christ likewise became a covenant sacrifice
of the peace offering type (cf. John 6:41 ff.). The covenant

meal of which the worshiper partook with Jehovah, in Old Testament symbolism, was an effective way of expressing a desire for, or realization of, communion. The virtue of Christ's life became available for man as a communion sacrifice on the basis of man's participation in the ethical quality of that life (Heb. 5: 9; John 15: 1 ff., esp. v. 10).

Paul declares that the ceremony Christ inaugurated calls our attention to two additional facts: Christ's death and promised return (I Cor. 11: 26).

3. Gethsemane (14: 26-52)

On the way to Gethsemane, Jesus predicted that all His disciples would desert Him in His hour of crisis. Peter boasted that all the rest might desert but he would not. Jesus then predicted Peter's three denials that very night, "before the cock crow twice." Peter responded vehemently, "If I must die with thee, I will not deny thee" (14: 31), and the others echoed his words.

In Gethsemane, taking only the selected three, He told them, "My soul is exceeding sorrowful even unto death: abide ye here, and watch" (14: 34). He went on to pour out the anguish of His soul in prayer and submission to the Father's will. Three times He returned to the three disciples, each time to find them sleeping instead of watching and praying. Trusting their own resources, they failed to realize that the crisis was facing them and that they were not adequate in themselves to overcome the strong temptations that were soon to beset them. Physically tired, they were insensitive to the anguish of Jesus and consequently unsympathetic in the hour of His greatest struggle. We can never know the intensity of Jesus' agony of spirit or the contents of the cup; but we can know that, in our Gethsemanes, Jesus will be utterly sympathetic and that inspired by His example we too can come forth with words of victorious submission, "Not what I will, but what thou wilt" (14: 36).

Awakening them from their slumber for the third time, Jesus announced that His betrayer was at hand. Before He had finished speaking Judas, "one of the twelve," came leading a mob armed with swords and clubs, perhaps Temple police delegated by the Sanhedrin to arrest Jesus. By a prearranged sign—a kiss—Judas pointed out Jesus to the mob, some of whom seized Him. In the melee Peter (John 18:10) cut off the right ear of a servant of the high priest. Jesus rebuked the mob for coming against Him as against a robber with swords and clubs, when for days He had taught openly in the Temple and they had not seized Him. The disciples then forsook Jesus and fled, in literal fulfillment of His prediction (14:27). A young man, often thought to be John Mark, followed Jesus, and when he was seized left his outer wrap and fled, clad only in his tunic.

4. *Tried Twice by the Sanhedrin and Denied Thrice by Peter* (14:53—15:1)

Jesus was led into the presence of the assembled Sanhedrin, the members of which sought testimony that would incriminate Him. False witnesses offered testimony that, because it did not agree, was invalid. Failing here, the high priest tried to provoke Jesus so that He would make a damaging admission in defending himself. The ruse failed; Jesus remained silent.

The high priest then asked Jesus if He were the Messiah, "the Son of the Blessed" (a circumlocution to avoid using the name of God); and Jesus without equivocation replied, "I am," and you will see Me as the heavenly Son of Man. According to strict Jewish theology Jesus made no assertion that would have involved blasphemy, even had He not been God's Son. But the infuriated hierarchs needed no further evidence. Tearing his mantle, the high priest asserted, "You have heard his blasphemy. What is your decision?" (14:64, R.S.V.) Unanimously they agreed on the death sentence. The guards began to spit on Jesus and to beat and revile Him. Blindfolding Jesus, they struck Him and challenged Him to prophesy by declaring who had smitten Him.

At this time Peter, who had followed Jesus into the courtyard of the high priest, was standing by a fire warming himself, when one of the maids of the high priest accused him of being one of Jesus' associates. Peter denied. Twice the accusation was repeated and Peter twice more denied—the last time with an oath. The second crowing of the cock suddenly made Peter aware of what he had done, and he wept.

At daybreak the chief priests, elders, and scribes again met to get the Roman government to take official action, thereby shifting the popular resentment that was certain to arise as a result of Jesus' execution from being directed against themselves. Since there were a number of illegalities involved in the earlier trials they probably hoped to give a semblance of legality to their charge of blasphemy.

5. Tried by Pilate and Mocked by the Soldiers (15:2-20)

Before Pilate they began to accuse Jesus of forbidding the payment of tribute to Caesar and of calling himself King-Messiah (Luke 23:2). When Pilate asked Jesus, "Are You the King of the Jews?" Jesus replied, "You are saying so" (Luke 23:3, original translation from the Gk.). The chief priests made many further charges; but when Pilate invited Jesus to reply, Pilate wondered at His silence.

Pilate wanted to get out of the awkward situation into which he was thrust. Callous and cruel as he was, he had no taste for the role he was forced to play. The custom of releasing a prisoner at the Passover season seemed to afford a way out. He would appeal to the crowds and they would surely demand Jesus' release.

The selection of the one who was to be released, however, lay in the hands of the people, who demanded that Barabbas, an insurrectionist and murderer, be released to them instead of Jesus of Nazareth. A variant reading of Matt. 27:16 indicates that the murderer's name was also Jesus, or savior. If this was the case, we have the people loudly and insistently demanding the release of Savior Bar-Abbas, an insurrectionist, and refusing their true Saviour and Messiah. Pilate, threatened with being accused before Caesar as one who aided and abetted treason, finally submitted to the demands of the angry mob and delivered Jesus to be crucified.

Some have seen in this incident the fickleness of the crowd which exultantly had proclaimed Jesus as Messiah just a few days before. However, probably few of Jesus' disciples were yet aware of what was going on, and it was those with a sadistic curiosity who would be attracted to the scene of judgment. Moreover, the hierarchs would certainly have their henchmen distributed in the crowds stirring up mob spirit against Jesus.

After Jesus had been scourged—an ordeal so severe that often the victim died under it—the soldiers made the charge pronounced against Him, "The King of the Jews," the subject of ridicule and crude and brutal derision. A wreath of twisted stalks of some thorn was made in mock imitation of the laurel wreath, a symbol of victory often worn by Roman emperors on festal occasions as a mark of military distinction. This thorny wreath was pressed on His head, and He was clothed in purple, while they did mock obeisance and heaped upon Him indignities similar to those accorded Him earlier by the servants of the high priest.

6. The Crucifixion of Jesus (15:21-32)

a. *Crucifixion.* Crucifixion, as well as scourging, was a penalty that the Romans usually reserved for slaves and the lowest criminals. Imported from the Carthaginians, crucifixion was one of the most horrible means of execution ever devised. The victim usually was made to carry the heavy crossbar to the place of crucifixion. There his hands were tied or nailed to this crossbar, which was then nailed or tied across or on top of the vertical pole. Sometimes the legs were allowed to straddle a peg or projection on the upright in order to bear the weight of the body. The feet were then tied or nailed to the vertical pole.

In case the hands and feet were nailed, as were those of Jesus (John 20:24-27), the immediate torture was extreme; but the other method prolonged the suffering, for the victim died of exposure and exhaustion. Stripped before he was fixed to the cross, the victim hung for interminable hours or even days exposed to the sun, the biting of insects, and the ridicule of brutal spectators. Extreme pain coupled with suffering occasioned by thirst combined to make this a horrible means of death.

b. *On the Way to the Cross* (15:21-22). Mark says that it was a Jewish proselyte from Cyrene—perhaps at Jerusalem as a pilgrim to the feast—who was given the task of carrying the crossbeam to the place of crucifixion, called the place of the skull. It may have been from his sons, who are named here presumably because they were known to Mark's readers (cf. Rom. 16:13), that Mark derived this bit of information about the Crucifixion, since the disciples, except possibly John, seem to have been absent.

c. *The Crucifixion and First Three Hours on the Cross* (15: 23-32). When they arrived at the Place of the Skull, Jesus was offered a drink of wine mixed with myrrh, which was an opiate for the deadening of pain. When He had tasted it and realized what it was He refused it, choosing to endure His sufferings to the very end with a clear mind. At about nine o'clock in the morning they crucified Jesus.

While Jesus hung in agony on the cross the soldiers cast lots for His garments and then sat and watched Him as He suffered. "Those who passed by scoffed at him, nodding at him in derision and crying, 'Ha! You were to destroy the temple and build it in three days! Come down from the cross and save yourself!' " (15: 29 f., Moffatt.)

The high priests also, along with the scribes, mocked Jesus. "He saved others; himself he cannot save," they said (15:31), voicing unknowingly a profound truth, for Jesus is able to save others just because His fidelity to His mission would not permit Him to save himself. In conformity to the custom in Roman crucifixions, the accusation was written on a placard affixed to the cross. From the words of this accusation, "The King of the Jews," they lifted up a taunt against Him, "Let the Christ, the King of Israel, now come down from the cross, that we may see and believe," they jeered. Even the criminals who were crucified with Him reviled Him.

7. The Death of Jesus (15:33-39)

At noon the light of the sun failed and until three o'clock in the afternoon, about the time of Jesus' death, great darkness prevailed. At the hour last mentioned Jesus with a loud voice cried, "My God, my God, why hast thou forsaken me?" which in the Semitic language led the bystanders to believe that Jesus was calling for Elijah. With this in mind they offered Him vinegar to drink from a sponge and waited to see if Elijah would come to His rescue.

Instead, Jesus gave a great Victor's shout and expired. The centurion who witnessed the end testified in awe, "Truly this Man was God's Son" (15: 39, Gk.). Simultaneously with Jesus' death the great Temple veil was torn from top to bottom, symbolizing that the way into the holiest was now open.

8. Burial of Jesus (15:40-47)

Three loyal women of a larger group, who from a distance beheld Jesus die, are named by Mark. Perhaps it is to them that we owe most of the Synoptic account of the Crucifixion. These women waited until they saw the place of Jesus' burial, so that they could return after the Sabbath to anoint His body. Jesus' body had been requested by Joseph of Arimathaea, a respected member of a council, and was granted by Pilate after he had proof that Jesus was already dead.[22] This request and the burial of Jesus would have required some courage on the part of Joseph, who won for his name immortality by the tender concern he manifested in performing the last rites for Jesus' mortal remains.

9. "He Is Not Here..." (16:1-8)

The same three women who watched the burial came very early Sunday morning to anoint His body. While they were discussing how they would roll back the great stone that barred access to the tomb, suddenly they realized that it had been rolled back. When they entered the tomb they were greeted by a young man in a white robe who told them not to be amazed, for the Jesus they were seeking "is risen; he is not here" (16:6).

Commanded to go and tell the disciples and Peter the good news, the women, astonished and trembling, "said nothing to any one; for they were afraid" (16:8).

10. Resurrection Appearances (16:9-20)

These last twelve verses, which are not in the two oldest Greek manuscripts, describe some of the appearances of Jesus after His resurrection. The first (vv. 9-11) was to Mary Magdalene. It is given in more detail in John 20:1-18. The second (vv. 12-13) is to the two disciples on the way to Emmaus. A fuller account of this is found in Luke 24:13-35. The Great Commission (v. 15) is given in another form in Matt. 28:18-20. The Ascension (v. 19) is described in Luke 20:50-51 and Acts 1:6-11. No new incidents in the life of Jesus are given in this section.

[22] It was contrary to Jewish law (Deut. 21:22-23) to leave corpses on the cross overnight, especially over the Sabbath (John 19:31).

CHAPTER VI
THE SON OF MAN
(LUKE)

A. Introduction

I. *Authorship and Date*

Luke's method and purpose in writing this beautiful Gospel have been noted already. His preface, in which he indicates these principles, is an indispensable aid in our understanding of the origin of the Gospels. The reasons for believing that the writer of the third Gospel and Acts was Luke, together with our information about the writer, are set forth in the chapter on Acts. Since both books are dedicated to the same man and Acts mentions a "former treatise," Luke's Gospel presumably was that "former treatise." For this reason the Gospel is usually dated slightly before Acts.

II. *Special Features*

The Gospel of Luke abounds in special features that endear it to every Christian reader. Written in a Greek style that is surpassed in the New Testament only by the Epistle to the Hebrews, Luke is the most literary of the Gospels. Observing naturally the rules of Greek style and using accurately his ample vocabulary, the writer pours his ideas into balanced periodic sentences. In spite of his literary polish, however, in the opening chapters of each volume Luke's style is rough and Semitic. Probably this indicates his fidelity to his sources.

The many references in Luke to contemporary history furnish the scholar with more data than do the other Gospels for establishing the approximate dates of important events. Thus Luke is of inestimable value for the historian. Without Luke's writings no connected account of the beginnings of Christianity would be possible.

Among the other traits that set Luke apart is its stress on prayer by its selection of Jesus' teaching and by its frequent mention of His example. Six times Luke mentions Jesus praying where the other Gospels do not.

Praise, too, is often found in Luke, who was the first hymnologist of the Church. In the third Gospel alone are found the *Magnificat* (1:46 ff.), the *Benedictus* (1:68 ff.), the *Nunc Dimittis* (2:29 ff.), the *Ave Maria* (1:28 ff.), and the *Gloria in Excelsis* (2:14).

Still other features that endear the Gospel to the followers of Jesus are its stress on Jesus' humanity and universality. He is the Saviour of sinners, who satisfies the deepest longings of the moral nature. His concern is not primarily with the Jew, but, as the genealogy indicates, Jesus is the Saviour of all men. He is presented as the Friend of the publican, the harlot, and the prodigal—the outcast (c. 15). He loves the Samaritan (10:25-37) and the Gentile.

The third Gospel is written by one who is dominated by a wise, generous, and serene spirit. He feels the throb of life. The joy of redeemed humanity is a favorite theme (2:14; 15:7, 10, 24, 32).

Jesus is greatly concerned for the poor, and demands of the rich proper stewardship of their wealth. In Luke's unique material this is especially prominent (6:20-26; 12:13-21; 16:19-31).

The role of women is stressed and Jesus' ability to understand them and sympathize with them indicated (8:1-3; 7:11-12, 36-50; 10:38-42; 23:28; 15:8-10; 18:1-8). Children are also more prominent in Luke than in other Gospels. While Mark omits completely the birth and infancy of Jesus and John, Luke devotes two long chapters to them. Twice he alone notes that a miracle of Jesus was performed on behalf of an only child (7:12; 9:38).

Luke is also the Gospel of the Spirit. The Spirit is mentioned frequently in the first two chapters. At His baptism Jesus was filled with the Spirit (3:22; 4:1), and after His temptation He returned to Galilee "in the power of the Spirit" (4:14). When He began His ministry at Nazareth the first words of His text were, "The Spirit of the Lord is upon me" (4:18). When the seventy returned from their successful mission Jesus "rejoiced in the Holy Spirit" (10:21). Luke records Jesus' words about "the promise of my Father" and His command to wait in Jerusalem (24:49). Thus the Gospel of Luke is necessary as an introduction to the companion volume which records the acts of Spirit-filled men.

B. CONTENTS

I. Preface (1:1-4)

Luke's formal preface, written in the stilted Greek style common to such productions, is the most ancient and important testimony about the origin of written Gospels. It tells us how and why Luke wrote and, by indicating the human element in Gospel writing, gives a mandate to the scholar to investigate the sources and methods of the Evangelists and other writers of Scripture. These opening verses serve as a preface for the two-volume work, Luke-Acts.

II. The Birth and Boyhood of the Saviour (1:5—2:52)

1. The Annunciations and Mary's Magnificat (1:5-56)

a. The Promise to Zechariah of the Birth of John (1:5-25). Luke traced the beginning of Christianity to the birth of John the Baptist, whose work was that of a forerunner to the Messiah. Thus, although John stands within the old order, his ministry points to the new and forms the bridge which helps us to connect the period of preparation with that of fulfillment.

The narrative begins with an aged couple who according to Old Testament standards were blameless. But no children had come to bless the home of Zechariah, the priest, and his wife, Elisabeth. One day while Zechariah was burning incense—an honor that he did not enjoy often, and so for him a time of great solemnity—an angel of the Lord appeared, announcing that his prayer had been heard and that his wife, Elisabeth, was to bear a son, whose name was to be John.

The detailed, poetic promise that followed indicated that many would share the father's joy because John would be great in God's estimate. A Nazarite, filled with the Holy Spirit from birth, he would fulfill the prophecy of Malachi (4:5-6). When Zechariah expressed doubts and a desire for a sign, he was made dumb.

b. The Promise to Mary of the Birth of Jesus (1:26-38). About six months later the angel Gabriel announced to Mary, a virgin who was betrothed to Joseph, that she had "found favor with God" (1:30) and would conceive and bear a son

who should be called Jesus (1:31). He would be the expected
Davidic Messiah, who would re-establish the Kingdom which
will never end. In beautiful, restrained simplicity the miraculous nature of Jesus' conception (1:34-35) and Mary's humble
acceptance of God's will (1:38) are indicated.

c. *Mary's Visit to Elisabeth and the Magnificat* (1:39-56).
Hastily departing for the home of Elisabeth, Mary upon her
arrival was greeted by Elisabeth, who pronounced a blessing
on Mary and her unborn child. Mary's response is recorded in
the poem that is commonly called the Magnificat, the theme
of which is expressed in her words, "My soul doth magnify
the Lord, and my spirit hath rejoiced in God my Saviour"
(1:46-47).

This poem reflects the language and spirit of the song of
Hannah (I Sam. 2:1-10). In joyous wonder it contemplates
the divine condescension in permitting the Messiah to be born
of a lowly maiden, making her name blessed, and proving
God's saving interest in His people. It should be noted that
along with its dominant spiritual theme there are echoes of
the popular idea of a Messianic kingdom that was national-
istic in character (1:51-55).

2. *The Births of John and Jesus* (1:57—2:20)

a. *The Birth of John* (1:57-80). Interest here centers
around the naming of the baby at the time of his circumcision
when he was eight days old. When Zechariah on paper confirmed Elisabeth's contention that the boy's name should be
John, immediately his tongue, which had been silent since
the angel's announcement that he would have a son, was loosed
and he blessed God.

There follows the prophecy of Zechariah, called the Benedictus from the first word of the song in the Latin Vulgate.
In it Zechariah gives thanks for a national deliverance based
on God's promise to Abraham (1:68-74a). The purpose of
this deliverance is that, being free from heathen interference
and defilement, His people might serve God "in holiness and
righteousness before him all our days" (1:75). To this end
John has been given as "the prophet of the Most High" (1:76)
to precede and prepare the way of the Lord and "to give
knowledge of salvation unto his people in the remission of
their sins" (1:77). John's mission will be completed when

"the dayspring from on high shall visit us" (1:78), when the Messianic age shall dawn. The light of the Messiah's coming will dispel the darkness, while He guides His people in ways of salvation.

b. *The Birth of Jesus and the Visit of the Shepherds* (2:1-20). Luke describes an enrollment for taxation that brought Joseph and Mary to Bethlehem, the ancestral home of Joseph. This first enrollment may have been timed to coincide with one of the Jewish festivals in order to allay the resentment that such an order would incite. In this case an influx of pilgrims may explain the circumstance that "there was no room for them in the inn" (2:7). The birth of Jesus is described in Luke's characteristic, beautiful simplicity in one sentence—"And she brought forth her firstborn son; and she wrapped him in swaddling clothes, and laid him in a manger, because there was no room for them in the inn" (2:7).

The story of the appearance of the angels to humble shepherds on the Judean hills enshrines a joyous announcement of the significance of Jesus' birth—"a Saviour, who is Christ the Lord" (2:11). It is no wonder that the angels sang, "Glory to God in the highest" (2:14a), on the night of the Saviour's birth. The better manuscripts explain why almost twenty centuries later we still do not have peace on earth. There is a condition attached. On earth there is to be "peace among men in whom he is well pleased" (2:14b).

In eager response to the angelic announcement the shepherds found the Babe, and when they had recounted their awesome experience "returned, glorifying and praising God for all the things that they had heard and seen . . . " (2:20). To Mary's vivid memory of these things (2:19) we may owe the facts reproduced so charmingly by Luke.

3. *The Infancy and Boyhood of Jesus* (2:21-52)

a. *The Circumcision and Presentation of Jesus in the Temple* (2:21-38). On the eighth day, as the law stipulated, Jesus was circumcised. This act symbolized the bringing of a Jewish boy into the covenant with Jehovah and the consecration of his life to God. At this time Jesus, like John, was given the name that had been revealed earlier.

Thirty-three days later Mary went up to the Temple to fulfill the purification ceremony required by the law. At this

time Jesus, as the first-born, was presented for redemption
(Exod. 13:2, 12). The offering (2:24) which was presented
for Mary's purification is another detail that bears witness to
the relative poverty of the family.

The center of interest in this section is Simeon, a righteous
and devout man who looked for the fulfillment of the Messianic hopes of his people. To him the Holy Spirit had revealed
that he would see the Lord's Messiah before he died. When
Simeon took Jesus into his arms he blessed God, saying:

> Now lettest thou thy servant depart, Lord,
> According to thy word, in peace;
> For mine eyes have seen thy salvation,
> Which thou hast prepared before the face of all peoples;
> A light for revelation to the Gentiles,
> And the glory of thy people Israel (2:29-32).

In his further words, addressed to Mary, Simeon predicts
the rise of those who accept Jesus and the fall of those who
reject Him. Men cannot remain neutral in His presence and
can never be the same after He has confronted them. Jesus'
rejection and crucifixion will bring piercing sorrow to the
heart of Mary.

The next verses (36-38) tell of the witness of an aged
prophetess, Anna, who spoke of Jesus to all the devout who
were "looking for the redemption of Jerusalem" (2:38).

b. *An Episode from Jesus' Boyhood* (2:39-52). After recording the return to Nazareth and Jesus' normal development, Luke presents the one incident of Jesus' boyhood that
links the infant Jesus with the Prophet of Nazareth. In the
story of Jesus in the Temple conversing with the Jewish theological experts, the first thing that impresses us is His amazing wisdom. Perhaps what should impress us even more is
His conception of God as His Father and the intensity of His
dedication to God's service. He is surprised that His parents
did not know where to find Him: "Knew ye not that I must
be in my Father's house?" (2:49.) These are the first recorded
words of Jesus.

These few verses tell us all that is known of Jesus' boyhood and youth. Two verses (2:40, 52) suggest that Jesus'
development proceeded along normal lines. The educative
influences of home, synagogue, school, worship, the Scriptures
—all contributed to the shaping of His religious nature. His

public ministry indicates that He had saturated His mind with the Scriptures and had thought deeply on spiritual problems.

The opening chapters of Matthew and Luke give us all the facts that we possess about Jesus' birth, infancy, and boyhood. The restraint of the accounts is striking when they are compared with the "marvelous and often grotesque and repulsive accounts of Jesus as an exhibitionist and as a boy wonder,"[1] which are found in the Apocryphal Gospels.

III. The Saviour's Preparation for His Ministry (3:1—4:13)

Beginning with an introduction that locates John the Baptist's ministry in its temporal, geographical, political, and ecclesiastical context, this section relates the work of John to that of Jesus. Calling his contemporaries "offspring of vipers" (3:7), John warned them that Abraham's merit would not save them. Baptism was a sign of the repentance that should make their lives bear fruit. To each group that requested specific instruction John replied pointedly. To the multitudes John said: Share your surplus food and clothing; to the tax collectors he said, "Collect no more than is appointed you" (3:13, R.S.V.); to the soldiers he replied, "Extort from no man by violence, neither accuse any one wrongfully; and be content with your wages" (3:14).

When John was asked if he were the Messiah he answered that One who was greater than he would come who would baptize with the Holy Spirit and fire. As a farmer with a winnowing fork separates the wheat from the chaff, storing the wheat and burning the chaff, the Messiah would separate evil men from the good. With fires of judgment the Messiah would purge the people of God and destroy the wicked. Fire also refers to the purging of sin from the believer's heart by the baptism of the Holy Spirit.

Luke alone records the fact that Jesus was praying at the time of the descent of the Spirit and the acclamation of the voice from heaven. The genealogy and account of the Temptation bring to a close this epoch of Jesus' life.

IV. The Galilean Ministry (4:14—9:50)

1. The Beginning of Jesus' Ministry (4:14-30)

"In the power of the Spirit"—a fact noted only by Luke —Jesus returned to Galilee, where He acquired great fame.

[1] S. M. Gilmour, IB, VIII, 66.

But the favor Jesus found in Galilee did not meet Him in His native Nazareth. In the synagogue when He was given the roll of Isaiah, He unrolled the scroll until Isa. 61:1-2 and 58:6 were exposed to view. Selecting these as His texts, Jesus read:

The Spirit of the Lord is upon me,
Because he anointed me to preach good tidings to the poor:
He hath sent me to proclaim release to the captives,
And recovering of sight to the blind,
To set at liberty them that are bruised,
To proclaim the acceptable year of the Lord (Luke 4:18-19).

After Jesus had finished reading, He declared, "To-day hath this scripture been fulfilled in your ears" (4:21). The people wondered at His gracious words, asking, "Is not this Joseph's son?" (1:22) His reply to their unbelief was: "Doubtless ye will say unto me this parable, Physician, heal thyself" (1:23)—repeat here the things You are said to have done in Capernaum. Noting that a prophet is not acceptable in his own country, Jesus proceeded to give two illustrations of His point (4:25-27). This angered His hearers so that they wanted to cast Him down from a bluff and kill Him. "But he passing through the midst of them went his way" (4:30).

2. *Jesus' Ministry in and near Capernaum* (4:31—5:16)

In the synagogue at Capernaum, Jesus taught with authority and cast out a demon (4:31-37). After this He healed Simon's mother-in-law and many others, and cast out demons, whose testimony to His deity He suppressed (4:38-41). Then Jesus departed from Capernaum and began to preach in the synagogues of Judea.

In this period of popularity Jesus, using Simon's boat for a rostrum, preached to the crowds who were gathered by the shore of the Lake[2] Gennesaret. After they had labored all night without success, Jesus, directing the fishing operations, enabled Simon, James, and John to take a great catch. The incident made a profound impression on Peter, who dated his call to catch men from that hour. Jesus now had three select disciples (5:1-11).

This portion of Jesus' ministry closes with an account of the healing of a leper (5:12-16). Luke, a physician, alone

[2] Luke accurately calls the "Sea of Galilee" a "lake." The other Gospel writers use the popular designation "sea."

notes that the man was "full of leprosy" (5:12). And only Luke reports Jesus' retirement from the needy crowds so that He might pray (5:16).

3. Controversies with the Pharisees (5:17—6:11)

In this section of Luke the healing of the paralytic, the call of Levi, the question about fasting, the controversy about plucking grain on the Sabbath, and the healing of the man with the withered hand are given. Two interesting touches added by Luke are the statement that "the power of the Lord was with him to heal" (5:17b) and the observation appended to the parable of the wineskins: "And no man having drunk old wine desireth new; for he saith, The old is good" (5:39).

4. The Sermon on the Plain (6:12-49)

Luke alone mentions that it was after a night of prayer that Jesus called the twelve disciples. In the sermon he does not include such a large block of teaching as does Matthew. The nine beatitudes in Matthew are given in the third person. Luke gives only four beatitudes in the second person plural but adds four woes.

Both records include Jesus' teaching on loving one's enemies (6:27-36; cf. Matt. 5:39-42, 44-48). Luke here does not include the statement found in Matt. 5:47 about saluting only one's brethren, but adds the illustrations given in 6:33-34 and part of the exhortation in verse 35: "But love your enemies, *and do them good, and lend, never despairing; and your reward shall be great,* and ye shall be sons of the Most High."

A slight addition is also made to Matthew's section on judging, including the admonition to be generous: "Give, and it shall be given unto you; good measure, pressed down, shaken together, running over, shall they give into your bosom" (6:38). Luke includes next a paragraph on the tests of goodness and concludes, as does Matthew, with the parable about the two builders.

There is also an interesting difference between the verse with which Matthew concludes this portion of the sermon and its parallel in Luke. In Matthew the statement is, "Ye therefore shall be perfect, as your heavenly Father is perfect" (5:48). In Luke the stress is on mercy: "Be ye merciful, even as your Father is merciful" (6:36).

5. *Two Acts of Mercy* (7:1-17)

A delegation of Jews came to Jesus in Capernaum to get Him to heal the servant of a centurion. It is interesting to note that the Jews in commending the centurion declared that he had built a synagogue for them. Remains of a beautiful synagogue at Tel Hum have been uncovered. This synagogue was probably built on the same location and according to the same plan as that which had been financed by the centurion mentioned here.[3]

The faith of the centurion deserves attention. He did not wish to trouble Jesus by having Him come. A word of command would be sufficient. He believed that Jesus' word was as final over disease as was his own command when addressed to an inferior. Jesus healed the servant and marveled over the man's faith, saying, "I have not found so great faith, no, not in Israel" (7:9).

Soon afterwards, as Jesus approached the city of Nain, He came upon the funeral procession of an only son of a widowed mother. Jesus, gripped with compassion, touched the bier and restored the young man to his mother. Mentioned only by Luke (7:11-17), this incident caused the people to fear and to glorify God.

6. *Jesus and John* (7:18-35)[4]

7. *Jesus and a Penitent Woman* (7:36-50)

In this incident while Jesus was reclining at a meal as a Guest of Simon the Pharisee, a sinful woman—probably a prostitute—came and stood behind Him, weeping. She wept so profusely that her tears wet His feet. So she dried them with the hair of her head and then began to kiss His feet over and over. Finally she anointed Jesus' feet.

Since Oriental custom permitted uninvited guests to come and go rather freely, Simon had not complained about the woman's presence. But he became inwardly offended that Jesus had permitted these demonstrations. Jesus, sensing Simon's attitude, told the parable of the two debtors, by means of which He wrung from Simon the admission that to be forgiven much means to love much. Simon, who had never been

---

[3] See Finegan, *Light from the Ancient Past* (Princeton: Princeton University Press, 1946), pp. 266 ff.
[4] This is discussed in the chapter on Matthew.

conscious of his sin, could not understand the gratitude of this woman whose life had been so marvelously transformed. He had failed to supply even the common courtesy—water with which Jesus could wash His tired feet. Turning now to the woman, Jesus reassured her with the words: "Thy sins are forgiven. . . . Thy faith hath saved thee; go in peace" (7:48, 50).

8. Jesus as Teacher and Miracle Worker (c. 8)

After an introductory verse describing Jesus' itinerant ministry, Luke alone tells of a number of women who, with the Twelve, followed Jesus and ministered to them out of their means. Three are mentioned by name, one of whom, Joanna, was the wife of Chuza, the chancellor of Herod Antipas.

The rest of chapter eight includes incidents mentioned in Mark and Matthew. The Parable of the Soils is followed by a statement of the reason for speaking in parables and then by its interpretation. Sayings about light and responsibility, the definition of Jesus' true relatives, the accounts of the stilling of the storm, the restoration of the Gerasene demoniac, the raising of the daughter of Jairus, and the cure of the woman with the hemorrhage complete the contents of the chapter. In the last incident Luke is kind to the physicians (cf. 8:43 with Mark 5:26).

9. Jesus and the Twelve (9:1-50)

Here Luke tells of the sending of the Twelve, Herod's reaction to Jesus' work, the return of the Twelve and the feeding of the 5,000, the Great Confession and first prediction of the Passion, Jesus' statement of the conditions of discipleship, the Transfiguration, the healing of the epileptic boy, the second prediction of the Passion, the dispute about greatness, and the exorcist who "followeth not with us" (9:49). Luke alone indicates that the disciples were sleepy (9:32) and that Jesus was praying at the time of the Transfiguration (9:29).

V. The Journey to Jerusalem (9:51—19:27)

Containing a large amount of unique material, this division of Luke includes a record of teaching given and events that happened while Jesus was on His way to Jerusalem (9:51; 13:22; 17:11).

1. The Discipline of Discipleship (9:51-62).[5]

The opening statement suggests the open-eyed courage of Jesus, who, although He realized that death awaited Him at the nation's capital, "stedfastly set his face to go to Jerusalem" (9:51). It was because His face was set toward Jerusalem that a village of Samaritans refused to receive Him. He had to rebuke two of the disciples—James and John—who suggested their desire to call down fire from heaven, that the village might be destroyed.

Three would-be followers next asserted their willingness to become His disciples. In answer to the first man who professed willingness to follow Jesus wherever He went, Jesus replied, "The foxes have holes, and the birds of the heaven have nests; but the Son of man hath not where to lay his head" (9:58). In other words, Jesus can offer His followers no settled abode but only constant exposure to opposition. To the second man, who wished time to bury his father, Jesus replied: Let the spiritually dead bury the physically dead, "but go thou and publish abroad the kingdom of God" (9:60). To the third, who wished to return home to bid farewell to his family, Jesus replied: "No one is any use to the Reign of God who puts his hand to the plough and then looks behind him" (9:62, Moffatt). It is as impossible for one with mixed motives or divided affections to render acceptable service to the Kingdom as it is for a man to plow a straight furrow while he is looking backwards.

2. The Mission of the Seventy (10:1-24)

Although none of the other Gospels mentions this incident, the instructions given to the Twelve when they likewise are sent out two by two is so similar that little added comment is needed (cf. Matt. 9:37-38; 10:7-16). Luke does not indicate here any order of Jesus forbidding work among the Gentiles and the Samaritans (cf. Matt. 10:5-7). This lends credence to the theory that while the Twelve represent the twelve tribes of Israel, seventy, the number expressing completeness combined with indefiniteness and magnitude, symbolizes all peoples. This interpretation accords with Luke's universalism.

Luke includes here woes against some of the cities of Galilee and Jesus' words of gratitude that the Father has

[5]Verses 51-56, 60-62 are found only in Luke.

chosen to reveal himself through the Son to those who were
babes in understanding—material that in Matthew is not related to the mission of the disciples (Matt. 11:21-25). Unique
in Luke's record are the joyous report of the disciples about
the success of their labors, Jesus' acknowledgment of their
success, a statement about the unusual immunities from danger that had been given to them, and a word concerning the
true ground for rejoicing. One is to rejoice primarily, not
because of spectacular achievements for God, but because his
life has divine approval.

3. *The Parable of the Good Samaritan* (10:25-37)

This beautiful parable was given in response to the lawyer's defensive question, "Who is my neighbor?" (10:29.)
The form of the reply, however, is addressed to the question:
To whom can I prove myself a neighbor? Anyone who stands
in need of assistance that I can give is my neighbor. It is of
interest that insofar as our records are concerned it was this
lawyer who first combined the two commands with which
Jesus later summarized the law (10:27; cf. Mark 12:28-31;
Matt. 22:34-40). However, it took Jesus to discover in them
their full meaning and to incarnate them in His life to a degree that no other has ever succeeded in duplicating.

4. *The Devotional Life* (10:38—11:13)

a. *Sitting at Jesus' Feet* (10:38-42). This incident, which
took place in Bethany at the home of Mary and Martha, a
favorite retreat of Jesus, is a corrective against the idea that
Christianity is entirely a matter of doing. Martha was distracted and irritable in her anxiety to prepare for her Guest
an elaborate meal. Jesus indicated that a simple menu was
adequate and a sympathetic audience such as that given Him
by Mary was the menu that He most desired.

b. *The Lord's Prayer* (11:1-4). Luke alone preserves the
fact that it was Jesus' practice of prayer that moved His disciples to ask for a form of prayer such as that which John
had given his disciples. More properly called "the disciples'
prayer," the model prayer is neither as long nor as liturgical
in Luke as the more commonly used version in Matthew.

c. *An Illustration of the Power of Persevering Prayer*
(11:5-13). Jesus told the now familiar story of the friend

who at midnight requested from his neighbor three loaves of bread, so that he could entertain an unexpected guest, to show that unusual persistence succeeds where less resolute action fails. If persistence means success in this instance, how much more will prayer be answered by the Heavenly Father, who delights in answering the prayers of His children! Nor will He mock them by offering a useless or harmful substitute for their real needs. Even an earthly father, who is tainted with racial evil, would not do this. "How much more shall your heavenly Father give the Holy Spirit to them that ask him?" (11:13.)

5. *Addresses to the Scribes and Pharisees* (11:14-54)

Luke includes here the Beelzebub controversy (cf. Matt. 12:22-30; Mark 3:22-27), the account of the return of the evil spirit (cf. Matt. 12:43-45), and a discourse against the Pharisees that closely parallels that found in Matthew 23.

6. *An Exhortation to Fearless Confession* (12:1-12; cf. Matt. 10:26-33)

Jesus, addressing the disciples in the presence of a vast throng, tells them that they have no right to condemn the Pharisees for their hypocrisy if through fear of the consequences they at the same time draw back from a bold proclamation of the truth. At the same time He cautions them about the unsleeping hatred of the Pharisees who are doing their utmost to stamp out the new movement. The Pharisees can only kill their bodies; their souls are in the hands of God.[6] In spite of the danger, they are, therefore, to trust in a God whose infinite love is reflected in a concern about the minutest detail that affects the lives of children.

7. *The Parable of the Rich Fool* (12:13-21)

Evidently the Master had scarcely concluded these challenging utterances when one of the crowd requested that Jesus compel his brother to divide the inheritance with him. Jesus found in the request—legitimate though it was—an occasion to warn His disciples against the ever-present temptation to be enamored with the appeal of earthly values. "Take heed," He said, "and keep yourselves from all covetousness: for a

[6]Commentators are divided as to who it is who is to be feared (v. 5).

man's life consisteth not in the abundance of the things which he possesseth" (12:15).

The parable which follows points to the plight of a man rich in material things but a pauper in spiritual values. Entirely wrapped up in himself and his own happiness, he concluded incorrectly that he could feed his soul with *things*. Forgetting that he was only a steward of the possessions in his hands, he paid no attention to his obligations to the poor and to God. Jesus said he was a fool, for he had not used his time wisely in preparing for eternity. This illustrates the case of everyone who "layeth up treasure for himself, and is not rich toward God" (12:21).

8. Distracting Cares and the Need for Alertness and Fidelity (12:22-48)

The warning about distracting cares is given in almost the same language in Matthew (6:25-33, 19-21). Also found in Matthew (24:43-51) are the parables of the householder and of the faithful and unfaithful servants. But only Luke preserves a brief exhortation to be alert like servants who await their master's return from the marriage feast (12:35-38). "Blessed are those servants, whom the lord when he cometh shall find watching . . . " (12:37a). Also peculiar to Luke is the statement concerning the principle of divine judgment (12:47-48). Severity of judgment will be in proportion to the amount of the knowledge of God's will attainable that is disobeyed. Much light implies much accountability.

9. On Interpreting the Present Time (12:49—13:9)

Jesus forecasts (12:49-53; cf. Matt. 10:34-35) that He will be the occasion of the division of families, a fact that many have experienced to their own sorrow. Where Christ comes into one's heart there is a distinct separation from the old life, which often involves a separation from family and friends and even a persecution by them. Jesus says not to be surprised at this.

To the crowds, Jesus said (12:54-56; cf. Matt. 16:2-3): You know how to read the weather by observing the wind and the sky but "why even of yourselves judge ye not what is right?" (12:57). One who is certain to lose a case at court should attempt to settle with his accuser on the way (12:57).

Repentance is an urgent matter. Let them not think that the Galileans whom Pilate slew with their sacrifices or the eighteen killed when the tower in Siloam fell were more guilty than the nation as a whole. Except they repent immediately —reverse the direction they are traveling—destruction lies right ahead.

The case of the Jewish nation is like that of a fig tree whose owner for three years vainly had sought fruit. It is given one last chance to bear fruit before it is cut down. God is giving the nation her last opportunity to repent.

10. *The Crippled Woman Healed and Two Parables Given* (13:10-21)

Jesus, preaching for the last time in a synagogue, saw a woman bent double and unable to straighten herself. Immediately feeling compassion for her, Jesus applied the healing touch. The president of the synagogue was scandalized and probably many others who considered themselves the spiritual members of the Jewish church. In a statement addressed to the congregation, but really aimed at Jesus, he indicated that there were six other days in which to perform the cure. It was not a matter of life and death. Therefore Jesus had broken the Sabbath law. But Christ exposed their inconsistency. They untied their *animals* on the Sabbath and led them to water, which was not a life and death matter but an act of kindness designed for the comfort of the creatures; but they would not permit Jesus to release from her bonds and sufferings on the Sabbath this daughter of Abraham who had been bound for eighteen years. No wonder Jesus addressed them as hypocrites! Their devotion to the law was only a pretense. The real motive for their professed religiosity was their hatred of Jesus.

11. *Teaching on a Journey* (13:22-35)

Close parallels to much of the teaching recorded here are found in Matthew (7:13-14; 25:10-12; 7:22-23; 8:11-12; 19:30). One may fail to be saved because he refuses to put forth the moral energy required (13:23-24), or because he knocks too late (13:25-27). "The time is short, and as there is an hour by which the ordinary householder expects his family to be indoors, so there is a time when God will close the gate of life, and those who come knocking after that will be treated as intruders."[7]

To have seen and associated with Jesus in the flesh will not be enough. There must be a genuine commitment of one's life to the way of righteousness. The Jews, who took it for granted that they would share in the Messianic banquet, will find themselves excluded. Sitting in the outer darkness, they will gnash their teeth in frustration and rage, and weep and wail, but they will not be admitted. The Gentiles will take their place at the banquet. "And they shall come from the east and west, and from the north and south, and shall sit down in the kingdom of God" (13:29).

Luke alone preserves the warning, given to Jesus by some friendly Pharisees, that Herod Antipas was seeking to kill Him. This was the occasion for Jesus' lament over Jerusalem (13:34-35).

12. Table Talk in the House of a Pharisee (14:1-24)

a. The Man with Dropsy Healed on the Sabbath (14:1-6). One Sabbath a synagogue-president invited Jesus to a meal. Since the host was a Pharisee, the rest of the invited guests were probably Pharisees. A man with dropsy appeared before Jesus. Presumably he had not been invited but had made use of the open door in Oriental fashion to beg alms or food. Jesus assumed the initiative, asking the scribes and Pharisees: "Is it right to heal on the sabbath or not?" (14:3, Moffatt.) When they remained silent, Jesus cured the man and sent him away. Then He asked, "Which of you shall have an ass or an ox fallen into a well, and will not straightway draw him up on a sabbath day?" (14:5-6).

b. Rules for Guests and Hosts (14:7-14). Jesus observed the care with which the guests chose the places of honor at the table and used it to enforce teaching on humility. Better to take the lowest place at a marriage feast and then to be bidden to come up higher than to take a place of honor and then be humiliated by being forced to give up one's place to some more important person. "For every one that exalteth himself shall be humbled: and he that humbleth himself shall be exalted" (14:11).

---

[7] Manson, *op. cit.,* p. 167.

Jesus now turns His attention to the practice of inviting to feasts only relatives, friends, and rich neighbors. Such invitations will probably be reciprocated. The only generosity God recognizes and rewards is that which is extended to those who are unable to repay it.

c. *The Parable of the Messianic Banquet* (14: 15-24). Jesus had mentioned the resurrection of the just. Apparently this led one of the guests to make the pious remark, "Blessed is he that shall eat bread in the kingdom of God" (14: 15). Jesus replied to this with a parable indicating that one may have a sentimental interest in God's kingdom without a desire strong enough to lead to entering the Kingdom when the invitation to do so is extended.

In the parable, the guests were invited well in advance; so they had no excuse for not being prepared when the hour arrived. In Oriental manner the guests were again invited when the time for the feast arrived. But the invited guests began to make excuse. They all had legitimate reasons for not responding to the invitation. Consequently the angry master of the house told his servants to "go out quickly into the streets and lanes of the city, and bring in hither the poor and maimed and blind and lame" (14: 21). These were probably intended to represent the outcasts of Israel. After the servant had done this he reported that there was still room at the feast. He was then instructed to "go out into the highways and hedges, and constrain them to come in, that my house may be filled. For I say unto you, that none of those men that were bidden shall taste of my supper" (14: 23b-24). This statement was probably intended to mean the call of the Gentiles and the exclusion of the Jews who refused Jesus' message.

13. The Conditions of Discipleship (14: 25-35; cf. Matt. 10: 37-38; 5; 13)

To be a disciple of Jesus means that one's love for Him is so complete that by comparison his love for all else—even his own life—might be termed hate. Discipleship involves daily cross bearing. Five times statements to this effect meet us in the Synoptic record.

Since the demands of discipleship are so high, one should count the cost before he decides to become a follower of Jesus.

A person does not begin to build a tower until he first takes inventory to see that he has sufficient resources to complete it. He does not want the foundation to be a monument to his foolishness. Likewise a king does not go to war unless he first calculates his chances of victory. So anyone "that renounceth not all that he hath, he cannot be my disciple" (14:33). Just as salt has value only as long as it retains its taste, disciples have value only when they possess this quality of being willing to make heroic sacrifice. When they lose this they have lost their very reason for existence. "He that hath ears to hear, let him hear" (14:35b).

14. Joy in Heaven (c. 15)

Three beautiful parables in this chapter illustrate the joy in heaven over the sinner who repents. Given by Jesus to defend himself for associating with the tax collectors and sinners, these parables would have afforded comfort and encouragement to the outcasts of His day.

a. *The Lost Sheep* (15:1-7). In this parable Jesus introduces the figure of the kind shepherd who leaves the ninety-nine sheep to seek the one who has gone astray and brings it back rejoicing. The universal appeal of the good shepherd has never ceased to move men Godward. The point of the parable is the joy of the shepherd because he has found his lost sheep. Jesus says, "Even so there shall be joy in heaven over one sinner that repenteth, more than over ninety and nine righteous persons, who need no repentance" (15:7).

b. *The Lost Coin* (15:8-10). In the first parable of the trio the sheep was outside of the fold, but here is a coin lost within the *house*. Perhaps this refers more pointedly to the lost sheep of Israel. Publicans, too, were children of Abraham. In the parable of the lost sheep a man occupies the center of attention. Here it is a woman.

The ten coins might have represented the life savings of a widow. She lighted a lamp because the Palestinian houses were not equipped with anything remotely resembling our modern picture windows. She rejoiced when she found the coin, because in her penury the drachma represented so much toil and sacrifice expended and so much security and satisfaction expected. Her joy over her recovery of the lost coin, as she calls in her friends and neighbors to celebrate with her, illustrates God's joy over one sinner who repents.

c. *The Lost Son* (15:11-32). In this parable there are two distinct parts, the first of which centers around the younger son and his restoration, and the second of which focuses on the attitude of the elder brother in contrast to that of the father. The entire sketch is so true to life that even the details of the story take on significance.

In the parable the younger son demands his share of his father's estate, which would be one-third (Deut. 21:17). The "far country" to Jesus' hearers probably suggested some Jewish colony in Alexandria or Rome.

Once in the far country and away from the restraining influences of home and old associates, the younger son spent his money recklessly, perhaps in dissolute living, as his older brother charged (15:30). When he had spent all a severe famine struck the land. In order to eke out a living, he began to tend swine. The Jewish attitude towards this occupation is reflected in the Talmud: " 'Cursed is the man who keepeth swine.' "[8] His fare was so poor that he even envied the swine the carob pods, which men ate only when they were in desperate circumstances.

At this point the story changes. The realization came to the young man that life as a servant in the father's house was better than existence as swineherd. Realization crystallized into resolution. He would return and confess his guilt and ask to be taken in as a servant. Resolution was coined into action. He arose and came to his father.

The reaction of the father was something he had not anticipated. Recognizing the returning prodigal at a distance, the father ran and embraced him and kissed him affectionately. The son then confessed: "Father, I have sinned against heaven, and in thy sight: I am no more worthy to be called thy son." But before he could ask to be made a servant his father requested that the son be clothed in the best robe—the one reserved for an honored guest—and that a ring be put on his hand and sandals on his feet in token of the fact that he was a son. The calf that had been fattened for a festal occasion was to be killed, and banqueting and celebration were

[8]*Baba Kama*, 82b, cited by Manson, *op. cit.*, p. 179.

ordered because "this my son was dead, and is alive again: he was lost, and is found" (15:24).

The merriment, however, was soon interrupted. The elder brother, who had been forgotten in the excitement, came in from the field and inquired what all the commotion was about. Discovering that the celebration was occasioned by his younger brother's return, he exploded with rage. When his father attempted to salve his injured feelings, he reminded his father of his years of faithful service, which had never been recognized, not even with a kid! "Lo, these many years do I serve thee, and I never transgressed a commandment of thine; and yet thou never gavest *me* a *kid,* that I might make merry with my friends: but when *this thy son* came, who hath devoured *thy* living with *harlots,* thou killedst for him the *fatted calf*" (15:29-30, italics added).

To this outburst the father replied: "Son, thou art ever with me, and all that is mine is thine. But it was meet to make merry and be glad: for this *thy* brother was dead, and is alive again; and was lost, and is found" (15:31-32, italics added). It is interesting that the father corrected the contemptuous "this *son of yours*" to "*your brother.*" Jesus was using this dual parable to show God's attitude toward the repentant sinner and to show that any criticism of this generous, gracious attitude is unjustified. We are not to criticize His attitude but to share it.

15. *The Use and Abuse of Wealth* (c. 16)

a. The Parable of the Unjust Steward (16:1-13). In the parable the manager of an estate was charged with wasting his master's goods and was told that he was to prepare a statement of his accounts before he was dismissed. The steward realized that he was in a bad situation. Too weak to work at manual labor, too proud to beg, he decided to use strategy instead. One by one he called in his master's tenants and instructed each to tear up the old bill and write out quickly a new, discounted one. Perhaps the differences in the discounts were due to his shrewd appraisal of the reaction of the men with whom he was dealing. His program was designed to place these tenants under lasting obligation to himself, so that they would give him help when he needed it. The master found out about his steward's clever plans and commended him for "looking ahead; for the children of this world look further ahead, in dealing with their own generation, than the children of Light" (16:8, Moffatt).

We need to remind ourselves that this is strictly a parable. The one lesson is the important factor. The "sons of light" ought to use the realism, resourcefulness, and energy in achieving their spiritual goal that the men of this world use in gaining their worldly ends. They should have the same ability to look the future squarely in the face and then take resolute, heroic, fitting action. The man is commended for one thing only—his shrewdness. Moreover, it should be noted that since this is in no sense an allegory the characters are not to be assigned an independent significance. It is not Christ, or God, who commended the dishonest steward, but the manager's earthly master.

In the application of the lesson, the disciples—disciples here may refer to the wider circle of Jesus' followers—are told to use their wealth wisely, so that when it fails, the friends they have made by means of their unrighteous mammon may receive them into "eternal tabernacles" (16:9, literal translation).

As a further precaution against the unwarranted inference that one may be careless or dishonest in financial matters and still receive God's approval, Jesus indicates that faithfulness and dishonesty in little things are not matters of no moment. Life is all of one piece. If a person is dishonest in little things, he is dishonest, and cannot be trusted with greater responsibilities. God's true riches, the blessings of spiritual wealth, will not be entrusted to one who is unfaithful in his stewardship of material wealth. If one is not faithful in his use of the currency of this world—foreign coinage to one whose citizenship is in heaven—who will give him the spiritual riches which are his true and abiding wealth? (16:10-12.)

b. *The Rich Man and Lazarus* (16:14-31). Since the Pharisees were lovers of money and since they could not defend their covetousness by logic, they resorted to abuse, often the last weapon of one defeated in argument. Jesus replied: "Ye are they that justify yourselves in the sight of men; but God knoweth your hearts: for that which is exalted among men is an abomination in the sight of God" (16:15). He then proceeded to give the parable of the rich man and Lazarus.

The word translated by "hell" in the King James Version is the Greek term *Hades,* which corresponds to the Hebrew *Sheol,* regularly used for hell in the Hebrew Old Testament. Originally Sheol meant only a dark, vast subterranean cave to which the shadowy, spirit remains of men were thought to go after death. Hades has two distinct parts. There is the fiery torment to which the rich man is subjected, but there is also the paradise where Lazarus is comforted in Abraham's bosom. Within sight and talking distance of each other, the two are separated nevertheless by an impassable gulf which is fixed.

The second part of the parable may be addressed to the query: Why, if eternal destinies are settled by choices made and activities performed in this life, does not someone come back from the dead to warn us? Jesus answers that they had the moral teachings given through Moses and the prophets, which contain adequate truth concerning the finality of the choices made in this life and the nature of God's rewards. Thus there is a moral explanation for the fate of the rich man and Lazarus. Lazarus is saved because he is righteous, but the rich man failed to obey the repeated injunctions in the law and the prophets to show mercy and justice.

16. Teachings on Forgiveness, Faith, and Man's Ingratitude (17:1-19)

There are two unique paragraphs in this section: the parable of the servant (17:7-10) and the account of the healing of the ten lepers (17:11-19). In the parable Jesus may have in mind the legalistic righteousness of the Pharisees who thought that they could do so many deeds of righteousness that God would be obligated to save them. Jesus says that when we have done our best salvation is still a matter of God's grace.

In the account of the healing of the lepers, although there were ten cleansed only one returned to thank Jesus for the benefit that was conferred. The others may have been only carrying out Jesus' command, but His approval of the Samaritan is unmistakable.

17. Teaching About the Coming of the Kingdom (17:20-37)

The most popular pastime of the apocalyptic writers was speculating about the signs that would precede the end. In portraying the "woes of the Messiah," the catastrophes that were to come before the end, they gave their imagination free reign. Jesus had announced that the Kingdom was at hand. Perhaps they were challenging Him to produce the evidence—the sign.

What did Jesus answer? He replied that "the kingdom of God cometh not with observation," or, "with signs to be observed" (17:20). He continued: "Neither shall they say, Lo, here! or, There! for lo, the kingdom of God is within you" (17:21).

The Kingdom was in their midst in the person of Jesus and His disciples, in whose lives God's will was being done, and so His reign had begun. The Pharisees would find salvation in the revelation Jesus brings or they would not find it at all.

Parallels to the rest of the chapter are found in Matthew's apocalyptic discourse (c. 24) and elsewhere except for verses 28-29, 32, and 34.

18. Parables on Prayer (18:1-14)

a. *The Parable of the Unjust Judge* (18:1-8). In this parable, which Luke alone preserves, the same lesson is taught as in the parable of the friend at midnight. In this case, although the unjust judge will not administer justice out of religious, ethical, or humanitarian considerations, he is afraid that at last the widow who demands vindication will become violent and create a scene. The literal translation of the Greek text behind the words "lest . . . she weary me" is "lest she come at last and beat me." Even more graphic is the translation "lest she give me a black eye," which the Greek permits.

Since this is a parable, of course the unjust judge is not to be identified with God. Jesus is saying that if an unjust judge will out of self-regard finally execute justice because of the persistence of a widow, how *much more* will God "vindicate his elect, who cry to him day and night? Will he delay long over them? I tell you, he will vindicate them speedily" (18:7-8, R.S.V.). The last part of verse eight indicates an anxiety about the courage and fidelity of the disciples.

b. *The Parable of the Pharisee and the Publican* (18:9-14). Jesus painted a vivid contrast between the proud, self-righteous Pharisee and the humble, penitent publican. Not he who congratulates himself on his own goodness is saved, but he who pleads for mercy. The only basis of our justification is the goodness of God shown in redemption.

19. Conditions of Entrance to the Kingdom (18:15-34)

Since this material is treated in the previous two chapters, its contents will be merely indicated here: Jesus and the children, the rich young ruler, the third prediction of the Passion, and the dispute about greatness.

20. Jesus in Jericho (18:35—19:27)

Here Jesus healed Bartimaeus, was a guest of Zacchaeus, and gave the parable of the pounds.

a. The Conversion of Zacchaeus (19:1-10). This beautiful story is so well known that little comment is needed. It should be noted that Zacchaeus volunteered to make restitution for any wealth he had acquired wrongfully. In accordance with the requirements of the Law (Exod. 22:1), he agreed to restore fourfold.

b. The Parable of the Pounds (19:11-27). This parable is similar to that of the talents recorded by Matthew (25:14-30); but the details and occasions of the two differ. There are two parts or strands of thought that run through the parable or allegory.

There is first of all the story of the nobleman who went to a far country to receive kingly authority and, having had his credentials verified, returned to rule. However, his citizens hated him and sent a delegation "after him, saying, We will not that this man reign over us" (19:14). The returning ruler wreaked vengeance on those who had attempted to prevent his confirmation as king. The story of Archelaus, which may have provided the background for at least part of this allegory, would have had a peculiar appeal if Jesus were still at Jericho—Jericho was not far from Jerusalem and Archelaus had constructed a palace and aqueduct at Jericho.[9]

In this account probably the nobleman is intended to represent Christ. The far country is heaven and the return is the Second Coming. The citizens who hated the nobleman are primarily the Jews who opposed Jesus. The execution of these enemies is the judgment which will be meted out to apostate Jews when He returns.

9 Josephus, *Ant.*, XVII.13.1.

The allegory is pervaded by another strand of thought also. The Lord's return will be delayed. The teaching was given "because he was nigh to Jerusalem, and because they supposed that the kingdom of God was immediately to appear" (19:11).

While the Lord delays His return there are duties to be performed diligently by the disciples. Instead of daydreaming about rewards and honors which will be theirs in the Kingdom, the disciples should devote themselves to fulfilling God's plans for their lives, investing wisely in the work of the Kingdom the capital that the Master has entrusted to them.

The amount of the returns on the original investment made by two of the servants singled out for special notice suggests the lapse of a considerable period of time—a delayed Second Coming.

Of the ten servants mentioned in the beginning of the account as recipients of the Master's capital, only three are singled out for special comment. Of these one brings back an increase on the original investment of 1,000 per cent and another of 500 per cent. These represent disciples who in gratitude alertly and diligently carry out their Master's commission and by proving themselves worthy and capable of greater responsibilities win for themselves approval and promotion.

The third servant, who returned only the original investment without interest, represents those who grasp greedily the office that has been entrusted to them but do nothing with their opportunities for service, justifying their failure to act by blaming their Master. Complaining that his master was so hard to please that he was afraid to attempt anything, the servant forgot that the greatest failure is the failure to attempt something worth-while.

VI. Ministry in Jerusalem (19:28—21:38)

In connection with the Triumphal Entry, Luke records the Pharisees' request that Jesus silence the praise of His disciples, and Jesus' reply (19:39-40). He also tells us that when Jesus neared Jerusalem He "wept over it, saying, If thou hadst known in this day, even thou, the things which belong unto peace! but now they are hid from thine eyes"

(10:41b-42). He speaks of the siege and of the devastating success of the attackers who "shall dash thee to the ground, and thy children within thee; and they shall not leave in thee one stone upon another; because thou knewest not the time of thy visitation" (19:44).

With the other two Synoptists, Luke records the question about authority, the parable of the wicked tenants, and the questions about tribute to Caesar and the resurrection. Luke has an earlier account of the Great Commandment (10:25-28) and so he does not include here the similar material which Matthew and Mark have at this point.

With Matthew and Mark, Luke shares the question about David's Son and a brief censure of the scribes (20:41-47). He includes earlier more of Jesus' statements against the Pharisees (11:39-44) and the lawyers or scribes (11:45-52) and the lament over Jerusalem (13:34-35). Luke shares with Mark the account of the widow's gift (21:1-4), and with both Matthew and Mark the apocalyptic discourse in which He interprets the desolating sacrilege as the appearance of the Roman armies in the environs of Jerusalem (21:20). Luke has some apocalyptic material at an earlier point which Matthew places here (Luke 17:23-24, 26-27, 34-35; 12:39, 42-46) and some shared with Mark and Matthew that he likewise places earlier (19:12-13; 12:40, 38). The last verses of chapter 21 indicate how Jesus spent His time during the last week of His ministry. Apparently He slept at Bethany every night.

VII. Closing Scenes and Death (cc. 22—23)

In the Passion narrative Luke notes that "Satan entered into Judas" (22:3). Luke also records Jesus' expression of His desire "to eat this passover" with His disciples before He suffered (22:15) and His statement that He would "not eat it, until it be fulfilled in the kingdom of God. For I say unto you, I shall not drink from henceforth of the fruit of the vine, until the kingdom of God shall come" (22:16, 18).

Reported only by Luke are Jesus' words to Peter about Satan's desire to sift him as wheat and His assurance, "I have prayed for you that your faith may not fail; and when you have turned again, strengthen your brethren" (22:32, R.S.V.). In the arrest Luke preserves a unique statement of Christ when one of the disciples had used his sword: "No more of this!"

(22:51, R.S.V.). He alone tells of Jesus healing the man who had lost an ear in the fracas (22:51), and he also describes Jesus' intense agony in the Garden and mentions the angel who strengthened Him (22:43-44).

In Luke is found Jesus' advice to the disciples to take their purses and bags, if they had them, and to procure a sword by selling their mantles if necessary (22:35-38). Perhaps the most plausible interpretation is that Jesus is speaking seriously but in symbols. When the disciples had been sent out two by two they went without purse or sandals and lacked nothing because the people had been hospitable. But now the situation is reversed. The disciples will need money and supplies and even instruments of defense. Probably the reference to the sword is an allusion to the antagonistic attitude of the Jews. The answer of the disciples indicates that they took the saying about the sword literally. Jesus' rejoinder indicates that they were mistaken, and the sequel corroborates this.

Luke places Peter's denials before Jesus was commanded to tell if He was the Messiah; Matthew and Mark, immediately afterward. Luke alone tells of Jesus' trial before Herod Antipas. Since the people were crying for blood, Pilate was glad for what he thought was an opportunity to get this innocent Man off his hands (23:4-7). Herod too was glad, for he hoped to have Jesus perform a sign. But, interrogated by Herod and in the presence of the chief priests and scribes who were vehemently accusing Him, Jesus remained silent. Herod and his soldiers then mocked Him and clothed Him in a royal garb and sent Him back to Pilate.[10]

Pilate interpreted this act of Herod Antipas as a confirmation of his own earlier verdict that Jesus was not guilty of the charges that had been brought against Him. Since Jesus had done nothing deserving the death penalty, Pilate said, "I will therefore chastise him, and release him" (23:16). Luke shows how Pilate attempted to stem the mob pressure (23:22) but finally acquiesced to its will (23:23-25).

Omitting the account of the mocking by the Roman soldiers, Luke tells of Jesus' sympathetic words to the women who were bewailing and lamenting Him (23:28-31). The

[10] Luke states that it was this incident that reconciled Herod and Pilate (23:12). Luke alone tells of Pilate's verdict at this point (23:4).

daughters of Jerusalem will of all women suffer in the days that lie ahead. Motherhood and the care of little children, instead of being a singular blessing, will be the essence of woe. In the distress and anguish that will attend the destruction of the city, mothers will call on the mountains and hills to fall on them, so that they might not see their infants subjected to such awful suffering and death. Perhaps the general meaning of verse 31 is: What is now happening to Jesus is insignificant when it is compared to what will happen to this people. Innocence is represented by the green tree, guilt by the dry tree.

It is Luke who records Jesus' words on the cross: "Father, forgive them; for they know not what they do" (23:34). These words constitute a high point of divine revelation. They show that God is forgiving even when our sins and wrong are causing Him infinite pain. The Cross is a window into the heart of the Eternal, who always suffers when we sin. Luke also preserves the words of Jesus to the penitent thief: "Verily I say unto thee, To-day shalt thou be with me in Paradise" (23:43). Someone has said that there was one such case recorded in the Gospels that none should despair; only one so that none should presume.

Jesus' last words: "Father, into thy hands I commend my spirit," (23:46) are found only in Luke. These words uttered in a loud cry were probably words of triumph. He had accomplished His task. His suffering was over. The New Covenant was a reality. Luke reports that "when all the crowds who had collected for the sight saw what had happened, they turned away beating their breasts" (23:48, Moffatt).

VIII. Resurrection and Ascension (c. 24)

The women who had followed Jesus from Galilee, Luke tells us, saw where Jesus' body was laid and returned to prepare spices and ointments. They did not proceed with the embalming of the body because it was the Sabbath (23:55-56).

When the women came to the tomb early Sunday morning they found the stone rolled back, and where Jesus' body had been were two men in dazzling raiment (24:4).[11] The women were asked: "Why seek ye the living among the dead?

[11] Mark has "a young man" (16:5); Matthew, "an angel of the Lord" (28:2).

He is not here, but is risen." When they told the eleven and
the rest what they had seen and heard, their words seemed
to the apostles "as idle talk; and they disbelieved them"
(24:11).

The beautiful story of the two on the way to Emmaus to
whom Jesus appeared and talked as they journeyed together
is recorded by Luke. To Him they unburdened their hearts,
telling how Jesus of Nazareth, the One they had hoped would
redeem Israel, had been crucified, and now His body was gone.
Some said that He was alive, but while they had confirmed
the reports of the women about the empty tomb, "him they
did not see" (24:24). Jesus then began to explain to them
that it was necessary for the Messiah "to suffer these things,
and to enter into his glory" (24:26). So He began with Moses
and all the prophets, interpreting "to them in all the scriptures the things concerning himself" (24:27).

Near Emmaus the disciples, still not knowing who their
Companion was, asked Him to spend the night with them. It
was only after He had blessed the bread that they knew Him,
but by that time He had vanished. Then they said to each
other, "Was not our heart burning within us, while he spake
to us in the way, while he opened to us the scriptures?"
(24:32.)

Excitedly the two rushed back to Jerusalem—probably
without even stopping to eat. There they were met by the
eleven and others, who said, "The Lord is risen indeed, and
hath appeared to Simon" (24:34). Then the two told them
of their experiences on the road and in the breaking of the
bread. At this juncture "he himself stood in the midst of them,
and saith unto them, Peace be unto you" (24:36). Supposing
that they had seen a ghost, they were afraid, but Jesus invited them to see His hands and feet and to handle Him, that
they might see that He was no mere spirit. Even after they
saw His hands and feet they "disbelieved for joy" (24:41).

Jesus told them that all the scriptures concerning himself must be fulfilled and "then opened he their mind, that
they might understand the scriptures" (24:45). Declaring that
it was written that the Messiah should suffer and rise from
the dead and that remission of sins should be proclaimed to
all peoples, Jesus indicated their mission: "Ye are witnesses
of these things" (24:48).

However, being witnesses in a require more than usual dynam this. Therefore, He told them to would be "clothed with power promise of my Father." This Spirit's indwelling presence, realized on the Day of Pentec Spirit is still indispensable if our live witness to the grace of Christ.

After this appearance of Christ at Bethany, whi was blessing the disciples He departed from them. The dis ciples, true to Jesus' command, returned to Jerusalem "and were continually in the temple, blessing God" (24:53).

CHAPTER VII

THE SON OF GOD
(JOHN)

A. Introduction

The first century of the Christian era was drawing to a close when the fourth of our canonical Gospels appeared. Most of the other books of the New Testament had already been written, and all of the original twelve apostles but John had died. The Christian Church was more than half a century old and had changed with the passing of the years from a predominantly Jewish membership with headquarters at Jerusalem to a strongly Gentile church with centers of influence at Antioch in Syria, Ephesus, Corinth, and Rome. This gradual change was largely the result of Paul the Apostle's victory over the Judaizers on the issue of justification by faith, along with the influence of Greek culture. The Church had grown and spread under the protection of the Roman Empire, which granted it favor in the sense that it was not antagonistic to it. Persecutions during the first century were largely local, inspired by local conditions, although at times they were brought on by enemies of Paul who followed him from place to place in order to stir up strife against him (Acts 17:13).

When the Gospel of John appeared, the second-generation Christians were giving leadership to the Church, and the author represents one of the last links with the original eyewitnesses. He sought to interpret Christ and the gospel for the new generation. There is some evidence that the new membership had lost some of the warmth of its fathers and that certain heresies had grown up within the Church against which the members needed to be warned.

I. Authorship

Five New Testament books have commonly been ascribed to John the Apostle: the Gospel of John, the three Johannine Epistles, and Revelation. The external evidence from the middle of the second century has been almost unanimously in favor of this opinion. The traditional argument on the

188

basis of internal evidence has also supported the authorship of John and has not been refuted with any high degree of conclusiveness. The argument may be stated quite briefly: The author was a Jew, a Jew of Palestine, an eyewitness of most of the events which he relates, and an apostle—all of which point to the Apostle John.

II. The Author

Very little is known about the Apostle John for the obvious reason that not much has been recorded about him. In Matthew, John is mentioned only three times, and seven times as much is told about John the Baptist as about John the Apostle. Mark mentions him ten times and Luke seven; while the Gospel of John does not call him by name at all. This latter fact has always been a strong argument in favor of the Johannine authorship. John was self-effacing to a fault.

The date of John's birth is not known, but he was probably the youngest of the apostles. He was the son of Zebedee and Salome and the brother of James. He was engaged in the fishing business with his father in his younger manhood. The family was apparently comfortably situated economically, since they had hired servants (Mark 1:20) and John was able to take Mary the mother of Jesus and care for her after the Crucifixion (John 19:27).

Since the population of Galilee was mixed and the business of the family was carried on with peoples of various nationalities, John from his earliest years was in contact with Hellenistic influences. Being a Jew, he would have visited Jerusalem many times, and he was probably acquainted with the high priest there (John 18:15). Jewish and Greek characteristics mingled in the man, and these two influences are dominant in his Gospel.

The Apostle was an early disciple of John the Baptist and needed no great persuasion to leave him and follow Jesus (John 1:37). He seems to have continued his fishing activities for a time after this—perhaps a year or so (Matt. 4:18-22; Luke 5:1-11; cf. John 1:29-46)—before becoming a full-time follower and disciple. During the closing half of Jesus' ministry the special group of three was formed, consisting of Peter, James, and John. They sustained a closer intimacy with Him than any other of the disciples. At the raising of the daughter of Jairus (Luke 9:49f), Jesus took the chosen three with Him. When Jesus was transfigured on the mountain (Matt. 17:1-8; Mark 9:2-8; Luke 9:28-36), these three were there to behold His glory. And in the last hours of our Lord's life on earth, when He struggled and prayed in Gethsemane, John, with Peter and James, was called upon to share His suffering. John, with Peter, prepared the Last Supper (Luke 22:8). Of the twelve they alone followed Jesus to the place of judgment (John 18:15-16), but only John followed Jesus to the cross (John 19:26). John and Peter are again found together as they ran to the tomb on the first Easter morning (John 20:3-4).

The Book of Acts has very little to say about John, and when mentioned he is cast in the shadow of Peter. He is also eclipsed by Paul, being referred to only once after Paul comes on the scene (15:6), and then not by name. But long after Peter had followed his Lord in death by crucifixion and Paul had been beheaded at Rome, John lived and preached the gospel of love. While others seemed to be more active in the extension of the Early Church, no one did more than John to establish the Christians in their faith. It may well be a fact that his were the teaching and influence which held the Church steady against the heresies which grew up within it. John is said to have been the bishop of Ephesus and to have died there, full of years and love for God and for his fellow man.

The keenest insight into the character of John was given by Jesus when He nicknamed him a son of thunder (Mark 3:17). What demonstrations of hot temper, of snap judgment, and of unbridled rage must have been observed by those who knew him! Indications of this characteristic are seen on three occasions. He forbade some men who were strangers to him to labor in the name of Jesus (Mark 9:38). He wanted to call down fire from heaven upon certain Samaritans who had refused to receive him (Luke 9:54). And on the last journey of Jesus to Jerusalem, John and his brother James sought to take unfair advantage of the other disciples by asking for the places of prestige in the new Kingdom.

There was nothing passive in John's character. His emotional reactions were strong. He could hate vehemently and love with equal intensity. Under the touch of the Master and the later baptism of the Spirit, the directions and motives of his life were changed. Hhis character became, not a soft, temperless something marked by a love that knew no moral distinctions, but strong to hate the evil and love the good. He was an ardent follower of the meek and lowly Nazarene who gave himself in meekness to save mankind, but who had also a short time before driven the money-changers from the Temple in holy anger.

III. Purpose for Writing

The devotional reader may find so many inspirational passages in the Gospel of John that it appears to him as a beautiful bouquet. But the book is much more like a multicolored mosaic. There are plan and purpose back of the author's work. Nor does he fail to inform us of that purpose. He writes: "But these are written, that ye may believe that Jesus is the Christ, the Son of God; and that believing ye may have life in his name" (20:31). He wrote with a purpose and for a decision.

Let us try briefly to catch John's meaning. To believe means to see and understand and accept something as truth, and, we must add, see with the heart as well as the head. He sought to make his readers believe that Jesus the Man, the One born in Bethlehem who lived and suffered and died, the One whom John saw and handled and touched, was the Christ. The Christ means the chosen of God, the anointed of God. And to the Jews that meant that Jesus was their promised Messiah. Their long hopes had been fulfilled; their Deliverer had come. John wrote that the Jews might believe that Jesus was their Messiah.

But to John He is more than the Jewish Messiah. He is also the Son of God. This was emphasized for the sake of the Greeks and those of Greek culture—those of philosophic mind. Their quest was not for a Messiah, but for the metaphysical, fundamental source of things. And to them John presents Christ as the Son of God, who is equal with God in creation. We must wait to see how John goes about to establish these astonishing claims, but he does so with a purpose, knowing that faith has assured results. Faith in Jesus as the revelation of God to all mankind results in life: a new life, eternal life, the life that was in Christ himself. Jesus said, "I came that they may have life, and may have it abundantly" (10:10).

IV. Manner of Writing

"Many other signs therefore did Jesus in the presence of the disciples, which are not written in this book" (20:30). John selected only those things which best suited his purpose, and it has been estimated that his Gospel refers to no more than twenty days of the whole ministry of Jesus. We do know that by the time chapter twelve is reached Jesus has come to the last week of His earthly ministry.

A casual reading of all four Gospels will reveal the wide difference between the material used by the Synoptic writers and by John. Much of the first four chapters of John's Gospel seems to cover a period of ministry prior to that recorded by the Synoptics. It has already been noted that John speaks of Jesus and John the Baptist preaching simultaneously while the Synoptics record Jesus' ministry only after the arrest of the Baptist. A study of the call of the various disciples will help to confirm this idea of the early ministry of Jesus. Then when we come to chapter thirteen, we find that all of the last discourse to the disciples through chapter seventeen is peculiar to John.

V. Characteristics of the Gospel

From the purpose as above stated it can be seen that Jesus is the center of this Gospel. John gives his readers the heart of the Christ. The good news of the Gospel is the news that one may sustain a personal relationship with Christ, the eternal Son of God. This "Spiritual Gospel," in contrast to the Synoptics, presents the earthly life of Jesus in its heavenly setting. The author reveals the Christ who came from heaven and who has already returned there. From the very beginning he sees Jesus as the Son of God, and pictures Him as also knowing that fact from the beginning of His ministry and sharing that knowledge with others. Not only the Jesus of history, but the Christ of eternity, is the center of this Gospel.

The Gospel of John is characterized by simplicity of thought and diction—yet by great depth of spiritual insight. John punctuates his writing with the plentiful use of key words, such as love, light, believe, and know. The word believe is used ninety-eight times. To John all the acts and words of Jesus are signs pointing in one direction, to prove the deity of Jesus. We find such figures of speech as hearing, eating, drinking, shepherding, and the shining of light. These make the Gospel simple to understand. And while John used the language of the common people, as did the other Gospel writers, the choice of his terms and the manner of their use lend richness and depth.

Aside from this simplicity of style, there is an excellency of arrangement which cannot be ignored. A very fruitful way of starting one's study of this Gospel is to study its literary features. Note the setting, the relation of the author to his subject, the local color of geography, and living habits among the people. Catch the plot which surrounds the Hero, the elements of suspense, tension, opposition, drama, and climax. Watch the central theme running from beginning to end, and observe how the different characters help to bring it out. Note also the personal, social, national, moral, and ethical applications of this theme. Study the characters themselves—their various motives, the Hero of the story, and the unusual events in His life. What can you learn about these individuals, and from them? What does the book reveal about the author? Is he an effective writer? Does he know human nature? To what extent did he share in the events which he recorded? Did he accomplish his stated purpose?

In the prologue (1:1-18) he gives the setting for this Gospel of witness. Then he brings John the Baptist forward as his first witness (1:19 ff.). In the first twelve verses of chapter two, Jesus is presented as giving witness to himself to Galileans at the miracle at Cana in Galilee, and, as a result, "his disciples believed on him." Following this, Christ's witness is to the Jews: traveling to Jerusalem, cleansing the Temple, discoursing with Nicodemus on the new birth, and laboring throughout Judea. At the close of this section we read, "He that believeth on the Son hath eternal life; but he that obeyeth not the Son shall not see life, but the wrath of God abideth on him" (3:36).

The witness of Jesus is next to a Samaritan, one of mixed race, as He talks with the woman at Jacob's well (4:1-42). The culmination of this event is "many of the Samaritans believed on him." Then He bears witness to a Gentile, an official at Capernaum, whose son He heals (4:46-54). There follows the main body of the Gospel (5:1—12:50), in which Jesus is revealed as witnessing by deed and discourse to people throughout the land. Note the universality of this witness to the deity of Jesus, also the mounting opposition of the Jews, closing with: "And Jesus cried and said, He that believeth on me, believeth not on me, but on him that sent me. . . . the things therefore which I speak, even as the Father hath said unto me, so I speak" (12:44, 50).

Starting with chapter thirteen and continuing through chapter seventeen, John gives Jesus' intimate witness of himself to the closed circle of the chosen disciples, with chapter seventeen His closing benediction. In chapters eighteen and nineteen He continues with the betrayal at Gethsemane, followed by the trial and crucifixion. Here the conflict between Jesus and the Jews is of the most intense sort, with shadows of every kind gathering around the scene, the work and witness of the Son of God seeming to come to naught as He dies on the cross and is buried in a tomb. John does not attempt to tell what the disciples did at this time, nor what their reactions were. The whole scene closes in darkness with the Hero of the narrative having died in shame on a cross and having been safely sealed in the grave. To those who might be unacquainted with the story, this would appear dramatic indeed, and those to whom it is familiar must take care lest that familiarity result in blindness.

But John has not told all of his story. The darkness symbolized by the closed tomb serves to emphasize the brightness which follows. In the early morning of the third day Mary Magdalene is seen wending her way through the still dawn to the place of burial—and action again breaks out as she runs and tells the disciples that the body of Jesus is gone. Peter and John come running and see that the tomb is indeed empty, but go away again heavyhearted, leaving Mary weeping alone. Unbelieving, but still somehow holding on to her Lord though she still thinks Him dead, Mary is fully confirmed in her faith by the appearance of the risen Lord himself. Again she hurries to the disciples with the word, "I have seen the Lord." Then Thomas, the doubter, appears as the last great personal witness to Christ. When Jesus appears before him in resurrected form, doubt vanishes, and he cries out: "My Lord and my God."

At this point John has brought us around the full crescent

of his purpose to show that Jesus is the Christ, the Son of
God, in the hope that his readers, like Mary and Thomas,
may also believe. Besides the witnesses already mentioned,
there are to be found the witness of the Scriptures, of the
Father, of the disciples, of the miracles, and of the Resurrection. The final chapter of this Gospel is the denouement. John
allows his readers to bask in the calm which follows the storm
and to linger for a short spell in the presence of the risen
Christ, giving time for the fact of His glorious triumph to lay
hold upon them.

B. Contents

I. The Prologue (1:1-18)

The prologue is a poetic masterpiece, having the Logos
as its theme, and it serves as an introduction to the whole
book. It is prophetic of all that follows and gives the essence
of God's revelation of himself to the world. Verses six through
eight and verse fifteen, in which John the Baptist is introduced,
are interruptions to the central thought of this prologue.

The Greek Logos was the divine reason or wisdom. This
thought was fused with the Hebrew idea of creative activity
and self-revelation by Philo, the Alexandrian Jewish philosopher, who used the term Logos "to express the conception
of a mediator between the transcendent God and the universe,
an immanent power active in creation and revelation, but
though the Logos is often personified, it is never truly personalized."[1]

John took this expression, which had become almost a
household word in the first century, personalized it, and used
it to denote God's highest revelation to man. When he says
"Logos" he means Jesus Christ, the incarnate Son of God,
and by the use of this term he endeavors to say that all that
both Greeks and Jews conceived as God's expression of himself to man is found in Jesus Christ. John does not speak directly of the Incarnation, neither does he tell of the Virgin
Birth, as do Matthew and Luke. But after this introduction
he goes on to discourse upon Him who is the Logos.

The Logos is presented as eternal in existence (v. 1), having fellowship with God (vv. 1-2), divine in nature (v. 1),
creative in activity (v. 3), and as the Source and Giver of all

[1] W. F. Howard, *Christianity According to St. John*, p. 38.

life, both physical and spiritual (v. 4). The Incarnation is suggested in verse five, and the whole conflict of Christ with the forces of sin in the world is introduced in the words: "The light shineth in the darkness; and the darkness apprehended it not" (v. 5). In other words, there is no compatibility between Christ, the Light, and the sin of the world; neither can the darkness extinguish the light.

Christ was; John the Baptist was sent, and being sent, he came as a witness to Christ, in order that men might believe in Him (vv. 6-7). He came into the world which He had made, but the people would not receive Him (v. 11). In contrast to Moses, who gave only the Law, He brought grace and truth and revealed the glory of God. To this minority came a new birth, a new life, and the right to be called the sons of God in a sense not comprehended in the idea of creation.

II. The Gospel of Witness (1:19—6:71)

It has been noted above that John endeavored to accomplish his stated purpose by bringing together many witnesses. Let us observe how each incident serves to bear witness to the Christ, the Son of God.

1. John the Baptist (1:19-51)

John the Baptist, whose birth is recorded in Luke's Gospel, came as the forerunner of Jesus and realized that his ministry was soon to give way to that of Jesus. He was willing that it should be so because he knew the limits of his calling and was satisfied with his lot in life. He was the voice; Jesus was the message. He baptized with water; Jesus would baptize with the Spirit. He felt himself unworthy to do much less than he was called upon to do. He was busy preaching, baptizing, and making converts for some time before he knew Jesus for what He was. But when that revelation came to him and he recognized Jesus as He approached one day, he began at once to turn the attention of his own disciples to Him. But of the baptism of Jesus by John, at which time the Spirit came according to the Synoptic record, nothing here is said.

This Gospel shows Jesus and John the Baptist preaching simultaneously for a time, while the other Gospels record only the preaching of Jesus following the death of John. The reason seems to be that this Gospel gives the first months of Jesus' ministry, of which the others say nothing. We find John again, in chapter three, still baptizing and people still coming to him. In a discussion with the Jews over purifying, he disclaimed any final authority and pointed them to Jesus for their answer. At the beginning of chapter four it may be observed that John's ministry was more and more giving way to that of Jesus. In 5: 33-36 Jesus speaks of him in highly complimentary terms. No other mention of him is made in this Gospel except in 10: 41, where many folk were saying that he did no miracles, yet everything he said of Jesus was true. What a significant reputation for a man to leave behind him when his life's work has been completed!

2. The Witness to the Galileans (2: 1-12)

The calling of the first three disciples mentioned above took place near the Jordan River. Jesus then went north with them into Galilee, where He met and called Philip, who brought Nathanael. His chief reason for going seems to have been the occasion of a wedding at Cana. He was accompanied by His mother and His new disciples, and there the opportunity was afforded for His first miracle: that of turning water into wine. John, who is usually careful to explain or interpret, does not give us any reason for this miracle; so we may judge it to have served as an introduction to His Galilean ministry. It is significant that this first miracle should have been performed in the realm of natural law. It invited the sincerest kind of faith and aroused no antagonism whatever.

3. The Cleansing of the Temple (2: 13-25)

After spending a few days in Capernaum with His mother and brothers (Joseph was apparently dead by this time), Jesus went to Jerusalem to attend the Passover Feast of the Jews. This was one of three great annual feasts, the others being Pentecost and the Feast of Tabernacles. The Passover was instituted at the time of Israel's deliverance from Egyptian bondage. We are not told to what extent Jesus may have entered into the festivities, but He seems to have been very soon detracted by the manner in which sacrifices were being sold to the worshipers. With the cry, "Take these things hence; make not my Father's house a house of merchandise," (v. 16) and with a whip of cords hastily fashioned, He drove out the animals, overthrew the money tables, and ordered the owners to take away their crates of pigeons. When the Jews challenged His authority, asking for a sign to confirm it, He answered, "Destroy this temple, and in three days I will raise it up" (v. 19).

Little wonder they did not understand Him. Actually He did give them a sign which they could afterward observe, for John tells us that His reference was to His body, which should be put to death and raised again. They could not see that Jesus was claiming himself to be the fulfillment of all for which the Temple stood, and that He was to stand superior to the Temple ritual after it would one day be destroyed. They could only scoff at His seemingly blasphemous boast and, remembering His claim, use it to condemn Him at His trial.

The selling of sacrifices to worshipers coming from a distance and the changing of money into Temple currency for the Temple tax were necessary. But this business had been allowed to encroach upon the Court of the Gentiles; the spirit of secularity had suppressed the spirit of reverence; greed and graft had become acceptable to the Temple authorities. Jesus sought to correct this abuse. His zeal for His Father's house would not allow Him to be quiet.

Some people, however, did believe on Jesus when they heard Him speak and saw the things which He did on this trip to Jerusalem. But He distrusted them because He knew their hearts. Their faith was only in one whom they saw as a miracle worker. When this same Doer of outstanding deeds began to make moral claims upon their lives and reveal the divine character of His mission, they were unwilling to follow His lead. Some became secret disciples, while others openly joined the opposition which soon rose.

4. Nicodemus and the New Birth (3:1-21)

If it be true here, as in some other places, that John uses one incident to illustrate and enforce another, Nicodemus may well be an example of those who believed at this time. A ruler of the Jews, a member of the Sanhedrin, he came to Jesus at the most convenient time for a conference, seemingly speaking for a group. "Rabbi, we know that thou art a teacher come from God . . . " (v. 2)—this was a good show of faith to be sure, but it needed to be directed into new channels;

hence the answer of Jesus concerning the new birth. To believe on Jesus must mean an entirely new approach to life; in fact, a new life—"Ye must be born again" (v. 7, K.J.V.). And then Nicodemus showed why Jesus could not fully rely on his declaration of faith by completely misunderstanding what Jesus was trying to say. He could think only in terms of physical birth when Jesus was speaking of spiritual birth. Jesus was not asking him to understand this but to accept the truth of it. The proselyte to the Jewish faith was supposed to have had a rebirth, and Nicodemus most certainly was acquainted with this concept. Jesus was referring to a new life which He had come to give. Truly it was a birth from above, and to enforce the truth of it Jesus followed with a homily on His own divine origin and His coming sacrificial death. The following verses (16-21) provide some of the deepest insight into the redemptive work of God. John 3:16 will always stand out as the classic expression of the plan of salvation.

Nicodemus seems to have listened and then departed in silence, perhaps to ponder these deep truths. We find him still in a very favorable attitude toward Jesus when he appears again (7:50). Later still (19:39) he assisted Joseph of Arimathaea in preparing the body of Jesus for burial. Perhaps Nicodemus forever remained a believer, but in secret: a deep sympathizer, but not a committed follower.

The expression "born again" is a descriptive rather than a definitive term. It is an analogy for a spiritual truth: the great truth that Jesus came that "ye may have life." The new birth is the impartation of the divine life of Christ to a human soul. "He that believeth on the Son hath eternal life" (3:36). "For God so loved the world, that he gave his only begotten Son, that whosoever believeth in him should not perish, but have everlasting life" (3:16, K.J.V.).

5. The Witness to the Samaritans (3:22—4:42)

Again Jesus returned to Galilee, because of jealousy which arose among the Pharisees over the growing popularity of Jesus as against John the Baptist. He chose to go straight north through Samaria rather than to go through Perea, across the Jordan River, as the Jews usually did. There was intense enmity existing between the Jews and their neighbors of mixed race. The Samaritans based their religious worship on the Pentateuch only, and they had had their temple on Mount Gerizim. Arriving in the heat of the day, Jesus stopped to rest while His disciples went into Sychar to buy food. Then there followed that very significant conversation of Jesus with the Samaritan woman who had come to get water from Jacob's Well.

At every point Jesus broke through the prejudices represented in that situation—prejudice of race and place, of worship and religious authority. He said, "Nowadays you are worshipping with your eyes shut" (v. 22, Phillips). He challenged the rabbinical prejudice against women by talking to this Samaritan woman and by revealing to her His messiahship (v. 26). He destroyed the Samaritan concept of their priority in religion by saying that salvation was from the Jews, and then said that even the Jewish system of religion must give way to a purer form of spiritual worship. "God is a Spirit: and they that worship him must worship in spirit and truth" (v. 24). He brought this great truth home to the woman by probing her inner heart life, drawing forth confessions of her own sinfulness, and then telling her that He, the Christ, had come to give "living water" to her thirsty soul, which would bring lasting satisfaction because its essence was eternal life. She left her water jar to go and tell others: "Come, see a man, who told me all things that ever I did: can this be the Christ?" (v. 29.) "And many more believed because of his word" (v. 41). Thus did Jesus bear His clearest witness to date to the Samaritans.

6. The Witness to the Gentiles (4:43-54)

After spending two days in Samaria, Jesus continued on to Galilee, where He received a warm welcome at Cana. The reference to a prophet having no honor in his own country (v. 44) presumably refers to His inhospitable reception in Judea, since He was a Jew and had been born in Bethlehem, even though Nazareth in Galilee had been His home. Word of His arrival spread to Capernaum and came to the ears of a nobleman, an officer in the service of Herod Antipas. He was probably a Gentile. On behalf of a sick son he came to Jesus asking Him to go to his home and heal the boy. Jesus saw his faith but demanded an even greater degree of faith on the part of this man by merely saying, "Go thy way; thy son liveth" (v. 50). The response of faith was immediate, and as he was returning home his servants met him and reported the recovery of the boy. As a result the man's household also believed on Jesus.

7. In Jerusalem at a Feast (c. 5)

"After these things" is very indefinite, but Jesus again went to Jerusalem at the time of a feast of the Jews. Since John apparently always mentions the Passover by name whenever he refers to it, this is perhaps not another Passover There are three Passovers mentioned (2:13; 6:4; 13:1).

John records for us just one event of this visit, the healing of the invalid at the Pool of Bethesda, followed by the controversy with the Jews. This healing of the invalid is the introduction to a period of great controversy between Jesus and the Jews which continues to the end of chapter six. John does not dwell upon the greatness of the miracle, for to him miracles are the normal thing for Him who is the Son of God. He accepts it as a testimony to Christ, and his purpose for relating it seems to be to show up the opposition of the Jews. Jesus had manifested himself thereby as the Giver of life, and He was opposed in this act of mercy because He had done it on the Sabbath and thereby had broken the Mosaic law. On one additional count they sought also to kill Him: He identified himself with God (vv. 17-18). Jesus replied that both He and Moses were directed by God in their work, and that in opposing Him they were also opposing the Law which they professed to honor. The Law itself condemned them. "For if ye believed Moses, ye would believe me; for he wrote of me" (v. 46).

8. Feeding of the Five Thousand (c. 6)

Again we find Jesus in Galilee, crossing to the east side of the lake. The crowds followed Him and became hungry—with no food and with apparently no means to buy. In response to the need, Jesus miraculously fed the crowd by multiplying the five loaves and two fishes of a lad who was present. Rather than opposition, as in Jerusalem, now popularity became a problem, for the people were ready to take Jesus and make Him their King. So He hurried away to the hills by himself. In the night Jesus, walking on the water, came to the disciples as they sought to cross the sea by boat. The next day the crowd sought Jesus and found Him and His disciples at Capernaum. In response to their question, "Rabbi, when camest thou hither?" (v. 25) He began His sermon which He had been prevented from delivering the day before, using the feeding miracle as a basis. His topic may be stated: The Giver of life is also the Sustainer of life. Realizing that their chief concern was physical bread, He exhorted them to work "for the food which abideth unto eternal life, which the Son of man shall give unto you" (v. 27). But they could not understand, thinking that He would perhaps somehow duplicate the giving of manna in the wilderness, and asked for a sign to assure them. He told them that not Moses, but God, gave them the manna from heaven and in like manner was giving His Son to be the Bread of Life to all the world: "I am the bread of life: he that cometh to me shall not hunger, and he that believeth on me shall never thirst" (v. 35).

But again popularity increased the enmity of the Jews. They objected to His claims because He was the son of Joseph. No one of such lowly origin should make such bold assertions, taking God for his authority. The fact that this was their complaint indicates that they were well able to understand His allegorical sermon; their trouble was an unwillingness to accept any of its implications. Jesus knew this and made no effort to make things easier for them, but rather pressed them at the point of their unbelief by such statements as, "Except ye eat the flesh of the Son of man and drink his blood, ye have not life in yourselves" (v. 53), and, "The words that I have spoken unto you are spirit, and are life" (v. 63).

There is something plaintive about the closing verses of this chapter. Many of Jesus' disciples drew back from following Him. Then in His first mention of the twelve as a group Jesus said, "Would ye also go away?" (v. 67.) Peter replied, "Lord, to whom shall we go? thou hast the words of eternal life" (v. 68). But Jesus was more conscious of unbelief than of faith among them, and, for the first time, stated that He already knew that one of them would betray Him to His enemies. And so He continued His ministry in the midst of growing and deliberate opposition—with the traitor Judas in His camp.

III. Jesus and the Jews (cc. 7—12)

We come now to the last great series of discourses given by our Lord at Jerusalem in the midst of the conflict with the Jewish authorities, which resulted finally in His death. Very little of the material in these chapters is paralleled in the Synoptics. Jesus preached and performed miracles before the great multitudes in Jerusalem, and then (cc. 13—17) discoursed privately to the closed circle of the twelve. The Jews continued their relentless endeavor to find cause to arrest Him. How darkened were their hearts and minds not to know that they were dealing with Deity, that they were waging warfare with the Almighty to their own destruction! Fortified with truth and watching the divine time clock, Jesus parried their thrusts, blunted their instruments, and threw them back in consternation again and again. But His was not their kind of warfare, nor did He seek only to defend himself. He knew that in due time He would give himself up to them to be crucified, but not until His work on earth was accomplished.

We are carried along as we read, even as John must have been transported in heart as he recalled and recorded what happened to Him who labored so magnificently and died so triumphantly for the salvation of mankind. Rising above the clamor and debate, Christ's voice is heard: "I am the light of the world" (8:12)—"Ye shall know the truth, and the truth shall make you free" (8:32)—"If therefore the Son shall make you free, ye shall be free indeed" (8:36)—"Before Abraham was born, I am" (8:58)—"I am the door" (10:7)—"I am the good shepherd" (10:11)—"I am the resurrection, and the life: he that believeth on me, though he die, yet shall he live; and whosoever liveth and believeth on me shall never die" (11:25-26)—"He that believeth on me, believeth not on me, but on him that sent me" (12:44). Here we see the divine Logos, the Word of God made flesh, living and speaking among men the truths of eternal life.

1. At the Feast of Tabernacles (c. 7)

Jesus remained in Galilee, where He was relatively safe from the Jews, because the authority of the Sanhedrin did not reach beyond Judea. They could harass Him, but could not take Him. The brothers of Jesus were among those who did not believe in Him at this time, and it is difficult to understand their motive in urging Him to go to Jerusalem, unless there was perhaps an undercurrent of feeling on their part that His presence there might bring an end to the affair which was apparently becoming a problem to His family.

The occasion at this time was the Feast of Tabernacles: a harvest festival, a time of thanksgiving to God for the blessings of the gathered harvest. Christ persuaded all the others to go without Him, and later He followed alone. Jesus was the chief topic of conversation at the feast, and people were asking where He was. When the celebrations were about half over, Jesus appeared in the Temple, preaching to the people. There was safety in the crowd, especially a divided crowd like this one. The people marveled at the wisdom of His teachings, to which He replied that anyone could prove the truth of His words by acting upon them. Obedience is the test of truth.

John tells us why the Jews did not take Him at this time: "because his hour was not yet come" (v. 30). Jesus was guarded by Deity and was working on a divine time schedule. The chief priests and the Pharisees even sent officers to arrest Him, but they returned with only one very unusual excuse to offer for their failure: "Never man so spake" (v. 46). Jesus would not subscribe to their dogmas, and they sought to destroy Him. It was not dogma He offered them, but truth; not creeds, but life. "If any man thirst, let him come unto me and drink. He that believeth on me, as the scripture hath said, from within him shall flow rivers of living water" (vv. 37-38). John tells us that this promise was to be made real at the subsequent giving of the Holy Spirit. Faith in Christ during His lifetime could be but an incomplete experience because the work He came to do was not finished until He had died on the cross, risen, and ascended to the Father, and the Holy Spirit was given in His stead. This is inherent in the teachings of Jesus at this time (vv. 32-39).

2. The Adulterous Woman (8:1-11) [2]

Realizing their inability to take Jesus by force, the Pharisees resorted to trickery, seeking to involve Him with some phase of the Law. Bringing a woman caught in an act of im-

---

[2] This passage is not found at this place in the two oldest Greek manuscripts, and in some it is found in Luke. So it is commonly thought it may not have been a part of the original Gospel of John. However, it is generally held to be a true incident in the life of Christ.

morality, they asked Jesus to judge concerning her in the light of the law of Moses, which said she should be stoned. If He agreed, they would demand that He rule all His actions by the Law. If not, they would condemn Him for opposing the Law, which was God-given. But, as usual, Jesus took a position neither for nor against the Law. First of all, He stooped and made marks in the dust, delaying His answer and inciting them to more heated demands. This was perhaps a device of Jesus by which He led them into false hopes in their attempts to catch Him. They were assuring themselves by their oft-repeated questioning, when Jesus turned the tables with one sweeping statement: "He that is without sin among you, let him first cast a stone at her" (v. 7). In utter defeat and frustration—for He had thus condemned them all—they slipped quietly away, still observing the details of the Law, as the elder preceded the younger of the group. Jesus resumed His doodling in the dust with perhaps a twinkle in His eye; yet how He must have yearned for them to acknowledge the truth and share with the woman His final verdict, "Neither do I condemn thee: go thy way; from henceforth sin no more" (v. 11)!

3. Jesus, the Light of the World (8:12-59)

Jesus' teachings at this time must be understood against the background of the Jewish situation politically and religiously. He was now teaching at Jerusalem—the very center of Judaism—and in the hearing of the religious leaders of the day. The Pharisees, Sadducees, and all other groups were represented there, and so we find Jesus speaking, not in parables of home and business and common themes, as in the Synoptics, but giving lengthy discourses on themes which transcend everyday life and have for their topic the person of Christ and His relation to God. Each group found reason for opposing Him, and their mutual hatred made companions in persecution of those who were enemies before. "It was the one great fact of a spiritual movement in the midst of them, the one great fact of a supremely spiritual personality among them, the one great fact of an absolutely spiritual claim before them that broke in upon the dream of their political ideals, that smote the indifference of their materialism, that crushed the self-conceit of their ceremonialism, and brought them all to realize that if the Galilean won His way their day of power and life was gone."[3]

The picture presented is that of God's chosen people hoping and looking for their promised Messiah, but blindly seeking to kill Him when He came to them. No wonder Jesus cried out against that darkness, "I am the light of the world" (9: 5). He had offered them bread, and drink, and light, and life, and they knew only to argue and take stones to throw at Him. Perhaps their rage was the more vehement because they did comprehend in a measure what He had said. They were condemned, not for lack of comprehension, but for lack of faith.

4. The Man Born Blind (c. 9)

Next there follows the story of the healing of the man who had been born blind. It is a beautiful illustration of Jesus, the Light of the World. After being healed, the man immediately became the center of an investigation. The people were divided in their opinion of the validity of his claim until his parents identified him and confirmed the fact of his earlier blindness. The parents refused to become involved, and the issue quickly shifted to the one who had performed the miracle. The man had not learned the stranger's name, but continued to persist in his claim that he was a good man. For this he was excommunicated from the Temple.

Behind the scenes the Jewish authorities were trying to learn for certain that it was Jesus and to use the incident as evidence to condemn Him, because He had made the cure on the Sabbath. Then Jesus came and identified himself to the man, who responded with a hearty, "Lord, I believe" (v. 38). Jesus warmed up to this man, who stood out in such contrast to most of the people, and confided in him the secret of those strange events. His physical sight was symbolic of the spiritual sight which He came to give. Those who had refused to believe were gradually losing what powers of spiritual sight they did possess. Herein lies the great truth of this miracle—the light is offered to all, but those who have never heard the truth of the gospel are often more susceptible than those who have heard and rejected it.

[3] *Addresses on the Gospel of St. John* (Printed and circulated by the St. John Conference Committee, Providence, R.I., 1905), p. 63.

5. *T*

disco
tinua
is un
the s
really
heale
were
revea
to ca

a do
herd
some
by th
the
shee
spee
Con
shep
shee
them
Or
tinu
shee
a re
who
beca
lowi
that
agai

6. F

ever
afte
tion.
Tem
Epip
it w

eclare specifically whe
ver may reveal the re
ye believe not: the w
e bear witness of me"
uestioning to their unl
to their desire to kill
se they were not His
n though they were Jev
m of identity with Goo
n, but He left them, t
n as before, and went
re He stayed for four
o at Bethany (11:1) an

The Raising of Lazarus

The miracles recorded
e simple turning of wat
dead man. This miracl
hrist's teaching about hi
ates His saying, "I am th
ohn began this great em
irth and closed it with an
oes not mention compass
s do the Synoptic write
xisting between Him and

Bethany was about
at the Mount of Olives (M
slope, a small village me
chiefly in connection wi
Christ's life on earth. Th
home to the Master, and
close friendships, aside fr
us some insight into the
was also human with the
during those troublesom
drawn to His friends. Joh
who anointed Christ with
her hair (John 12:1-5). M
give the account of the
wiping of His feet. The
cannot be a reference to

her or not He was the Christ. His
son for their asking. "I told you,
rks that I do in my Father's name,
(v. 25). He attributed their need
lief, and their reason for question-
Him. They did not know Him be-
eep; neither did they know God,
. A brief reiteration of His former
brought on more attempts to take
at same divine dignity protecting
ross into the land beyond Jordan.
onths, spending some of this time
at Ephraim (11:54).

11:1-54)

by John have moved in kind from
into wine to the raising to life of
stands by itself as the climax of
self as the Giver of life. It illus-
resurrection, and the life" (v. 25).
asis with the teaching of the new
ct of resurrection. As a rule, John
n as a motive for Christ's miracles,
, but in this case the great love
he Bethany household is primary.
o miles from Jerusalem (v. 18)
t. 21:1; Luke 19:29) on its eastern
oned few times in Scripture and
events in the last few days of
Bethany household was a second
is account shows one of His few
n that with the twelve, and gives
son of Christ. Though divine, He
tural yearning for fellowship; and
closing days He was particularly
tells us that Mary was the woman
intment and wiped His feet with
k (14:3-9) and Matthew (26:6-13)
ointing, but do not mention the
milar account in Luke (7:36-50)
e same event because it is placed

earlier in the ministry of Jesus and takes place in the home of a Pharisee, apparently in Galilee rather than in Judea; and the woman is called a sinner, which does not fit what we know about Mary of Bethany.

The fellowship was mutual, for when Lazarus became ill, the sisters sent for Jesus. Against the protest of His disciples (v. 8) He answered the summons, because He knew that by God's reckoning nothing could befall Him until He had completed His work. The words of the sisters, "Lord, if thou hadst been here, my brother had not died," (vv. 21, 32) reveal not only the sorrow of both Martha and Mary over the death of their brother, but constituted a rebuke to Jesus for His two-day delay in coming. He was very much troubled that they should question His friendship for them and wept—both for His own sorrow and for theirs.

When Jesus asked where the body of Lazarus was, He revealed a curious mingling of human limitation with divine foreknowledge. His power to discern without being instructed was not always in evidence, seeming to be used by our Lord only on special occasions and for specific purposes. Amidst the questioning of the people present, Jesus turned His attention to Lazarus, and after a brief prayer cried, "Lazarus, come forth" (v. 43). And Lazarus arose. How quickly all doubt must have vanished, and how gloriously did Jesus demonstrate His claim that He had come to be the great Life-Giver!

No longer could anyone present deny Jesus' claim to powers normally attributed to God. Some believed on Him, but the chief priests and the Pharisees had been convinced against their will and were of no mind to change. One of their number, Caiaphas, saw what was transpiring. Rebuking his colleagues for their ignorance, he told them that their nation would not be saved by a Messiah such as they in their traditional prejudice envisioned, but by One who would die for the people. John tells us that he spoke, not of his own accord, but by inspiration (v. 51). He must speak the truth as it came to him, even though he was unwilling within himself to accept it and take the consequences. His prophecy that Jesus should die thus became the great warning to the Jewish leaders that they were about to destroy their own Messiah. God is faithful and will not allow anyone to proceed to his own destruction unwarned. But "from that day forth they took counsel that they might put them to death" (v. 53). Jesus soon retired with His disciples to the city of Ephraim, to avoid the Jews. He was waiting His time.

8. Last Public Ministry at and near Jerusalem (11:55—12:50)

This portion of the Gospel of John comes at the very close of the above-mentioned four-month period and brings us to the spring of the year, probably in April at the close of the week preceding Passion Week. We have seen that Jesus raised Lazarus during this period, but what else occupied His time John does not say. The Synoptic account fills in this gap with what is known as the "Later Perean Ministry."

a. The Anointing at Bethany (12:1-11). The third Passover of Christ's public ministry drew near. Again attention began to focus upon Him in Jerusalem as people began to speculate whether or not He would come to the feast, especially since the Pharisees had asked for public support in their endeavor to catch Him (11:57). Their organization was now perfected, and their nets were out. Six days before the Passover, Jesus and His disciples came to Bethany, where a special supper was given in His honor, probably at the home of Simon the Leper (Mark 14:3), with the Lazarus household cooperating, for Martha served and Mary was there.

Mary, the most spiritually-minded one of the family, took a jar of costly ointment noted for its high fragrance—worth about fifty dollars by some calculations—and anointed the feet of Jesus (apparently in addition to His head as recorded in Mark, and a greater evidence of her devotion), wiping them with her hair. We need to use Mark's account to learn that she did this in anticipation of His soon-coming death, and that perhaps Jesus' remark meant that she be allowed to use the remaining portion for His burial rather than to sell it and give the money to the poor as Judas suggested. Mary thus revealed a spiritual insight shared by very few at that time. This is the first intimation from anything Judas had done that he was different essentially from the other disciples. His interest in the poor was a camouflage. He wanted the money put into the treasury which he controlled, and from which he had been helping himself, for "he was a thief" (12:6). John fails to tell us that Judas went immediately to the high priest and negotiated the agreement to betray Jesus.

b. *The Triumphal Entry* (12:12-19). The chief priests were seeking to put Lazarus to death because his fame was drawing the people, and many were believing on Jesus. Their attempts to take Jesus were being thwarted by public opinion. Thus a great crowd was on hand when Jesus started for Jerusalem the next day. Insofar as they were able, the crowd gave Him the honor designed for royalty, placing palm branches in His path and shouting, "Hosanna [save we pray]: Blessed is he that cometh in the name of the Lord, even the King of Israel" (v. 13). His enemies could do nothing, and they knew it. He sadly disappointed the multitude, for He took no advantage of their popular enthusiasm to set himself up in power. He knew what they did not know—that He was to be the Suffering Servant as well as the Messiah King. His entry was triumphal in the sense that it was a sign of His kingship. It was prophetic of His reign over the hearts of His true followers and also prophetic of that day when it shall be proclaimed, "The kingdom of the world is become the kingdom of our Lord, and of his Christ: and he shall reign for ever and ever" (Rev. 11:15).

c. *Sir, We Would See Jesus* (12:20-43). John omits the second cleansing of the Temple as found in the Synoptics and adds the story of some Greeks who desire to see Jesus. The disciples bring them and He receives them, but He has no time or thought for questions they may want to ask. He is altogether absorbed. "Except a grain of wheat fall into the earth and die, . . . ," He says and continues in allegorical fashion, describing His own present humiliation and coming death, and at the same time giving the secret formula for citizenship in His kingdom. To lose oneself in Christ is the one sure way of saving oneself for eternity.

There followed a brief experience, framed in the atmosphere of the Gethsemane agony, where Christ seemed to lose himself from the crowd and hold converse with the Father. "Father, save me from this hour. But for this cause came I unto this hour. Father, glorify thy name." And then the voice from the other world: "I have both glorified it, and will glorify it again" (vv. 27-28). This was the assurance He needed and received in that dark hour. It was a voice from heaven to the crowd, confirming Christ's own words. "While ye have the light, believe on the light, that ye may become sons of light," (v. 36) were His parting words to them. These are almost His last words to the gathered throng. He soon left them, some believing, some doubting. Even those who believed were afraid to acknowledge it openly for fear of the Pharisees, "for they loved the glory that is of men more than the glory that is of God" (v. 43).

d. *Christ's Last Message to the World* (12:44-50). The closing verses of chapter twelve are the concluding words of Jesus' public ministry. They were spoken to the crowd, yet not to the crowd directly. More like an echo of His previous teachings and weighted with all the passion of His soul, "Jesus cried and said, He that believeth on me, believeth not on me, but on him that sent me" (v. 44). The words that follow need but to be read to be understood.

IV. Jesus and His Disciples (cc. 13—17)

1. The Last Supper (13:1-20)

With the knowledge of His imminent death heavy upon Him, Christ's heart went out in love to His little band of disciples. On the evening before the Passover, He and His disciples sat down to their last meal together. After the meal was finished, Jesus began to prepare the way to give them His parting message. Some preparation was necessary because their hearts were proud—and there were both a traitor and a denier among them. Humility and faith must be strong within them if they were to face the coming storm successfully. The first lesson came in the form of an acted parable— Jesus washed His disciples' feet. But it was more; it was a living example of the character of Christ himself, true to what they had known Him to be during their years together. "I have given you an example, that ye also should do as I have done to you" (v. 15). They must be able to stoop to the necessary tasks of life and bend under their weight, or break beneath them.

2. The Betrayer Revealed (13:21-30)

Following this, in great anguish of spirit Jesus revealed the traitor to the group. Judas' hour had also come. He had already bargained to sell his Lord. He was now one of the

disciples in name only. The words of encouragement which
Jesus had for the beloved little flock were not for his ears.
He must be dismissed. "Verily, verily, I say unto you, that
one of you shall betray me" (v. 21). "Lord, who is it?" said
one of them. Jesus pointed to Judas by giving him a morsel
of food, and John tells us that Satan entered into him about
that time. He immediately arose and went out. But Jesus
mourned for Judas. In His closing prayer a few hours later,
He made a sad reference to Judas, and later still at the Garden
of Gethsemane, Jesus gave him a chance to repent (18:8).

3. Peter's Denial Foretold (13:31-38)

To the astonished group Jesus sought to reveal the true
meaning of what was going on. He broke the news gently by
saying that He was going to leave them in order to be glorified. They could not come, but were to remain behind in a
fellowship of love. If ever Peter spoke without really thinking, it was now. "Lord, why cannot I follow thee even now?
I will lay down my life for thee" (v. 37). But Jesus answered
him, "Wilt thou lay down thy life for me? Verily, verily, I
say unto thee, The cock shall not crow, till thou hast denied
me thrice" (v. 38). First the betrayer is dismissed, and now
a denier is revealed.

Chapter fourteen might be called table-talk since it is in
reality a continuation of the conversation between Jesus and
the eleven disciples as they sat at the table. When they finally
arose to go (14:31), they became silent while Jesus continued
to speak in more extended and lofty tones (cc. 15—17). In all
three chapters He spoke of the highest and most intimate relationships of the Christian life, and from those closing hours
of conversation John has recorded for posterity a veritable
treasure chest of divine truth.

4. The Way, the Truth, and the Life (14:1-7)

Jesus is the Way for going, the Truth for knowing, and
the Life for growing. He is the Way to God the Father, the
Truth from God the Father, and the Life of God the Father.
He is the Way to God now, the Truth from God eternally, and
the Life of God everlasting. To know Christ is to know God,
and to know Him here is the guarantee of knowing Him in
the house of many mansions.

5. *Christ and the Father Are One* (14:8-17)

Many times previous to this Jesus had testified to doing the will of His Father. Now He claims identity with God the Father—"He that hath seen me hath seen the Father" (v. 9). At least three things should have convinced the disciples of this fact. First was His presence with them. Could anyone be in His presence so long and not know who He was? Second, the words which He spoke to them were not His own, but the Father's, freighted with divine truth. And third, the miracles were witness to His divinity. None of these by itself was proof positive; altogether they gave an ample ground for faith.

6. *I Go Away; I Come unto You* (14:18-31)

The thought of His leaving them brought sorrow to their hearts. Now He says, "I come unto you" (v. 18). Later, speaking of the Father, He says, "We will come unto him, and make our abode with him" (v. 23). And again, "I will pray the Father, and he shall give you another Comforter" (v. 16). Christ will come; He and the Father will come; They will send the Comforter. Which does He mean? The blessed unity of Father and Son is extended to include the Holy Spirit (v. 26). In Him both the Father and the Son will be ever present with those who love and serve Him. And when the Spirit is come, not to the world, but to the believers, He will reveal to them the fact of Christ's oneness with the Father, of which they were now in doubt. All the things which Christ had taught will be brought to their memories and understanding. And the Spirit in coming will bring peace, the peace that Christ himself was then manifesting in the face of impending death. And it is not for their sakes alone that all this will happen, but that the world may also know. Whether or not the world believes and accepts, the objective truth of God's great plan of redemption has been manifested in Christ and will be perpetuated by the Holy Spirit.

7. *The Vine and the Branches* (15:1-16)

Christ's talk with His disciples could very well have ended here, for at this point He said, "Arise, let us go hence" (14:31). But all were loath to leave, Jesus no less than the rest. It was a moving scene as they lingered, the disciples listening as Jesus continued to talk. The darkness of doubt and misunderstanding was still upon them, and He longed to dispel it. Still holding out the light of truth, He gave them the allegory of the vine and the branches, which illustrates the unity which must exist between himself and His disciples. They are dependent the one upon the other: they, for life; He, for fruit. The relationship is a relationship of life—"for apart from me ye can do nothing" (v. 5). He also implies that apart from them He can do nothing more to save the world. Fruit-bearing branches are pruned and dressed and made to produce more fruit. Fruitless branches will be destroyed. Only the fruit-bearing life is a joyful life.

This life of discipleship is also a relationship of love— both with Christ and with other disciples. "This is my commandment, that ye love one another, even as I have loved you" (v. 12). They already knew what it was to love, for at least some of them were family men. But Christ gave them a new standard of love—"as I have loved you." To this high state He has called them—to be His friends and to bear fruit —with the guarantee that the Father through the Holy Spirit would constantly supply their need, "that whatsoever ye shall ask of the Father in my name, he may give it you" (v. 16).

8. No Fellowship with the World (15:17-27)

In this section Jesus is shown pointing out the fundamental difference between His disciples and the world system of evil men. The followers of that system hate the followers of Christ because they hate Him, and in hating Christ they hate the Father too. Their hatred, expressed in unbelief and persecution, is assured because Christ, the Light of the World, came and revealed sin. When that light is received, the individual is transferred from the realm of darkness to the realm of light. When that light is rejected, the darkness of the individual becomes more intense; and sin increases, along with the added responsibility for sin. In the face of these prospects Jesus again promises the Holy Spirit, the Spirit of truth, whom the Father will send to testify of Christ (v. 26).

9. The Promise of Persecution (16:1-6)

The promise of persecution—yea, even death—was no pleasant prospect. But Christ was now preparing them for it, by precept, and soon by example. He was near the Cross and He knew it. They too would have their crosses to bear and suffer. But again He promised them the one great sustaining force. The coming of the Spirit would be even better than if He himself stayed with them.

10. The Comforter (16: 7-33)

Up to this time the security of the disciples had rested upon Christ and His presence with them. Soon He would not be with them, and they would be scattered as sheep without a shepherd. He could not tell them everything they needed to know because they were unable to bear it. He could not speak of the Cross directly, nor of its meaning to the world. But again He falls back in dependence upon the Holy Spirit. If He could stir in them an expectant faith in the coming of the Spirit, He could feel that they were secure. "I have yet many things to say unto you, but ye cannot bear them now. Howbeit when he, the Spirit of truth, is come, he shall guide you into all the truth: for he shall not speak from himself; but what things soever he shall hear, these shall he speak: and he shall declare unto you the things that are to come" (vv. 12-13).

Let us look briefly at what Jesus has taught concerning the Holy Spirit in this great discourse. He is the Spirit of truth (14:17; 16:13). He will come to Christ's followers in response to their obedience (14:16). Christ will ask the Father to send Him (14:16). He is another Comforter, Christ himself also being an Advocate, or Comforter (I John 2:2). The Father will send Him in Christ's name (14:26). He will remind the disciples of what Christ taught and will make the truth plain to them (14:26; 16:13). Christ will send Him after He himself goes away (16:7). He will be a convicting force in the world of men (16:8-11). This work of convicting or convincing is with a view toward winning them to Christ. In doing these things He will glorify Christ (16:14). This, of course, is a limited concept of the person and work of the Spirit compared to the complete picture in the New Testament. But there are here resident many great truths which were in time made plain by the Spirit. We find them in the writings of Paul and others, as well as in the individual hearts of believers.

11. Christ's High Priestly Prayer (c. 17)

This is universally recognized as the great high priestly prayer of our Lord and was uttered at the close of His ministry, only a few hours before His death. John alone records this prayer, and, in contrast to Christ's prayer in Gethsemane recorded in the Synoptics, where Jesus falls on His face, here He lifts His eyes to heaven. There is nothing of despondency or gloom in this prayer; all is triumph and trust. He knows where He is going and goes forward unhesitatingly. Previously He had said, "No one taketh it [My life] away from me, but I lay it down of myself" (10:18). Melanchthon, the reformer, said of it, "There is no voice that has ever been heard, either in heaven or in earth, more exalted, more holy, more fruitful, more sublime, than this prayer offered up by the Son of God Himself."[4]

The prayer divides itself naturally into three parts. The first part is for himself (vv. 1-5). The second is for His disciples (vv. 6-19). The third is for the whole Church (vv. 20-26).

a. *For Himself* (vv. 1-5). With the true intimacy of sonship Jesus addressed the Father. He reported that He had now finished the work assigned Him on earth and had thereby given glory to His Father, and then asked for the return of that glory which He had with the Father previous to the Incarnation. He knew that He had been following the divine time schedule and that the clock would soon strike the final hour. In a few hours He would place himself in a favorable position to be arrested, and His work of redemption would be completed on the cross. As a result men could have eternal life.

b. *For the Disciples* (vv. 6-19). To Jesus, His disciples were His in a very peculiar way, given Him by the Father. He was proud of them (v. 10), not as slaves, but as friends (15:15). To them He had revealed the name and true nature of God (v. 6). He had given them the truth about God (v. 14) and the messages received from God (v. 8). They had received them and believed in His deity, even though they had fallen far short of full comprehension of it. While He was with them He had kept all of them but Judas Iscariot (v. 12), but now that He must leave them He prayed for them a threefold prayer. This should be associated with His earlier promise of the giving of the Holy Spirit, and it is not too much to say that the coming of the Spirit would accomplish that for which He now prayed.

[4] Marcus Dods in *Expositor's Bible, John,* II, 248.

He first of all prayed for oneness among them. The standard He set was high—"That they may be one, even as we are" —even as He had earlier exhorted them to love as He loved (15:12). It was union with Christ and unity with one another—a spiritual unity akin to that between the Father and the Son.

He also prayed that they might be kept from the evil of the world. The disciples of Christ are to live above evil even while they must live in the midst of it. Seclusion from life is not the way to be a Christian, neither is death necessary to the cleansing from sin. Christ's prayer was for the here and now. His own can be kept from the evil of the world, for, in fact, they do not belong to the world.

Then He prayed that they might be sanctified. First Christ prayed, "Sanctify them in the truth," and then, "I sanctify myself." The word translated "sanctify"—the same verb being used in both instances—has a breadth of meaning; sometimes it is used in a limited sense, while at other times it is used in its complete sense. The meaning must be determined from the context.

In 10:36 Jesus spoke of being sanctified by the Father and sent into the world. This assuredly means that He was dedicated to the work of redemption. Here He speaks of sanctifying himself, the meaning being that, whereas the Father had earlier given Him to this task, He was now willingly devoting himself to it. This idea of dedication or consecration is the primary meaning of the word, and it could not be made to denote more when applied to Jesus.

For the disciples it had this significance—and more. They had been chosen by God and given to Christ (v. 6) and now in a new sense were being consecrated to the task of representing their Master in the world. Moreover, this consecration was incomplete unless they, like Christ, made it their own wholehearted choice. In addition it was still necessary—and this, too, is inherent in the word—to be made fit for the task. Consecration to God and His service has always included the idea of fitness—of moral rectitude. The lamb on the Jewish altar was without spot or blemish. The lips of the prophet Isaiah were purged before he was sent to prophesy. Moral fitness must always accompany the commission for service. So

Jesus prayed that, as the disciples were to be sent into the world as His witnesses, they should be made ready. Thus for the disciples the word sanctify is used in its fullest sense. They were to be cleansed from all sin that they might be fit to be dedicated to His service.

c. *For the Church* (vv. 20-26). The news now comes that this prayer was not for the twelve alone, but "for them also that believe on me through their word" (v. 20). This last portion of the prayer does not differ materially from what has gone before, but it does strengthen it. The unity becomes "I in them, and thou in me" (v. 23). The unity of Christ's disciples will be the great convincing testimony to the world. And while they have been the recipients of His glory here, both by observation and by experience, He prays that they may one day be with Him to behold His restored glory, and we can be assured that this prayer for all those who have been sanctified through the truth will be answered by the Father.

V. The Passion (cc. 18—19)

1. The Betrayal (18:1-11)

Immediately following this great benediction, Jesus and the eleven left the upper room and made their way out of the city of Jerusalem and across the Kidron Valley to the western slope of the Mount of Olives, "where was a garden." This was the Gethsemane of which the Synoptics tell. John tells nothing of Jesus' agony there, but takes up the story where He came out of the garden to meet Judas, who had brought the band of soldiers and officers armed "with lanterns and torches and weapons" (v. 3). The hour had come, and Jesus stepped out to meet His destiny.

2. The Arrest and Trial (18:12—19:16)

The actual arrest was comparatively simple. Jesus gave himself up; there was no struggle. They took Him, tied His hands together, and led Him to Annas, high priest emeritus, at the home of Caiaphas, his son-in-law and high priest. Annas was an old man with great prestige and influence and "was the virtual, though not the formal, head of the Sanhedrin."[5] He asked Jesus a few questions and turned Him over to Caiaphas, the president of the Sanhedrin. John does not go into all the details of the trial. During this phase of it an officer

[5] J. Stalker, *Life of Christ*, p. 128.

struck Jesus because he did not like an answer He gave to a question. Peter was there, just outside the door of the high priest's court, and then it was that he denied ever having known Jesus.

The Sanhedrin was the ruling body of the Jews and exercised civil jurisdiction over all Judean communities. Its origin is somewhat in doubt. It consisted of seventy-one members who elected their own successors, and was made up largely of Sadducees with some Pharisees. The other Gospel writers tell of the indignity heaped upon Jesus by this ecclesiastical group. With no witnesses for the defense and no interest in justice, their rage knew no bounds when at last they had this Man in their power. They would have killed Him themselves, but they feared the people and the Roman authorities. Any sentence of death passed by them had to be ratified by Pilate, and that is why they soon hurried Him to the Praetorium, the palace of Herod the Great, where Pilate was.

So the Prisoner was taken to Pilate, the Roman governor. He had become procurator of Judea in A.D. 26. He hated the Jews and was in constant conflict with them. By this time the fate of Jesus had already been determined by the Sanhedrin, which had met at the home of Caiaphas. The explanation of their being together at that early hour is that they expected Jesus to be brought and were waiting for Him, endeavoring to have the trial finished and the verdict settled before the populace was around in the morning.

The only accusation brought against Jesus was that He was an evildoer, and Pilate refused to have anything to do with the case until the Jews told him that a death sentence was involved. The proceedings which followed were not so much a trial as a struggle for power between Pilate and the Jewish leaders, with Jesus in the middle.

The story of this part of the trial as John gives it is straightforward and graphic. Pilate had to meet the Jews outside the Gentile hall of judgment, lest they defile themselves by entering. Three times he interviewed Jesus within the hall, and three times he sought to release Him. Perhaps in irritation and certainly in an attempt to placate the Jews, he had Jesus scourged and sat by while soldiers crowned Him with thorns and mocked and abused Him. He weakened his position by thus punishing One whom he had declared innocent, and when Jesus was brought out again, the passions of the crowd were aroused and they began to cry, "Crucify him, crucify him!" Pilate heard someone say that Jesus claimed to be the Son of God, and his acquaintance with Greek mythology may have caused him to believe at least the possibility of a son of one of the gods coming to earth. For this reason he again questioned Jesus, "Whence art thou?" to which he received no answer. Then he challenged Him, "Knowest thou not that I have power to release thee, and have power to crucify thee?" to which Jesus replied, "Thou wouldest have no power against me, except it were given thee from above." Pilate got his answer. Maybe this Man was after all what He claimed to be. We can only imagine his consternation as he went before the Jews again, determined to set Jesus free. He was laboring against tremendous odds. But soon he went down beneath their last great pressure, "If thou release this man, thou art not Caesar's friend: every one that maketh himself a king speaketh against Caesar." He had fought a losing battle. Hurling a last few futile taunts at them—"Behold, your King!" and "Shall I crucify your King?"—he gave Jesus over to be crucified. In one last thrust he ordered to be placed over the cross a sign which said, "JESUS OF NAZARETH, THE KING OF THE JEWS." Pilate was weak as well as wicked. It would have taken a stronger man than he to save Jesus and at the same time save his own position. Since he could not do both, he chose the latter.

3. The Crucifixion (19:17-30)

Again we find John leaving out of his account some details of this tragic event. He mentions that two others were also crucified with Jesus; that the soldiers cast lots for His seamless robe; that four women—Mary, His mother; her sister; Mary, the wife of Clopas; and Mary Magdalene—were at the cross; and that He was given "sour wine" in answer to an appeal for something to drink. John's abbreviated account is not that of one who did not know the facts, but of one who was too deeply moved by the remembrance of those facts to dwell upon them at length. For John too was at the cross. As he was helpless to interfere, only a strong faith could have sustained him. He does not say that Jesus died, but that "he bowed his head, and gave up his spirit" (v. 30). God's clock

had struck the appointed hour, and John was there. Some of
Jesus' last words were spoken to him and Mary: "Woman,
behold, thy son! . . . Behold, thy mother!" And "from that hour
the disciple took her unto his own home" (vv. 26-27).

4. *The Aftermath* (19:31-42)

Lest their Sabbath be defiled by the dead bodies, the
Jewish leaders requested Pilate to remove them. The soldiers
did not break the legs of Jesus, as was the custom in such
cases, because they found Him already dead. The phenomenon
"there came out blood and water" has had many and varied
explanations. Christ seems to have died before the natural
causes of death could accomplish their purpose; and, if so,
John is saying that the blood and water are evidences of the
supernaturalness of Christ's death. His cry, "It is finished,"
bears this out to an extent—it being, not the last gasp of a
spent life, but the triumphant cry of One who had come to
do the Father's will and now knew that it was accomplished.

At this time two secret disciples come on the scene—
Joseph of Arimathaea and Nicodemus. Joseph asked for and
obtained the body, and Nicodemus assisted with spices for the
burial. Together they wrapped the body in linen with the
spices, "as the custom of the Jews is to bury," and put it in
an unused tomb in the garden nearby.

VI. The Resurrection (c. 20)

1. *The Empty Tomb* (20:1-18)

The shadows have fallen. The crowd has dispersed. The
members of the Sanhedrin have gone about their preparations
for the Passover celebration after having disposed of their
tormentor. Judas had preceded his Lord in death by a few
hours. The disciples were secreted by themselves, waiting
what might befall them next. The third morning came, but
still they waited. But Mary Magdalene was at the tomb before the sun had risen. Finding it open and not daring to look
in, she hurried away and brought Peter and John, who went
in but found no body. John says that they saw and believed
and returned home. Mary also wished to see her Lord and
lingered at the tomb, weeping. She could not share the ready
faith of Peter and John. Seeing first two angels, to whom
she voiced her lament, she then turned and saw Jesus behind
her, but did not recognize Him. Doubtless her own disturbed

emotions and tear-dimmed eyes made recognition difficult. The early morning with its dim light may have been a factor. Also, Jesus in His resurrected form may have given a somewhat different appearance. Perhaps an element of faith was necessary in order to recognize the risen Lord, for nowhere is it stated that others than believers ever saw Him after the Resurrection. To her anguished question He had but one word, "Mary." It was a transforming word and drew quickly from her the answer, "Rabboni; which is to say, Teacher."

2. Jesus Appears to the Disciples (20:19-31)

This miraculous appearance of Jesus through closed doors is meant by John to confirm the Resurrection and to give a minor description—if not a definition—of what a resurrected body is like. It could be seen and touched, and could speak as a normal man, but was not circumscribed by the restrictions of time and space. Jesus' coming to them had a threefold purpose: to confirm their faith, to commission them to carry on His work, and to bestow upon them the Holy Spirit. The first was accomplished by His very presence. The second was based upon His own commission from the Father. In one sense Jesus had fulfilled it, but in a greater sense it was still in progress, and they were to take up where He was leaving it. "Take Him" is what is literally meant in verse twenty-two. "There was therefore a Paschal as distinct from a Pentecostal gift of the Holy Spirit, the one preparatory to the other. It should be noticed that 'Holy Spirit' is without the definite article in the Greek, and this seems to imply that the gift is not made in all its fullness."[6]

Eight days later Jesus again appeared to the eleven (for Thomas was now present) in the same manner as before. Thomas had previously declared his unwillingness to believe in the Resurrection without some tangible evidence. Jesus turned to him and said, "Reach hither thy finger, and see my hands; and reach hither thy hand, and put it into my side: and be not faithless, but believing" (v. 27). That was more than Thomas had asked for, and his response was immediate and wholehearted: "My Lord and my God."

Here is the grand climax to this great Gospel. After all the many testimonies to Jesus down through the years with

[6] *Cambridge Bible*, p. 362.

Thomas as witness to most of them, he still doubted. But we do both John and Thomas a disservice when we label him a doubter. Rather he is the doubter who believed. Faith is the great truth here. In masterly style John has concluded his thesis of proving that Jesus is the Son of God. The Resurrection is the last piece of evidence to conclude his case.

VII. The Epilogue (c. 21)

1. The Risen Lord (21:1-14)

Chapter twenty-one comes as a supplement, written in the style and language of the rest of the Gospel and probably added by John himself before the work was given to the public.

This chapter serves historically as a prelude to the Book of Acts, in the first part of which Peter and John are prominent. In it a few of the disciples seem to have rallied around these two, making seven in all. They had gone to Galilee, and Peter suggested that they go fishing. While some have depicted these men as defeated and going back to their original occupation, let us be reminded that they were believing disciples who had seen their risen Lord and were in Galilee waiting further orders from Him (Matt. 28:7; Mark 16:7). It is all to their credit that they were gainfully employed while they waited.

As was the custom, they fished at night; but they caught nothing. In the early dawn they saw a Man on shore who inquired of their success and suggested that they put their nets down on the right side of the boat, with the result that the net was filled. Then the characteristics of these two leading disciples came to the fore. "St. John is the first to apprehend; St. Peter the first to act."[7] John said, "It is the Lord." Peter sprang into the shallow water and waded to shore to meet Him. Shortly they all sat in His presence, eating that which He had prepared over a fire on the shore.

2. Jesus and Peter (21:15-24)

While this conversation took place between Christ and Peter, it could have occurred with any one of the disciples participating and was apparently meant for all. The atmosphere is the old, familiar one of pre-Crucifixion days. Jesus

[7] *Cambridge Bible*, p. 369.

probed Peter for a confession of his loyalty, at the same time revealing to Peter his inner heart as he could not have seen it himself. The theme was love.

Much has been written and preached on the two words here translated "love": the Greek *philein* and *agapan*. Suffice it to say that they do not mean human love as over against divine love, because both are used in various places in the New Testament for the love of both God and man. The difference is in the quality of love as determined by its object and the intent or purpose of that love. *Philein* is the weaker of the two, being essentially of an emotional or affectional nature. *Agapan* is of a volitional nature, "the love that makes distinctions, choosing its object and holding to it." The first is warmer; the latter is stronger.

Peter wished to be sure that Jesus was making the same demands of others as of him. Indicating John, he said, "Lord, and what shall this man do?" Jesus answered, "What is that to thee? follow thou me." And on this significant note John closes his Gospel.

C. CONCLUSION

John has written as an eyewitness whose reputation for accuracy had been unquestioned among those who knew him. He has chosen his material carefully and presented it well, and, to those who will accept his evidence, he has proved beyond a doubt that "Jesus is the Christ, the Son of God." He has also shown that faith in Christ has its reward: the new life which He imparts. He writes what he himself knows.

To John knowledge is more than intellectual comprehension—it is also experience. He himself knows, because he has experienced. His acquaintance with the Christ covered the length of Christ's early ministry—and more. He had had fellowship with the resurrected Christ for many years since that night he leaned on Jesus' bosom at the Last Supper. He had lived in His presence in a fellowship of love. More than any other writer John catches the spirit of Christ, until his Gospel is more than biography, and teaching, and history, and narration; it is also divine insight, the record of a man who wrote in the light that shone from the other world. By the help of the Holy Spirit he was enabled to give us the greatest portrait ever drawn of the Son of God, who walked this earth as Son of Man.

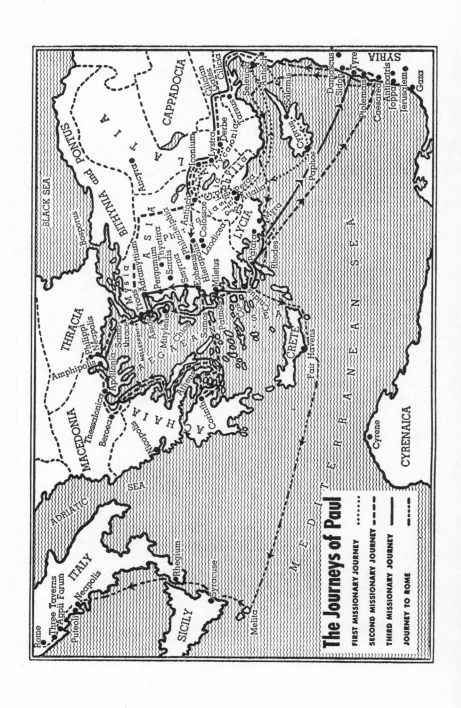

The Journeys of Paul

FIRST MISSIONARY JOURNEY ·········
SECOND MISSIONARY JOURNEY ‒ ‒ ‒
THIRD MISSIONARY JOURNEY ———
JOURNEY TO ROME ‒ · ‒ · ‒

ITALY
Rome
Three Taverns
Appii Forum
Puteoli
Neapolis
Rhegium
Syracuse
SICILY
Melita

ADRIATIC
SEA

MACEDONIA
Thessalonica
Beroea
Amphipolis
Neapolis
Philippi
THRACIA

ACHAIA
Corinth
Athens
Nicopolis

BLACK SEA

Bosporus

BITHYNIA and PONTUS

Ancyra

CAPPADOCIA

GALATIA

MYSIA
Troas
Thrace
Adramyttium
Assos
Pergamum
Thyatira
Sardis
Philadelphia
Smyrna
ASIA
Ephesus
Hierapolis
Laodicea
Colosse
Antioch
Iconium
Lystra
Derbe
LYCAONIA
PISIDIA
PAMPHYLIA
Perga
Attalia
Miletus
Samos
Mitylene
Chios
Patmos
Cos
Cnidus
Patara
Rhodes
Myra
LYCIA
Tarsus
CILICIA
Cilician Gates

CYPRUS
Salamis
Paphos

Seleucia
Antioch
SYRIA
Damascus
Sidon
Tyre
Ptolemais
Caesarea
Antipatris
Joppa
Jerusalem
Gaza

CRETE
Fair Havens

CYRENAICA
Cyrene

MEDITERRANEAN SEA

CHAPTER VIII
PENTECOST AND MISSIONS
(ACTS)

The Book of Acts is the first church history. It gives us the high lights in the story of Christianity from about A.D. 30-60; that is, during the first generation. Hence it is one of the most important documents in all literature. For the spread of Christianity has been the most significant movement in the last two thousand years.

A. INTRODUCTION

I. Authorship

Almost all New Testament scholars are agreed that the third Gospel and Acts were written by the same man. Early church tradition identifies this author as Luke, "the beloved physician" (Col. 4:14).

What do we know about him? Luke is mentioned by name only three times in the New Testament, all in Paul's Epistles (Philemon 24; Col. 4:14; II Tim. 4:11). These passages indicate that he was a companion of Paul. When we turn to the Book of Acts we find the author frequently speaking in the first person plural, indicating that he was traveling with Paul on his journeys.

These so-called "we-sections" begin at 16:10, showing that the author of Acts joined the missionary party at Troas on the second journey. The writer accompanied Paul to Philippi, but evidently remained there. For when the missionaries left Philippi for Thessalonica (17:1) the use of the third person is resumed.

But when Paul returned to Philippi on this third journey we find "us" and "we" occurring again (20:5-6). It would appear that Luke had remained there to pastor the new flock during the intervening half-dozen years (about A.D. 49-55). After that he apparently stayed rather close to Paul until the latter's death.

But why should we identify this companion as Luke? The answer is that of the companions of Paul mentioned by him in his Epistles only two prominent ones are unnamed in Acts:

227

Titus and Luke. When we arrive at this point in our reasoning we may let the very strong Early Church tradition settle the matter in favor of Luke.

We could wish that we knew more about this "beloved physician." He was evidently the very finest type of Christian gentleman, cultured, well-educated, widely traveled. He was large in both heart and mind. Very probably he and Lydia were responsible for the fact that the church at Philippi was the most thoughtful of Paul's needs, frequently sending him love offerings when others were forgetting him (Phil. 4:15-18). His companionship and medical care were doubtless a great comfort and blessing to the aging apostle in those days of strenuous activity and trying opposition.

II. Date

The Book of Acts closes with the account of Paul's imprisonment of two years at Rome (probably A.D. 59-61). The most natural conclusion would be that the book was written then. Was Paul condemned and executed at that time? If so, why does not the writer tell us? Was Paul released to make further journeys? Why, then, do we not have the account of them? No satisfactory answers have been given to these questions. So it seems best to assume that Luke chose to conclude his story with the climax of Paul's travels, his arrival at the capital of the Roman Empire. There are several hints that this was one goal that the great apostle had in mind,[1] taking in Rome on his way to Spain. The book, however, may not have been published until around A.D. 70.

III. Purpose

One purpose of the writing of Acts is suggested in the first verse. "The former treatise" clearly refers to the Gospel of Luke. This is acknowledged by all. In this earlier treatise he had recorded "all that Jesus began both to do and teach." The implication of *began* might be that in Acts he is going to give what Jesus *continued* to do and teach through His disciples.

But another purpose becomes apparent as one reads the account carefully. The Book of Acts is an apologetic for Christianity, written to show that though the Jews persecuted the new sect the Roman officials protected its propagators.

[1] See Acts 19:21; 23:11; Rom. 1:15; 15:23.

Over and over again—at Corinth, at Ephesus, at Jerusalem, at Caesarea—the Roman government gave protection to the preachers of the gospel.

In this connection we should note to whom the book is addressed. In Luke 1:3 he is called "most excellent Theophilus." This would suggest that he may have been a Roman official of high rank. That he was a convert to Christianity is probably indicated in Luke 1:4. The writer may have been hoping to reach the ear of the Roman government when he said, "O Theophilus."

It is universally agreed that the Book of Acts is the second volume of a two-volume history of the beginnings of Christianity. It bridges the gap between the Gospels and the Epistles. Without it we should find it very difficult to piece together the materials of Paul's Epistles into anything like a harmonious pattern. Acts gives us a very important, though incomplete, chronological framework for the history of the Christian Church during the first thirty years after the death of Christ in A.D. 30.

A word should be said about the title of the book. Acts does not give us "The Acts of the Apostles." Rather, it records some acts of some apostles—and several disciples. The oldest Greek manuscripts have simply "The Acts," which is a far more accurate title. Actually we find here "Acts of the Holy Spirit" in and through the Early Church.

B. CONTENTS

The key verse of Acts is 1:8. Here we find both the power and the program of Christianity. Its power: the Holy Spirit; its program: world evangelization.

We also find here the outline of the book:

    I. Witnessing in Jerusalem, cc. 1—7

   II. Witnessing in Judea and Samaria, cc. 8—12

  III. Witnessing in the Gentile World, cc. 13—28

The book also divides very naturally into two main sections. In chapters 1—12 Peter is the prominent figure; in chapters 13—28 Paul is the main character. One could also say that in the first twelve chapters we have a record of home missions while the rest of the book deals with foreign missions.

I. Witnessing in Jerusalem (cc. 1—7)

1. Introduction (c. 1)

The first chapter of the book is introductory. It gives the story of the ascension of Jesus and the choice of Matthias.

Luke is the only New Testament writer who records the Ascension. We find it in the last chapter of his Gospel and in the first chapter of Acts. In both places he includes the command of Christ to His disciples to tarry in Jerusalem until they received the Holy Spirit. Connected with the Ascension, in Acts, is the promise of His second coming.

After Jesus left them the disciples returned from the Mount of Olives to Jerusalem, "a sabbath day's journey" (v. 12)—about half a mile. There they gathered in an Upper Room where the eleven apostles were staying. It is interesting to note that several women, including Mary, the mother of Jesus, were there. Also present were "his brethren." Formerly they had not believed in Him (John 7:5). But it is comforting to know that they had now joined the group of believers who were waiting for the coming of the Holy Spirit. Altogether 120 waited in the Upper Room (v. 15).

How long did they wait? Ten days, you say. We derive that figure from the fact that the feast of Pentecost came fifty days after the Passover. Jesus was crucified at the time of the Passover feast. Acts 1:3 tells us that His post-Resurrection appearances continued for forty days. Subtracting, we assume ten days for the period of waiting in the Upper Room. Probably "a week or ten days" would be more accurate, since the exact length of time from the Resurrection (two or three days after the Passover) to the feast of Pentecost would be difficult to determine. Then, too, we are told in Luke 24:53 that after the Ascension the disciples "were continually in the temple."

One item of business was taken care of during that period. Peter, still the main spokesman for the twelve, called for an election to fill the place in the apostolic circle made vacant by the defection of Judas Iscariot. The group chose two candidates and then prayed for God to show which of the two was His choice. Matthias was elected. But we hear no more of him.

2. Pentecost (c. 2)

The most important event in the Book of Acts is Pentecost. About that there can be no question. For if there had been no Pentecost there would have been no book to write. It is the acts of Spirit-filled men that we find recorded here.

Pentecost is the New Testament name for what is called the Feast of Weeks in the Old Testament. It is described in Lev. 23:15-21 and Deut. 16:9-12. The feast was held fifty days after the waving of the first fruits, which prefigured the resurrection of Jesus. Hence its Greek name, "Pentecost," which means "fifty."

The Jewish rabbis held that Pentecost commemorated the giving of the law at Sinai. This gives us a cue for interpreting the accompanying signs of that original Pentecost and assessing their permanent value.

A glance at the account in Exod. 19:16-19 will show some striking similarities with Acts 2:1-4. Back there we read of thunders and lightnings, a thick cloud, the sound of a trumpet, smoke, fire, an earthquake. Here we read of a tornado-like sound, flames of fire, speaking in tongues.

Why all this startling display? The answer is the same in both cases. A new era was being inaugurated, and God introduced it with spectacular signs. He wanted the people to realize the sacredness of the law, and so He put on a display of pyrotechnics they would never forget, one that would fill them with a wholesome reverence for His law and a fear of disobeying it.

So it was with Pentecost. Perhaps the disciples were a bit drowsy from their days of prayer. At any rate, they were alerted that something tremendous was taking place. First there was a tornado-like roar that swept through the building and roused everyone to full attention. Then with wide-open eyes they saw a mass of flame move into the room. It separated into tongues of flame, one of which settled on each person present.

But the essential thing was that they were all "filled with the Holy Spirit"—the key phrase of the Book of Acts. All the other things were just accompanying signs, of sound and sight. But here was the reality: the infilling of the Spirit, the fulfilling of the promise of Jesus (1:5).

Immediately they began speaking with other tongues (v. 4). And so some have assumed that all those who are filled with the Holy Spirit today will speak in tongues. But the Scriptures do not support this. Only twice more in Acts do we read of this phenomenon (10:46 and 19:6). There is no mention, for instance, of the Samaritans speaking in tongues when they were filled with the Holy Spirit (8:17). Nor is it suggested anywhere else in the entire New Testament. It was one of those "signs" accompanying the inauguration of the dispensation of the Holy Spirit. But to demand it today as an evidence of the baptism with the Spirit is to go beyond what the New Testament teaches.

The purpose of the speaking in tongues on the Day of Pentecost is indicated in the verses that follow. Fifteen nationalities—composed of "Jews" and "proselytes"—were gathered in Jerusalem for the feast, and they all heard the gospel story in their mother tongue. This emphasized the universality of the gospel.

The best reading of verse 6—"when this sound was heard" —suggests that it was the tornado-like roar which brought the crowd together, not a report of the happenings in the Upper Room. At any rate, Peter seized the opportunity to give a gospel message to the assembled multitude.

His sermon provides an interesting study. By way of introduction he refuted the charge of drunkenness and quoted Joel 2:28-32. "This is that," he declared. In its larger context "the last days" means the whole of the Church age. It is the last era, the dispensation of grace in and through Jesus Christ.

After this introduction Peter preached about Jesus, using as his three main points: (1) His crucifixion (vv. 22-23); (2) His resurrection (vv. 24-32); (3) His exaltation (vv. 33-36). His conclusion was that Jesus—the One they had crucified—was the Messiah. Then he gave the invitation to repent and accept Christ as Saviour. Three thousand responded and that day the Church of Jesus Christ was launched on the ocean of time.

3. The Healing of the Lame Man (c. 3)

For some time after Pentecost the disciples continued worshiping in the Jewish synagogues and Temple. This was only natural. As yet there were no Christian church buildings. So we find Peter and John going up to the Temple at the hour of prayer. This was "the ninth hour," or three o'clock in the afternoon, the time of the offering of the evening sacrifice.

At the Beautiful Gate—probably facing the east side of the Temple area—they found a lame beggar. Though Peter had no money he gave something far more valuable: healing, and with it the ability to work and earn a living.

When the healed man began "walking, and leaping, and praising God"—for the first time in his life—the crowd came rushing together in Solomon's Porch, on the east of the Temple. Again Peter quickly seized the opportunity and preached his second sermon. After stating that it was divine power, not human, that had healed the man, he proceeded to bring solemn accusation against the assembled Jews. He charged them with killing the Prince of Life and asking a murderer (Barabbas) to be granted to them. That is what everyone does today who refuses to accept Jesus Christ as Saviour.

As in his first sermon, Peter called on the people to "repent" (v. 19). But this time his message was cut short before he could finish his invitation. The rulers of the Temple intervened and arrested him (4:1-3).

4. The First Persecution (c. 4)

Probably the people were listening eagerly to Peter. But the priests understood the implications of what he was saying and decided to put a stop to his preaching.

It will be noted that this first persecution originated with the Sadducees. The chief priests belonged to this party. The thing that offended them was the Resurrection, for the Sadducees did not believe in any resurrection (Matt. 22:23). During the greater part of Jesus' ministry He met opposition mainly from the Pharisees. But after His cleansing of the Temple on Monday of Passion Week we find the Sadducees heading the efforts to kill Him. They are the ones who carried on the early persecution of the disciples, over the issue of the preaching of the Resurrection.

In spite of the arrest and imprisonment of the apostles (v. 3), many hearers accepted the message. It should be noted that verse 4 does not indicate that 5,000 more believed. The Revised rendering accurately represents the Greek: "The

number of the men came to be about five thousand." That was
the total number of accessions to date.

The next day the supreme council met. "Rulers and elders
and scribes" (v. 5)—these were the three constituent parts
of the Sanhedrin. The "rulers" were mainly Sadducees. The
"scribes" were largely Pharisees. The "elders" probably came
from both parties. It is thought that there were some twenty-
two to twenty-four of each group, making a total of about
seventy members of the Sanhedrin. Some authorities say
seventy-one or seventy-two, which would include the high
priest, who acted as chairman.

When the apostles were called before the Sanhedrin, Peter
acted as spokesman. As defendant, he turned prosecuting at-
torney and boldly charged these Jewish rulers with having
murdered their Messiah. He went on to say that salvation was
only through believing in Jesus Christ, no longer through
Temple sacrifices.

Was this the same Peter who cringed before the accusing
finger of a maid that sad night of his denial of Jesus? Yes
and no. It was Simon Peter, but Peter "filled with the Holy
Spirit" (v. 8). That was what made the difference. Peter
was a changed man after Pentecost. He now had the power
that Jesus had promised (1:8).

A significant principle is suggested in verse 23—"And
being let go, they came to their own company." It is not what
we do when under close supervision that reveals, and determines, our character. It is what we do in our leisure, when
the restraints are off and we are "on our own." What do we
do then, and where do we go?

When the apostles came to their own group they held
a prayer meeting. Their petition is most amazing. They did
not pray for protection, but for power to preach (v. 29)—
and take the consequences. Their prayer was literally answered. The place was shaken and "they were all filled with
the Holy Spirit, and they spake the word of God with boldness" (v. 31). We are not surprised to find them in jail once
more in the next chapter.

Again, as at the end of chapter two, we find a description
of a community of goods in the earliest church. But the Greek
clearly indicates that there was not a general disposal of all
personal property, with the proceeds put into a common

treasury. Rather, from time to time people "were selling" and "were bringing" the money to the apostles. Then, from time to time, distribution "was being made" to those who happened to be in need. That is the meaning of the imperfect and present tenses used here. As needs arose they were met by the generosity of someone who sold property to meet the need.

That is also indicated by the fact that special mention is made of one who did sell some land, perhaps on the island of Cyprus. Barnabas is an Aramaic word which can mean either "son of consolation" or "son of exhortation." Actually Barnabas was both, as the later story in Acts clearly shows.

5. *Ananias and Sapphira* (c. 5)

The story of Ananias and Sapphira shows what God thinks of hypocrisy. Here are two hypocrites posing as consecrated Christians. Probably appreciation and public recognition had been given Barnabas for his generous gift to the church. Ananias and Sapphira wanted to be honored likewise.

Ananias did not say anything untrue, but he acted out a lie. He intended to give the impression that he had brought the complete price of the sale of his possession. Sapphira went a step further and told a deliberate lie with her lips. That is the way sin grows.

Swift sentence was executed on these first two hypocrites. Thereby God let it be known that He hates hypocrisy. Of course there have been a lot of hypocrites in the church since then. But a solemn warning was given back there as a deterrent, so that people would not flock carelessly into the church.

The twofold result is indicated in verses 13 and 14. Insincere people were afraid to join the church, yet "believers were the more added to the Lord, multitudes both of men and women."

Soon a second persecution arose (vv. 17-42). Again the Sadducees took the lead. This time when the apostles were put in prison the angel of the Lord let them out.

Summoned to face the Sanhedrin again, the apostles did not quail before that semicircle of scowling faces. Boldly they declared, "We must obey God rather than men" (v. 29). Once more they accused them of crucifying Jesus. Apparently the apostles would have been put to death, as their Master was, had not Gamaliel intervened, advising caution. So the disciples escaped with only a beating—which, incidentally, was not a pleasant experience.

With large welts on their backs from the thirty-nine stripes each had received,[2] they yet left the Sanhedrin "rejoicing that they were counted worthy to suffer shame for his name." Instead of keeping quiet now to avoid further persecution, "they ceased not to teach and to preach Jesus as the Christ." The power of the Holy Spirit was being displayed in their lives.

6. The Seven Deacons (c. 6)

A larger church means more problems, for every person is a potential problem. The late Dr. R. T. Williams once said to a group of pastors: "If you want to get rid of all your problems, chloroform your present members, and don't take in any new ones."

The internal problem described in this chapter posed a more serious threat to the church than the persecution from without. There arose a "murmuring"—and the Greek word suggests the buzzing of bees—on the part of one group against another. The "Grecian Jews"—that is, Hellenists, or Greek-speaking Jews—claimed that their widows were being neglected in the daily dole of food. A church split was in the offing.

With sanctified common sense the apostles handled the matter promptly. They suggested that seven men be appointed to administer the funds for the care of the needy, so that they would be free for the spiritual work of the church.

The qualifications for these "deacons," as we call them, are striking. They must first of all have a good reputation in the community. Then they must be "full of the Spirit and of wisdom," or tact. In dealing with the delicate situation in the Jerusalem church they would need all these qualifications.

The matter was also handled tactfully, for the men chosen were probably Hellenists; at least, they had Greek names. Then, too, the case was handled effectively, for "the word of God increased," there were many accessions to the church, and a large group of priests accepted Christ. All this came

2Cf. II Cor. 11:24; Deut. 25:3.

from solving a serious problem quickly and wisely, before it grew to proportions such as would make it impossible to handle.

Stephen overflowed his job in the commissary and soon was preaching. But Stephen's very success brought him into conflict with the Hellenists. Not able to "withstand the wisdom and the Spirit," with which he spoke, they resorted to violence as the only way they could answer his arguments.

When Stephen was brought before the Sanhedrin, false witnesses accused him of blasphemy. But instead of his face clouding darkly with anger it shone as the face of an angel. Here was powerful proof of the grace of God.

7. Stephen's Defense and Death (c. 7)

When Stephen was given the opportunity to speak he presented a resume of God's dealings with His people. He spoke at length of Abraham (vv. 2-8), Joseph (vv. 9-16), and Moses (vv. 17-44). Then very briefly he mentioned Joshua, David, and Solomon. This brevity may have been due to the fact that he sensed a growing opposition to his message. The abrupt change of tone at verse 51—"Ye stiffnecked and uncircumcised in heart and ears, ye do always resist the Holy Spirit" —seems to reflect a sudden outbreak of hostility on the part of the Sanhedrin. As Peter had already twice done, Stephen charged these Jewish leaders with the murder of Christ, "the Righteous One."

The scene that followed is a sad commentary on the Judaism of Jesus' day. Like a pack of hungry, snarling wolves they "gnashed on him with their teeth." But Stephen, "full of the Holy Spirit," looked up to heaven, where he saw Jesus waiting to receive him. When he testified to what he saw, the members of the Sanhedrin "cried out with a loud voice, and stopped their ears, and rushed upon him with one accord; and they cast him out of the city, and stoned him."

What a contrast is Stephen's conduct! Kneeling down, with the death-dealing stones flying around his head, he prayed God to forgive his persecutors. Then he "fell asleep." The Greek word gives us our name "cemetery"—strictly speaking, a place where the bodies of those who sleep in Jesus await the resurrection day.

Thus died the first Christian martyr, in a truly Christian spirit. Appropriately his name, Stephen, means "crown." He was the first, but not the last, to receive a martyr's crown.

II. Witnessing in Judea and Samaria (cc. 8—12)

1. Philip the Evangelist (8:1-25)

Saul, whose name appears for the first time in 7:58, in connection with the stoning of Stephen, consented to the latter's death. That would seem to suggest that, though a young man, he was a member of the Sanhedrin.

The aftermath of Stephen's stoning is rather amazing. One would have thought that the sanctimonious Sadducees and Pharisees after acting as beasts of the jungle would have slunk away in shame. Instead there arose "on that day" (v. 1) a great persecution against the Jerusalem church.

This persecution resulted in a dispersion of the believers from Jerusalem to the neighboring territories of Judea and Samaria. Saul, like a wild boar in a vineyard, "laid waste the church," even entering private homes and "dragging men and women, committed them to prison" (v. 3).

But those who were scattered abroad went "preaching the word" (v. 4). Because it is stated in verse 1 that the apostles stayed at Jerusalem, this has been called "the laymen's missionary movement" of the first century.

Stephen, one of the seven deacons, had turned preacher. Now another of that group, Philip, takes his place as evangelist.

Caught in this dispersion, Philip "went down to the city of Samaria" (v. 5). Anywhere from Jerusalem was "down," though Samaria was forty-five miles north of Jerusalem and at about the same altitude.

The Samaritans were a mixed race, largely Gentile. They worshiped the God of Israel, accepting only the Pentateuch (Torah) as their Scripture. The Jews despised them as half-breeds and treated them with scorn. Yet to these people Philip preached Christ. There were many conversions and, as always in such cases, "there was much joy in that city" (v. 8).

When word of this great revival reached Jerusalem the apostles Peter and John were sent to Samaria. They prayed for the new converts, "laid their hands on them, and they received the Holy Spirit" (vv. 15, 17). Here is one of the clearest examples of two distinct experiences of grace to be found in the Book of Acts. Under the preaching of Philip these Samaritans were converted to Christ; under the ministry of Peter and John they received the Holy Spirit. No one can deny two works of grace in this passage.

Simon Magus ("the sorcerer") wanted to purchase the power to confer the Holy Spirit. Thus he gave his name to that deplorable practice called "simony," the buying and selling of offices in the church. It is interesting to note that when Peter called on him to repent, Simon asked for prayer for his protection from evil consequences of his sin, not for salvation from sin. There are many like him today.

2. *Philip and the Ethiopian* (8:26-40)

Perhaps the greatest test that ever came to Philip was when he was instructed by the Lord to leave Samaria, with its great revival meeting, and go far south to a wilderness road. Many a lesser man might have argued the folly of such a move. Not so Philip. The aorist tenses—"he arose and went" (v. 27)—suggest prompt obedience. And because he obeyed at once, he met his man. A few hours of dawdling or argument and he would have missed him.

It was an Ethiopian eunuch, treasurer of the queen of Ethiopia. ("Candace" was a title for a dynasty, like "Pharaoh" of Egypt.) He was a proselyte to Judaism, who had just been up to Jerusalem on a pilgrimage to the Temple. Riding back in his chariot, he was reading the prophecy of Isaiah.

Guided by the Spirit, Philip approached the chariot. Hearing the man reading aloud, he asked, "Understandest thou what thou readest?" Invited into the chariot, Philip explained the meaning of the passage from the fifty-third chapter of Isaiah, where the eunuch was reading. There could have been no better place in the Old Testament from which to preach Jesus as the Messiah.

The eunuch's heart was open to receive the new truth. Soon he was baptized and went on his way rejoicing. Philip, meanwhile, was caught away by the Spirit, and proceeded to Caesarea.

3. Saul's Conversion (9:1-31)[3]

After the interlude describing the public and personal evangelism of Philip, we return to Saul (cf. 8:3). We find him still "breathing threatening and slaughter against the disciples of the Lord" (v. 1). To the high priest he went, and asked to be furnished with letters to the synagogues of Damascus giving him permission to arrest any followers of Jesus—called those of "the Way"—he found there and bring them back to Jerusalem. He was determined to stamp out this new heretical sect even in foreign cities. ("The Way" was one of the earliest designations of Christianity.)

But God had other plans for him. As he neared Damascus he was suddenly struck blind and prostrate by a bright light from heaven. When he answered the voice of Jesus he was instructed to go into Damascus.

The next three days were spent in prayer, seeking to adjust his mind to this new faith. At the end of that time Ananias, a disciple in Damascus, came to him on Straight Street—still a part of the famous bazaar in Damascus—and laid his hands on him. Paul received his sight and was filled with the Holy Spirit.

The most zealous persecutor immediately became the most ardent preacher. In the synagogues he declared that Jesus was the Son of God, proving to the Jews that He was their Messiah. This was rank heresy, and soon his life was sought (v. 23). Saul escaped over the wall and returned to Jerusalem.

Here the disciples were afraid of him, but bighearted Barnabas championed the cause of the new convert. However, Saul's vigorous preaching in Jerusalem resulted in his life's being threatened here also. The only solution was to take him down to the seaport, Caesarea, and ship him home to Tarsus. Then everything quieted down again!

4. Peter at Lydda and Joppa (9:32-43)

Peter takes the center of the scene again and holds it most of the time until the end of chapter 12. First he visited the saints at Lydda, near which is now located Israel's big airport. It is between Jerusalem and Tel-Aviv (on the coast) and serves both cities today.

[3] Recorded also in 22:6-16 and 26:12-18.

At Lydda, Peter healed Aeneas and at Joppa (modern Jaffa) he raised Dorcas from the dead. Then he stayed in Joppa with Simon, a tanner.

5. Peter and Cornelius (c. 10)

In the opening paragraph (vv. 1-8) of this chapter we are introduced to Cornelius, a centurion of the Italian Cohort. He is called "a devout man"; that is, he worshiped the God of the Jews. He was a man of generous giving and much prayer. An angel appeared to him one day and told him to send for Peter, who would give him further instruction.

Meanwhile the Lord had been working on Peter at the other end, preparing him for this important assignment. A vision appeared to him which showed him that in God's sight the Gentiles were not considered unclean.

As Peter was contemplating the meaning of this vision, the messengers from Cornelius arrived. The latter had received his vision at three o'clock in the afternoon (v. 3), while Peter's was at noon the next day (v. 9). Meanwhile those sent by Cornelius had covered the thirty miles from Caesarea down to Joppa—having stopped overnight on the way—and were inquiring for Peter. Instructed by the Spirit to go with them, Peter first brought them in and kept them overnight. The next morning they set out, probably covering the normal day's walk of twenty miles. About noon on the fourth day after Cornelius' vision (v. 30) they arrived in Caesarea. Here they found a congregation assembled, waiting.

Peter informed these Gentiles that they could receive remission of sins through believing in Jesus Christ (v. 43). While he was preaching, the Holy Spirit fell on his hearers and they were thus sanctified wholly (cf. 15:8-9). They were baptized in the name of the Lord and became members of the Christian community. Thus Peter used the keys Christ had given him (Matt. 16:19) to open the door of the new faith to the Gentiles. This incident is sometimes called the Gentile Pentecost. Hence the speaking in tongues (v. 46) to mark the inauguration of a new era for them.

6. Peter's Defense at Jerusalem (11:1-18)

When Peter returned to Jerusalem he was criticized for having eaten with uncircumcised Gentiles. Fortunately he had taken six Jewish brethren with him from Joppa to Caesarea and they could testify that God had poured out the Holy Spirit on the group in Cornelius' house without any official action on Peter's part. When the leaders of the Jerusalem church saw that it was the Lord's doing, not Peter's, they said in surprise: "Then to the Gentiles also hath God granted repentance unto life." It is hard for us to realize now what a revolutionary idea that was to them.

7. Christians at Antioch (11:19-30)

Verse 19 takes us back again to 8:1. The scattered believers were preaching only to Jews. (We have seen slight exceptions in chapters 8 and 10.) But fortunately some open-minded men from Cyprus (an island) and Cyrene (on the north coast of Africa) began preaching to the Greeks in Syrian Antioch. This was apparently the beginning of a new policy, and the Lord honored it with many converts (v. 21).

The mother church at Jerusalem was again concerned as to what was going on. Very fortunately it was Barnabas who was sent to investigate. With his usual large spirit he gave his blessing to this new movement among the Gentiles.

At Antioch we find the believers for the first time called "Christians." Whether they adopted this name themselves or it was given in derision by outsiders we cannot be sure. But the latter is more likely. At any rate, we who bear the name of Christ are obligated to act like Him.

The nobility of Barnabas' character is shown by the fact that he realized the work in Antioch was too big for him. Third largest city in the Roman Empire (after Rome and Alexandria) and with half a million population, Antioch was to become the home base for the evangelization of the Gentile world. It is to the everlasting honor of Barnabas that he sought out a man with more brilliant ability, Saul of Tarsus, to help in this work at Antioch.

Paul's own statement in Galatians (1:21) suggests that he had spent the intervening half a dozen or more years since leaving Jerusalem (Acts 9:30) in evangelizing his home province of Syria and Cilicia. Now he was ready for his great lifework.

8. Peter's Deliverance (12:1-19)

Herod Agrippa I executed James the son of Zebedee, one of the three leading apostles (with Peter and John). Seeing that it pleased his subjects, the king decided to put Peter to death too. But since it was the time of the Passover he put him in prison until the feast was over.

The night before his scheduled execution, Peter was miraculously delivered from prison. He went to the house of Mary, the mother of John Mark, where he found many praying for him. Instructing them to tell James—brother of Jesus and head of the Jerusalem church—he went into hiding.

9. Herod's Death (12:20-25)

After Herod had executed the sentries he went down from "Judaea" (i.e. Jerusalem) to Caesarea, the headquarters of the Roman government in Palestine. There representatives from Tyre and Sidon, wanting to gain his favor, hailed him as a god. Because he accepted this misplaced honor he was smitten by the Lord. The death of Herod Agrippa I, as we know from secular records, occurred in A.D. 44. The account given here of his horrible death is corroborated by Josephus,[4] a contemporary Jewish historian.

III. Witnessing in the Gentile World (cc. 13—28)

The end of the twelfth chapter marks the most important division point in the Book of Acts. Heretofore the main base of operations has been Jerusalem and the work has been carried on largely among Jews. With chapter 13 we come to the beginnings of the great foreign missionary enterprise. Antioch becomes the new center for the evangelization of the Gentiles. Paul takes the place of Peter as the main character.

1. The Inauguration of Foreign Missions (13:1-3)

As we have already noted, Pentecost is the most important event recorded in Acts. Perhaps Saul's conversion (c. 9) should rank second, as his ministry consumes the larger part of the book. But a close third would be the beginning of foreign missions recorded in this chapter.

The foreign missionary enterprise began in a prayer meeting. A striking parallel is the famous "haystack prayer meeting" in Williamstown, Massachusetts, which gave birth to American foreign missions.

As the leaders of the church at Antioch were waiting before the Lord in fasting and prayer, the Holy Spirit said,

[4] Ant., XIX.8.2.

"Separate me Barnabas and Saul for the work whereunto I have called them." God asked this church to give its very best workers for the foreign missionary cause.

The leaders laid their hands on them and sent them away (v. 3). At the same time they were "sent forth by the Holy Spirit" (v. 4). This is the proper combination: called by God, ordained by the church, sent forth by the Holy Spirit.

2. Paul's First Journey (13:4—14:28)

a. *Cyprus* (13:4-12). The small missionary party sailed from Seleucia, the seaport of Antioch, about fifteen miles away. Since Barnabas was from Cyprus they went there first. Cyprus is a large island (150 x 40 miles) about sixty miles off the coast of Syria and some one hundred miles from Antioch. They landed at Salamis, on the eastern end of the island, and evangelized their way across the island, preaching in the Jewish synagogues. John Mark was their attendant, or assistant— not "minister" in the modern sense.

Paphos, at the west end of the island, was the headquarters of the Roman government in Cyprus. Sergius Paulus was the "proconsul" of the island. A few years ago some scholars claimed that the author of Acts was mistaken in using this term. They said that Cyprus was an imperial province, governed by a propraetor, rather than a senatorial province, ruled by a proconsul. But archaeology has completely vindicated Luke. On the north coast of Cyprus there has been discovered an inscription dated "in the proconsulship of Paulus."

A significant change took place at Paphos. Now that he was working among Gentiles, Saul chose to be called by his Roman name, Paul. Probably he had been given both names at birth, since he was born a Roman citizen (22:28).

b. *Perga* (13:13). Leaving Paphos, they sailed some 170 miles to Perga in Pamphylia, on the mainland of Asia Minor, or modern Turkey. Here John Mark left them and returned to Jerusalem. He was a young man and may have been homesick. He may have feared the rugged, dangerous mountain regions that lay ahead. Probably, too, he resented the fact that Paul had replaced his cousin Barnabas as leader of the missionary party. It is significant that when they left Paphos this phrase is used: "Paul and his company." Hitherto it had been "Barnabas and Saul." Hereafter, with few exceptions, it is "Paul and Barnabas."

c. *Antioch of Pisidia* (13:14-52). Paul's first recorded sermon was preached in the Jewish synagogue at Pisidian Antioch. Here on the Sabbath day he took advantage of the prevailing custom which gave the privileges of the floor to any stranger who wished to speak. It is interesting to note the similarity between this sermon and Stephen's recorded in the seventh chapter. Both give a brief historical sketch of God's dealings with Israel. But Paul had more time to preach Christ, and salvation through Him, than did Stephen.

The consequences of this preaching of Jesus as Saviour and Messiah were to be repeated many times in the succeeding months. The Jews, on the whole, rejected the message. When they saw how enthusiastically the Gentiles received the new truth, they were filled with jealousy and persecuted the preachers. The missionaries met this opposition with the declaration: "We turn to the Gentiles" (v. 46). Expelled from Antioch, they moved on to Iconium, some sixty miles eastward. How amazing the statement that in the face of this persecution "the disciples were filled with joy and with the Holy Spirit" (v. 52)!

d. *Iconium* (14:1-7). In Iconium a large number of both Jews and Gentiles believed in Christ. But again the Jews who rejected the gospel message stirred up opposition against the apostles, so that the latter had to flee from the city. They turned southward to Lystra, some twenty miles away, a day's journey on foot.

e. *Lystra* (14:8-20). Two interesting events happened in this city. First, Paul healed a helpless cripple at the gate of the city. The astonished onlookers decided that he and Barnabas must be gods, and so they attempted to worship them with sacrifices. With great difficulty the apostles restrained them. Then when the Jews from Antioch and Iconium followed the missionaries' trail thither, bent on persecution, the people of Lystra listened to them and stoned Paul. Though they thought they had killed him, he revived. Then the apostles went on to Derbe, another twenty or thirty miles to the east.

f. *Derbe and Return* (14:21-28). The missionaries preached briefly in Derbe, then retraced their steps to Perga in Pamphylia. On the way they appointed elders in each church, so that the work would remain permanent. Sailing from Attalia, near Perga, they returned to Antioch.

3. The Council of Jerusalem (15:1-35)

Perhaps the fourth most important event in the Book of Acts was the council at Jerusalem, between Paul's first and second journeys. The issue at stake was whether the Gentile Christians should be required to observe the law of Moses. Fortunately for all future generations the decision of the council was in favor of Gentile liberty. Otherwise Christianity would have been just another sect of Judaism.

It all started with some Judaizers who came down from Jerusalem. To the Christians at Antioch they said: "Except ye be circumcised after the custom of Moses, ye cannot be saved." When Paul and Barnabas opposed this effort to strangle the new faith in the swaddling clothes of Judaism, the church decided to send the two apostles[5] to Jerusalem to confer with the leaders there about the matter.

Right away the Pharisees insisted that all Gentile converts must be circumcised and commanded to keep the law of Moses (v. 5). This was evidently at a general church meeting (v. 4).

So the apostles and elders met in special session to deal with this problem. After much argument Peter made an important speech. He referred to his experience in the house of Cornelius, concluding with a plea for Gentile freedom from the Jewish law.

Verses 8 and 9 are very important. It is often averred that, while the Book of Acts has a great deal to say about being filled with the Holy Spirit, the subject of sanctification is not even mentioned once. But Peter in these two verses identifies the receiving of the Holy Spirit with the cleansing of the heart. So we maintain that when the believer is filled with the Spirit his heart is cleansed from all sin.

After Peter finished his speech Barnabas and Paul related their experiences in evangelizing the Gentiles (v. 12). Then James, acting as moderator of the Church, gave the decision of the council. It was incorporated in a letter which freed the Gentile believers from the Mosaic law but requested only

---

[5] Both Paul and Barnabas are called "apostles" in 14:14.

that they avoid food offered to idols, blood, things strangled, and fornication (v. 29). The Jerusalem leaders claimed the authority of the Holy Spirit for this decision (v. 28). The letter was received with real joy by the Christians at Antioch.

4. Paul's Second Journey (15:36—18:22)

a. *Syria and Cilicia* (15:36-41). After some time spent at Antioch, Paul expressed to Barnabas his concern to revisit the churches they had founded on their first journey. The latter wanted to take John Mark, who had left them the former time. Paul objected strenuously. When they could not come to an agreement they separated. Barnabas took Mark and sailed again for Cyprus, his old home. We do not hear of him again in Acts. Paul chose a new companion, Silas—called Silvanus (I Thess. 1:1; II Thess. 1:1)—and they journeyed northward through Syria and around the corner of the Mediterranean through Cilicia, his home province.

b. *Lystra* (16:1-5). At Lystra, where he had been stoned on the first journey, Paul took on another, younger associate, named Timothy. To placate the Jews of that area he had him circumcised. Since his father was a Greek, he would not otherwise be acceptable to the Jews.

c. *Troas* (16:6-10). Having passed through the Phrygio-Galatic region, Paul wished to preach in the province of Asia, at the west end of Asia Minor. Being forbidden by the Spirit to do this, he tried to turn northward to Bithynia. But again the Spirit said, "No." So there was nothing else to do but keep going straight ahead to land's end at Troas, the site of the ancient Troy of Homer's *Iliad*. Here he received the call to Macedonia.

The leadings of the Lord must have seemed strange to Paul at that time. It was as if a person were walking down a corridor and finding all the doors on either side locked against him. At the end seemed to be a blank wall. But suddenly, when he reached it, double doors flung open, revealing a much larger room than those he had passed. God had a greater work for Paul in Europe, and so for the time being He closed the doors of Asia Minor against him. God always has His plans—far better than ours—which He reveals in due time to those who patiently wait and obey.

d. Philippi (16:11-40). Sailing from Troas, the missionary party—now augmented by Luke ("we," vv. 10-11)—reached the island of Samothrace in one day. The next day they sailed on to Neapolis ("New City"), the seaport of Philippi. From there they walked inland ten miles to the city which was named for Philip of Macedon, the father of Alexander the Great. Here there was no synagogue, but Paul and his party found a group of devout women gathered for prayer by the river's edge outside the city. If ten Jewish men in any community wanted a synagogue they must have one; the women didn't count.

Paul found here his first convert in Europe, Lydia, from Thyatira, a seller of purple goods. She believed and was baptized, with her household. Her commodious home became the missionaries' hotel.

But where was the man of Macedonia whom Paul had seen in the vision at Troas? The apostle had to go to jail to find his man! When he cast the demon out of the soothsaying slave girl, her masters hailed him before the magistrates. Cleverly they brought a charge which would carry weight in a Roman court: "These men, being Jews, do exceedingly trouble our city, and set forth customs which it is not lawful for us to receive, or to observe, being Romans" (vv. 20-21).

Paul and Silas were beaten and thrown into prison. But an earthquake set them free, and the jailer was converted.

The next morning the magistrates sent word to have them released. But Paul insisted on a public vindication, for the sake of the new church.

e. Thessalonica (17:1-9). Leaving Luke as pastor of the little flock—the "we" drops out at this point—Paul and his party set out westward along the Egnatian Way. After about thirty miles they passed through Amphipolis, and another thirty miles brought them to Apollonia. Forty miles more and they reached Thessalonica. The one hundred miles on foot might normally consume the week between two Sabbaths.

At Thessalonica, Paul followed his usual custom of beginning in the Jewish synagogue. For three Sabbath days he reasoned with them from the Scriptures (the Septuagint Old Testament), showing that their Bible taught that the Messiah was to suffer and rise again from the dead. His reasoning would be this: The Scriptures teach a suffering and resurrected Messiah; Jesus died and rose again; therefore Jesus *could* be the Messiah.

Those who rejected the message instituted an uproar against Paul, accusing him of turning the world upside down (v. 6)—an accusation most of us need never fear! Like those at Philippi, they were clever enough to bring a political charge against the missionaries: "These all act contrary to the decrees of Caesar, saying there is another king, one Jesus" (v. 7). Paul was running true to his pattern: first a revival, then a riot.

f. Beroea (17:10-15). Forced to slip out of Thessalonica under cover of darkness, Paul and Silas escaped to Beroea, fifty miles southwest. Here they found the Jews "more noble than those in Thessalonica," because they received the word readily and searched the Scriptures daily to see whether Paul was preaching the truth. The result was that many Jews here believed.

But the Jews at Thessalonica followed Paul's trail, so that he was forced to flee to Athens. They were acting the same way as did the Jews of Antioch and Iconium when they followed Paul to Lystra and had him stoned.

g. Athens (17:16-34). At Athens, Paul had an interesting twofold ministry. First, he reasoned in the synagogue with the Jews and proselytes ("devout persons"). Secondly, he reasoned daily in the market place with the Greeks he met there. He was playing the double role of Jewish rabbi and Greek philosopher.

But some Epicureans, who held that the highest good was pleasure, and Stoics, who held that the highest good was self-control, met him. Cynically they asked: "What would this babbler [lit. 'seed picker'] say?" So they brought him to the Areopagus—the court which originally met on Mars' Hill, and gave its name to that eminence, but which at this time may have been meeting in the Stoa adjacent to the Agora, or market place. Here[6] Paul made a speech. Tactfully he noted that they were "very religious" (v. 22). Using the inscription "To AN UNKNOWN GOD" as his starting point, he told them of the true God. But when he mentioned the resur-

[6] "Areopagus" (v. 19) and "Mars' Hill" (v. 22) are the same expression in the Greek.

rection these materialistic philosophers laughed him out of town. One wonders if this did not hurt Paul more than the violent mobs he met in other cities. The results were meager here, and we do not hear of a Christian church at Athens until the second century, though the few converts—one of which was Dionysius the Areopagite—doubtless did form a fellowship.

  h. Corinth (18:1-17). It was probably with something of a disappointed spirit that Paul walked or sailed—we are not told which—the seventy miles to Corinth. Perhaps he thought through his approach in preaching to Gentiles. At any rate, he wrote to the Corinthians: "For I determined not to know anything among you, save Jesus Christ, and him crucified" (I Cor. 2:2).

At Corinth, Paul found Aquila and Priscilla, who were tentmakers. Probably his work with them not only furnished him with needed funds but also healed his spirit, as manual labor often does.

Meanwhile Paul taught in the synagogue every Sabbath. When Silas and Timothy rejoined him, he pressed more strongly the truth that Jesus was the Messiah. The usual reaction resulted. Again Paul declared—this time perhaps with more finality than at Pisidian Antioch (13:46)—"From henceforth I will go unto the Gentiles" (v. 6).

Leaving the synagogue, Paul continued his ministry at Corinth in the house of Justus, who lived next door. An amazing result was that the ruler of the synagogue believed. Paul stayed in Corinth a year and a half, the longest of any place on his second journey.

Again we find Paul facing a Roman court. The judge was Gallio, who became proconsul of the province of Achaia (Greece) in the summer of A.D. 51. (So Paul's stay in Corinth was probably from the spring of A.D. 50 to the fall of A.D. 51.) The Jews were clever in wording their charge: "This man persuadeth men to worship God contrary to the law" (v. 13). They intended to convey the impression that they meant Roman law. But Gallio saw through their duplicity and threw the case out of court, because it related to Jewish, not Roman, law.

It is a slander to call him "Careless Gallio." Actually this man, who was brother of Seneca and had the highest reputation for noble character, was doing the only fair thing as judge.

The new ruler of the synagogue, Sosthenes, was beaten instead of Paul. One wonders if this beating resulted in his salvation, for Paul later mentions a Sosthenes as co-worker (I Cor. 1:1).

i. Ephesus and Return (18:18-22). Soon after the attempted trial Paul left Corinth. He took Priscilla and Aquila —evidently she was the stronger personality—along with him, sailed 250 miles to Ephesus, and left them there. After only one session in the synagogue, he sailed on to Caesarea. "He went up and saluted the church" (v. 22)—probably the Jerusalem church—then went down to Antioch to report again to the home base. Thus ended Paul's second journey.

5. Paul's Third Journey (18:23—21:16)

On this third journey Paul apparently started out in the same direction as on his second journey, going northward by land to Asia Minor. Revisiting the churches he had founded on his first journey in the southern part of the province of Galatia, he strengthened the disciples there.

a. Ephesus (c. 19). This time Paul paid more than a passing visit to Ephesus. In fact, he stayed three years, longer than we read of his staying in any other place.

Here he found a dozen disciples who did not give evidence of the Holy Spirit in their lives. When he questioned them he found that they, as Apollos (18:25), knew only John's baptism. So he told them of salvation through Christ and they "were baptized in the name of the Lord Jesus" (v. 5). Then, as a subsequent, second experience they received the Holy Spirit, in what is called the "Ephesian Pentecost." Thus these disciples of John the Baptist became Christians and then were filled with the Spirit.

As at Corinth, so in Ephesus, Paul's ministry had two stages. For three months he reasoned with the Jews in the synagogue. When he met resistance there he moved, with his followers, to the lecture hall of Tyrannus. Here each day he carried on a ministry among the Gentiles for two years. From this center the gospel spread throughout "Asia"

(v. 10)—not the continent (a much later designation), but the Roman province of Asia at the west end of Asia Minor.

An interesting incident here was the big bonfire, when the people burned their symbols of superstition and "books" —magical papyrus scrolls, of which many have been discovered by archaeologists.

But of course Paul could not stay in a city for three years without causing a riot. This time the opposition came from commercial sources, as at Philippi; elsewhere it was religious. The silversmiths were losing money as the result of the revival. So they agitated a mass meeting.

The temple of Diana—the Greek name of the goddess was Artemis—was one of the seven wonders of the ancient world. It was built to house a piece of black rock (meteorite) which had fallen to earth and was worshiped as a goddess from heaven.

b. *Macedonia and Greece* (20:1-5). After the uproar at Ephesus had subsided Paul made a trip through Macedonia —Philippi and Thessalonica, possibly also Beroea—and then spent three months in Greece, which would mean Corinth. He next planned to sail for Syria, but discovered a plot to assassinate him—probably on board ship, where it would be very easy. So instead he returned on foot by way of Macedonia.

He was accompanied by representatives of the churches at Beroea, Thessalonica, Derbe, Lystra, and Ephesus ("Asia"). These would go with him to Jerusalem to present the offering from the Gentile churches to the poor saints at Jerusalem (cf. I Cor. 16:3-4).

c. *Troas* (20:6-12). Luke joined the missionary party at Philippi ("we," v. 6) and apparently stayed near Paul throughout the rest of the latter's life. On this return trip it took five days between Philippi and Troas, contrasted with two on a previous voyage (16:11). The reason for this was adverse winds.

At Troas, Paul stayed one week. Here we have the first clear mention in Acts of the new Christian day of worship, "the first day of the week" (v. 7), when the disciples met together for a communion service. Paul preached until midnight and a young man fell out the window, evidently breaking his neck. But Paul restored him to life and, undaunted, preached till daybreak.

d. Miletus (20:13-38). Perhaps seeking solitude, Paul walked twenty miles to Assos and met his ship there—an interesting commentary on the speed of sailing vessels in those days. The ship evidently anchored for the night at Mitylene, on the island of Lesbos, since it was dangerous to navigate among the many islands in the dark. The next night they anchored at Chios, an island five miles offshore and famed as the birthplace of Homer. The following day they passed the island of Samos, birthplace of the philosopher Pythagoras, and anchored for the night at Trogyllium, on the coast of Asia Minor. Then they sailed past Ephesus to Miletus.

These detailed travel notes probably reflect two things in Luke, the writer. He was evidently an appreciative student of Greek literature and philosophy. He was also a great traveler and loved the sea.

From Miletus, where the ship stayed for a few days, Paul sent to Ephesus for the elders of the church there to come to him. Since that city was thirty-five miles away, three or four days would have passed before they could arrive.

To these Ephesian elders Paul recounted his unselfish, sacrificial ministry during the three years (v. 31) he had spent among them. He confided in them his forebodings about his coming visit to Jerusalem (vv. 22-23), and declared he would not see them again (v. 25). Then he gave these elders a solemn charge to take heed first to themselves and then to the flock. He quoted a saying of Jesus not recorded in the Gospels (v. 35), prayed with them, and said a tearful farewell.

e. Tyre (21:1-6). Leaving Miletus, the ship sailed to Cos. Next day they reached the famous island of Rhodes. From there they went to Patara, on the coast of Lycia. Changing ships there, they sailed past the west end of Cyprus and landed at Tyre, some four hundred miles away.

While the ship was unloading, Paul and his party spent a week with the disciples there. His visit ended with prayer on the beach.

f. Ptolemais and Caesarea (21:7-16). From Tyre the party went southward twenty-five miles down the coast to Ptolemais. This is the modern city of Acre, the last stronghold of the Crusades (1291). The massive crusader ruins there can still be seen.

After one day with the Christians there Paul's company went thirty miles farther down the coast to Caesarea. This had been built by Herod the Great as his main seaport. He had constructed a breakwater of very massive stones. Here Paul stayed with "Philip the evangelist," who was prominent in chapter eight. He had four daughters who were preachers.

Again Paul was warned of the persecution that awaited him at Jerusalem. But he declared his determination to go there, even if it meant death.

6. Paul at Jerusalem (21:17—23:35)

a. *The Conference with James* (21:17-26). Paul made a report of his missionary work to James and the elders of the church at Jerusalem. They requested that he quiet the criticism against him by taking a vow in the Temple. This would prove that, while he advocated Gentile freedom from the Mosaic law, he himself was acting as a good Jew.

Because he was willing to "become all things to all men" (I Cor. 9:22) for their salvation, Paul complied with the request. But his presence in the Temple offered the occasion for the trouble that followed.

b. *The Seizure of Paul* (21:27-40). Shortly before the period of the vow was ended, Paul was mobbed in the Temple by Jews from the province of Asia. Because they had seen him on the streets with a Gentile from Ephesus they concluded—with typical human logic—that he had brought Greeks into the Temple and thus defiled it. This was one of the most serious sins in the eyes of the Jews of that time. There has been found a Greek inscription from the Temple of Jesus' day, which reads thus: "No foreigner may enter within the balustrade and enclosure around the Sanctuary. Whoever is caught will render himself liable to the death penalty which will inevitably follow."[7]

As the Jews were trying to kill Paul, the tribune of the Roman Cohort in Jerusalem heard the uproar and rescued the apostle. So violent was the action of the mob that the

[7] Jack Finegan, *Light from the Ancient Past* (Princeton University Press, 1946), p. 246.

soldiers had to carry Paul bodily up the steps into the barracks, called the Tower of Antonia, at the northwest corner of the Temple area. But before he was taken inside the apostle asked for the privilege of addressing the crowd. This he did in Aramaic—called "Hebrew" in the New Testament—the common language of the Jews in Palestine at that time.

c. *Paul's Speech on the Stairs* (22:1-21). In his defense Paul informed his hearers that he had been brought up a strict Jew and trained in the school of the prominent Rabbi Gamaliel. Furthermore, he had zealously persecuted the Christians as dangerous heretics. But on the road to Damascus, Jesus had appeared to him and changed his life's course.

d. *Paul's Plea of Roman Citizenship* (22:22-30). When Paul mentioned Christ's command to him to go to the Gentiles, the crowd once more became a howling mob. The tribune ordered the prisoner carried into the barracks and examined by scourging. Not relishing this terrible torture—men sometimes died under the lash of the thongs with pieces of metal attached—Paul asserted his Roman citizenship. It was the rule at that time that no Roman citizen could be scourged without having first been tried and condemned.

The question might well be raised as to why Paul did not plead his Roman citizenship at Philippi and thus save himself a beating. The answer probably is that there was so much hasty confusion that he was not given the opportunity. For he did stand on his rights the next morning (16:37).

e. *Paul Before the Sanhedrin* (23:1-10). When Paul was brought before this highest Jewish tribunal he declared his clear conscience in the sight of God. The cruel high priest ordered that he be slapped on the mouth. Paul retorted with a warning of God's judgment.

It has been asked how Paul could say (v. 5) that he did not recognize the high priest. Perhaps the latter was not sitting in his usual chair as head of the Sanhedrin, or Paul's poor eyesight may have been responsible.

Then the apostle employed a very clever tactic. By asserting his belief in the resurrection, as a true Pharisee, he split the Sanhedrin. The Pharisees defended him against the Sadducees. By dividing his opponents, Paul saved himself from condemnation by the court.

f. The Plot Against Paul's Life (23:12-35). More than forty men bound themselves under oath that they would not eat or drink until they had killed Paul. Presumably these would-be assassins either broke their vow or committed suicide!

Realizing he had a serious situation on his hands, the tribune sent Paul immediately to Caesarea on the seacoast, the seat of Roman government in Judea. The measure of his fright is shown by the size of the military escort. Paul "rated" a guard of 400 infantrymen and 70 cavalry. The next day the foot soldiers returned from Antipatris, while the cavalry escorted this notable prisoner the rest of the way to Caesarea. The entire trip covered about sixty-five miles. But this time Paul rode (v. 24), probably on horseback.

7. Paul at Caesarea (cc. 24—26)

a. Paul Before Felix (c. 24). The Jews had hired an orator, Tertullus, to present their case to the governor. The flattery with which he opened his speech was anything but sincere and deserved, for Felix was a cruel ruler and much hated by the Jews.

Paul was accused of being a public nuisance, an insurrectionist, "a ringleader of the sect of the Nazarenes," and a profaner of the Temple. This last charge the apostle emphatically denied. One thing only would he admit: that he was guilty of the "heresy" of believing in Jesus. His motto in verse 16 is a good one for all of us today.

Felix had influenced Drusilla to leave her former husband and marry him. No wonder the governor trembled when Paul reasoned of righteousness and judgment (v. 25). Felix never found, as far as we know, "a convenient season" for repentance. Instead he sought a bribe from Paul. Hoping to please the Jews, he left Paul in prison when he was recalled to Rome. But the Jews, instead, lodged a complaint against Felix with the emperor.

b. Paul Before Festus (25:1-12). Festus has the reputation of being a more honest procurator than Felix. He refused the request of the Jews that Paul be brought to Jerusalem for trial. Instead he held the hearing at Caesarea, the location of the government palace.

Pressed by the Jews, Festus finally asked Paul if he would consent to go to Jerusalem for further trial. Then Paul once more stood on his rights as a Roman citizen and appealed to Caesar. This meant that he would be tried by the imperial court at Rome.

c. *Agrippa and Bernice* (25:13-22). Herod Agrippa II was the son of Herod Agrippa I—whose death is recorded in chapter 12—and the great-grandson of Herod the Great. Drusilla, wife of Felix, was his sister. Bernice was also his sister. Josephus[8] tells us that Agrippa's relations with his sister Bernice were creating quite a scandal at this time. It was typical of the Herods that this godless couple should appear "with great pomp" (v. 23) at the governor's palace.

d. *Paul Before Agrippa* (25:23—26:32). After Festus had explained that he wished Agrippa to help him frame a charge against Paul to send to the emperor, the king invited the prisoner to say what he wished in his own defense.

Paul first expressed his pleasure at addressing a man who was well acquainted with Jewish customs. He then proceeded to relate the story of his conversion. But when he became earnest in his preaching about Christ and His salvation (v. 23), Festus interrupted, crying that Paul was out of his mind because of his much learning.

After briefly but courteously denying the charge, Paul turned his attention once more to Agrippa and asked him if he believed the Old Testament prophets. Before the startled king could stammer out a reply Paul said, "I know you believe." After the moment of silence that ensued Agrippa said, "With but little persuasion thou wouldest fain make me a Christian." It could be that these words were spoken as much sarcastically as seriously.

8. *Paul's Voyage to Rome* (cc. 27—28)

Some two or three years before, Paul had written a letter from Corinth to the Christians at Rome. In it he mentioned his great desire to visit them (Rom. 15:23). But he felt it necessary at that time to take the Gentile offering to Jerusalem. So he had headed east instead of sailing west.

Now at last he was going to Rome. Little had he thought, however, that he would travel to the imperial city as a prisoner. The Lord had assured him that he would see Rome

[8] *Ant.*, XX.7.3.

(Acts 23:11). But it certainly looked for a while as if he would never reach it.

The description of Paul's voyage across the Mediterranean is the most vivid that has come down to us from ancient times. The copious, and yet correct, use of nautical terms current in that day shows that the writer, Luke, was accustomed to traveling on the sea.

Although Luke was not a prisoner, he accompanied Paul on this voyage. Leaving Caesarea, they stopped briefly at Sidon, sixty-five miles up the coast. Then they sailed on to the coast of Asia Minor.

It may seem strange that a grain ship from Alexandria, Egypt, would sail northeast to Asia Minor on its way to Rome. But that was done commonly because of the prevailing west winds which made it difficult to sail directly from Egypt to Italy. By means of northerly winds the ship could make it from Myra to Sicily and then work its way up to Puteoli.

On the lee (south) side of Crete the ship put in at Fair Havens. After the middle of September it was dangerous to sail on the Mediterranean. But now it was already after the Fast (v. 9)—the Day of Atonement, which fell on about October 5 in A.D. 59. During the months of November, December, and January all sailing on the Mediterranean ceased because of the severe winter storms.

So Paul advised against going any farther. But the majority wanted to push on along the coast some forty miles to Phoenix, where there was a more commodious harbor. When the south wind blew softly they took it as a good omen and set sail (v. 13). But soon after the ship ventured out from the safe harbor it was caught in a terrible northeast gale and driven for fourteen days and nights of awful darkness across the sea. Finally it was wrecked on the island of Malta, and the passengers spent the rest of the winter there. Spring found them sailing safely the rest of the way to Italy. Landing at Puteoli (Naples), they walked the 125 miles to Rome, entering it on the Old Appian Way, which one may still follow today. Some believers came forty miles from Rome to meet Paul at Appii Forum. Ten miles farther on, at The Three Taverns, another group met him. This was a great blessing and comfort to the apostle.

"And so we came to Rome" (28:14). How much is packed into that little word *so!* Yet even in the darkness and despair of the awful storm Paul had never doubted God (27:25). Faith had made him the hero of the hour. "Through many trials"—yes, but he arrived!

The Book of Acts ends with the statement that Paul spent two whole years in his own hired house at Rome. Whether he was acquitted then, or released for lack of having been tried within the legal period of two years, we cannot know. What we do know is that even as a prisoner Paul preached (28:31).

CHAPTER IX

PROBLEMS OF THE PRIMITIVE CHURCH
(THE EARLIER EPISTLES OF PAUL)

INTRODUCTION: THE PAULINE EPISTLES

1. Value of the Epistles

Of the twenty-seven books of the New Testament the Apostle Paul wrote thirteen. One of eight writers, he yet is responsible for one-fourth of the contents. Only Luke, with his two books, wrote more—and that only slightly more. But the material in Paul's Epistles is far more concentrated than that in Luke and Acts. Probably no one would question Paul's priority in giving us the most important single contribution of any writer of the New Testament. Certainly the Church has leaned more heavily on him for its theological support than on anyone else.

Not only have Paul's writings been the mainstay of theology; they have also produced sweeping revivals. Dr. George Croft Cell, of Boston University, said one day in class: "The Epistles of Paul have been the ferment of every great revival in the Christian church." D. A. Hayes writes: "It would be safe to say that no great church revival anywhere down the centuries or on any of the continents has failed to base itself on the teaching of Paul as recorded in his epistles."[1]

Three of the leading characters in the history of the Church are Augustine, Luther, and Wesley. Each of these men owed his conversion to Paul more than to anyone else.

In his *Confessions*, Augustine tells us how he was struggling with the chains of sin that bound him tightly. One day he went into the garden behind his lodgings in Milan. There he heard a voice say, "Take and read." He picked up the New Testament, and his eyes fell on Rom. 13:13-14. Suddenly God's power and peace swept through his soul, transforming him from a sensualist to a saint.

In his study of and lecturing on Romans at the University of Wittenberg, Martin Luther, still a monk, discovered the

[1] D. A. Hayes, *Paul and His Epistles* (New York: The Methodist Book Concern, 1915), pp. 123-24.

260

great truth that "the just shall live by faith." That became the keynote of the Protestant Reformation.

John Wesley likewise sought salvation through his own strivings and struggles. But one memorable night everything was changed. In his *Journal* he tells us what happened.

> In the evening I went very unwillingly to a society in Aldersgate Street, where one was reading Luther's preface to the *Epistle to the Romans*. About a quarter before nine, while he was describing the change which God works in the heart through faith in Christ, I felt my heart strangely warmed. I felt I did trust in Christ, Christ alone for salvation; and an assurance was given me that he had taken away *my* sins, even *mine*, and saved *me* from the law of sin and death.[2]

That was May 24, 1738, a day that has gone down in history as marking the beginning of one of the greatest revivals in all church history. Wesley's conversion has resulted in the conversion of millions more in the two hundred years since that time.

Paul, Augustine, Luther, Wesley—what a glorious succession! It all started back there on the Damascus road and found its greatest outlet through the apostle's pen. The Epistles of Paul have flowed down across the centuries like living waters, leaving healing behind them wherever they have gone.

2. Form of the Epistles

The Epistles of Paul follow a rather similar pattern as to form. First there is the *salutation*, which includes: (1) his name, with the addition often of one or more of his colleagues; (2) the name of the individual or church to which the letter is sent; (3) the greeting—usually "grace and peace." Then there is the *thanksgiving*. Next comes the *doctrinal* section, usually the longest portion of the Epistle. Fourth comes the *practical* portion, often fairly lengthy. The Epistle usually ends with *personal greetings* and a *benediction*.

3. The Greetings

In Paul's day, as we now know from the many papyrus letters of that period, it was the custom for a letter writer to put his own name at the beginning. So Paul begins all thirteen of his Epistles with his name.

[2] John Wesley, *Journal* (Curnock's Standard Edition; London: Epworth Press, 1938), I, 475-76.

Then he usually adds his title "apostle." The only exceptions are the two Thessalonian letters, Philemon, and Philippians. It is obvious that in the case of these four he felt no
need of asserting his apostolic authority. But in writing to
such places as Corinth and Galatia it was very important to
do so.

The ordinary Greek greeting in the papyrus letters was
"joy." The Hebrew salutation then, as now, was "peace"
(*shalom*). Paul combines these two in the greetings of all
his Epistles. Christianity fulfilled the highest hopes of both
Jews and Greeks. It is the one universal religion.

4. Classification of the Epistles

The letters of Paul fall rather naturally into four groups:

(1) Those of his second missionary journey, written in
A.D. 50 and 51. These include I and II Thessalonians. The
main topic of this group is *eschatology*, or the doctrine of future
things.

(2) Those of the third missionary journey, written about
A.D. 55 or 56. These include I and II Corinthians, Galatians—
which may have been written earlier—and Romans. The main
topic here is *soteriology*, or the doctrine of salvation.

(3) The Prison Epistles, written during Paul's first imprisonment at Rome, A.D. 59-61. These include Philemon, Colossians, Ephesians, and Philippians—probably in that order. The
main theme of this group is *Christology*, the doctrine of the
person of Christ.

(4) The Pastoral Epistles, written between Paul's release
from his first Roman imprisonment and his death, and so between 61 and 67. This group includes I Timothy, Titus, and
II Timothy. The main topic is *ecclesiology*, or the Church.

5. The General Character of the Epistles

With the exception of Romans and Ephesians, the Epistles
of Paul are not theological treatises but occasional letters.
By "occasional" letters we mean that they were written spontaneously because of some occasion that arose. Paul wrote
to the Thessalonians to correct some misconceptions they held
about the Second Coming; to the Corinthians to correct some
sad conditions existing among them; to the Galatians to combat the Judaizing influences threatening to undo his work in
that province; to Philemon about his runaway slave, Onesimus;

to the Colossians to combat the Gnostic tendencies there; to the Philippians to thank them for their love gifts; to Timothy and Titus to advise them in church administration. Romans and Ephesians were probably intended for more general use.

One very striking fact about Paul's Epistles is that they were missionary letters, written to meet the needs arising on the mission fields. It was the missionary movement which caused the New Testament to be written.

FIRST THESSALONIANS

A. INTRODUCTION

I. The City

In the time of Paul, Thessalonica was the chief city of Macedonia, a great shipping center with about 200,000 population. It is still an important seaport for the surrounding country. The Egnatian Way, which led from Rome to the East, passed through the city. As a commercial center on the Aegean, Thessalonica was rivaled only by Corinth to the south and Ephesus to the east.

II. The Church

On his second missionary journey Paul had founded the church at Thessalonica. The account in the seventeenth chapter of Acts indicates that the church was mainly Gentile, because the Jews rejected the gospel. Various references in the Epistle corroborate this, showing that Paul is writing mostly to Gentiles.

III. The Occasion

Paul had to leave Thessalonica by night because of the persecution raised against him by the Jews. He went to Beroea, and then, forced to flee from there, on to Athens.

When Paul arrived in Athens he was much concerned for his converts back at Thessalonica, who would be undergoing persecution from the Jews. So he sent Timothy to check on the situation there.

Paul's stay at Athens was cut rather short. So when Timothy returned he found the apostle at Corinth. He reported that the Thessalonian Christians were remaining true under persecution. But some of them were concerned about the fact that believers were dying before Christ's return. Would they miss out on that important event? Paul quickly dictated a letter to them to assure their minds in the matter.

IV. The Purpose

It seems clear that there were two purposes for which Paul wrote: (1) to encourage and comfort the Christians at Thessalonica in the persecutions they were enduring; (2) to correct a misunderstanding in their minds about his teaching on the second coming of Christ. He assured them that their deceased loved ones would share in that event.

V. The Place and Time of Writing

Both the Thessalonian letters were written from Corinth, during Paul's stay of a year and a half there on his second missionary journey. The date, as established now by archaeology, would be A.D. 50 or 51. This is derived from an inscription at Delphi which names Gallio as proconsul of Achaia and indicates that he took office in either A.D. 51 or 52. So Paul probably arrived in Corinth in A.D. 50.

B. CONTENTS

First Thessalonians is such a spontaneous, personal letter that it is a bit difficult to outline. Paul did not construct an outline and then compose his letter from that outline. Rather, he wrote from his heart to these recent converts of his. Every true pastor knows what a fatherly feeling one has for his own converts. They are his children in the Lord.

There do seem to be, however, two main divisions of the Epistle. The first three chapters are primarily personal, while chapters four and five are more doctrinal and practical.

I. Personal Matters (cc. 1—3)

1. Salutation (1:1)

In the writing of this Epistle, Paul associates with himself his younger colleagues, Silas and Timothy. This shows a beautiful spirit of magnanimity. It also shows the close association of Paul and his fellow workers.

As already noted, Paul combines the typical Greek greeting, "Joy," and the Hebrew greeting, "Peace," in his salutation to the churches, modifying "joy" to "grace."

2. A Model Church (1:2-10)

In almost all of his Epistles, Paul follows the salutation with a thanksgiving to God. Gratitude was spontaneous with Paul, a habit that is worth cultivating.

Though of recent origin—or perhaps because of recent origin—the church at Thessalonica was almost a model one. Paul mentions their "work of faith," their "labor of love," and their "patience of hope." These expressions remind us of the great Pauline trilogy in I Cor. 13:13—"faith, hope, love."

It seems that, intended or not, these three phrases in verse 3 find their counterpart in verses 9 and 10. Their "work of faith" was that "ye turned unto God from idols"; their "labor of love" was "to serve a living and true God"; their "patience of hope" was "to wait for his Son from heaven." Paul's use of trilogies is a marked characteristic of his Epistles.

Three things are said about the members of this model church: (1) they were genuinely converted—"Ye turned unto God from idols" (v. 9); (2) they were living exemplary lives —"Ye became an example" (v. 7); (3) they were aggressive in propagating the faith—"From you hath sounded forth the word of the Lord" (v. 8). This church was certainly far from backslidden.

Verse 6 sums up the attitude of the Thessalonian believers —"Ye became imitators of us, and of the Lord, having received the word in much affliction, with joy of the Holy Spirit." Young converts who eagerly imitate their pastor, seek to imitate Christ, in the midst of persecution are filled with joy— that is the picture at Thessalonica.

3. *Paul's Relations with the Thessalonians* (cc. 2—3)

a. *His Ministry Among Them* (2:1-12). In spite of Paul's persecution and imprisonment at Philippi, when he came to Thessalonica he was bold to preach the gospel to them "in much conflict." The account in Acts (17:1-9) indicates that opposition from the Jews was strong from the beginning. But that did not deter Paul.

The large heart of the apostle is shown very beautifully in verses 7 and 8. Instead of asserting his authority as an apostle (v. 6), he was as gentle as a nurse with her own children, and "being affectionately desirous of you, we were well pleased to impart unto you, not the gospel of God only, but also our own souls, because ye were become very dear to us." He dealt with them "as a father with his own children" (v. 11). Paul had a true pastor's heart.

While in Thessalonica, Paul had worked "night and day," so that he might not be a financial burden to them. In between his times of preaching he worked at his trade of tent-making. It is said that one of the main industries in Thessalonica at that time was the manufacture of coarse cloth for tents. So it would probably be easy for Paul to get work.

The apostle could call their attention to "how holily and righteously and unblamably" he had behaved himself among them (v. 10). Happy is the pastor who leaves such a record behind him.

b. *His Thanksgiving for Them* (2:13-16). Paul was thankful that the Thessalonians had received his message, not as man's opinion, but as the word of God. He was also grateful for their faithfulness under persecution.

c. *His Longing for Them* (2:17-20). It had been with great regret that Paul had left them. Often he would have visited them, but "Satan hindered." They were his loved ones, and he longed to see them.

d. *Timothy's Mission* (3:1-10). When the apostle found that he could not visit them himself he sent Timothy, "to establish you, and to comfort you concerning your faith; that no man be moved by these afflictions" (vv. 2-3). Those words also express well the purpose of the Epistle.

The humanity of Paul is revealed in the repeated phrase: "when we [I] could no longer forbear" (vv. 1, 5). The apostle was a man of very intense emotions, and he felt things keenly. He was anxious about his new converts.

When Timothy brought to him at Corinth a good report of the conditions in the church at Thessalonica, Paul was much comforted (v. 7). His heart overflowed with thanksgiving for their loyalty.

e. *An Apostolic Benediction* (3:11-13). So rejoiced was Paul that he broke out in a beautiful benedictory prayer. This passage also reveals the secret of how to keep sanctified—"increase and abound in love one toward another, and toward all men" (v. 12). If we do that we shall be established in holiness and ready for the second coming of Christ.

II. *Practical and Doctrinal Teachings* (cc. 4—5)

1. *The Will of God* (4:1-8)

One of the great passages in the New Testament is I Thess. 4:3—"This is the will of God, even your sanctification." It is worth observing that this declaration is addressed to the people described in the first chapter as converted, exemplary, aggressive Christians. The experience Paul is talking about is not for sinners or backsliders; it is for God's own children.

It may seem strange that the apostle should give as the purpose of their sanctification "that ye abstain from fornication," emphasizing thus the ethical aspect of holiness. But we must remember that Paul was writing to those who had recently been saved from paganism, and who were still surrounded by heathen immorality. It is difficult for us today to realize the unspeakably low moral conditions of that period. The excavations at Pompeii have given us vivid proof of the indescribable licentiousness of Paul's day. The modern parallel would be found only in the low morals of some of our heathen mission fields.

The commentators are almost evenly divided as to whether "vessel" (v. 4) means one's body or one's wife. In favor of the latter is the fact that the verb "possess" is better rendered "acquire" or "get possession of." In any case, the emphasis is that God has not called to uncleanness, but to holiness (v. 7).

2. A Quiet Life (4:9-12)

One of the important exhortations of this Epistle is found in verse 11—"that ye study to be quiet, and to do your own business." That is a much-needed admonition in our restless "Aspirin Age."

3. The Second Coming (4:13-18)

This paragraph contains one of the most definite descriptions of the so-called "Rapture" phase of Christ's second coming. Paul first declares that the deceased saints will have a part in the Rapture. Those who are alive at the time will not "precede"—"prevent" (K.J.V.) is the old English equivalent—those who have died. First will take place the resurrection of the righteous (v. 16). Then all the saints will be caught up together "to meet the Lord in the air" (v. 17). The Thessalonians are to "comfort one another with these words" (v. 18).

4. The Day of the Lord (5:1-11)

This expression is particularly prominent in the Minor Prophets. There it always means God's day of judgment, a day of darkness and desolation. Here it seems to refer in general to the time of the Second Coming.

As in the Olivet Discourse of Jesus, the main emphasis is on readiness for the coming of Christ—"Let us watch and be sober" (v. 6). That should always be our main interest in connection with the Second Coming.

5. Miscellaneous Exhortations (5:12-22)

Into this paragraph the apostle packs a whole series of things he would like to say to his converts at Thessalonica. Each one of them will reward careful meditation in our devotional reading.

6. Closing Items (5:23-28)

"And the God of peace himself sanctify you wholly" (v. 23) is the basis of the term "entire sanctification." The Greek word for "wholly" is found only here in the New Testament. It is a compound term meaning "wholly-completely." Perhaps the best translation is "through and through." It describes a thorough sanctifying of our entire being.

Greek letters of this period commonly close with the wish: "I hope that you are in good health." How much more beautiful is Paul's brief benediction: "The grace of our Lord Jesus Christ be with you"!

SECOND THESSALONIANS

A. INTRODUCTION

I. The Place and Time of Writing

Paul wrote his second letter to the Thessalonians only a few months after his first. Both were written from Corinth, about A.D. 50 or 51.

II. The Occasion

After Paul had sent his first letter he learned that some at Thessalonica had misinterpreted his teaching on the Second Coming. They had taken so seriously his emphasis on its imminence that they had quit working and were waiting around for the great event to take place. This was causing an unfortunate situation.

III. The Purpose

The purpose of this second letter was to correct the misunderstanding about the Second Coming and to urge the people to go back to work.

B. Contents

I. Salutation (1:1-2)

Again, as in I Thessalonians, Paul associates with himself Silas and Timothy. And again he greets them with grace and peace.

II. Faithfulness in Affliction (1:3-12)

Paul begins by thanking God for their growth in faith and love (v. 3). Apparently their sufferings were drawing them more closely together. As often happens, outside persecution united the church more firmly.

III. The Second Coming (c. 2)

Paul now proceeds to correct the misunderstanding on this point. The Thessalonians are not to become shaken and troubled with the idea that Christ is coming right away (v. 2). Even though one of their number might have had a false impression ("by spirit"), or some supposed saying of Paul had been reported ("by word"), or a forged letter purportedly from him had been presented ("by epistle as from us"), yet they were to hold steady and not get agitated. The date-setters are still with us, getting people excited every now and then. A sane study of the New Testament will save us from going astray here.

Paul gives two signs that will precede the Second Coming: (1) an apostasy, or falling away; (2) the manifestation of "the man of sin." The description of this person fits that of the beast in Revelation (13:1-10), what is commonly called "the Antichrist."

In verse 6 the word "let" (K.J.V.) means "restrain" or "hinder." The "one that restraineth" has been interpreted as the Roman Empire—particularly the emperor Claudius at this time—or the Holy Spirit. The latter fits into the premillennial view that the Holy Spirit will leave this world at the Rapture —when Christ comes for His Church—and that the result will be an outbreak of sin accompanied by terrible judgments from God—what is called the "Great Tribulation." This will be followed by the Revelation, when Christ returns with His Church to set up His millennial kingdom on earth.

A terrible truth is stated in verses 11-12. If people willfully reject the truth and refuse to believe it, then they become a prey to delusions, so that they finally can sincerely believe a lie. As in other places in the New Testament—especially the Gospel of John—we are reminded that unbelief is primarily moral rather than mental.

The Thessalonian Christians are admonished to "hold the traditions which ye were taught, whether by word, or by epistle of ours" (v. 15). We do well to recognize that orthodox Christianity has stood the test of nineteen centuries, and we are foolish to leave it for some modern fancy.

The chapter closes with one of Paul's frequent benedictions (vv. 16-17). These sprang spontaneously from a heart filled with devotion to God and love to man.

IV. Final Admonitions (3:1-16)

In this closing chapter Paul exhorts his readers to be steadfast in Christ (v. 5). He speaks out forcibly against the idea of waiting idly for the coming of Christ, declaring emphatically: "If any will not work, neither let him eat" (v. 10). He chides those who instead of being busy are "busybodies" (v. 11), and exhorts them that "with quietness they work, and eat their own bread" (v. 12), rather than living on others.

V. The Close (3:17-18)

The apostle calls attention to his autograph with which every genuine Epistle of his closes (cf. 2:2). Since his letters were dictated to secretaries, this personal signature was all-important to prove genuineness. The Thessalonians were not to accept any letter without this.

FIRST CORINTHIANS

A. INTRODUCTION

I. The Corinthian Correspondence

Paul spent a year and a half at Corinth on his second journey. As we have noted, this was probably A.D. 50-51.

Our I Corinthians was apparently not the first letter Paul wrote to Corinth. For in I Cor. 5:9 he says: "I wrote unto you in my epistle to have no company with fornicators." When this earlier epistle was written, or where, we do not know. But this reference shows that Paul wrote letters, probably many, which are not preserved to us.

Also the Corinthians had written to Paul, for in 7:1 he says: "Now concerning the things whereof ye wrote unto me."

Probably a considerable correspondence was carried on between Paul and this important church.

II. The Place and Time of Writing

First Corinthians was written from Ephesus during Paul's stay of three years there on his third journey. The date would be around A.D. 55. About five years had passed since Paul's pastorate there, and conditions had risen in the church that needed correction.

III. The City

Corinth was one of the great commercial centers of the eastern Mediterranean world in Paul's day. Lying at the crossroads of East and West, it caught the traffic going both ways. It was situated on a narrow isthmus separating the southern part of the peninsula from the rest of Greece. Today a canal some four miles long cuts across the isthmus. But in Paul's day small ships were sometimes pulled across on rollers; large ships unloaded their baggage for transfer. Corinth had a seaport on both sides of the isthmus, Cenchreae on the east (Aegean) and Lechaeum on the west (Adriatic).

The city of Corinth was noted not only for its wealth but also for its wickedness. "To Corinthianize" meant to corrupt morally. Excavations have uncovered thirty-three taverns behind a colonnade one hundred feet long.

Realizing the strategic importance of Corinth—in whose streets could be seen sailors, travelers, and merchants from all over the world—Paul spent a year and a half founding a church there. Yet this church gave him more trouble than any other. The atmosphere was not conducive to holy living.

IV. The Occasion and Purpose

Some visitors from the household of Chloe in Corinth had reported to Paul that there were serious divisions in the church (I Cor. 1:11). He also heard of a bad case of immorality tolerated in the church membership (5:1). These reports greatly disturbed him and made him feel that he must write.

Then, too, the Corinthians had written him (7:1), asking his advice on certain questions such as marriage and things sacrificed to idols. It was time he was answering their questions. Through it all was his purpose to enlighten the Corinthian Christians and help to correct abuses in the church.

B. Contents

The Epistle has two natural divisions: I. Things About Which He Had Heard (cc. 1—6); II. Things About Which They Had Written (cc. 7—16). In the first part are discussed three problems: (1) Divisions (cc. 1—4); (2) Immorality (c. 5); (3) Lawsuits (c. 6). In the second part six problems are discussed: (1) Marriage (c. 7); (2) Things offered to idols (cc. 8—10); (3) Church customs and conduct (c. 11); (4) Spiritual gifts (cc. 12—14); (5) The resurrection (c. 15); (6) The collection (c. 16). These nine problems constitute the table of contents the Epistle and should be familiar to every student.

I. Things About Which He Had Heard (cc. 1—6)

1. Divisions (cc. 1—4)

a. *Salutation* (1:1-3). In writing to the Corinthians, Paul immediately mentioned his position as apostle, for he was going to have to assert his authority in dealing with conditions in the church. He associated with himself Sosthenes, who may have been the former ruler of the Jewish synagogue at Corinth (Acts 18:17).

b. *Thanksgiving* (1:4-9). As usual after the salutation, Paul thanks God for these Christians. The language in verse 7 indicates that this church was outstanding for its ability.

c. *The Four Parties* (1:10-17). But this was largely spoiled by the fact that the church was split up into four parties—those claiming to be of: (1) Paul, (2) Apollos, (3) Peter, (4) Christ. Paul had been the founder of the church, and many would hold him in highest esteem. But Apollos was an eloquent orator, and some people liked his preaching much more. The Judaizing party claimed Peter as its leader. Had he not been the foremost of the apostles? The fourth party held itself aloof, on a pedestal of spiritual pride. They were the real "Christians." It is probable that this group was the most fanatical and troublesome.

d. *The Word of the Cross* (1:18-25). In contrast to this petty bickering, Paul points to the Cross. There is the secret of God's power manifested in the salvation of humanity. The Corinthians were proud, boastful, quarrelsome. They prided themselves on their human wisdom. But in this paragraph Paul draws a striking contrast between "the wisdom of the world" (v. 20) and "the wisdom of God" (v. 21). The former is foolishness in God's sight.

"The foolishness of preaching" (v. 21) should be "the foolishness of the thing preached." It is the message rather than the method that is indicated here. The Jews "ask for signs" and the Greeks "seek after wisdom" (v. 22). Christ crucified is the answer to both quests, for He is "the power of God" (signs) and "the wisdom of God" (v. 24). As in Colossians, Paul points to Christ as the only adequate answer.

  e. *The Instruments God Uses* (1:26-31). Paul calls attention to the fact that after all there were not many wise or noble members—as the world looks at it—in the church. There is no justification for their pride. The fact is that God often uses weak and despised human instruments, the better to display His power.

  f. *Man's Wisdom Versus God's Wisdom* (c. 2). When Paul came to Corinth he "determined not to know anything among you, save Jesus Christ, and him crucified" (v. 2). This may reflect his reactions to his seeming failure at Athens. At Corinth he did not try to depend on eloquence or argument, but only on the power of the Spirit.

But though he avoided human wisdom in his dealing with these who prided themselves so much on their superior knowledge, yet he did preach "God's wisdom" (v. 7), which is the mystery of redemption through Christ. He warns the Corinthians that the "natural man" cannot understand spiritual truth (v. 14). Only by the aid of God's Spirit can we understand the things of God (v. 13).

  g. *Carnal Corinthians* (3:1-9). On the surface it seems difficult to harmonize 3:1 with 1:2. In the latter place Paul addresses the Corinthians as "sanctified in Christ Jesus." Here he says they are "carnal." It is obvious that the term "sanctified" in 1:2 is used in its partial meaning of "consecrated, set apart to God," which all Christians are. Even as carnal babes in Christ they belong to God. Regeneration includes initial sanctification, or cleansing from the pollution of our own sinning.

But the point that Paul is emphasizing here is that a schismatic spirit is an evidence of carnality. Pride always leads to divisions, and pride comes close to being the essence of carnality.

Paul's answer to the quibbling, quarrelsome attitude of the Corinthians is: Apollos is nothing; Paul is nothing (v. 7). God is everything. Furthermore, he and Apollos are one (v. 8).

Verse 9 looks both ways. "Ye are God's husbandry" (Moffatt, "farm") points back to Paul's discussion of planting and watering in verses 6-8. "Ye are God's building" points forward to verses 10-15.

h. *God's Building* (3:10-23). Paul states that as a wise master builder he laid the foundation of the church at Corinth as its founder. Now let everyone be careful how he builds on it. The only foundation is Christ—not Paul, Apollos, or Cephas. Only lasting materials are to be used in building.

Then Paul makes the figure a bit more specific by stating that the church at Corinth is a temple of God, and adds: "If any man destroyeth the temple of God, him shall God destroy" (v. 17). This was a solemn warning to the schismatics. By dividing the church they were destroying it.

These first three chapters have really turned out to be a discussion on the subject of *wisdom*. Now Paul concludes his treatment of that topic with the emphatic declaration: "The wisdom of this world is foolishness with God" (v. 19). That is the divine characterization of all merely intellectual wisdom which leaves God out. Since God is the source of all wisdom, no one can be truly wise who ignores God.

i. *Paul's Defense of His Ministry* (c. 4). There were some sharp critics of Paul at Corinth. He reminds them that he is not concerned about their judgment (v. 3). He asserts: "I know nothing against myself" (v. 4).

In the next paragraph (vv. 6-13) Paul again warns the Corinthians against pride, their besetting sin. He asks them a question which ought to close the mouth of every boaster: "What hast thou that thou didst not receive?" (v. 7.) The answer to that question—"Nothing!"—leaves absolutely no place for pride.

One cannot understand Paul's Epistles unless he realizes that the apostle is often answering his opponents. Many times words he uses should be put in quotation marks, for Paul is using them, not in their true sense, but in the sense that his opponents give to them. Such is the case with verse 10, where "fools," "wise," "weak," and "strong" should all be in quotation marks.

After Paul's stern strictures on the Corinthians for their pride and schismatic spirit, he ends this section on a tone of tenderness (vv. 14-21). He says—"I write not these things to shame you, but to admonish you as my beloved children." Yet if, as children, they will not heed then he will have to use the rod (v. 21).

2. *Immorality* (c. 5)

With all their boasted wisdom and spirituality, the Corinthians were tolerating an obnoxious case of incest. One of the church members was living with his stepmother. Instead of mourning over the situation, they were puffed up with pride (v. 2). Paul declares that, though absent, he is sitting as judge in the case and giving sentence against the offender.

The language of verse 5 seems very harsh. But what Paul refers to is probably expulsion from the church. "The destruction of the flesh" may mean either mortification of fleshly desires, or physical suffering as punishment for sin, or both.

The apostle reminds them that in a previous letter he had told them not to fellowship with fornicators (v. 9). He gives his final orders in this case: "Put away the wicked man from among yourselves"; that is, put him out of the church.

3. *Lawsuits* (c. 6)

a. *The Christian Attitude* (vv. 1-11). The spirit of division had led some of the church members actually to go to law with one another. Paul chides them for this. If the saints are going to judge angels, can they not even take care of cases within the church? Is there no one capable of judging? Then Paul states a striking truth—"Nay, already it is altogether a loss to you, that ye have lawsuits one with another" (v. 7, margin). As Moffatt renders it: "Even to have lawsuits with one another is in itself evidence of defeat." That is, even if a man won the lawsuit, he had lost spiritually more than he gained materially.

The Christian attitude is to suffer wrong, rather than to sue at law. So far from this were some of the Corinthians that they were inflicting wrong, and that on fellow Christians.

The three terms "washed," "sanctified," "justified" (v. 11) evidently refer to the one experience of conversion in its different aspects. It is clear that "sanctified" here refers to initial sanctification.

b. *Warning Against Fornication* (vv. 12-20). It is very probable that the repeated phrase, "All things are lawful for me" (v. 12), was the watchword of some party at Corinth. In that case the words should be put within quotation marks, and the second clause in each half of the verse should be treated as Paul's answer. Probably, also, the expression, "Meats for the belly, and the belly for meats," should be treated as a quotation. Evidently there were some of the Corinthian Christians who had libertine tendencies. They probably considered themselves more enlightened than the rest.

Paul bases his uncompromising denunciation of fornication on the premise that the body of the Christian is a temple of the Holy Spirit (v. 19). That is the noblest conception of the human body ever expressed in language.

II. *Things About Which They Had Written* (cc. 7—16)

1. *Marriage* (c. 7)

a. *Marriage and Celibacy* (vv. 1-9). It is very evident that Paul favored celibacy (vv. 1, 7-8). Yet because of the prevalent "fornications"—note the plural—at Corinth he thought that marriage might be safer. In any event both husband and wife are to be unselfish and thoughtful each of the other (v. 3).

The statement of verse 9, "It is better to marry than to burn," is sometimes interpreted as referring to hell fire. But the correct meaning is given in the Revised Standard Version: "It is better to marry than to be aflame with passion." Of course, the proper procedure is to keep the body under the control of the spirit.

b. *Marriage of Believers and Unbelievers* (vv. 10-16). In verse 10 Paul is addressing married Christians and warns against separation. But in verse 12 he speaks "to the rest"; that is, non-Christian couples.

It would appear that some of the Corinthians found themselves in the position of living with a companion who was not a Christian. Should they seek a divorce? "No," said Paul, "stay together." The union is still a valid marriage and is consecrated by the fact that one is a Christian. ("Sanctified" in verse 14 is obviously used in its partial meaning of "consecrated.") Consequently the children are not "unclean" (illegitimate). Paul says that marriage is a sacred union even if one partner is unsaved.

Of course, this in no way condones Christians marrying non-Christians. Paul is dealing with a situation where the husband or wife has accepted Christ and the companion refuses to do so—a common occurrence.

c. *Christians and Society* (vv. 17-24). Paul did not advocate the overthrow of the social and economic customs of his day. Christianity revolutionizes from within, not from without. The slave was not to demand his freedom because a Christian (v. 21).

d. *Concerning Virgins* (vv. 25-40). The language of Paul in verse 25 is very interesting. He says that he has no command from the Lord, but that he is giving his personal judgment. His advice is that the married remain together, but that the unmarried remain single. Why? "The time is shortened" (v. 29). Paul was expecting Christ to come at any time. So why become involved in marriage? Then too, the children would only suffer in the persecutions beginning to fall on Christians—from the Jews at this time. We are glad that Paul is careful to state that he is giving his own opinion in the matter. For celibacy has not proved practical for most Christians.

In verse 36, the Revised Standard Version gives the clearest rendering: "If any one thinks that he is not behaving properly toward his betrothed, if his passions are strong, and if it has to be, let him do what he will, he does not sin; let them marry." However, Paul would rather see them remain single (v. 37).

2. *Things Offered to Idols* (cc. 8—10).

Dr. Tenney gives a four-part outline in this section.[3] It is so good that we are using it (with slight adaptation).

a. *Evaluated by the Idol* (c. 8). Another problem that plagued the Corinthian Christians was whether they should eat meat that had been offered to idols. This was a very practical problem, for much of the meat sold in the public markets had been so offered.

[3] Merrill Tenney, *The New Testament* (Grand Rapids: Wm. B. Eerdmans Publishing Co., 1953), p. 310.

Probably the words, "We know that we all have knowledge," are quoted by Paul from the lips of the proud "wise men" at Corinth, and so should be placed in quotation marks. Paul's answer is: "Knowledge puffeth up, but love edifieth." The last word is literally "builds up," as one would build a house. So it may be translated: "Knowledge blows up, but love builds up." One reason "a little knowledge is a dangerous thing" is that it inflates a person with false pride. But true education is like laying one brick upon another, building a solid structure.

Probably the last half of verse 4 and perhaps all of verse 8 should be put in quotation marks as reflecting the attitude of the "wise" at Corinth. We can almost hear them saying repeatedly, "We know."

Paul's solution is unselfish love, the best solution to every problem. It is true that idols are nothing—just so much wood, stone, or metal. But we should not do anything to offend the weak conscience of a Christian brother. ("Weak" here means "unenlightened.") Then the apostle closes this section of his discussion with one of the most magnanimous statements ever made—"If meat causeth my brother to stumble, I will eat no flesh for evermore, that I cause not my brother to stumble" (v. 13). Note the repeated expression, "my brother." Love is the highest test in life.

b. *Evaluated by Freedom* (c. 9). Paul's discussion of this problem raised by the Corinthians gave him the opportunity for a masterful essay on the general subject of Christian liberty. While he takes up the question of idols again in chapter 10, this chapter is devoted to the broader topic.

There are two fundamental philosophies of freedom. The first might be tagged, "License to do what I please." The other is, "Liberty to do what is right and best." Paul's was the second. He reminds the Corinthians that he had a lot of "rights": (1) "to eat and drink"—that is, to be provided with free entertainment because he was a preacher; (2) "to lead about a wife that is a believer"—a "sister" in the Lord; (3) "to forbear working"—that is, to cease doing manual labor for his living. But Paul had not been one to demand his rights.

However, the apostle teaches definitely (vv. 7-14) that it is God's ordained plan that a minister of the gospel should be compensated for his services, so that he will not have to do secular work for his living. But because Paul was the target of so much criticism he had not availed himself of this right (v. 15).

The basic principle on which Paul operated is expressed clearly in verse 22: "I am become all things to all men, that I may by all means save some." Then he adds: "I do all things for the gospel's sake" (v. 23). What a tremendous consecration! No wonder that Paul has made a greater impression on Christianity than anyone else since Christ founded it.

c. *Evaluated by Relation to God* (10:1-22). Paul returns now to the subject of idols. In chapter 8 it seems that he endorses the view that idols are nothing. But here he shows the other side of the picture: there is a real danger in idolatry. For that he cites the example of what took place at Mount Sinai, when the people worshiped the golden calf. It led to immorality, as idolatry always does. Five warnings he gives from the history of Israel (vv. 6-10). Then he caps them all with this general warning: "Let him that thinketh he standeth take heed lest he fall" (v. 12).

But he does not stop. The thirteenth verse gives us one of the most comforting promises in God's Word: "There hath no temptation taken you but such as man can bear: but God is faithful, who will not suffer you to be tempted above that ye are able; but will with the temptation make also the way of escape, that ye may be able to endure it." That is God's guarantee to the tempted.

In view of what happened to Israel, Paul admonishes: "Flee from idolatry" (v. 14). Though idols themselves are nothing, yet they represent the demons which the heathen worship (v. 20). So the safest course is to avoid any contact with them.

d. *Evaluated by Relation to Others* (10:23-33). In this paragraph Paul comes back to the original discussion. For the third and fourth times (cf. 6:12) he quotes, "All things are lawful." But the correct principle is that of unselfish love: "Let no man seek his own, but each his neighbor's good" (v. 24). That is, liberty is limited by the law of love.

Verses 31 and 32 indicate the two great motives that should govern Christian action: (1) God's glory; (2) man's salvation.

3. Church Conduct (c. 11)

a. *Women at Worship* (vv. 1-16). Paul definitely advised that the Christian women should follow the custom of the day by keeping veiled in public. To fail to do so would only open the church to criticism from the outside. It would seem that some of the women in the church wanted to demonstrate their Christian liberty by disregarding all proprieties. Paul warned against such procedure.

b. *The Lord's Supper* (vv. 17-34). The church at Corinth in Paul's day was very far removed from perfection. People were actually getting drunk at the Lord's Supper.

In the Early Church the agape (love feast) and the Eucharist (Lord's Supper) were celebrated together. But finally it became necessary to separate them in order to protect the sacredness of the latter. For people were making the love feast an orgy of eating and drinking.

In verses 23-25 Paul describes the inauguration of the Lord's Supper. It is natural that his description should agree most nearly with Luke's, for these two men were closely united. The apostle's interpretation of the significance of the Lord's Supper in verse 26 is that it is a memorial of Christ's death and also an anticipation of His second coming.

Paul's discussion of the Lord's Supper here was intended to emphasize its great sacredness. That is what the Corinthians had forgotten.

4. Spiritual Gifts (cc. 12—14)

a. *Unity in Diversity* (c. 12). The unity of the Trinity is the basis for the unity of the Church (vv. 4-5). While there are diversities of gifts, one Spirit should be working through all the activity.

Nine gifts are listed here (vv. 8-10), beginning with wisdom and knowledge, and ending with tongues and the interpretation of tongues. But, again, it is one Spirit working through all (v. 11).

The word "body" occurs eighteen times in vv. 12-31. This long paragraph has one topic: the unity of the body of Christ, the Church. Every member has his place. There should be no self-depreciation (v. 15) or depreciation of others (v. 21). For all parts of the body are important.

In verse 28 we have another list, this time of eight orders in the Church. Apostles, prophets, and teachers are named first, and tongues again is named last. Then the apostle says: "But desire earnestly the greater gifts"—certainly not tongues, which is last in both lists. But there is something above and beyond these gifts—"a most excellent way." This is the way of love described in chapter 13.

b. Love, the Greatest Thing (c. 13). This beautiful chapter sets the way of love over against the unfortunate emphasis in Corinth on spiritual gifts. What they needed was love.

The first verse shows the connection with what precedes: "If I speak with the tongues of men"—eloquent oratory—"and of angels"—an unknown tongue—and do not have love, "I am become sounding brass, or a clanging cymbal." The gift of tongues without love means only clamor and confusion.

This chapter divides rather naturally into three sections: (1) values of love (vv. 1-3); (2) virtues of love (vv. 4-7); (3) victories of love (vv. 8-13).[4] The middle paragraph (vv. 4-7) reads most beautifully in the Revised Standard Version. We have space only to quote verse 5: "It is not arrogant or rude. Love does not insist on its own way; it is not irritable or resentful." That comes very close home to daily living.

Every clause and phrase of this great love chapter is trenchant. The student would do well to read it in a number of different translations. Each new version throws a little added light on this gem and makes it sparkle a bit more brightly.

c. The Gift of Tongues (c. 14). Paul picks up here where he left off at the end of chapter 12. He says: "Follow after love," or, as Moffatt has it: "Make love your aim." What a motto! Then he adds: "Desire earnestly spiritual gifts, but rather that ye may prophesy." Prophesying, or preaching, is listed as the greatest gift.

Paul declares that there is no value in speaking in public in a language that nobody understands. To do so is to be a "barbarian" (v. 11). The Greeks could not understand foreigners. So they called them *barbaras;* in other words, "ba-

---

[4] G. Campbell Morgan, *The Corinthian Letters of Paul* (New York: Fleming H. Revell Co., 1946), p. 161.

ba-ba." To speak in an "unknown tongue" is no better than that. It is much better to "prophesy" (preach) in a language that everyone can understand (vv. 23-25).

So Paul lays down definite rules to curb the orgy of over-emotionalism in the Corinthian church, which was producing disorder and confusion. Not more than two or three were to speak in tongues, and then not unless someone could interpret. Two or three could also preach.

In verses 34-36 Paul admonishes the women to keep silence in the churches. This must be interpreted in the light of the historical situation. The Christian women at Corinth were glorying in their new-found freedom and acting like children with a new toy. They were disturbing the church services by talking out loud. Paul told them to ask their questions at home, not in public worship.

The last verse sums up the general emphasis of the apostle: "Let all things be done decently and in order."

5. *The Resurrection* (c. 15)

This is the great resurrection chapter of the New Testament. It is also the longest chapter in this Epistle.

There are two main divisions of the chapter: (1) The Certainty of the Resurrection (vv. 1-34); (2) The Nature of the Resurrection (vv. 35-58). The first part answers the question of verse 12—"How say some among you that there is no resurrection of the dead?" The second answers the questions of verse 35—"How are the dead raised? and with what manner of body do they come?"

a. *The Certainty of the Resurrection* (vv. 1-34). The apostle begins with a brief summary of the post-Resurrection appearances of Jesus (vv. 1-11). The interesting thing is that Paul lists his vision of Jesus as on the same level with the Resurrection appearances described in the Gospels. He says, "He appeared to me also," using the same verb exactly as in the case of the other appearances. In other words, Paul claimed to have seen Jesus.

In verses 12-19 the apostle shows that to deny the resurrection is to deny the entire scheme of salvation. If there is no resurrection, then Christ did not rise. In that case we have no hope of redemption.

But in verses 20-28 Paul asserts emphatically that Christ has risen. That assures us of our resurrection if we are in Him.

In verses 29-34 the apostle points out the great importance of believing in the resurrection. Without that hope we might as well "eat and drink" (v. 32). If we are going to die like animals, we might as well live like animals. That is the logic of our day, too.

b. *The Nature of the Resurrection* (vv. 35-57). The important statement on this subject is found in verse 44: "It is sown a natural body; it is raised a spiritual body." This language is so clear that there seems to be no excuse for arguing for a physical body in the next life. Doubtless our glorified bodies will be so far beyond these physical bodies that they will surpass our wildest dreams. We do not need to know all about it now. Heaven will be better than our best conceptions of it.

Verses 51-57 are somewhat parallel to I Thess. 4:13-18. In both places we find a striking description of the second coming of Christ. Both passages emphasize its suddenness.

In view of our glorious prospects we can well afford to be "stedfast, unmovable, always abounding in the work of the Lord." The hope of the resurrection and immortality is the highest incentive to Christian character and service.

6. The Collection (c. 16)

Paul was taking up a collection in the Gentile churches for the poor saints at Jerusalem. Thus he hoped to bind the Jewish and Gentile churches more closely together. Verse 2 indicates God's plan for regular giving: (1) It should be systematic—"on the first day of the week"; (2) It should be proportionate to one's income—"as he may prosper." This fits in well with our tithing program. It is a plan that works, as has been proved time and again.

Paul is planning on a visit to Corinth (v. 5). But he wants them to have their offering already collected before he arrives (v. 2). The apostle was careful in handling public monies: chosen delegates were to accompany the offering to Jerusalem (v. 3).

A great general principle is enunciated in v. 14: "Let all that ye do be done in love." The Corinthians certainly needed that admonition. But so do we.

Paul closes with his own autograph signature: "The salutation of me Paul with mine own hand" (v. 21). It was essential that this very important Epistle be accepted as genuine and authoritative.

SECOND CORINTHIANS

A. Introduction

I. The Place and Time of Writing

The Second Epistle to the Corinthians was written from a city in Macedonia, probably Philippi. The date was a few months after I Corinthians, about A.D. 56.

II. The Unity of the Book

The outstanding problem in relation to II Corinthians is the matter of its unity. Many scholars hold that chapters 10—13 were written before chapters 1—9.

In 2:4 Paul says: "Out of much affliction and anguish of heart I wrote unto you with many tears." In 7:8 we read: "For though I made you sorry with my epistle, I do not regret it: though I did regret it." Scholars generally refer to this previous epistle as the "stern letter" or "severe letter." But when did he write it?

One solution is that the severe letter is our I Corinthians. In it there are definitely some stern passages and places where Paul speaks with strong emotion. In the absence of any manuscript evidence whatever for the division of II Corinthians we may hold to its unity.

III. The Occasion and Purpose

Paul reveals the occasion for writing this Epistle more clearly than he does in the case of some of his other letters. In 1:8 he says: "For I would not have you ignorant, brethren, concerning our affliction which befell us in Asia, that we were weighed down exceedingly, beyond our power, insomuch that we despaired even of life." This experience took place in Ephesus during his stay of three years there on his third journey. Very much disturbed by reports of conditions at Corinth, he had sent Timothy thither with the First Epistle to the Corinthians, urging the church there not to mistreat or despise this messenger (I Cor. 16:10). He had wanted Apollos to go and try to straighten matters out, but the latter declined (I Cor. 16:12). Perhaps he wisely judged that his presence in Corinth would further agitate the party strife there and actually work out to Paul's disadvantage.

What the outcome was of Timothy's mission we do not know. But the implication seems to be that he failed to help matters. It is commonly thought that at this juncture Paul himself made a quick trip to Corinth, for in II Corinthians he says of his anticipated visit at that time: "This is the third time I am ready to come to you" (II Cor. 12:14; cf. 13:1). The second visit is unrecorded in Acts but probably occurred between the writing of the two Epistles. From what Paul says in II Corinthians we judge that he was insulted by some at Corinth and returned to Ephesus with a broken heart.

His next step was to send Titus, who was perhaps a little older than Timothy and seems to have been somewhat more firm in disposition. After he sent Titus, Paul was so overcome with anxiety about the Corinthian situation that he "despaired even of life." Worn down by his almost superhuman labors, it seemed this extra burden was more than he could carry.

Finally he left Ephesus and went to Troas. There he found a wide-open door of opportunity awaiting him. But he was so terribly distressed by his concern for the Corinthians that he could not even settle down and preach! So he went on across to Philippi. Here are his own words: "Now when I came to Troas for the gospel of Christ, and when a door was opened unto me in the Lord, I had no relief for my spirit, because I found not Titus my brother: but taking my leave of them, I went forth into Macedonia" (II Cor. 2:12-13).

Titus had stayed in Corinth longer than expected. To Paul this seemed a bad omen and only increased his anxiety. Though he had come to Troas to preach, he could not stand the suspense of waiting any longer for Titus. So he crossed over to Philippi, perhaps planning to go on to Corinth if Titus did not appear soon.

Finally the suspense was broken; Titus arrived! Paul tells us about it in II Cor. 7:5-6—"For even when we were come into Macedonia our flesh had no relief, but we were afflicted on every side; without were fightings, within were fears. Nevertheless he that comforteth the lowly, even God, comforted us by the coming of Titus."

Thereupon the apostle wrote to the Corinthians, expressing his relief at their changed attitude. The purpose of II Corinthians was to assure them of his love, and at the same time to defend himself against those in Corinth who were still challenging his authority.

IV. The General Character of the Epistle

Second Corinthians is the most personal of Paul's Epistles. Here his heart is bared to us and we see the intensity of his emotions. In this Epistle the great apostle is very human. Strong man that he was, he could be crushed to the ground with a heavy burden of anxious care for his converts. His autobiography as we find it in this Epistle is a comfort to us, for we see that the greatest of men are still human.

The difference between I and II Corinthians is well pointed out by D. A. Hayes. He writes:

> First Corinthians tells us more about the inside history of the early church, its troubles and its triumphs, its practices and its principles, than we can learn from any other book in the New Testament. Second Corinthians tells us more about the heart history and the inmost character of the apostle Paul than any other source of information we have.[4a]

B. CONTENTS

The Epistle has three main divisions, very clearly marked: I. Defense of His Ministry (cc. 1—7); II. The Collection for the Saints (cc. 8—9); III. Vindication of His Character (cc. 10—13).

I. Defense of His Ministry (cc. 1—7)

1. Salutation (1:1-2)

Paul associates Timothy with himself in the writing of this Second Epistle to the Corinthians. He also gives it a wider address: "with all the saints that are in the whole of Achaia." It was to be a sort of circular letter to the whole province.

2. Comfort in Affliction (1:3-11)

The keynote of this section is "comfort." The word occurs ten times in the first five verses of the paragraph. Only by finding comfort in our own sufferings are we able to comfort others in their afflictions (v. 4).

[4a] D. A. Hayes, *Paul and His Epistles* (New York: Methodist Book Concern, 1915), p. 229.

3. *Vindication of His Conduct* (1:12—2:13)

a. *His General Behavior Pattern* (1:12-14). Paul states that he has the testimony of his own conscience that "in holiness and sincerity of God, not in fleshly wisdom but in the grace of God, we behaved ourselves in the world." And he adds that he was especially careful of his behavior toward them.

b. *Explanation of His Change of Plans* (1:15—2:13). The apostle had first planned to go directly across to Corinth by ship from Ephesus and then to visit Macedonia—probably Thessalonica and Beroea—return to Corinth and then go to Jerusalem from there (vv. 15-16). But his plans had changed. Consequently some Corinthian critics were accusing him of being fickle (v. 17), of not knowing what he wanted to do. But it was to spare them that he postponed his visit (v. 23). Evidently he feared a serious clash because the atmosphere was tense at that time.

So instead of going in person Paul wrote them a letter. Out of much anguish of heart he wrote, with many tears, to show them his love (2:4).

The apostle was glad to learn that the church had taken action against the immoral person, concerning whose case he had written in his previous letter (c. 5). Now he urged them to forgive this man, who apparently had repented of his sin (2:5-11). So that case was cleared up.

4. *Vindication of His Apostleship* (2:14—6:10)

a. *The Nature of the Ministry* (2:14—3:18). In 2:14 Paul uses the figure of a Roman triumphal procession. But as he faces the gigantic task of the ministry, he asks: "Who is sufficient for these things?" (2:16.) The answer to that question he gives in 3:5—"Our sufficiency is of God." Certainly no man, of himself, is adequate for the demands of the ministry. Only with God can he succeed.

A beautiful thought is expressed in 3:18—"But we all, with unveiled face beholding as in a mirror the glory of the Lord, are transformed into the same image from glory to glory." The Greek word for "transformed" is *metamorphoo*. It is found in Rom. 12:2. The only other occurrences in the New Testament are in connection with the transfiguration of Jesus (Matt. 17:2; Mark 9:2). It suggests that the Christian life should be "the transfigured life."

b. *The Honesty of the Ministry* (4:1-6). If any man should be honest, certainly the preacher should be in handling the Word of God. For eternal souls are at stake. Paul says that he does not handle the Word of God deceitfully (v. 2). He does not preach himself, but Christ (v. 5).

c. *The Sufferings of the Ministry* (4:7—5:10). In 4:8-9 Paul says that we are pressed, perplexed, pursued. Phillips has a very striking translation of the last part of verse 9—"We may be knocked down but we are never knocked out!"[5]

One of the outstanding passages of this Epistle is to be found in 4:17-18—"For our light affliction, which is for the moment, worketh for us more and more exceedingly an eternal weight of glory; while we look not at the things which are seen, but at the things which are not seen: for the things which are seen are temporal; but the things which are not seen are eternal." That is one of the grandest statements of the life of faith that one could find anywhere.

Paul calls the human body a tent ("tabernacle") which will someday disappear. But in heaven we have our eternal home. In the midst of sufferings down here we sometimes groan, wishing to be clothed upon with immortality (5:1-4). In view of all this, "We walk by faith" (v. 7).

d. *The Motive of the Ministry* (5:11-19). Nowhere is the highest motive of the ministry expressed better than in 5:14 —"The love of Christ constraineth us." The expression "the love of Christ" may be interpreted three ways: (1) Christ's love for me; (2) my love for Christ; (3) Christ's love in me. All of these constrain me to unselfish sacrifice and selfless service.

The main message of the ministry is given in 5:19—"God was in Christ reconciling the world unto himself." That packs into a nutshell the very heart of the gospel.

e. *The Example of the Ministry* (5:20—6:10). The minister has the highest office on earth: he is an ambassador for Christ. That should make every minister square his shoulders and look the world in the face. The job of the ministry is to beseech men to be reconciled to God (5:20).

[5] J. B. Phillips, *Letters to Young Churches* (New York: The Macmillan Co., 1947), p. 73.

Yet this very glory of the ministry involves the high responsibility of being an example. For the ambassador represents Christ, and so must act like Him. He is to give "no occasion of stumbling in anything" (6:3), so that the ministry may not be blamed. In outward hardships (vv. 4-5), in inward graces (vv. 6-7), and in innocence of accusation (vv. 8-10) the preacher must commend himself as a minister of God.

5. *Concluding Appeal for Reconciliation* (6:11—7:16)

a. *Paul's Large Heart* (6:11-13). The apostle declares that his heart is enlarged towards the Corinthians. He begs them to enlarge their hearts: "You are not restricted by us, but you are restricted in your own affections" (R.S.V.).

b. *Parenthesis: Threefold Appeal* (6:14—7:1). Paul wants the Corinthians to be largehearted, but not so as to take in heathenism. So he issues a threefold appeal: (1) "Be not unequally yoked with unbelievers" (v. 14); (2) "Come ye out from among them, and be ye separate" (v. 17); (3) "Let us cleanse ourselves from all defilement of flesh and spirit, perfecting holiness in the fear of God" (7:1).

c. *The Foundations of Reconciliation* (7:2-16). There are three adequate bases for reconciliation: (1) Paul's affection for the Corinthians (vv. 2-4); (2) the obedience of the Corinthians in eliminating sin from their midst (vv. 5-12); (3) the affection of Titus for them and his good report about them (vv. 13-15). Paul concludes, with evident relief: "I rejoice that in everything I am of good courage concerning you" (v. 16).

II. The Collection for the Saints (cc. 8—9)

Paul had made brief reference to this matter in his first Epistle (I Cor. 16:1-9). Now he treats the matter at greater length. It is plain that this collection for the saints at Jerusalem was a major concern with him at this time.

1. *The Example of Macedonia* (8:1-7)

The churches of Macedonia—Philippi, Thessalonica, and Beroea—had set a wonderful example of liberality. Though poor, they had given richly. Not only that, but they demonstrated the primary principle of Christian stewardship by first giving themselves (v. 5). Three times in this paragraph Paul refers to giving as "this grace."

2. Exhortations to Giving (8:8-15)

The great example for our giving is Jesus Christ, who, though rich, yet for our sakes became poor to make us rich. If we have His grace, we shall give.

The Corinthians had begun their collection the previous year (v. 10). Paul now urges them to complete the project (v. 11). He desires that there shall be an equality of giving (v. 14), each church giving according to its ability.

3. The Handling of the Collection (8:16—9:5).

Paul is sending Titus to take care of getting the collection ready, and with him he is sending "the brother whose praise in the gospel is spread through all the churches" (v. 18). Origen and Jerome identify this one as Luke, the writer of the Gospel. Paul adds that this "brother" was "appointed by the churches to travel with us in the matter of this grace" (v. 19).

The principle which Paul enunciates in verse 21 should be followed by every pastor and church: "We take thought for things honorable, not only in the sight of the Lord, but also in the sight of men." One cannot be too careful in the handling of church finances.

The reason why Paul is sending Titus and this brother is partly that he has been boasting of the forwardness of the Corinthian church in the matter of the collection (9:2). Now he does not want them to let him down, lest they both be embarrassed (v. 4).

4. Exhortation to Give Liberally and Cheerfully (9:6-15)

Stingy givers cheat themselves (v. 6). But Paul wishes the giving to be entirely voluntary; for "God loveth a cheerful giver" (v. 7). The Greek word for "cheerful" is our word hilarious. That is the kind of giving the Lord loves, and nothing will bring the glory of God on a service any more quickly or surely than hilarious giving.

In verse 8 we have one of the most inclusive promises in the whole Bible: "And God is able to make *all* grace abound toward you; that ye, *always* having *all* sufficiency in *all* things, may abound to *every* good work" (K.J.V., italics added). This wonderful promise especially highlights Paul's love of the word "all."

What is the greatest incentive for giving? Paul suggests it in the closing doxology of this section: "Thanks be to God for his unspeakable gift" (v. 15). We can never outgive God. Since he gave His best, we should give Him our best.

III. *Vindication of His Character* (cc. 10—13)

1. *Paul's Apostolic Authority* (c. 10)

As we have noted before, we cannot understand this Epistle unless we realize that Paul is frequently answering the jibes and slanders of his critics at Corinth. For instance, the first verse here indicates that those critics were saying: Paul is a very lowly person when among us, but when he is absent he waxes very courageous. In other words, he was essentially a coward. Verse 2 shows that some accused him of walking according to the flesh.

But the meanest thing they did was to ridicule his personal appearance: "His letters, they say, are weighty and strong; but his bodily presence is weak, and his speech of no account" (v. 10). Paul assures them that he can speak and act strongly in their presence (v. 11).

Fundamentally, Paul was a pioneer preacher. For him "the regions beyond" were always calling (v. 16). As missionary, pastor, general superintendent, theologian, writer, Paul was a genius of the first order.

2. *The Meek Boaster* (11:1-15)

The Corinthians had pushed the great apostle into a corner with their malicious, unjust slander, so that he feels compelled to defend his character and position. He says something naturally very un-Pauline: "I reckon that I am not a whit behind the very chiefest apostles" (v. 5). He had earned his own living in Corinth, so as not to be a burden to them, but now that was thrown back into his face (v. 7). It was implied that he knew his services were not worth anything.

3. *The Apostle's Sufferings* (11:16—12:13)

The catalogue of sufferings which Paul gives us here is almost unmatched elsewhere. Just to read over 11:23-33 makes one feel ashamed that he has ever complained of his own lot.

The nature of Paul's "thorn in the flesh" (12:7) has aroused a great deal of curiosity. Poor eyesight, chronic malaria, and epilepsy have all been suggested, along with other afflictions. Perhaps it is purposely not identified, so that every sufferer can find consolation here. The important thing

292   EXPLORING THE NEW TESTAMENT

is to accept for ourselves the promise which the Lord gave to
Paul: "My grace is sufficient for thee: for my power is made
perfect in weakness." God does not always choose to heal.
He did not heal Paul. But He made him and thousands of
other afflicted people a greater blessing to the world because of
their weak bodies.

4. *Paul's Anticipated Visit* (12:14—13:10)

The apostle is looking forward to making his third visit
to Corinth (12:14; 13:1). He hopes that he will find them
obedient, so that there will be no unpleasant situation when
he arrives (12:20-21). But if they need to feel his authority
he will assert it (13:1-10). He hopes that will not be necessary.

5. *Farewell* (13:11-14)

In spite of what he has had to say, Paul closes with a
Christian farewell filled with tender feeling. The trinitarian
benediction here (v. 14) has always been the favorite one
for closing church services.

CHAPTER X
THE MEANING OF REDEMPTION
(THE DOCTRINAL EPISTLES OF PAUL)

Galatians and Romans naturally go together. They both treat primarily of the doctrine of redemption. In both a dominant theme is justification by faith. Galatians clearly was written first. Romans is a more extensive, calm, reasoned presentation of the same ideas, from a positive point of view. Hence we shall study these two Epistles in the same chapter.

GALATIANS

A. INTRODUCTION

I. Destination

The letter is addressed to "the churches of Galatia." But what does "Galatia" mean?

The North Galatian theory holds that the Epistle was written to what might be called Galatia proper, or Galatia in the popular sense. This was a region in the north central part of Asia Minor, where a large number of Gauls had settled in the third century before Christ, giving their name to that area. In Paul's day this was the northern part of the Roman province of Galatia.

The South Galatian theory takes the word Galatia in its provincial sense. It then holds that Paul wrote this Epistle to the cities in the southern part of the province of Galatia, where he had founded churches on his first missionary journey —Pisidian Antioch, Iconium, Lystra, and Derbe. Paul usually concentrated on the great centers of population, where his work would reach the most people. Furthermore, the Judaistic controversy, which caused the letter to be written, would be more apt to reach the nearer cities in the southern part of the province. All in all, the South Galatian theory seems more likely.

II. Date

Gal. 4:13 seems to imply two visits to Galatia before Paul wrote the Epistle. Paul revisited Lystra, Iconium, and Antioch on his return trip of the first journey, so that on the basis of the South Galatian theory he could have written this letter between his first two journeys, near the time of the Jerusalem Council, when the Judaistic controversy was at its height.

At best the date is uncertain. It could have been written as early as A.D. 48. We have placed it with the Corinthian letters, about A.D. 55 or 56, for this reason: psychologically, with its strong feeling, it is most closely related to II Corinthians; theologically it lies closest to Romans. So one is tempted to place it between the two, as the majority of scholars in the past have done. However, many today favor the earlier dating, making it the first of Paul's Epistles.

III. Occasion and Purpose

Paul learned to his great distress that Judaizers were undoing his work in Galatia. They were telling his converts that unless they were circumcised and kept the law of Moses they could not be saved. Paul recognized that this meant a denial of salvation through Christ. So he quickly composed a letter to the churches of Galatia.

The purpose of the Epistle, then, was to combat the work of the Judaizers in Galatia. The theme of Galatians is justification by faith. This was Paul's answer to the Judaistic teaching of salvation by works.

B. CONTENTS

The Epistle to the Galatians has three clear divisions: (1) Personal (cc. 1—2); (2) Doctrinal (cc. 3—4); (3) Practical (cc. 5—6). These with the Salutation and Conclusion give us the outline of the Epistle.

I. Salutation (1:1-5)

Paul begins by asserting and defending the divine origin and authority of his apostleship. He declares that it was not from a human source ("from men") nor through human agency ("through men"). His authority as apostle was not derived from any man-made decree, nor was it received through ordination by any official of the church.[1] Instead it came to him directly from God through Jesus Christ.

Probably the Judaizers claimed that Paul had not been ordained by Jesus, as had Peter and the other original apostles. But Paul affirms that the *risen* Christ had given him a divine ordination as apostle, which was just as valid as Peter's.

[1]"Through men" could just as accurately be translated "through a man."

II. *Personal History* (1: 6—2: 21)

1. *Introduction* (1: 6-10)

After the salutation Paul usually has a thanksgiving. But this time he was so extremely agitated and concerned that he burst out immediately in surprised indignation: "I marvel that ye are so quickly removing from him that called you in the grace of Christ unto a different gospel." They were just in the process of falling away. So Paul was hastening to write them at once in an effort to rescue them before they fell completely away from Christ.

Paul declared that this supposed "gospel" of the Judaizers was no real gospel at all (v. 7). It was not good news of deliverance but a sad bondage. So strongly did the apostle feel about it that he declared that even if an angel from heaven were to preach any other gospel than salvation through faith in Jesus Christ he should be accursed.

2. *The Divine Origin of Paul's Gospel* (1: 11-12)

In verse 2 Paul had stated the divine authority of his ministry; here he affirms the divine authority of his message. He had received both his apostleship and his gospel directly from God.

Of his gospel he says: "For neither did I receive it from man, nor was I taught it, but it came to me through revelation of Jesus Christ." Probably the Judaizers were saying that Paul received his gospel secondhand; he never saw Jesus. This Paul most emphatically denies. He was not taught it; he received it himself from Christ by revelation.

3. *Saul's Conversion* (1: 13-17)

As a young Jew, Saul had advanced beyond his contemporaries. His zeal had shown itself both in rigorous adherence to the law (v. 14) and in severe persecution of the Church (v. 13). But his conversion changed the whole course of his life.

The particular point he is making here, however, is that he did not counsel with others as to what he should preach (v. 16), nor did he go up to Jerusalem to receive instruction (v. 17). Instead he went away into Arabia, where doubtless this clear revelation of the gospel of Christ came to him. How long he stayed there we are not told. It is nowhere stated that he spent three years in Arabia.

4. His Limited Contact with Jerusalem (1:18-24)

Again Paul is emphasizing the fact that he did not receive his theology from the original apostles. Three years after his conversion—or his return from Arabia—he had made a very brief visit of two weeks with Peter at Jerusalem. But he did not see any other apostles.[2]

Then he spent some years in "the regions of Syria and Cilicia." This sounds definitely as though he was busy evangelizing in his home province.

5. Paul's Second Visit to Jerusalem (2:1-10)

Paul presented to the apostles the gospel which he was preaching and they endorsed it. They extended to him the right hand of fellowship and gave their blessing to his ministry among the Gentiles.

The point that Paul is making is clear. He did not receive his apostolic authority or his gospel message from the leaders at Jerusalem. It came to him directly from Christ. However, those leaders had endorsed his work. Though not subservient to the Jerusalem apostles, he was in good fellowship with them.

6. Paul's Rebuke of Peter (2:11-21)

When Peter paid a visit to Antioch he at first ate freely with the Gentile Christians. But when some strict Jewish Christians came down from Jerusalem, he feared this disapproval so much that he separated himself from the Gentiles. To Paul this was sheer "hypocrisy" (Greek word for "dissimulation"). So he rebuked Peter publicly.

Verse 20 is a strong holiness text. The word "nevertheless" does not appear in the Greek, which reads very clearly: "I have been crucified with Christ; and no longer do I myself [Greek, ego] live, but Christ lives in me." It is an emphatic, repeated declaration that the old self has been crucified and no longer does the ego live, but Christ has taken the place once held on the throne of the heart by the carnal self. When translated correctly the verse gives a much stronger emphasis to holiness.

III. Doctrinal Polemic (cc. 3—4)

1. Justification by Faith (3:1-14)

Having established the divine origin and authority of his apostleship and gospel, Paul now confronts the Galatians with

2"Save" (v. 19) should probably be "but only."

an indignant question: "O senseless Galatians, who bewitched you, before whose eyes Jesus Christ was placarded crucified?"[3] With Christ before their gaze they should not have been bewitched by the "evil eye" of the Judaizers.

Then Paul proceeds to give the example of Abraham to prove the validity of his doctrine of justification by faith. The Jews held Abraham in very high veneration as the father of their nation. The apostle points out the fact that Abraham was justified by faith, not by works. The true sons of Abraham are those who follow faith rather than works (v. 7).

2. The Function of the Law (3:15-29)

The covenant which God made with Abraham was not abrogated by the coming of the law (v. 17). But that covenant was based on promise, not on works (v. 18).

Why, then, was law brought in? Paul's answer is: "It was added because of transgressions" (v. 19). That is, the law was given to strengthen man's moral weakness and to educate man's conscience. It was intended to bring a keen consciousness of sin and guilt.

In verse 24 we have an interesting figure used for the law. Paul writes: "The law is become our tutor to bring us unto Christ." The Greek word for "tutor" (K.J.V.—"schoolmaster") is paidagogos, which gives us "pedagogue." This term was used for a slave who acted as guardian for a youth. It does not suggest the idea of a schoolteacher, although the slave might give some instruction.

3. Christian Sonship, Not Slavery (4:1-11)

In the fullness of time God sent His Son to redeem us, that we might be adopted as His sons (v. 4). That is certified to our hearts by His Spirit, who makes our relationship real (v. 6).

With such a glorious sonship why should one turn back to the "beggarly rudiments" of the old regime? (v. 9.) Why exchange freedom in Christ for the bondage of the law?

4. The Galatians' Former Zeal for Him (4:12-20)

Paul now states the cause of his first visit to them. He says: "Because of an infirmity of the flesh I preached the gospel unto you the first time" (v. 13). Evidently it was for

[3]Literal translation of verse 1.

reasons of health that Paul first visited Galatia. This may have been malaria contracted in the swampy lowlands along the coast, which drove him inland to higher ground. Or it may have been ophthalmia (sore eyes), which was very common near the coast. The expression, "Ye would have plucked out your eyes and given them to me," is taken by some as suggesting this. But it could be just a figure of speech for zealous devotion.

5. The Allegory of Hagar and Sarah (4:21-31)

Paul uses these two characters as an allegory representing the difference between the slavery of the law and the freedom of the gospel. The true Israelites are children of promise, as was Isaac.

IV. Practical Application (5:1—6:10)

1. Christian Freedom (5:1-15)

The apostle urges these Christians to stand fast in their liberty in Christ, not returning to the slavery of the law. He says that if they become circumcised they forfeit Christ (v. 2), they fall from grace (v. 4).

But this liberty does not mean license (v. 13). Love is the key to liberty (v. 14).

2. The Spirit Versus the Flesh (5:16-26)

The flesh—the sinful, selfish, carnal self—brings division ("works"). The Spirit brings unity ("fruit"). The list of "works of the flesh" (vv. 19-21) is a black picture indeed, ugly and repulsive. But there is no more beautiful picture in the Bible than this lovely cluster of the "fruit of the Spirit." It is "love, joy, peace, longsuffering, kindness, goodness, faithfulness, meekness, self-control."

Two observations might be made on this passage. One is that fruit does not grow as soon as a tree is planted. It takes time. Hence, the lack of the fruit of the Spirit in mature abundance is no evidence that the Holy Spirit has not come in His fullness.

But the converse is also true. A good tree, under proper conditions, will ultimately bear fruit. If a sanctified person does not soon begin to manifest some of the fruit of the Spirit in his life, then something is wrong.

3. Spiritual Meekness and Love (6: 1-5)

Christians should seek humbly to restore any brethren who may fall. There is no place for pride; any of us might fall but for the grace of God. We are to carry our own load of responsibility (v. 5) but help lift the crushing burdens of others (v. 2).[4]

4. Christian Giving (6: 6-10)

The word "communicate" means "share." The one receiving spiritual instruction should share his material resources with the teacher. That is God's plan. But the one who is too sparing in his giving will impoverish himself.

V. Conclusion (6: 11-18)

It has been suggested that verses 11-16 are in the nature of a postscript which Paul added himself. Probably he dictated the letter to this point. Then he took the pen from the amanuensis and added a personal word in his own handwriting. Possibly because of poor eyesight he wrote with large letters.[5]

The brand-marks on Paul's body (v. 17) probably refer to the scars won in his campaigns for Christ. Paul had no stars on his shoulders or stripes on his chest, but he was a real five-star general whose scars testified to the many battles he had fought.

ROMANS

A. INTRODUCTION

I. Value of the Epistle

In the Introduction to his *Commentary on St. Paul's Epistle to the Romans*, Godet says of this letter: "The Reformation was undoubtedly the work of the Epistle to the Romans, as well as of that to the Galatians; and the probability is that every great spiritual revival in the church will be connected as effect and cause with a deeper understanding of this book." He calls it "the cathedral of the Christian faith."[6]

Luther, in the Preface to his famous commentary on Ro-

---

[4] Two different Greek words for "burden" are used in these verses.

[5] The Greek does not at all say "how large a letter"—*epistole*—but "with how large letters"—*grammasin,* from which we get "grammar," meaning primarily letters of the alphabet.

[6] F. Godet, *Commentary on St. Paul's Epistle to the Romans,* trans. A. Cusin (New York: Funk & Wagnalls, 1883), p. 1.

mans, says: "This Epistle is the chief book of the New Testament, the purest gospel."

Probably most Bible students would agree with Luther that we have here the most important single book of the New Testament. If we had no other, we would still know the way of salvation clearly. As we have seen, it was the reading of Luther's Preface to the Epistle to the Romans which caused Wesley's conversion.

Romans is the most theological of Paul's Epistles. Here we have the nearest to a systematic theology of any book in the New Testament. However, one particular branch of theology is treated most comprehensively here—soteriology, or the doctrine of salvation.

II. Place and Time of Writing

The Epistle to the Romans was written in Corinth around A.D. 56, near the close of Paul's third missionary journey. It came out of his wide experience in preaching the gospel across the eastern Mediterranean world.

III. Occasion and Purpose

When Paul made his last visit to Corinth, on his third journey, he planned to go on westward to Rome and Spain. A man of his vision and consecration could not but feel the call of distant fields. Especially would Paul wish to see the capital of the great Roman Empire.

But he was deterred from his plan by a tremendous concern about the offering being collected for the saints at Jerusalem. It was not just a matter of financial aid, important as that was. What Paul hoped to accomplish by means of this offering was a closer unity between the Jewish and Gentile churches. Jesus, the night before His crucifixion, prayed three times for the unity of His followers (John 17:11, 21-23). This same burden now lay heavily on Paul's heart.

He finally decided that he had better go in person with the offering to make sure that it was accepted (Rom. 15:30) and that it actually did help to cement the churches together. So he set aside his plans for visiting Rome and Spain (Rom. 15:22-29). Instead he returned to Jerusalem.

In lieu of a visit he felt that he must write a letter. The apostle realized full well the strategic importance of Rome. Being at the capital, the church there would naturally have a dominant influence throughout the empire. It was important that the Roman church should be carefully indoctrinated. The wisdom of Paul's strategy is shown in the fact that the church at Rome did gain a reputation for orthodoxy. That was one of the reasons that it became the mother church of the West.

The Epistle to the Romans was a worthy document to be sent by the great apostle to the imperial city. It sets forth the essential doctrines of sin and salvation in a comprehensive way. Since the Romans were legally minded the Epistle is forensic in character.

B. Contents

The Epistle to the Romans has three main divisions, besides the introduction and conclusion. The first eight chapters are doctrinal; chapters 9—11 are prophetical; chapters 12—16 are practical. One might list these three divisions as: (1) Doctrinal; (2) Dispensational; (3) Devotional. The middle section (cc. 9—11) seems to be somewhat parenthetical to the main drive of the Epistle.

The doctrinal section may be divided into three parts: (1) The Doctrine of Sin (1:17—3:20); (2) The Doctrine of Justification (3:21—5:21); (3) The Doctrine of Sanctification (cc. 6—8).

Again, the doctrine of sin may be subdivided. In chapter one we have the sin of the Gentiles; in chapter two we have the sin of the Jews; in chapter three we have the sin of the whole world.

I. Introduction (1:1-17)

1. Salutation (1:1-7)

Paul begins his great Epistle to the Romans by calling himself a servant (lit., bond servant) of Jesus Christ, and then an apostle. The thought of service, rather than authority, was uppermost in his mind as he wrote to the Romans. This is a beautiful touch of humility.

Having named himself as the writer, in verse 1, Paul states about whom he is writing (vv. 3-6). Everything that the apostle wrote had relation to Jesus Christ. He mentions His humanity in verse 3 and His deity in verse 4. The Resurrection is cited as the outstanding proof of His deity.

Then in verse 7 Paul indicates to whom he is writing. The Epistle is addressed to all the saints at Rome.

2. Paul's Desire to See Them (1:8-15)

The apostle thanks God that "your faith is proclaimed throughout the whole world" (v. 8). He reminds them that he is praying for them constantly (v. 9), and expresses his great longing to see them (vv. 10-15).

Included here is Paul's famous statement, "I am debtor." The apostle's tremendously busy life of sacrificial service was just one continuous effort to pay back the debt he owed to Christ. Only in service to others can we repay our debt to God.

3. The Gospel (1:16-17)

Even at Rome, the center of imperial authority and military might, Paul was not ashamed of the gospel. Why? Because "it is the power of God unto salvation to every one that believeth." The Romans prided themselves on their power. Rome was the strongest empire the world has ever seen. But Paul would declare that their vaunted power was like that of a 22-rifle compared with God's atomic power to transform lives. Rome could subjugate whole nations, but she could not change the heart of a single individual.

The gospel is a revelation of God's righteousness which is given to those who believe. The reference here is not primarily to righteousness as an attribute of Deity, but to that righteousness which God imparts to those who will receive it by faith. The statement here in verse 17 is central to the entire book. It is a faith-righteousness rather than a work-righteousness. Paul is here reiterating the main emphasis of the Epistle to the Galatians.

II. Doctrinal Exposition (1:18—8:39)

1. Sin (1:18—3:20)

a. *The Sin of the Gentiles* (1:18-32). Much study has been given during the last century to the origin of religion and religions. But the most authoritative statement anywhere in literature is to be found in this first chapter of Romans.

Here we read that man began with monotheism and then descended to gross polytheism. The path downward is clearly marked. Starting with a knowledge of God as revealed in creation (vv. 19-20), four steps are indicated in verse 21: (1) indifference; (2) ingratitude; (3) vain philosophy; (4) spiritual blindness. Then came: (5) intellectual pride

(v. 22); and (6) idolatry (v. 23). The final step was: (7) moral abandonment (v. 24). This is the true story of "The Descent of Man."

Three times in this passage we read: "God gave them up" (vv. 24, 26, 28). This is divine judgment in answer to willful disobedience. The most fearful thing that can happen to men is for God to give them up. Since the people would not follow God, He let them follow their own sinful desires. The result has been a horrible trail of sin and suffering.

There is no blacker picture of sin in the Bible than we find here in the first chapter of Romans. But a reading of the secular writers of the first century will show that Paul has not painted the picture a bit more lurid than it was. We cannot appreciate the New Testament properly unless we recognize the very low moral background against which it was written.

b. *The Sin of the Jews* (c. 2). The twin sins of the Gentiles were *idolatry* and *immorality,* which always go together. But in this chapter Paul gives us the twin sins of the Jews, *insincerity* and *inconsistency.*

The sins of the flesh, enumerated in hideous detail in chapter 1, are very repulsive indeed. But not less serious in God's sight are the sins of the spirit, such as pride and hypocrisy.

That Paul is addressing Jews in this chapter is indicated clearly in verse 17. That gives us the proper interpretation of "O man" (v. 1). The parallel for us today would be church members.

The key phrase of chapter two is "the judgment of God." It is declared that one's judgment will be "according to truth" (v. 2); "according to his works" (v. 6); and "according to my gospel" (v. 16).

It is also indicated in verses 12-15 that people will be judged according to their light. Those who have the law (Bible) will be judged by it. But those who have had no Bible will be judged according to their consciences (vv. 14-15). God is just. He will not condemn men for what they do not know. But in every man there is the light of conscience. Everyone who has reached the age of accountability has disobeyed his conscience and so is guilty before God.

The Jew (church member) is pictured in this chapter as one who judges others and justifies himself. That is altogether too common an attitude even among Christians. But it is severely condemned in this chapter.

c. The Sin of the World (3:1-20). Having "before laid to the charge both of Jews and Greeks, that they are all under sin" (v. 9)—as he has done in the first two chapters—Paul now declares that all the world is guilty before God, and "under the judgment of God" (v. 19). He ends this section by asserting that "by the works of the law shall no flesh be justified in his sight" (v. 20). That is one of his main emphases in Galatians and Romans.

2. Justification (3:21—5:21)

a. The Means of Justification (3:21-31). Paul begins this important section with a majestic statement: "But now apart from the law a righteousness of God hath been manifested, being witnessed by the law and the prophets; even the righteousness of God through faith in Jesus Christ unto all them that believe." This is one of the several summaries in this Epistle of what the gospel is. God's righteousness is given to those who believe. Faith is the means of our justification.

Verse 23 declares that "all have sinned." The apostle declares that all men fall short of God's glorious ideal.

The expression, "the redemption that is in Christ Jesus," might be taken as the theme of this Epistle. One could then construct an outline like this: (1) The need of redemption (1:1—3:20); (2) Redemption applied to the sins of man (3:21—5:21); (3) Redemption applied to the sin of man (6:1—8:11); (4) Redemption applied to material creation (8:12-39); (5) Redemption applied to the Jewish people (cc. 9—11); (6) Redemption applied to practical living (cc. 12—15); (7) Redemption applied to personal relationships (c. 16).

The great problem of salvation is: How can God "be just, and the justifier of him that hath faith in Jesus"? The solution is the Cross. There Christ paid the penalty for man's sin. As a result, God can justify those who accept Jesus' sacrifice for their sins.

b. An Example of Justification (c. 4). In this chapter Paul calls attention to the example of Abraham. That patriarch "believed God, and it was reckoned unto him for right-eousness" (v. 3).

Added to the example of Abraham is the testimony of David, quoted from Psalms 32, one of the great penitential psalms. There David declared the blessedness of those whose sins are forgiven and to whom the Lord does not reckon sin.

But, says Paul (v. 9), is this blessing just for the circum-cision, or is it also for the uncircumcision? He answers by scoring an important point. The statement that Abraham's faith was reckoned to him for righteousness is quoted from Gen. 15:6. But Abraham's circumcision is recorded in chap-ter 17, some fourteen years later. If Abraham was justified by faith long before he was circumcised, then one does not have to be circumcised to be justified in God's sight. That cut the foundation right out from under the Judaizers, who claimed that one had to be circumcised in order to be saved.

Being circumcised does not make one a true son of Abra-ham. Those Jews are sons "who also walk in the steps of that faith of our father Abraham which he had in uncir-cumcision" (v. 12).

One of the great definitions of faith is found in verse 21: "being fully assured that what he had promised, he was able also to perform." In other words, faith is a full assurance that what God has promised He will do. The important point to note is that faith is always based on the Word of God.

There is a significant combination in verse 25: "Who was delivered up for our trespasses, and was raised for our justifi-cation." Without the resurrection of Christ, His death for us on the cross would not have availed. The Resurrection is the assurance to us that the atonement made in our behalf is acceptable to the Father and is therefore efficacious for us. We do not make as much of the Resurrection today as did the Early Church, which realized how crucially it was involved in salvation.

c. *The Results of Justification* (c. 5). One of the results of justification is "access by faith into this grace wherein we stand." That could be referred to entire sanctification as the establishing grace of God—"wherein we stand." But one should not be dogmatic in insisting that this is the intended meaning or the only one.

Another result of justification is ability to rejoice in tribulations (v. 3). The apostle also notes that Christ died for us: (1) "while we were yet weak" (v. 6); (2) "while we were yet sinners" (v. 8); and (3) "while we were enemies" (v. 10). Note the progression: weak, sinners, enemies. But Christ died for them all.

The closing paragraph (vv. 12-21) seems almost to personify sin and death, so that those two words could be spelled with capitals. Sin and Death reigned from Adam to Moses. Through Adam's disobedience "the many" (all) were made sinners; through Christ's obedience "the many" are made righteous (v. 19). This last statement, of course, is potential and provisional.

The law "slipped in" (v. 20) to give the consciousness of sin. That was its function. But it could not save.

3. Sanctification (cc. 6—8)

a. *Through Death to Self* (c. 6). There are two aspects to sanctification. The negative is death to self, crucifixion of the old man, cleansing from the carnal nature. The positive is the fullness of the Holy Spirit, perfect love, complete devotement to God.

Apparently some antinomians had been saying: "Why not continue in sin, that grace may abound?" (cf. v. 1.) The more I sin, the more God's grace abounds. Therefore, more sin, more grace.

Paul refutes this emphatically. The expression "God forbid" is used fourteen times by Paul and once in Luke (20:16). It literally means "May it not be." But since it obviously is emphatic, perhaps the best translation is, "By no means!"

In chapter 6 we have: (1) an analogy—death (vv. 1-11); (2) an exhortation (vv. 12-14); (3) an illustration—slavery (vv. 15-23). For death to self Paul uses the image of baptism (vv. 3-4). Here we have: (1) immersion=death; (2) submersion=burial (ratification of death); (3) emergence=resurrection. So we are to be buried with Christ and then rise with Him to newness of life.

Rom. 6:6 is another important text on sanctification: "Knowing this, that our old man was crucified with him, that the body of sin might be done away, that so we should no longer be in bondage to sin."

There are those who say that "was crucified" (aorist tense) refers only to our potential crucifixion with Christ nineteen hundred years ago. But unless that becomes actual in us by the crisis of death to self it has no practical value for us.

What are we to do with the provisions of Calvary for our sanctification? The answer is found in verse 11: "Even so reckon ye also yourselves to be dead unto sin, but alive unto God in Christ Jesus." The word "reckon" is in the present (continuous) imperative: "keep on reckoning yourselves." There is necessary the continuation as well as the crisis. And the only way to stay dead to sin is to keep "alive unto God."

In verses 12-14 we are exhorted to "present," in one decisive act (aorist tense) ourselves to God and our bodies to be used as His instruments. That is a high conception of the sanctified life.

Again, Paul meets an objection, in verse 15: "What then? shall we sin, because we are not under law, but under grace? God forbid." His answer is that though we have been freed from the law we have become bond servants to God. So we must serve Him, not sin.

b. *Through Union with Christ* (7:1-6). As long as a woman is married she is bound by law to her husband. But if he dies she is freed from further obligation. In the same way, says Paul, "Ye also were made dead to the law through the body of Christ; that ye should be joined to another, even to him who was raised from the dead, that ye might bring forth fruit unto God" (v. 4).

Throughout this Epistle, Paul is concerned to make it clear that Christians are freed from the Mosaic law. The coming of Christ meant the death of the law. No longer is anyone under obligation to keep the law.

Union with Christ is the secret of victory in the Christian life. It is *His* power and strength that makes us victorious.

c. *The Need of Sanctification* (7:7-25). This autobiographical section has been the subject of much debate. Most scholars agree that Paul is writing about some period in his life. But when was it?

The most prevalent view is that Paul is here describing his struggles as a Pharisee under the law. With the law came the consciousness of sin (v. 9). He tried to obey the law but found within himself a different law, with which he was constantly struggling (v. 23). This he defines as "sin which dwelleth in me" (vv. 17, 20).

It is obvious that some of the language here could be applied to the state of regeneration.[7] In the life of the converted person there is a conflict between the Christ nature and the carnal nature. This struggle can be fully ended only by the crucifixion of self.

    d. *Through the Indwelling Spirit* (c. 8). Cleansing from the carnal nature, or death to self, is not all there is to sanctification. It is only the indwelling presence of the Holy Spirit which makes us holy. Holiness is more than the absence of sin. Put in briefest terms, holiness is Christlikeness. But it takes the constant presence of the Spirit of Christ to make us like Christ.

Paul pictures it as a new law operating in our members. He says: "For the law of the Spirit of life in Christ Jesus made me free from the law of sin and death" (v. 2). That is, the Holy Spirit functions in our hearts as the Successor to the old law of sin and death.

The true nature of the carnal mind is described in verse 7: "Because the mind of the flesh is enmity against God; for it is not subject to the law of God, neither indeed can it be." Carnality is essentially an attitude of rebellion against the will of God. Entire sanctification means complete submission to the will of God. That is the very essence of it.

The Spirit-filled, Spirit-led life is the truly Christian way. "For as many as are led by the Spirit of God, these are sons of God" (v. 14). Only by letting the Spirit lead us can we feel the gracious assurance of sonship and also demonstrate to the world that we really are "sons of God."

In verses 18-25 Paul deals with redemption in relation to creation. Through man's disobedience all creation was put under a curse. Through Christ's obedience "creation itself also shall be delivered from the bondage of corruption into the liberty of the glory of the children of God" (v. 21). It is a grand prospect.

The Holy Spirit helps us in our prayer life, making intercession for us in accordance with the will of God (vv. 26-27).

---

[7] See John Wesley's sermon on "Repentance of Believers."

Jude also speaks of "praying in the Holy Spirit" (v. 20). This is one of the privileges of the Spirit-filled Christian.

One of the most comforting promises in the New Testament is that found in Rom. 8:28. In two out of the three oldest Greek manuscripts (Papyrus 46 and Vaticanus) it reads thus: "And we know that to those who love God, God works all things together for good, to those who are called according to His purpose."

The closing paragraph (vv. 31-39) forms a grand climax to the doctrinal section of the Epistle. The guarantee of God's providence is expressed with the tremendous force of an unanswerable question in verse 32—"He that spared not his own Son, but delivered him up for us all, how shall he not also with him freely give us all things?" The fact that God gave His most precious possession, His own Son, is proof positive that He will not withhold any good thing from us.

The tone of the whole chapter is reflected in verse 37— "Nay, in all these things we are more than conquerors [super-victors] through him that loved us."

There is nothing outside a Christian which can separate him from God (vv. 38-39). Only the wrong attitude of his own will can do that.

The word "Spirit" occurs some twenty times in the eighth of Romans. This is probably the outstanding single chapter on the Holy Spirit in the New Testament. It stands right beside the fourteenth and sixteenth chapters of John's Gospel as a great passage on a great theme.

III. Prophetical Interpretation (cc. 9—11)

1. Israel's Remnant Among God's Children (c. 9)

Paul was a man of strong feelings. His large heart carried large burdens. This is reflected strikingly in the language of verses 2 and 3: "I have great sorrow and unceasing pain in my heart. For I could wish that I myself were anathema from Christ for my brethren's sake, my kinsmen according to the flesh." Although he was the great apostle to the Gentiles he carried a crushing burden for the people of Israel.

One thing that Paul seeks to demonstrate in this chapter is that God's promises to Abraham have not failed (v. 6). The true Israel has been preserved. Though the nation lost its independence because of its disobedience, yet there will always be an Israel; the spiritual remnant cannot be destroyed. He documents this assertion with a quotation from Isaiah (v. 27).

One of the most difficult problems in Romans has to do with the doctrine of predestination, especially as expressed in verses 14-18. But it must be noted that the foreordination described here relates to national prosperity rather than individual salvation.

Griffith Thomas has a comment to make on verses 22-23 which is worth quoting. He says: "Men fit themselves for hell; but it is God that fits men for heaven."[8] That is a sound interpretation of what this passage declares.

2. Israel's Rejection of God's Righteousness (c. 10)

The Jews continued to seek God's favor through their own righteous acts, instead of accepting the righteousness which Christ provided. This rejection of Christ amounted to rebellion against God (v. 21).

The way of salvation is stated simply, but clearly, in verses 9-10: "Because if thou shalt confess with thy mouth Jesus as Lord, and shalt believe in thy heart that God raised him from the dead, thou shalt be saved: for with the heart man believeth unto righteousness; and with the mouth confession is made unto salvation."

3. Israel's Restoration to God's Favor (c. 11)

In chapter nine Paul indicated that some of Israel were already saved; in chapter ten, that all Israel might be saved except for unbelief. Now in this chapter he states that all Israel will ultimately be saved (v. 26). Perhaps this statement suggests a spiritual revival as well as the national restoration which has already taken place. (The new nation of Israel was established May 14, 1948.)

The chapter may be divided into two parts: (1) Rejection of Israel is not total (vv. 1-10); (2) Rejection of Israel is not final (vv. 11-36). Those two statements sum up the teaching of this chapter.

Paul sounds a warning to his Gentile readers. If Israel was rejected for her unbelief, how much more will the Gentiles forfeit God's blessings if they likewise fail to believe and obey!

---

[8] W. H. Griffith Thomas, *St. Paul's Epistle to the Romans* (Grand Rapids: Wm. B. Eerdmans Publishing Co., 1946), p. 261.

But though Israel was cut off as an unfruitful branch, God is able to graft her in again (v. 23). The revival of Israel as a nation in our own day ought to quicken our hope of Christ's return.

IV. Practical Application (cc. 12—15)

1. The Religious Life of the Believer (c. 12)

On the basis of God's mercies in providing redemption for us, Paul pleads that we "present" (aorist tense, once for all) our bodies a living sacrifice to God. And if we do so we must stop conforming ourselves to the world, but rather be continually transformed (transfigured) by the renewing of our minds. One way to be transfigured more and more into the image of Christ is to have the mind of Christ, to think the kind of thoughts He would think. What we think has everything to do with what we become.

This twofold plea for a crucial consecration (v. 1) and a continual transformation (v. 2) is followed by an exhortation to humility (vv. 3-8). One who reads the New Testament carefully will note that humility is one of the main emphases of its writers.

After urging his readers to exemplify various Christian virtues in their lives, Paul closes this chapter with the statement of an important secret of success: "Be not overcome of evil, but overcome evil with good." The best way to avoid evil is to *fill* our lives with good thoughts and actions.

2. The Civil Life of the Believer (13:1-7)

The teaching of the thirteenth chapter of Romans is in line with that of Christ—"Render to Caesar the things that are Caesar's" (Matt. 22:21)—and of the First Epistle of Peter. We are to be in subjection to civil government (v. 1), pay our taxes (v. 6), and show proper respect to those who are in authority (v. 7). This is because God has ordained government for man's protection (vv. 1-4). That does not mean that every person in high position is God's choice. But it does mean that God has ordered the fact of human government and we should respect its officers.

3. The Social Life of the Believer (13:8-14)

Christians are exhorted to pay their debts (v. 8) and to love their neighbors (vv. 8-10). The only way that one can truly fulfill the law is to have love (v. 10). Without it all else is incomplete.

Then Paul warns his readers to be ready for the coming of Christ, when their salvation will be completed (v. 11), and to guard themselves against the sinful pleasures of the world. It was the reading of verse 13 which precipitated Augustine's conversion.

4. The Relation of the Strong to the Weak (14:1—15:13)

By "weak in the faith" (v. 1) Paul means either a new convert or, perhaps, those who thought they were saved by works as well as faith. In any case such a person is to be received into the membership of the church but not given a position of responsibility. Both novices and legalists can cause a great deal of trouble if given a little authority.

The best help for our understanding of the term "weak" is Paul's use of it in the eighth chapter of I Corinthians. There he defines the "weak" person as one who is unduly concerned with nonessentials—what we today call "legalist."

The main point of this whole passage is summed up in 14:13—"Let us not therefore judge one another any more: but judge ye this rather, that no man put a stumblingblock in his brother's way, or an occasion of falling." The legalist is not to condemn the liberty of the strong, enlightened Christian; nor is the strong one to hold the legalist in contempt (v. 3). Both censoriousness and contempt are equally sinful in God's sight.

The true nature of Christianity is well expressed in verse 17. It is not a religion of externalities—"eating and drinking"—but of inward realities—"righteousness and peace and joy in the Holy Spirit." Legalism majors on the external appearance; love majors on the inner spirit.

But we must not hurt the consciences of those who are weak, and we are not to please ourselves (15:1). Our purpose should always be to treat others as Jesus would treat them.

This section ends with one of Paul's many beautiful benedictions: "Now the God of hope fill you with all joy and peace in believing, that ye may abound in hope, in the power of the Holy Spirit" (v. 13).

5. Paul's Devotion to Christ (15:14-33)

Paul was one of the greatest pioneer preachers of all time. He had "fully preached the gospel of Christ" around the eastern end of the Mediterranean, "from Jerusalem . . . even unto Illyricum" (v. 19). The latter faces across the Adriatic towards Italy.

But he was not content to stop with even this wonderful achievement. He must go far westward to Spain, stopping at Rome on his way (vv. 24, 28). But first he must go to Jerusalem, accompanying the offering for the poor saints there (vv. 25-27). He asks them to pray that his offering may be accepted (vv. 30-31).

V. Personal Communication (c. 16)

The last chapter is a mosaic of personal greetings. Their beautiful hues reveal something of the heart of the apostle. Altogether some thirty-five individuals are named.

1. Recommendation (vv. 1-2)

Paul commends to his readers Phoebe, a deaconess of the church at Cenchreae—the eastern harbor of Corinth. She has been a faithful worker in her local church and also a helper of Paul. It is interesting to note that the apostle includes a considerable number of women in these closing salutations.

2. Greetings to His Friends (vv. 3-16)

Priscilla and Aquila head this list of Paul's friends. Evidently she was the stronger of the two, for she is usually named first. The local church was meeting in their home (v. 5).

A beautiful spirit of Christian love and unity pervades the atmosphere of this chapter. It is a revelation of the wonderful fellowship which brothers and sisters in the Lord enjoy with one another.

3. Warnings Against Schismatics (vv. 17-20)

It would appear that even at Rome the Judaizers were causing trouble, stirring up confusion and inciting divisions. Paul pleads with his readers to ignore such. He notes that the Roman church has a widespread reputation for its faithfulness (v. 19).

4. Greetings from Fellow Workers (vv. 21-24)

Timothy was Paul's main co-worker at this time. Three of his kinsmen were with him. Tertius, the scribe who wrote the Epistle, inserted his personal note of greeting. Gaius was host to Paul and to the whole church. Erastus, "the treasurer of the city," was a member of the Christian group.

5. *Benediction* (vv. 25-27)

What would Paul's letters be without his benedictions? So no gathering of Christians—whether at church, in the home, or out in the open—is quite complete without a closing word of prayer.

CHAPTER XI

PREACHING FROM PRISON

(THE PRISON EPISTLES)

Four Epistles—Philemon, Colossians, Ephesians, and Philippians—are known as the Prison Epistles. In each of them are found references to imprisonment or bonds: "I Paul, the prisoner of Christ Jesus" (Eph. 3:1)—"in my bonds" (Phil. 1:7—"I am also in bonds" (Col. 4:3)—"Paul the aged, and now a prisoner also of Christ Jesus" (Philemon 9). It seems probable that he wrote the Prison Epistles during his two-year imprisonment in Rome (Acts 28:16-31). He was allowed to live in his own house (Acts 28:30), and large numbers of people came to him, to whom he expounded the gospel. This would give him ample time for reflection upon the gospel and for writing. Moreover, the references in Phil. 1:13 to the Praetorian Guard and in 4:22 to Caesar's household greatly strengthen the case of Rome as the place of writing. Thus we can date these Epistles at A.D. 60-61.

The above order of the Prison Epistles is followed because that was the probable order in which they were written. The incident of Onesimus, the runaway slave, which precipitated the letter to Philemon, seems to have been the initial occasion for the prison correspondence. Tychicus was to return to Colosse with Onesimus, bearing Paul's letter to Philemon. At about that time Epaphras had arrived from Colosse with word from the church, so Paul decided to write the church and send the letter with Tychicus and Onesimus, who would also convey personal information concerning Paul's imprisonment (Col. 4:7-9). It seems logical to suppose that Paul took the same opportunity to send a letter addressed to all the churches of Asia, the one known to us as the Epistle to the Ephesians, since Tychicus was also the bearer of this Epistle (Eph. 6:21). The fact that the Colossian and Ephesian letters are so much alike would support this idea. The Epistle to the Philippians, while written during the same imprisonment, was probably written after the other three.

PHILEMON

The letter of Paul to Philemon is the only strictly personal letter among all of his writings which have been preserved. The Pastoral Epistles were written to individuals, but their messages were for groups or churches as well as for the recipient, while the message here was for Philemon alone, although greetings to the church were included (v. 2).

There are five persons involved in this letter: Paul, Philemon, Apphia, Archippus, and Onesimus. Timothy is also mentioned as being present with Paul, along with Epaphras, Mark, Aristarchus, Demas, and Luke.

Paul was the author. The Epistle has been recognized as Pauline from the earliest times. It was written at Rome and carried to Colosse by Tychicus, who accompanied Onesimus back home (Col. 4: 7-9). In all probability it was the first of Paul's Prison Epistles.

Philemon was a layman of Colosse and one of Paul's converts, in whose house the Colossian church met. Paul calls him a "fellow-worker" (v. 1) and a "partner" (v. 17). He may have been actively engaged at one time in Paul's evangelistic efforts. Hayes suggests that "he may have been a partner with Paul in some business enterprise."[1] He was a slaveowner.

Apphia was probably the wife of Philemon, but there is no evidence available to identify her definitely. Archippus was probably their son. He held some responsible place in the Colossian church (Col. 4: 17). Paul terms him "our fellow-soldier" (v. 2).

Onesimus was the object of the writing of this letter. A slave of Philemon, he had run away (v. 12) after having robbed his master (v. 18). Arriving in Rome—the best possible place to hide—he had come in contact with Paul and had been converted. He would have known Paul, because of the association of Paul and Philemon, and may have contacted him when his freedom proved less profitable than he had expected, or when his conscience began to trouble him. He remained thereafter with Paul, becoming very useful to him, until it finally became evident to him that the Christian thing to do was to return to his master, regardless of the conse-

[1] D. A. Hayes, *Paul and His Epistles*, p. 332.

quences. Tychicus agreed to accompany him, and Paul determined to try to guarantee the outcome by writing a letter to Philemon.

Slavery was common in the Roman Empire. Many of the rich owned hundreds of slaves, while a man with as few as ten was considered a poor man. The slave was the property of his master and could claim no rights of his own. The privileges granted him depended, of course, upon the good graces of his master, but by law the smallest crime was punishable by death. He had no legal right to marry, and in all respects he was but the chattel of his master.

The gospel does not legislate against slavery. To do so would be to set one class in society over against another in the name of Christ, thereby alienating the class ruled against. Slavery is only one of many evils in the world. The gospel is meant for everyone and offers salvation to all. It contains the power to remedy all of the ills of society and make brothers of all men. When a man begins to look upon his slave as a brother, recognizing him to be of equal value with himself in God's sight, that man is on the way to give freedom to his slave.

Paul knew all this, and he was too wise to tell Onesimus that he should be set free or to tell Philemon to free him, although he knew that such freedom would be the inevitable outcome if both of them walked in the light of God's truth. Paul shows us here that some results of the gospel must be given time to develop.

Paul had learned the psychology of a good approach when he had a difficult situation to deal with. In this Epistle he is at his best. He knew what Philemon's rights were as a slaveowner, and he also knew what Philemon as a Christian should do in the case of his runaway slave. But he was not quite so sure of what he would do. With the courtesy of a gentleman, the compassionate interest of a brother, and the spiritual insight of an apostle, he began by expressing joy over Philemon's reputation for love and faith and his interest in the salvation of others. This could not fail to put Philemon in a good frame of mind.

Then Paul made his appeal to Philemon. Although he had the right to command, he preferred to appeal to him on behalf of Onesimus. Although a willful, runaway slave, the latter had become converted and was like a son to Paul and a brother to the saints. Paul would have liked to keep him because of his valued services. But because he was the property of Philemon, he was sending him back. Perhaps there was something providential in the whole circumstance, because Philemon could now receive him as a brother in the Lord and not as a slave. Paul pleaded on the basis of their mutual friendship and on the basis of his own imprisonment. As for any debt that Onesimus may have owed his master, whether through robbery or failure to perform his duties, Paul would become responsible for it. At the same time he suggested that Philemon should even go so far as to cancel the debt since he owed his very life to Paul—for had not Paul led him to Christ? This he asks Philemon to do, not just for the sake of Onesimus, but for his own sake. "Brother, let me have joy of thee in the Lord: refresh my heart in Christ" (v. 20).

Paul appealed to his friend in the full confidence that he would do as he had been requested, even more than that which was necessary. Furthermore, he asked to have the spare bedroom made ready against his probable visit to Colosse. He had faith in the prayers of his friends and hoped to be released from prison. Following this, Paul closed his Epistle with greetings from friends and his own benediction.

We are not told the outcome of this request. We may fondly hope that Philemon responded to the great apostle and gave Onesimus his eventual freedom. We trust also that Onesimus conducted himself in a manner worthy of that freedom. We are certain of this: Paul's little Epistle points the way to the remedy for all the social evils which afflict mankind. Through Christ the brotherhood of man can become an accomplished fact.

COLOSSIANS

A. INTRODUCTION

I. The Occasion

Paul had probably never visited the Colossian church (2:1). While he was a prisoner in Rome, Epaphras had come to him from Colosse with word from the church. This visit coincided with the proposed departure of Tychicus and Onesimus to Colosse. So Paul took the opportunity to attempt a solution of some problems in the church at Colosse, and he sent this letter by them. Timothy and Luke were with Paul at the time of writing.

II. The City

Colosse was located in Asia Minor, due east of Ephesus, near the junction of the Meander and Lycus rivers. It was not far from Laodicea and Hierapolis, and it gradually gave way in importance to these two cities. It was well known for the production of wool. The people were worshipers of angels.

III. The Church

The church at Colosse was probably established during Paul's three-year stay at Ephesus on his third missionary journey (Acts 19). Epaphras and perhaps Timothy were the evangelists under Paul who were instrumental in its organization. For this reason it was natural for Paul to feel a particular responsibility for the church, which met in the home of Philemon.

IV. Purpose and Plan

The problem in the Colossian church to which Paul directed his letter was of a philosophical nature (2:8). It laid stress upon ritualism (2:16), upon asceticism, the worship of angels, and superior knowledge received through visions (2:18). There are strong elements of Judaism, as seen from verse 16; and elements of Gnosticism, as seen from verse 18. There may have been a strange mingling of the two, which, though essentially different, possessed tendencies toward identical errors—asceticism particularly. Paul may be speaking of a dual heresy, as the introductory phrases of verses 16 and 18 might well suggest. It is certain that he was more interested in combating the error than in describing it. Paul saw it as a serious challenge to Christ in Colosse.

B. Contents

I. Greetings (1:1-12)

1. Salutation and Thanksgiving (1:1-8)

Although Paul had termed himself "the least of the apostles" (I Cor. 15:9), it was not done through any doubt of his calling. He was bold to proclaim that he was "an apostle of Christ Jesus through the will of God." This is found at the beginning of most of his Epistles. It serves not only to introduce him to his readers, but also to establish in their minds a certain sense of authority which Paul had and which he exerted when the need required it. There was no false humility about the apostle, but he manifested a directness and an objectivity which kept him from partiality and helped him to place the gospel above personalities, even his own.

Timothy was with Paul at the time of writing and is included in the opening salutation, "to the saints and faithful brethren in Christ that are at Colosse." Together they greet the church with, "Grace to you and peace from God our Father."

It is characteristic of Paul, when he wished to correct some error in a church, first of all to find something good to mention and for which to thank God. This is especially true in the case of the Corinthian church, in which he found so much that needed to be corrected. To the Colossian church he related the many fine things which he had heard—their faith in Christ, their love for the saints, and their hope of heaven. The three primary Christian virtues were found in this church: faith, hope, and love. They had been true followers of the gospel which Epaphras had preached to them. Epaphras had also brought this good report to Paul.

2. *A Prayer for the Church* (1: 9-12)

Paul's deep concern for the churches is revealed by his frequent reference to his habit of praying for them. Here he records another sample of his prayers. He prays for them daily. He prays that they may be filled with the knowledge of the will of God, having spiritual wisdom and understanding, living worthy of the Lord and pleasing to Him. He prays that they may be made strong with the strength of God—a glorious, triumphant strength, which will give them a joyful patience and continual thanksgiving to God. He does not forget that there is an inheritance of the saints in which they may share, because they have been redeemed from the darkness of sin through Jesus Christ. Always direct, always spiritually minded, Paul reveals in his prayers the quality of his own Christian life.

II. Doctrinal (1: 13—2: 3)

1. *The Nature of Redemption* (1: 13-14)

One of the most remarkable things about Paul's writings is the very little trace of Jewish legalism and ritualism found in any of them. Paul had been the strongest type of the ultra-religious Jew, and his conversion to Christianity had wrought a great reversal in his thinking. Redemption had but one source: Jesus Christ, crucified and risen. It had one purpose: to transfer men from the kingdom of darkness to the kingdom of light. It resulted in the forgiveness of sins. These are the essentials of salvation. Thus simplified, it is not difficult to comprehend Paul's insistence that justification is by faith alone.

2. The Person of Christ (1:15-19)

Paul's summary of the nature of redemption is transitional, leading him directly to his main topic—Christ. This paragraph is one of the strongest Christological passages in all of the New Testament and is Paul's attempt to give Christ His rightful place in the life and teaching of the Colossian church. As we have seen above, the error found in this church constituted a direct challenge to Christ, and, as elsewhere, Paul answers error with truth.

Christ is described in His relation to God, to the created universe, and to the Church. In relation to God, He is the "image of the invisible God." The concept here expressed is very similar to the Logos idea of John: Christ in His person is the representation and the manifestation of God. In opposition to the idea of many angels which were in some way supposed to represent God, Paul believed that Christ alone reveals God. God is invisible except as He is seen in Christ. As in the Epistle to the Hebrews, He is the "very image of his substance" (1:3). In Him God manifests himself to man. He is at once both God and man. "A Savior not quite God is a bridge broken at the farther end."[2]

In relation to the universe Christ was prior in existence to creation. He was the Agent of creation, and the Object for which all things were created (v. 16). He himself was not created. Being separate from the created universe, He preserves it in balance and controls its orderly course (v. 17). This refers to His essential being in relation to the universe and not to His incarnate being.

[2]H. C. G. Moule, quoted by W. H. Griffith Thomas, Christ Preeminent, p. 41.

In relation to the Church, Christ is "the head of the body" (v. 18). He is its sovereign Ruler. In Ephesians the emphasis is upon the body, in Colossians it is upon the Head. Christ is also the beginning of the Church by virtue of His resurrection, being thus its source. Elsewhere (Col. 3:1; Eph. 2:1; Gal. 2:20) Paul thinks of the conversion of the members of the Church in terms of a resurrection. In this passage he says that the Church itself had its beginning in the resurrection of Christ. The Church is thus likened to His resurrected body.

Because He has priority in these respects, He is entitled to pre-eminence in everything. For all the attributes of God are in Him by God's own pleasure, and through Him and His death on the cross, God wills to make reconciliation of all things in the universe. The deity of Christ in Paul's mind was thus firmly established.

3. The Work of Christ (1:20-23)

Paul thought of redemption as a work of reconciliation as well as of forgiveness. Among other things, sin is hostility to God, resulting in acts of unrighteousness. When one is reconciled, both his disposition and his actions are changed, in order "to present you holy and without blemish and unreprovable before him" (v. 22). This last achievement, however, is dependent upon the Christian's continuing faithful in the hope of the gospel.

4. Paul's Share in This Work (1:24—2:3)

Paul interpreted his imprisonment as sharing with Christ in His sufferings for the sake of the Church in general, and, in the present instance, for the sake of the Colossian church in particular. This he considered to be a part of his calling as a minister of the gospel—and he rejoiced in it. As a minister, he shared in the revelation given to Christians of the mystery which had been hidden during all previous ages, that mystery being, "Christ in you, the hope of glory" (1:27). To this end he had exerted all of his energies in order that every man, both Jew and Gentile, might personally experience the truth of this revelation.

One purpose of Paul in writing was to let the church know how deeply he was concerned for them, even though he had never met them. His great desire was that they might be encouraged through their mutual love, and that they might come to a more perfect understanding of Christ. In Him is hidden an inexhaustible reservoir of "the treasures of wisdom and knowledge" (2:3). Paul also wrote to warn them against those who would mislead them "with persuasiveness of speech" (2:4). In spirit he would always be with them, upholding the truth.

III. Polemical (2:4—3:4)

1. The False Teachers Versus Christ (2:4-15)

Paul now begins to argue the claim of Christ as opposed to these false teachers. They were deceitful, speculative traditionalists (v. 8), essentially opposed to Christ. In fact, there was no place for such philosophy as they taught in the gospel of Christ, and the life which such doctrine produced was totally unchristian.

Christ had put an end to any need of other intermediaries between God and man, such as Gnosticism taught, and by His death had abolished the old Jewish ceremonialism.

The fullness of God's revelation of himself to man was found in Jesus Christ. In place of the rite of circumcision in the flesh, there was a Christian circumcision which brought about a separation from all the old, degenerate nature, and a separation unto Christ. The rite of baptism was raised from a mere ritual to a blessed analogy of the death and resurrection of the sinner—dying to sin and rising to newness of life in Christ.

Paul continues to remind the Colossian Christians of what they had already experienced in Christ. They who were dead in sins had been made alive, having received forgiveness of sins and cancellation of the debt owed to God because of sin. This was accomplished by the cross of Christ. By the Cross, Christ also achieved victory over all the powers arrayed against Him.

2. Obligations (2:16—3:4)

As a consequence of this work of Christ on behalf of man, certain obligations of necessity fall to the Christian. He is obliged to defend himself against all errors and to resist all who would lead him astray. There will be those people who judge the Christian by their own standards, who are greatly impressed with their own ideas, but who do not know Christ. Apparently some church members in Colosse had succumbed to such heresy, and Paul argues with them.

After having died to sin and been made alive to Christ, why do they live like the world around them, submitting to regulations which could in no way contribute to lives of righteousness? The only attitude for the Christian to take is that of striving after the spiritual values as found in Christ. His life has been "hid with Christ in God," and he should live in continual expectation of Christ's return and the glory to follow.

IV. Practical (3:5—4:6)

1. Personal Life (3:5-17)

The apostle has already anticipated the emphasis he now makes upon the personal life. He gives two rather long lists: things to put off and things to put on. Christians are to make real in common life what has been ideally wrought in their hearts at conversion. The practical life must conform to the inner experience.

First, put off or "put to death." This expression is a strong one, speaking of an act resulting in a complete separation. Put to death "fornication"—"sexual immorality" (Phillips); "uncleanness"; "passion"—uncontrolled appetites; "evil desire"—wishing for that which is forbidden; "covetousness, which is idolatry"—setting up some object of desire in place of the worship of God. God is angry with all who practice these things. In addition put away "anger, wrath, malice, railing, shameful speaking out of your mouth: lie not one to another" (vv. 8-9). They must not engage in these things which belong to the old, sinful nature which they have also "put off." They have the new nature. To them all men are equal, and all distinctions of race and religion and social standing count as nothing—"Christ is all, and in all."

Second, "put on." As children of God, put on "a heart of compassion, kindness, lowliness, meekness, longsuffering" (v. 12). These virtues will create right attitudes of forbearance and forgiveness in the church. Christ is the pattern for this. "And above all these put on love, which binds everything together in perfect harmony" (v. 14, R.S.V.). Love is the crowning virtue. "Love is the golden chain of all the virtues" (v. 14, Phillips). There will follow, then, peace and thanksgiving. Christians should receive instruction from one another through the use of the Scriptures, and by the singing of psalms and hymns and spiritual songs. Everything the Christian does is to be done in the name of Christ.

Paul realized the human tendency to resist advice and instruction; so three times in this paragraph (vv. 15-17) his admonition is to be thankful. One who is truly thankful to God for the manifold blessings provided by Christ will not find the requirements of the gospel difficult to fulfill. Duty will be a pleasure and service a joy.

2. Domestic Life (3:18—4:1)

This section seems to contain the nucleus of what Paul wrote on this subject to the Ephesians (5:21—6:9). For the treatment of this, turn to the discussion of Ephesians.

3. In Relation to the World (4:2-6)

Like Jesus, Paul thought of the Christian as a man who took his place in the life of the world about him. Rather than his experience of salvation separating him from the world of men and their activities, it was to fit him to live above the evil of the world. The advice which here follows is simple, yet very practical. Maintain a consistent prayer life. Take account of danger spots and thank God for grace to overcome. Pray for the called workers that they may speak the truth with boldness and clarity at every opportunity. Be wise in the contacts with the unsaved, lest they misunderstand and be driven away, and make the most of every opportunity to win them. Speak graciously and with care, striving for a proper answer to questions which may be asked. Paul considered every church member as vitally important to the spread of the gospel.

V. Personal (4:7-18)

1. Mission of Tychicus and Onesimus (4:7-9)

Tychicus has been visiting Paul at Rome during his imprisonment. He is to accompany Onesimus, the runaway (but now converted) slave, back to his owner, Philemon. They will deliver Paul's letter to the church and give a further report of Paul's welfare.

Tychicus, a native of Asia Minor (Acts 20:4), was one of a band of younger men who served under Paul's direction in his missionary work. He is not as well known as Timothy and Titus, to whom Paul wrote letters, nor as well known as Barnabas and Silas, with whom Paul shared the trials of the missionary road. Paul later mentions Tychicus in connection with Crete (Tit. 3:12) and Ephesus (II Tim. 4:12). But Paul's estimate of him is the highest. He calls him a "beloved brother and faithful minister and fellow-servant in the Lord" (v. 7). No doubt more credit for the success of the Early Church should go to the little-known men such as Tychicus than is customarily given.

Paul terms Onesimus a "faithful and beloved brother, who is one of you" (v. 9)—not only a brother in the Lord to Paul, but to all the members at Colosse. We trust that Paul's suggestion was sufficient to insure Onesimus a cordial reception.

2. Greetings and Benediction (4:10-18)

Aristarchus was "a Macedonian of Thessalonica" (Acts 19:29; 27:2). He accompanied Paul to Jerusalem at the close of this third missionary journey (Acts 20:4). He was with Paul on his journey to Rome (Acts 27:2). He was a prisoner at Rome with Paul (Col. 4:10). This may reveal him as a convert from Judaism with Paul, and with him a sharer in his sufferings.

Mark, the cousin of Barnabas, deserted Paul's first missionary party (Acts 13:13), but later served as the teammate of Barnabas after Paul had refused to take him on his second missionary journey (Acts 15:39). He was apparently reconciled to Paul by the time of the writing of Colossians. Paul's parenthetical statement, "touching whom ye received commandments; if he come unto you, receive him" (v. 10), is apparently an attempt on his part to reinstate Mark in the fellowship of the churches.

Besides these two there were Justus, of whom little is known, and Epaphras, the founder of the Colossian church, who still labored greatly for all three churches of that area: Colosse, Laodicea, and Hierapolis. These, along with Luke, the physician, send greetings to the church. In turn the church is asked to convey Paul's greetings to the church at Laodicea and to Nymphas. He makes request that the Colossian letter be read to the Laodicean church (v. 16), and sends a last-minute exhortation to Archippus to be faithful in the ministry. He closes with a personal salutation, a request for their prayers and a final "Grace be with you."

EPHESIANS

A. INTRODUCTION

I. The Nature of the Epistle

Since the three earliest and best manuscripts of this Epistle omit the words "at Ephesus," it is quite generally thought that Ephesians was a circular letter addressed to all of the churches of Asia. Some have thought that it was the letter to the Laodiceans mentioned in Col. 4:16. The probable occasion for the writing of this Epistle is given in the introduction to the Prison Epistles, page 315, together with an explanation of the similarities between it and Colossians. There are no personal greetings in Ephesians such as are found in the other letters of Paul, all of which were sent to a specific destination. Paul had spent three years at Ephesus, and it would seem strange for him to write to the church and fail to remember any of the many friends he must have had there, or to have been thus silent in writing the Laodiceans. We conclude that Ephesians is a circular Epistle, written by Paul to the churches of Asia.

II. The City

Ephesus was located at the mouth of the river Cayster on the Aegean Sea and was a great trading center. It was at times the capital of Proconsular Asia. Northeast of the city was located the temple sacred to Artemis ,(Acts 19:35). It is not known who founded the Ephesian church, perhaps some believing Jews from Asia who were at Pentecost (Acts 2:9). Paul first visited the church near the close of his second missionary journey (Acts 18:18-21). His second visit was during his third missionary journey and lasted three years (Acts 20:31). Very little is said of his work there at that time, but Luke wrote that during Paul's visit all the people in Asia heard the gospel (Acts 19:10, 26).

III. The Purpose and Plan

There is no evident problem to which Paul specifically refers in this letter. It contains many instructions to the

Christian Church and reveals the great eternal purpose of God for the Church, grounded in His own sovereign will.

It is rather characteristic for Paul to divide his Epistles between the doctrinal emphasis (which always comes first) and the practical. Ephesians is divided after this fashion at the close of chapter three.

B. CONTENTS
I. Salutation (1:1-2)

The author calls himself an apostle and addresses his readers as saints. These two titles are used because of the relationship of both parties with Christ, a relationship grounded in the will of God. For his readers he wishes grace and peace from God the Father and the Son. This is a typical Pauline introduction.

II. Doctrinal (1:3—3:20)
1. The Origins and Blessings of the Church (1:3-14)

This paragraph emphasizes the great fact of the foreordination of God—that God has chosen the saints "before the foundation of the world" (1:4), according to the purpose and counsel of His will. This concept may be broken down into five divisions: the object, the Agent, the spirit, the purpose, and the effects of God's foreordination.

The saints are the primary object of the foreordination of God; or, in other words, God foreordains that men should be saints. It is only by inference that one could say that He has also foreordained godlessness for some persons—an inference altogether unwarranted. The will of God seeks man for redemption, for sonship, for His glory; and nowhere in Scripture does it say that God's will is to drive men away from Him. He foreordains to inclusion, not to exclusion. It is not His will that any shall be lost. He "is longsuffering . . . not wishing that any should perish, but that all should come to repentance" (II Pet. 3:9). Jesus himself expressed the reason for man's destruction in explaining the case of those killed by the fall of the Tower of Siloam: "Except ye repent, ye shall all likewise perish" (Luke 13:5). Man, not God, wills his own destruction.

The Agent of God's foreordination is Christ. Men are chosen "in him" (v. 4); they are sons "through Jesus Christ" (v. 5); they have redemption "through his blood" (v. 7); and in Him "we should be unto the praise of his glory" (v. 12). God's purpose, so wondrously expressed in the atoning work of Christ, is to save men from sin. Christ came to save, not to damn.

The spirit of God's foreordination is love, not hatred. His approach to man is one of love. God "in love foreordained us" (v. 5, margin).

The purpose of God's foreordination is fourfold. First, He wills that men "should be holy and without blemish before him" (v. 4). Second, He wills that men who are already His sons creatively should become His sons redemptively (v. 5). Third, He wills that they should be restored to Him along with all creation in the work of redemption of the universe in "the fulness of the times" (v. 10). Fourth, He wills that man shall live to God's glory (v. 12). All phases of this purpose are good and for man's benefit as well as God's glory.

The effect of this foreordination is twofold. First, it results in "redemption through his blood"—the forgiveness of sins (v. 7). Second, it results in a sealing by the Holy Spirit (v. 13), which is the promise of a yet greater inheritance in the future. "The dynamic of the church's life is the Holy Spirit, who is the seal of acceptance (1:13), the means of access to God (2:18), the source of revealed truth (3:5), the secret of universal power (3:16), the bond of unity (4:3, 4), the mentor of thinking and of speech (4:30), the stimulus of joy (5:18), and the armorer for conflict (6:17)."[3]

The foreordination of God does not interfere with the will of man. The wisdom of God in this regard is seen in Christ (vv. 8-9), who was the revelation of God—God in man. In Him we see love, and pleading, and self-giving, and prayers —even for His murderers. But at the same time there is freedom of choice for all. "He saved others [that is what He came to do]; himself he cannot save" (Matt. 27:42)—when men choose to kill Him. Men themselves choose for or against the will of God.

2. A Prayer for the Church (1:15-23)

The plan of God for the salvation of man, which Paul has thus outlined, is not easily comprehended. And so he prays for the church. Upon analysis this prayer will be seen

[3] M. C. Tenney, The New Testament, p. 332.

to be similar to the prayer in Colossians (1:9-12). After expressing his gratitude to God for their faith and love, he reveals the substance of his prayer for them. Paul's concept of God has, for the moment, been enlarged as the result of his contemplations, and he addresses Him as "the God of our Lord Jesus Christ, the Father of glory" (v. 17). He prays that Christians may receive through the Holy Spirit a revelation of truth and the wisdom to comprehend it, in order that they may come to an experiential knowledge of the things of Christ. These he describes as, first, "the hope of his calling" (v. 18). With the acceptance of the call to salvation comes the hope of salvation—a hope which can be realized only at the final resurrection and the consummation of all things. Second, there are "the riches of the glory of his inheritance in the saints" (v. 18). Ours is the hope, His is the inheritance. Christ's inheritance is not in worlds or universes, neither in the glory which was restored when He returned to the Father on the day of Ascension; His inheritance is in the saints. The reward for His sufferings will be a host of people who have been saved through the merits of His death. Finally, there is "the exceeding greatness of his power to us-ward who believe" (v. 19). That power is within the Christian, and is the God-given strength whereby he does the will of God. In order to show its "exceeding greatness," Paul identifies it with the power of the resurrection of Christ, the power whereby He arose from the dead and ascended from the earth to the presence of the Father. As a continual demonstration of that power, God has made Christ the Head of the Church, "which is his body," the tangible evidence of the efficacy of His grace and its far-reaching influence.

3. Regeneration (2:1-10)

The Church is made up of those to whom Paul says, "By grace have ye been saved through faith" (v. 8). To Paul sin is death and salvation is life. Living in sin is twofold: first, living "according to the course of this world" (v. 2); second, living "according to the prince of the powers of the air" (v. 2). That prince is manifestly the devil, whom Paul calls by name later in the Epistle (4:27; 6:11). The majority of mankind have the spirit of the devil and are disobedient to the will of God. They live to satisfy the natural appetites of their depraved natures, and the imaginations of their minds are therefore subject to the wrath of God.

In opposition to this Paul places God—"But God" (v. 4). In His great mercy and love He has taken those to whom Paul refers and resurrected them to newness of life in Christ and into a spiritual experience and relationship with Christ which Paul describes as "the heavenlies" or "the heavenly places." This expression is found several times in this Epistle (1:3; 1:20; 2:6; 3:10; 6:12). It emphasizes the fact that salvation has a heavenly source and a heavenly fellowship.

Those thus saved are saved by the grace of God and not by their own works, but they are saved in order to do good works. Thus the riches of God's grace will be manifest for all time through His redeemed Church, "his workmanship" (v. 10). Paul's emphasis here is that salvation is of God, both in its planning and its accomplishment, and it is to His glory.

4. A Twofold Reconciliation (2:11-22)

The Church of Christ is the universal Church. Paul, a Jew, knew that salvation had come by the crucified Jew, Jesus. But unlike many of his day, he did not conclude that salvation was for the Jews alone. He was the great champion of justification by faith for all men. In this paragraph Paul reminds the Gentiles among his readers of their separation from Christ, not only because of sin, but also because they had not been included in God's covenant with Israel. But through Christ, God had bridged the great gulf between Jews and Gentiles. In His death Christ completely fulfilled the ordinances of the law by making atonement for sin once for all, and thus both Jews and Gentiles may come to God in the name of Christ. Both are reconciled to God by this same means, and both Jews and Gentiles become united in Christ. The "middle wall of partition" (v. 14) has been broken down, and the Gentiles may now be counted among God's saints. "No more strangers and sojourners," they are "fellow-citizens with the saints, and of the household of God, being built upon the foundation of the apostles and prophets, Christ Jesus himself being the chief corner stone" (vv. 19-20).

5. An Afterthought—a Gospel Minister (3:1-13)

"For this cause I Paul, the prisoner of Christ Jesus in behalf of you Gentiles,—" (3:1). With this Paul began another prayer for the church, but he was arrested by his own description of himself, and became awe-struck at the thought that God had given him the revelation of the gospel and had called him to preach it. To him had been revealed the mystery, hitherto hidden, that the Gentiles were included in the plan of redemption. He thrilled at the thought that he could preach the "unsearchable riches of Christ" (v. 8) to everyone, and bring men to a knowledge of this great mystery. In this moment of ecstasy he laid down some of the outlines of Christian doctrine: the universality of the gospel (v. 9); the missionary task of the Church (v. 10); the fact that the Author of salvation is also the Creator of the universe (v. 9); salvation through Christ is the fulfillment of the eternal purpose of God (v. 11); and faith thus founded gives boldness to proclaim the truth, and confidence of continual access to God (v. 12). Suffering on behalf of the gospel was suffering for the sake of Christ and the souls of men. Why then should Paul's brethren be discouraged over his imprisonment? He had found the gospel of Christ to be the answer to all the basic problems of life.

6. *Another Prayer, with a Benediction* (3:14-20)

This prayer originally arose out of Paul's concept of the universal Church built as a temple in which God by His Spirit should dwell (2:22). He returns now to that thought, but stresses the truth of the individual being indwelt by Christ (3:17). However, the Church is also the "family" of the Father, which family has members both in heaven and on earth. For this "temple," for the earthly members of this "family," Paul prays like a good Trinitarian, stressing the dwelling of the "Spirit in the inward man" (v. 16)—Christ dwelling in the heart through faith (v. 17)—and being "filled unto all the fulness of God" (v. 19). He prays that, having been strengthened by the Spirit, and having the whole heart filled with Christ (essentially one petition), they may proceed to be built up, collectively and individually, into the "holy temple in the Lord" (2:21). With the love of God as the foundation, they are to build a four-dimensional structure with breadth and length and height and depth (v. 18). The blueprint is found in the love of Christ (v. 19), which will always exceed one's complete comprehension, and thus this building must always be in the making. Peter expressed the

same idea: "But grow in grace and knowledge of our Lord
and Saviour Jesus Christ" (II Pet. 3:18). The purpose of this
"temple" is that it "may be filled unto all the fulness of God"
(v. 19).

This concept of the indwelling of Deity in the Christian
is paramount to Paul.

> Christ and the Christian are one. The believer's identifi-
> cation with Christ is set forth in this epistle more clearly than
> ever before. It is a chief theme in all of the Pauline epistles.
> The life of the Christian is to be a life in Christ. The two words
> 'in Christ' sum up the Pauline Theology. They occur one
> hundred and seventy-six times in Paul's epistles, thirty-six
> times in the Epistle to the Ephesians, and only once in the
> Epistle to the Colossians. They express the absoluteness of the
> union between Christ and the Christian. For the Christian
> to live is Christ. In spirit and in experience he is one with his
> Lord.[4]

This prayer has sounded the depths of Christian experience. It is boundless in its scope, endless in its possibilities,
and it scales the heights of Christian perfection. Yet, God "is
able to do exceeding abundantly above all that we ask or
think, according to the power that worketh in us" (v. 20).
The standard is high, yet attainable. This is normative for
Paul. It is God's will and for His honor and glory. "Unto him
be the glory in the church and in Christ Jesus unto all generations for ever and ever. Amen" (v. 21).

III. Practical (4:1—6:20)

Paul knew that one must build a foundation in doctrine
before he can exhort effectively. He has built his foundation
well and is now ready for the practical aspects of the Christian
life. He also knew that spiritual truth cannot stand alone—
it must be balanced with practical applications. The two must
always go together. While the second half of the Epistle is
practical, the spiritual is never absent for very long. "Scripture always brings the doctrinal into the practical, as reason
and mainspring; and nowhere more than in this Epistle."[5]

1. Exhortation to Unity (4:1-16)

Paul's first "therefore" is "keep the unity of the Spirit in
the bond of peace" (v. 3). This may be considered a dimen-

[4] D. A. Hayes, Paul and His Epistles, p. 393.
[5] H. C. G. Moule, Ephesians, The Cambridge Bible (Cambridge:
Cambridge University Press, 1902), p. 103.

sional thought. The unity of God's people, which results from
the indwelling of the Spirit, must be maintained within the
limits of peaceful living. Fellowship is broken when one goes
beyond the bounds of peace. Strife, envy, and the like, are
"out of bounds" for the Christian. Paul dwells on the positive
rather than on the negative aspects of peaceful living. He
argues from principle—"There is one body [the Church], and
one Spirit, . . . one hope . . . , one Lord, one faith, one baptism,
one God and Father of all" (vv. 4-5). There should, therefore, be unity in the church. That unity is jeopardized, however, because different gifts have been bestowed by Christ
upon the various members of the church, and grace provided
commensurate with the gift (vv. 7-11). Jealousy may creep
in on the one hand, or the abuse of the gifts on the other.
Paul exhorts the members "to walk worthily of the calling
wherewith ye were called" (v. 1). Unity will be maintained
if each exercises his gifts in a peaceable manner, "with all
lowliness and meekness, with longsuffering, forbearing one
another in love" (v. 2).

These gifts have been given for a purpose, the same as
stated in Paul's second prayer above. It is for the building
of God's "temple," representing both the Church and the individual, both of them temples for the Spirit of God. He
states it this way: "for the perfecting of the saints, unto the
work of ministering, unto the building up of the body of
Christ: till we all attain unto the unity of the faith, and of
the knowledge of the Son of God, unto a fullgrown man, unto
the measure of the stature of the fulness of Christ" (vv. 12-13).
A united church is necessary to the accomplishment of this
purpose. A divided church is like a group of children, unstable, never knowing what they want and easily carried away
by evil designs. Paul exhorts the Christian to speak the truth
in love (v. 15), and thereby grow up in every way in Christ,
from whom comes the grace which makes every part of the
church function properly and causes it to be built up in love
(vv. 15-16).

2. Break with the Old Life (4:17-24)

To Paul there was a distinct contrast between the Church
and the world, between the Christian and the non-Christian.
In this paragraph he points out this distinction, using the term
Gentiles to represent the non-Christian. Apparently he was

thinking of the Church as the true Israel of God. Christians
are to live differently from the Gentiles. In contrast to Christians, the Gentiles are estranged from God because their understanding is darkened, they are ignorant, and their hearts
are hard (vv. 17-18). They have given themselves over to
lives of rebelliousness and greed. All this is indicative of a
sinful nature, the "old man." Contrary to this, the Christian
must put off this nature and put on the new nature, which
is patterned after God's own nature of righteousness and holiness. Apparently some Christians of Paul's day were demonstrating some traits of the old sinful life, and he says the
reason is that the sinful nature remains in them. This they
must be rid of. It takes a change of nature to change the life.

3. Some Things to Avoid (4:25-32)

The negative element in religion is necessary to the full
realization of the positive. Stop lying in order that the truth
may be told. The unity of the Christian community disallows
anything but honesty and truthfulness. "Be ye angry, and
sin not" (v. 26). The sin of anger rises out of the reason for
the anger. "Anger, as the mere expression of wounded personality, is sinful; for it means that self is in command. Anger,
as the pure expression of repugnance to wrong in loyalty to
God, is sinless, where there is true occasion for it. The Apostle
practically says, let anger, when you feel it, be *never* from the
former motive, but always from the latter."[6] Put away sinful
anger and deny the devil any opportunity to enter. Do not
steal, neither take that for which you have not labored. Honest labor becomes the Christian, and makes him both able
and willing to help others in need. Avoid all evil speech, but
practice conversation which is both edifying and instructive.

All these evils—lying, anger, stealing, and evilspeaking—
were primary characteristics of the heathen society of Paul's
day. And they grieve the Holy Spirit. All such should be put
away, along with the old nature which produces them. In
their place are to be found kindness, tenderheartedness, and
a forgiving spirit such as Christ himself has shown.

4. The Christian's Walk (5:1-20)

The Christian need not be ignorant of the kind of life he
should live. "Be ye therefore imitators of God, as beloved

[6] H. C. G. Moule, *Ephesians*, p. 122.

children" (v. 1). As a son seeks to be like his hero-dad, so the Christian must seek to imitate his Heavenly Father. That pattern may be seen in Christ, who gave himself in love for others, and lived His life as a "fragrant offering . . . to God" (v. 2, R.S.V.). Paul describes the life of the Christian as a walk, perhaps to emphasize the importance of the day-by-day, the moment-by-moment, the step-by-step aspect of it. Twice in the preceding chapter the Christian walk has been referred to (4:1, 17); so no new thought is being introduced here.

Three additional phases of this truth are stressed. First, "Walk in love" (v. 2). Love is the atmosphere in which Christians should live, because that is the attitude of Christ toward them. Paul has already exhorted that they have a forbearing attitude toward one another in love (4:2). Second, "Walk as children of light" (v. 8). This is the positive of which 4:17 is the negative. As with John, darkness is sin; light is righteousness. The light of God's truth will reveal the darkness of unrighteousness. The life of one who walks in light will expose sin and serve as an agent for its removal. The Christian will be a convicting force in the life of sinners (v. 13), and Christ through him will give them light (v. 14). This, however, can come to pass only as the Christian keeps sinfulness out of his own life (vv. 3-6). Neither can he associate with sinners in their sin (vv. 7, 10); and "the things which are done by them in secret it is a shame even to speak of" (v. 12).

Third, "Look . . . carefully how ye walk" (v. 15). A man who does not look where he is going is unwise. If he is going somewhere he will watch the time, lest he fail to keep his appointment. So, too, the Christian; he will be wise to know the will of God and follow it, not allowing the evil of his day to retard him (vv. 16-17). Paul speaks of drunkenness as an evil to be avoided. A drunken man finds it difficult to walk carefully or straight, and Paul may be using drunkenness as illustrative of all those forms of sin which cause one to err from the way and become involved in dissipating activities. The antidote to waywardness and sinfulness is to be "filled with the Spirit" (v. 18); and the diversions which relieve the tedium of a journey, which is sometimes rough, are not detours to worldly pleasures, but are found in "speaking one to another in psalms and hymns and spiritual songs, singing and making melody with your heart to the Lord" (v. 19).

Mingled with this will be thanksgiving to God the Father in the name of our Lord Jesus Christ (v. 20). How beautifully Paul again brings the Trinity into the life of the Christian! This experience is that which the twelve men received at the Ephesian Pentecost (Acts 19:1-7).

5. *The Christian's Home* (5:21—6:4)

So far Paul's practical points have dealt more or less with generalities. Now he seeks to apply what he has been saying to the everyday life of the home. This might be considered a sermonette with verse 21 as the text: "Subjecting yourselves one to another in the fear of Christ."

The relationship of husband and wife is compared to the relationship of Christ and the Church. The wife is to be subject to her husband even as the Church is to Christ as its Head. However, equally important and more pertinently stated, just as Christ has loved the Church and has given himself for it in order to make it "a glorious church, not having spot or wrinkle or any such thing; but that it should be holy and without blemish" (v. 27), so the husband's attitude toward his wife must demonstrate the same solicitude for her welfare. The mystical union of Christ and His Church —which is called the body of Christ—is somehow re-enacted in the union of the husband and wife. This is a great suggestive truth, a "mystery," a revealed truth, not altogether comprehended by the mind, yet of great spiritual significance. Paul seems to say, among other things already suggested, that the Church and the home are closely related, not only by analogy, but also in fact. They give mutual support.

As Paul finds in Christ and His Church the analogy of the relationship of husband and wife, he finds in the Ten Commandments the authority for the obedience of children to their parents (6:1-2). Children need authority over them until they learn the lesson of willing obedience. The commandment has promise of long life (v. 3), and authority must be administered with love and with the purpose of teaching obedience to the will of God (v. 4).

6. *Christian Masters and Servants* (6:5-9)

Paul recognized different levels in human society. Elsewhere he exhorted respect and obedience to acknowledged civil authority (Rom. 13:1). Many early Christians came from the large number of slaves abounding in every city. Nowhere does the New Testament condemn slavery directly, but it does teach a standard of human values and of brotherly love that would deal a mortal blow to the evils of slavery and finally sound its death knell. However, the Christian life is not dependent upon any required social status—it is meant to make a man Christian in heart and life wherever the fortunes of life have placed him. It will make him a good slave or a good master.

The way to be a good slave is to consider oneself first of all a bond servant of Christ. God will reward. The way to be a good master is to be a servant of Christ. God has a reward for him, too. That makes the difference between servant and master essentially slight. These human relationships are but for a time and are best maintained with spiritual values in view.

7. *Having Done All, Stand* (6:10-20)

The sharp contrast which Paul has emphasized between righteousness and unrighteousness, between the Christian and the sinner, brings him now to the consideration of the Christian life as a warfare. The Christian does not fight the sinner, but he fights the devil and all of his reinforcements in this life. Just as God has blessed His people "with every spiritual blessing in the heavenly places in Christ" (1:3); as Christ, following His resurrection, was made to "sit at his [God's] right hand in the heavenly places" (1:20); as the Christian by conversion is made "to sit with him in the heavenly places, in Christ Jesus" (2:6); and as "unto the principalities and the powers in the heavenly places might be made known through the church the manifold wisdom of God" (3:10); so the Christian warfare is "against the spiritual hosts of wickedness in the heavenly places" (6:12). These hosts are not "flesh and blood" but "principalities" and "powers" and "world-rulers of this darkness" (v. 12). The warfare is spiritual, and there is spiritual armor suitable to it. The girdle which holds together the warrior's dress and equipment is "truth." The "breastplate" which protects the heart is "righteousness." The equipment for the feet which determines his place in the battle is "the gospel of peace." The protection against the attacks of the enemy is the "shield of faith." The mind is kept clear by the "helmet of salvation." It will be

noticed that everything thus far is for defense. Only one
weapon of offense is given, "the sword of the Spirit, which
is the word of God" (vv. 13-17).

At this point Paul leaves his figurative language and
exhorts the Christians to lead lives of perpetual prayer. When
all is said, the Christian fights his battles on his knees. He
now includes himself as one of the band to whom he has been
writing and requests that they pray for him—not just mention
his name in prayer, but that all their prayers may be with
supplication—with a piling up of prayer upon prayer, because
he himself feels the need of strength in his task of preaching
the gospel.

IV. Conclusion (6: 21-24)

This letter was to be delivered to its destination by Tychicus, who would also carry additional news from Paul. He
would obtain information for Paul upon his arrival and seek
to encourage the hearts of the brethren—for he was a "beloved brother and faithful minister in the Lord" (v. 21).

The benediction is typically Pauline: "Peace be to the
brethren, and love with faith, from God the Father and the
Lord Jesus Christ. Grace be with all them that love our Lord
Jesus Christ with a love incorruptible" (v. 24).

PHILIPPIANS

A. Introduction

"We find Philippians more peaceful than Galatians, more
personal and affectionate than Ephesians, less anxiously con-
troversial than Colossians, more deliberate and symmetrical
than Thessalonians, and of course larger in its applications
than the personal messages to Timothy, Titus, and Philemon."[7]

I. The City

The city of Philippi was located on the east border of
Macedonia, about ten miles from the coast. Neapolis was its
seaport on the Aegean Sea. It received its name from Philip II
of Macedon in the fourth century B.C., became a port of the
Roman Province of Macedonia in 146 B.C., and became a Roman colony in A.D. 42. It had a small Jewish colony in the
time of Paul, but apparently it had no synagogue (Acts 16: 13)

[7] H. C. G. Moule, *Philippian Studies* (London: Hodder and Stoughton,
n.d.), p. 5.

II. The Church

Paul had founded the Philippian church, the first church in Europe, on his second missionary journey (Acts 16). The households of Lydia and the jailer, with the fortunetelling girl, made up the charter membership. The church had been established about ten years when this Epistle was written and, during that time, had been a source of great joy to Paul. No other church had been so mindful of Paul's personal needs in giving him assistance. In fact, the occasion of the writing of the Philippian letter was the arrival of Epaphroditus from Philippi with gifts for Paul. In no other Epistle does he write in such intimate terms. Paul visited the church at least three times (Acts 16:12; II Cor. 2:13; Acts 20:6). After the initial organization, Luke seems to have been left in charge of the new church for a time. For the most part it was apparently left to itself.

III. Authorship

There is little doubt that Paul was the author of Philippians. This Epistle contains some of the strongest evidence found in the Prison Epistles that the imprisonment of Paul was at Rome, and that he wrote from there. Paul's situation at the time of writing was somewhat changed from his situation as revealed in Ephesians and Colossians. Only Timothy was with him, whom he planned to send to Philippi with Epaphroditus (2:19). This fact may be no more significant than perhaps to point to Paul's having sent the other men, such as Demas and Luke and Tychicus, on other missions. Paul is hopeful of his release from prison (1:19-26), and from this it may be judged that he wrote this Epistle toward the close of his two-year imprisonment in Rome.

IV. Purpose and Plan

The Philippian church had grown steadily, and its members were quite free from division, except for the case of two women who were having some difficulty (4:2). Paul's primary aim in writing was to thank the church for the offering which it had sent by Epaphroditus. In addition to this he stressed two things—personal details and the need of Christian unity.

However, there were some signs of trouble in the making. There is a note of anxiety in the first chapter (vv. 3-11).

There is a strong reference to the teachings of the Judaizers (3:2-4), with the consequent inclination to antinomianism (3:17-21). The reference to preachers with bad motives (1:15-18) probably has no application to the membership of the church at Philippi.

While Paul wrote much about himself, the Epistle is not Paul-centered. It is Christocentric. His personal testimony was: "By the grace of God I am what I am" (I Cor. 15:10). His life was so bound up in Christ that he could speak of himself to the glory of God. It was not strange for him to speak of the sufferings of Christ and his own imprisonment in the same breath. He could sincerely proclaim the great desire of his heart, that "Christ shall be magnified in my body, whether by life, or by death" (1:20).

V. The Occasion

The arrival at Rome of Epaphroditus, possibly the pastor at Philippi, was followed by his very severe illness (2:27). Upon his recovery Paul planned to send him back to the church with the Epistle, accompanied by Timothy (2:19).

The Philippian Epistle gives a remarkable insight into the character of Paul. In prison, practically alone (the church at Rome was seemingly uninterested in his welfare), and with death hovering near at all times, he nevertheless wrote the most joyful of his Epistles. "In every way, whether in pretence or in truth, Christ is proclaimed; and therein I rejoice, yea, and will rejoice" (1:18). No doubt the years had mellowed him. There is no note of complaint or bitterness, only triumph throughout.

B. CONTENTS
I. Greetings (1:1-11)

1. Salutation (1:1-2)

From the first verse it might be understood that Paul and Timothy were the coauthors of this Epistle, except that later Timothy is referred to objectively (2:19). Apparently Timothy shared very intimately with Paul in his prison experiences. They present a lonely, yet a triumphant, pair against the black background of the Roman prison.

Paul wrote "to all the saints in Christ Jesus that are at Philippi." The "all" speaks of the unity of the church and is conspicuous at several other points in the Epistle. In most of the churches the unity among "all" the members was lacking. Little wonder that Paul found such joy in writing to the Philippians.

The inclusion of "bishops and deacons" (v. 1) reveals that the church had grown into an organization large enough to require a system of leadership.

To this great church he wishes "grace . . . and peace from God our Father and the Lord Jesus Christ."

2. Thanksgiving and Prayer (1:3-11)

Every time Paul prayed he remembered the saints at Philippi and thanked God for them, principally for the fact that they had been his unceasing partners in the spread of the gospel from the day the church was founded. There had been no lapse in their loyalty. And he was confident that God would help them to continue faithful in heart and work until Christ should return. It must have been with a lump in his throat that he claimed his right to feel as he did toward them (v. 7). They were in his heart because their faithfulness had been the same when he was free to preach the gospel and when he was a prisoner. In Paul's mind there may have been the recollection of some churches which had not been loyal to him at the time of his arrest.

It is not difficult to understand Paul when he wrote, "I long after you all" (v. 8). But since he must be separated from them, he prayed that their love might continue to grow, and that their lives might be fruitful to the glory of God.

II. Personal Considerations (1:12-26)

1. Paul's Imprisonment Furthers the Gospel (1:12-18)

In the normal process of cause and effect the imprisonment of Paul would have been a great blow to his evangelistic work, and the Philippian church shared in this feeling. But he assured them that what may seem disastrous may in fact be a plan of God—his imprisonment had resulted in the gospel's being preached throughout the barracks of the imperial bodyguard at Rome. In addition, many Christians had been made strong in the face of persecution because of Paul and were preaching with greater boldness.

But some preachers, perhaps Judaizers, chose to take unfair advantage of Paul, preaching the gospel in a spirit of envy and strife. Some of them envied Paul's success and popularity and sought to turn people against him, using the gospel as a weapon. Others defended Paul and his character, preaching the gospel with love and good will. The significant thing to Paul was not what people thought about him or said against him. It was that a new impetus had been given to preaching the gospel. "Whether in pretence or in truth, Christ is proclaimed; and therein I rejoice, yea, and will rejoice" (1:18).

2. *Living and Dying* (1:19-26)

Moreover, Paul was assured that the total experience would "be for the good of my own soul" (v. 19, Phillips). He was not concerned about being released from prison. If Christ were being honored through him, what happened to him was of small consequence. He only hoped that he could bear his trials with courage—and unashamed. He had no personal choice between life and death. Death would mean eternal companionship with Christ; life would mean more labor and hardships. It was a difficult decision to make. His first choice was death, but he would not be selfish, since the church needed him. So he began to be convinced that he would be released and continue to preach the gospel. "For to me to live is Christ, and to die is gain" (v. 21).

III. Exhortations (1:27—2:18)

1. *Live Worthy of the Gospel* (1:27-30)

To Paul, the standard for life in all of its ramifications was found in the gospel of Christ. This is the basis for all his exhortations to godly living. As will be seen later, he did not offer the gospel as a magic formula or as a short cut to successful living. But in it were to be found the principles by which one's soul may be saved from sin and his life saved to righteous living. Thus he could say, "Let your manner of life be worthy of the gospel of Christ" (1:27).

Paul desired the same consistent unity of purpose in the church in his absence as in his presence. To seek only to please him on the one hand, or to be frightened into inactivity by enemies on the other, was unworthy of the gospel. Faithfulness to Christ is the only sure means of defeating the enemies of the church and the only sure way of achieving one's own salvation. The fact that the Christian must not only believe in Christ, but also suffer many things for His sake, should in no way influence his faithfulness. Paul's own imprisonment was the result of the inherent conflict between the Church and its foes, and so the members at Philippi must be made aware of sharing in the same conflict. All Christians alike share with Christ in the battle against sin, and Paul did well to remind the Philippians of their part in the struggle and the consequent need of unity among them.

2. Have the Mind of Christ (2:1-11)

Confident of the affectionate bond between himself and the Philippian Christians, Paul made a strong appeal to them to complete his joy in them by heeding his exhortation to unity. The "if" is not one of doubt but of certainty. There is "encouragement in Christ"; there is an "incentive of love"; there is "participation in the Spirit"; there are "affection and sympathy" (v. 1, R.S.V.). Therefore, Paul was saying, since these things are certain and an integral part of the gospel, let your unity be just as certain. Let it be a unity of heart and mind as well as of endeavor, each one seeking to serve the other without conceit or selfishness.

The pattern for this kind of life is found in Christ himself. Here follows (vv. 5-8) one of the gems of Scripture, dropped spontaneously from the heart and mind of the great apostle. It is one of the great Christological passages. Christ, who was in the form of God and on an equality with God, did not consider it a thing which He should retain, but emptied himself of that equality by taking upon Him the form of man, a servant of God, being born as a man. In addition to this, He humbled himself to the extent of dying on the cross, as a consequence of which God has exalted Him to the position that every other name is below His in rank, with the promise that the day will come when every knee will bow at the sound of that name, and every tongue will confess His lordship. This, in paraphrase, is Paul's statement. He has proclaimed the deity of Christ, His incarnation, His sacrificial death, His resurrection, and His subsequent coming to reign as King of Kings and Lord of Lords. In His humanity is seen His deity; in His deity is seen His humanity. Christ is the example, the argument, the incentive, and the motivation for the Christian life.

3. Work Out Your Own Salvation (2:12-18)

There is a note of authority in the writings of Paul. He considers himself to be exercising a certain authority over his followers. His exhortation to Christian unity has now become a command. Their own salvation depends upon their compliance with his demands. God is doing His part—now they must do theirs. They must work out what God has worked in (vv. 12-13).

Paul has here given the remedy for a perennial problem in the Church. The blood of Christ is unavailing to the man who will not mind the rules and labor at the task of being a Christian. An experience of conversion is no substitute for careful living. A soldier is disqualified—or even shot to death —if he fails to obey commands and heed the rules of warfare. A soldier in the Christian army disqualifies himself in the same way.

"Murmurings and questionings" are not the signs of a good soldier, neither are they good examples of conduct to set before the world which is watching the Christian. Nor do they make the captain happy. The leader is dependent upon his followers. Paul, as their leader, pleaded with the church in this manner, in order that his efforts might not prove altogether fruitless. He was now largely dependent upon them because he was in prison. As their captain he was ready to sacrifice his life for them for the success of the gospel. He would do it joyfully, and they too should rejoice.

While Paul's references to disunity at Philippi are few, his exhortations to unity are many and strong. Perhaps he was dealing with symptoms more than with cases.

IV. *Personal Hopes* (2:19-30)

As we have noted, Timothy alone of Paul's helpers was left with Paul at Rome at the time of the writing of this Epistle. Epaphroditus had come from Philippi with a gift from the church to Paul. He remained some time there because of illness (v. 26), but was probably detained also by Paul for some work in Rome, since Paul spoke of him as a brother and a fellow worker and soldier. He may have asked to have the Philippian pastor assist him for a time. He hoped to send Timothy (v. 19), but he thought it necessary to send Epaphroditus (v. 25).

At the time of writing Paul was uncertain of his fate as a prisoner (v. 23), yet having hope of release (v. 24). His chief purpose in sending Timothy was to obtain news from

Philippi, which he knew would be good news (v. 19). His recommendation of Timothy was high indeed. Timothy was interested in the Philippian church, probably because he had joined Paul's missionary party at Lystra only shortly before it crossed from Troas into Macedonia when this first European church was established. In contrast to other men—Paul does not name them—Timothy was committed to the interests of the gospel rather than to selfish interests (v. 21). He had been as a son to Paul in the work of evangelism.

Nothing is known about Epaphroditus except what is found in this Epistle. Having come from Philippi, he had risked his life, either on the journey or by his labors on Paul's behalf at Rome. In fact he nearly died as a result. This is a good index to his Christian character. Moreover, he longed to return home, and he was concerned because the church had heard of his illness. Paul counted him a brother and fellow laborer. Paul does not say why he was sending him back to Philippi—perhaps to take the letter, and to enforce its precepts.

V. Exhortations (3:1—4:9)

1. Rejoice—but Beware of Evildoers (3:1-11)

At this point Paul seems to have come to the close of what he had to say. "Finally, my brethren, rejoice in the Lord" (v. 1). But then a new thought strikes him. Perhaps word of some new danger has come to him. He may have heard that the Judaizers are on the move—and he is deeply stirred. Those who demand circumcision as necessary to salvation are "dogs" and "evil workers." His tone is much more severe than it was in his previous reference (1:15). To the Jews a Gentile was a dog, an unclean outcast from God's covenant. Paul used their own terminology to say that they were the true outcasts. In contrast, Christians alone follow the true ritual of worship, which is "worship by the Spirit of God" (v. 3). Their confidence is not in anything external and sinful, but in Jesus Christ.

And then all the argumentative fervor in Paul's nature bursts forth. He could say, and does say, that no one has more and better reasons for depending upon traditional Judaism than he. All that it had to offer has been his, and he has reaped its highest benefits. But then one day he met Christ and dared to look upon Him with an honest and open heart. All of life was changed for him, and—but Paul's own words will best tell what happened: "Howbeit what things were gain to me, these have I counted loss for Christ. Yea verily, and I count all things to be loss for the excellency of the knowledge of Christ Jesus my Lord: for whom I suffered the loss of all things, and do count them but refuse, that I may gain Christ, and be found in him, not having a righteousness of mine own, even that which is of the law, but that which is through faith in Christ, the righteousness which is from God by faith: that I may know him, and the power of his resurrection, and the fellowship of his sufferings, becoming conformed unto his death; if by any means I may attain unto the resurrection from the dead" (vv. 7-11).

Paul had learned that the gains of the law must sooner or later turn to loss, and that justification (righteousness) comes only through Christ. He himself was then, and had been for many years, the glad possessor of the gain of the Cross. He knew the power of the resurrection which had made him alive from the death of sin. He was, even as he wrote, joyfully experiencing the fellowship of the sufferings of Christ. And he was coming daily nearer to sharing in Christ's death. As a result of this he had a hope of one day experiencing also resurrection from the dead.

How quickly the heat of Paul's argument changed into the ardor of Christian testimony! This is a second time in this short Epistle that Paul has borne us aloft on the wings of inspiration as his thoughts have dwelt on Christ. How well might he have sung Bernard of Clairvaux's old hymn!

> *Jesus, the very thought of Thee*
> *With sweetness fills my breast;*
> *But sweeter far Thy face to see,*
> *And in Thy presence rest.*

2. *This One Thing I Do; Be Imitators of Me* (3:12—4:1)

By now Paul has forgotten the "dogs" and "evil workers." He has lost himself in "wonder, love, and praise." And he stands humbled before his Lord. Lest anyone misunderstand him, he hastens to add that he does not consider himself perfect (v. 12). That is, he has not attained to resurrection perfection, which we shall know only in the next life. Yet he numbers himself among those who have been made perfect (v. 15). Those who enjoy "Christian perfection" should continue to press on to the final goal of perfect Christlikeness.

However, he has not strayed from his subject. In tears he speaks again of the "enemies of the cross of Christ" (3:18). The course they follow will lead to certain destruction. But Christians are citizens of heaven, and one day Christ will return to earth and change their material bodies into spiritual bodies by His sovereign power. For this reason Paul exhorts the brethren to be true to the Lord.

3. Help Those in Disagreement (4:2-3)

Returning to the idea of unity in the church, Paul requests the help of a "true yokefellow" in settling some difficulty between two women members. This individual cannot be identified with certainty. The ladies had previously been valuable laborers with Paul and must be spared the evil effects of disagreement.

4. Rejoice; Pray; Think Virtuous Thoughts (4:4-9)

In these verses Paul exhorts the Philippian brethren concerning certain virtues which were evident in his own life. He has demonstrated throughout the Epistle his joyous disposition in the face of persecution. He possessed forbearance to a high degree—that quality described as love which "suffereth long, and is kind" (I Cor. 13:4). He lived with the consciousness that God was always near. He had learned to meet life, not with anxiety, but by making known his needs to God in prayers of thanksgiving and entreaty. He found, as a result, that God gave him a peace which held him steady both spiritually and intellectually. Though not fully understood, it was blessedly real (v. 7).

Paul was a man of discriminating intellectual taste. Only the best was worthy of his thought. Truth, honor, justice, purity, and such virtues were what occupied his mind and gave tone to all his life. He was a man of noble character, and so without fear of hypocrisy he could exhort the church to follow what they saw in him. Peace always attends such a well-ordered life (v. 9).

VI. *Personal Thanksgiving* (4:10-20)

Paul's gratefulness was not just the result of his having received their gifts. Rather, he recognzied their generosity as evidence of their own well-being. His concern for his own welfare at this time, as before (1:19-26), is one of indifference. God's grace was always sufficient to make him a victor under every circumstance and oblivious to unfavorable surroundings.

Some may feel that Paul was boasting of his spiritual attainments beyond what Christian humility would allow. But that is failing to recognize the spirit in which he wrote. To have denied his own spiritual attainments would have been hypocrisy. To give God the glory and exhort others to follow his example was Christlike. Not everyone can evaluate himself as objectively as Paul could, but he had died to self and sin and had consecrated himself wholly to his task of spreading the gospel. He demonstrated an assurance of his acceptance with God and an insight into the requirements of the Christian life that have probably never been excelled.

VII. *Greetings and Benediction* (4:21-23)

Paul wished to be remembered to all the saints at Philippi and sent them the greetings of the brethren who were with him, including the new Roman converts in the employ of the imperial government.

Having spoken several times of peace, he omits mention of it in his benediction: "The grace of the Lord Jesus Christ be with your spirit."

To Paul, Christ was the totality of life. To "know" Christ was the great incentive of his life. To "be found" in Him was his consuming passion. His desire for his converts was that they should live Christ-centered lives.

CHAPTER XII

PASTOR AND PEOPLE
(THE PASTORAL EPISTLES)

Three Epistles—I and II Timothy and Titus—are commonly known as the Pastoral Epistles. They were written to two of Paul's young preachers and contain instructions to Timothy and Titus and to the churches under their charge. They contain also a strong personal element. A more accurate description recognizes I Timothy and Titus as pastoral Epistles and II Timothy as personal.

I. AUTHORSHIP

The claim of the Epistles themselves to be from the pen of Paul, plus the many personal touches in them which are true to his character, combined with traditional opinion in favor of Paul, are sufficient grounds for holding to Paul as the author of these Epistles.

II. TIME AND PLACE OF WRITING

It is agreed that Paul could not have written the Pastorals before or during his first Roman imprisonment. The circumstances which they reveal are such as to make this opinion conclusive. Some time later, then, must be found. If Paul's death had occurred immediately following the events of Acts, it is strange that Luke did not mention it. The assumption is that Paul was released from prison after two years, because original charges were not pressed against him, and that he went on another missionary tour. He had previously planned to go to Spain (Rom. 15:24, 28). Clement of Rome in his letter to the Corinthians speaks of Paul's having gone to the West, which would be Spain. There is other early evidence in support of this idea. The Epistles "themselves provide the most decisive evidence, that Paul was released from the imprisonment of which we read at the end of Acts, and allowed to engage for a period in travel and active missionary work before he was again arrested and brought to Rome, this time to face martyrdom."[1]

[1] A. M. Stibbs, in *The New Bible Commentary* (Grand Rapids: Eerdmans, 1953), p. 1063.

On this basis, I Timothy and Titus were written during this final missionary tour, and II Timothy was written in prison just before Paul's death. His final testimony (II Tim. 4:6-8) is the word of a man who has received the sentence of death. We therefore hold to this late date, placing the writing of the Pastoral Epistles at approximately A.D. 63-67.

III. THE MAN TIMOTHY

Timothy was one of several young men whom Paul gathered around him and initiated into the gospel ministry. His home was in Lystra (Acts 16:1), and he was converted to Christianity probably at the time of Paul's first visit there (Acts 14:6). He soon became one of the leading members of the church in that place (Acts 16:1-2). On Paul's second missionary journey Timothy joined the party (Acts 16:3). He had a Jewish mother, Eunice, and a Greek father. His maternal grandmother's name was Lois. His mother and grandmother are commended by Paul (II Tim. 1:5) for their faith, which had so greatly influenced Timothy, and they too were probably converts of Paul. The father's name is not given, perhaps because he remained unconverted.

Timothy accompanied Paul and his party to Troas and crossed with them into Macedonia. He escaped imprisonment at Philippi, apparently because he occupied only a minor position in the party. He was with Paul at the organization of the church at Thessalonica, stayed for some time at Beroea, joined Paul at Athens, made a second trip to Thessalonica, and met Paul again at Corinth. He assisted Paul in the evangelization of Asia. Later Paul sent him to Macedonia and to Corinth, and he accompanied Paul when he started back with the offering to the Jerusalem church at the close of his third missionary journey. He was with Paul during Paul's first Roman imprisonment, apparently serving as his representative in dealing with the various churches (Phil. 2:19). He is named co-author, or at least a very close associate, with Paul in the writing of several Epistles: Colossians, Philippians, I and II Thessalonians, and Philemon. When Paul wrote his First Epistle to Timothy, he had left him at Ephesus in charge of the work there. Paul sent for him from Rome just before Paul's death (II Tim. 4:9).

IV. The Man Titus

Titus was another young companion of Paul. He first comes to attention in the New Testament at the close of Paul's first missionary journey. Supposing that Acts 15 and Galatians 2 refer to the same occasion, Titus was with Paul in Jerusalem at the first church council. He was chosen by Paul to supervise the work of the most difficult of churches— Corinth. From the many references to Titus in the Corinthian correspondence we gather that he was capable, highly trustworthy, and a wonderful asset to Paul in his work. The wonder is that he is not mentioned by name in the Book of Acts. When the Epistle to Titus was written, Paul had left him on the island of Crete, which Paul seems to have evangelized following his first Roman imprisonment. At the time of the writing of II Timothy, Titus had gone to Dalmatia (II Tim. 4:10) on another difficult assignment for Paul. All that we can learn of Titus is good. He could be depended upon in hard places.

FIRST TIMOTHY

A. Introduction

This first Epistle is written to a young pastor concerning his ministerial duties and his own personal conduct in the ministry. Instructions were included which were to be passed on to the church or churches. Certain teachers had been teaching doctrines contrary to the gospel. The heresy was similar to that found at Colosse, having elements of both Greek speculative philosophy and Jewish legalism. Paul does not describe it very definitely, but calls it "vain babblings," "old wives' fables," and "wranglings of men corrupt in mind." Paul had discovered the truth in Christ and had no sympathy for those who taught false doctrines for personal gain.

This Epistle shows the close attachment between Paul and Timothy. They were as father and son. Paul was Timothy's spiritual father and was old enough to be his physical father. Timothy had come to Paul shortly after the desertion of John Mark. Paul had guided him in the new life of a Christian, had drawn him into the ministry, and had watched over him with godly solicitude in the midst of all the temptations common to young men and in the face of the many problems which they met together in the churches. When the churches became more numerous and the organization more complex, it became more and more necessary for Paul to turn over the reins of control to others. Timothy was one whom Paul could trust above all the rest (Phil. 2:20). The two Epistles which bear his name reveal somewhat of this period of transition and how Paul sought to make the adjustment.

This Epistle is not clear in its outline. Paul wrote as he thought, one thing suggesting another. He deals with the situation as he found it (1:3-17), he gave charge to Timothy concerning the church (1:18—3:16) and to Timothy personally (4:1—6:19).

B. CONTENTS
I. Salutation (1:1-2)

This salutation is more formal than would normally be expected from Paul to one as close as Timothy. This is evident when it is compared with the greetings to Philemon. But Paul is not now in prison, thinking of a slave and his master, but out in the field with the weight of the campaign upon him, sensing also that his time is short. There he was comparatively inactive; here he is in full harness. He is in a businesslike mood. Moreover, while he writes to "my true child in faith," he is also addressing a co-worker on official church business. Paul knew when to relax into informality and when to display the dignity of his position.

II. The Existing Situation (1:3-17)
1. The Situation in Ephesus (1:3-11)

Timothy was well aware of the errors being taught at Ephesus. Paul needed only to exhort him how to meet them. Timothy is to exert his authority and to charge certain persons not to teach heresy. There is only one true doctrine: that which Paul had preached concerning Christ and the gospel. Speculations, genealogies, and mythologies do not build up people in faith, but serve only to confuse and divert them from the truth. Those who engage in these things become self-centered and self-made teachers, with no true understanding of what they teach (v. 7).

Error is often misrepresentation of the truth. The error in question pertained to the law. Lest Paul seem to condemn the law by condemning its perverters, he hastens to proclaim that the law itself is good. And because it is good, it condemns those whom Paul has condemned (vv. 8-10). They are using the law as a tool of the gospel to control the lives of Christians, when in fact it was laid down only for the ungodly (v. 9). Those who do not obey the gospel are condemned by the law; those who live by the gospel do not need the law. The very emphasis of these self-made teachers upon the law is proof enough of their error.

2. The Situation of Paul (1:12-17)

Paul could not forget the fact that he had at one time been a persecutor of the Church and an enemy of Christ. But the grace and mercy of God had been extended to him because he had done it "ignorantly in unbelief." In fact he considered himself the chief of sinners, yet he received mercy— an example of encouragement for others who should believe. Paul seems to say that his own case was proof positive that Christ could save anyone. Having saved the worst sinner, all others would be easy cases. At the thought of what Christ had done for him and would do for others, Paul breaks out into a benediction of praise: "Now unto the King eternal, immortal, invisible, the only God, be honor and glory for ever and ever. Amen" (1:17).

III. The Charge to Timothy for the Church (1:18—3:16)

1. The Purpose of the Charge (1:18-20)

In the background of Timothy's life somewhere had been predictions that he would be a minister. Perhaps his old grandmother, Lois, had seen some qualities in the lad which seemed to her to mark him for the work of the Lord. Perhaps his mother, Eunice, had dedicated him to the Lord with a peculiar leading that pointed toward the Christian ministry (cf. II Tim. 1:5). At a time when circumstances might shake his faith and cool his passion for the work, Paul exhorted him to steadfastness, reminding him of those who believed in him and his call to the ministry. The urgency of this appeal is emphasized by the reminder of those who had made shipwreck of their lives by failing to remain true. These two men, Hymenaeus and Alexander, had been "delivered unto Satan" by Paul. "It seems to have been something done by mere apostolic authority, under the direction of the Spirit of God."[2]

[2] Adam Clarke, Commentary on the New Testament (New York: Methodist Book Concern, n.d.), II, 589.

2. The Charge Concerning Prayer (2:1-8)

Prayer was to Paul the primary function of the household of faith. It is a pastoral duty to exhort the congregation to pray. Note that here it is not for personal needs or benefits, neither for the church, that prayer is urged, but "for kings and all that are in high place" (v. 2). Civil and world affairs can be influenced by the prayers of the church. It is God's will that all men be saved, and it is the duty of the church to pray to that end. Prayer is urged in four of its aspects, with no apparent regard for the order in which they are listed: supplications—the earnest pleadings of a humble petitioner; prayers—the all-inclusive expression; intercessions—in one's prayers putting himself in the place of the one needing salvation with the purpose of achieving his reconciliation with God; thanksgivings—the normal and necessary accompaniment to petition. To pray thus for all men is praying in accordance with God's will for them. "For there is one God, one mediator also between God and men, himself man, Christ Jesus, who gave himself a ransom for all" (vv. 5-6). This was the only kind of gospel that Paul knew, and it was what he expected his preachers to preach. For this reason he exhorts that men shall pray wherever they meet for worship. The custom in the East was to raise the hands when one prayed, and Paul exhorts that these hands shall be free from all unjust or impure deeds.

3. The Place of Women (2:9-15)

The social status of women in Paul's day was low, and while the gospel has raised the level of women, it has done so gradually as a leavening influence rather than by direct instruction. Thus, in this Epistle, the men are exhorted to do the praying, while instructions are given the women on how they should dress and act in the place of worship. Given in this way, these directives would hardly fit church life at the present time. Both men and women must pray and, at the same time, conduct themselves with respectability in the church.

The women were to come to the place of worship in a quiet, orderly, inconspicuous manner. Gaudy and expensive attire is inappropriate when one appears before God in worship, because it is the mark of worldliness and not of godliness. The money could be better spent on deeds of mercy. Moreover, women should leave the leadership of the church to the men, since Adam was given priority over Eve. A woman's place of prominence is in the home, where she will achieve her life's purpose if she lives a life of "faith and love and holiness, with modesty" (v. 15, R.S.V.).

As has been suggested, these instructions are given in keeping with the social standing of men and women in Paul's day in that part of the world. We, in our application of these instructions, must consider the change that Christianity has achieved in this regard. It is still true, however, that holiness with modesty, marked by love and good deeds, is the badge of Christian womanhood.

4. The Office of Bishop (3:1-7)

Instructions to the church are quite naturally followed by instructions to the officers of the church. It is difficult to be certain as to the nature of Early Church organization. That referred to in the Pastorals is of a more advanced type than that found in Paul's earlier Epistles. Three distinct offices are named here: those of bishop, deacon, and elder. It is also difficult to know exactly the duties ascribed to these offices, or to distinguish clearly between them. Bishop comes from the Greek *episcopos,* meaning "overseer." Deacon is a transliteration of the Greek *diakonos,* and means "servant." Elder comes from the Greek *presbyteros,* meaning "older" or "older man." In Tit. 1:5-7 "elder" and "bishop" seem to be used interchangeably. This much we can say: besides such a one as Timothy, whom we might call the pastor, there were the two offices of bishop and deacon, and the first seems to outrank the second. Timothy and Titus exercised the authority of pastors as we know them today, but they are never called by that title.

The bishop must be a good man, "without reproach" in every phase of life. He must be "the husband of one wife" (v. 2). He must be able to regulate his own home in an orderly fashion as proof of his ability to direct the work of the church. "He must not be a recent convert" (v. 6, R.S.V.), and he must have the respect of "outsiders." Otherwise, he becomes an easy target for temptation.

5. The Office of Deacon (3:8-13)

In like manner the deacons must be above blame. They must prove themselves qualified before they assume office. The women (v. 11), probably the wives of the deacons, are also required to be exemplary Christians. In other respects, the instructions to deacons are much the same as to the bishops.

The importance of these instructions cannot be overestimated. "If one's religion better not his morals, his moral deficiencies will corrupt his religion."[3]

6. A Personal Parenthesis (3:14-16)

Paul pauses long enough to suggest the possibility of his seeing Timothy soon in Ephesus; but until that time the letter which he is writing will suffice to regulate the life of the church.

As he labors at this great task of organizing the Church of Jesus Christ in the midst of all of the forces which threaten it, striving for permanency as well as genuineness, he is overwhelmed at the thought of the majesty of the Christian religion and of Jesus Christ, its Founder. In one of his flashes of exaltation he writes of Christ:

> He who was manifested in the flesh,
>   Justified in the spirit,
>   Seen of angels,
> Preached among the nations,
>   Believed on in the world,
>   Received up in glory (v. 16).

IV. Personal Charge to Timothy (4:1—6:21)

1. Conduct as a Young Minister (c. 4)

Timothy was a young man with responsibilities usually given only to much older men. He found himself embarrassed at times because of an unwilling acceptance of his authority on the part of some church members. In addition, he was faced with the problem of preserving the truth and spirit of the gospel in the face of self-appointed teachers who were substituting external regulations of everyday life for the inner spirit of Christianity—those who were putting law above grace. Out of Paul's fund of experience he counsels young Timothy.

[3] Jamieson, Fausset, and Brown, Commentary on the New Testament, in loco.

Concerning the false teachings, Paul does not tell Timothy to meet them one by one. If it were possible to refute single issues, their number would be endless and the pastor would never settle anything. Rather, Paul goes back to the question of what is primary. Things of themselves are good, and are made evil only by the use to which they are put. "Everything God made is good, and is meant to be gratefully used, not despised. The holiness or otherwise of a certain food, for instance, depends not on its nature but on whether it is eaten thankfully or not" (4:4, Phillips).

Paul continues: Have nothing to do with teachings foreign to the gospel. Seek to excel in godly living rather than in physical excellence. "For bodily exercise is profitable for a little; but godliness is profitable for all things, having promise of the life which now is, and of that which is to come" (v. 8). By both speech and life demand the respect that you and your position deserve. Be faithful to the charge given you, continue your ministry of preaching from the Scriptures, give yourself to your task in such a way that success will be assured. This is necessary to the salvation of both pastor and people.

2. Social Relationships (5:1—6:10)

Paul continues with special instructions to Timothy concerning certain classes of people in the church. The work of a pastor succeeds in the measure that he himself succeeds in dealing with the different classes of people in his congregation and in regulating their associations with one another and the church.

a. *The Old and the Young* (5:1-2). Timothy, as a young man, must be careful to show respect for people of different age groups. Older folk are to be respected and treated as one would treat his parents. Younger men are to be treated as brothers. "Treat the younger women as sisters, and no more" (5:2, Phillips).

b. *Widows* (5:3-16). They were of particular concern in the church, because they had very little if any opportunity to earn their own living. There was the danger of their seeking support by immoral means, or of becoming unnecessary burdens upon the church. It was the first duty of relatives, especially children and grandchildren, to support them. The widows themselves must live lives of great prayerfulness in order to strive against the temptations common to them.

It was the custom of the church to enroll widows in a special service organization for the purpose of assisting people in need. They thus became the counterpart of the deacons. Timothy is instructed to set the minimum age limit of sixty years upon those who could be thus enrolled, the reason being that by that time it was supposed that they would have outgrown their flirtatious ways (5:11-13) and gone beyond the possibility of remarriage. The best possible course for young widows to follow is to remarry and occupy themselves with their homes and families. Note how careful Paul is to guard the church against anything that would curtail its usefulness or mar its reputation.

c. *Elders* (5:17-22). There was apparently an order of elders in each church—for Paul is giving instructions to Timothy that pertain to a wider sphere of church work than the church at Ephesus. However that may be, the duties of the elders were those of preaching and teaching. They are worthy of "double honor," evidently meaning twice as much remuneration as they were accustomed to receive for their labors. They are to be honored highly, and Timothy is not to listen to any charge against an elder except it be supported by two or three witnesses. If one of them is found to be in sin, he should be publicly rebuked as an example to the others. But in order to circumvent as far as possible such difficulty, elders should be selected with great care, and impartiality shown to all.

d. *Physical Care* (5:23-25). Verses 23 to 25 contain advice to Timothy concerning his own physical care, and an observation on sin and righteousness. Some men sin openly and are known as sinners, while others are able to hide their sin beneath a cloak of outward rectitude. But with godly people, whether a man is an extrovert or an introvert, his righteousness cannot be hid.

e. *Slaves* (6:1-2). Paul's instructions to Christian slaves is identical in substance with his instructions in Col. 3:22-25.

f. *False Teachers* (6:3-10). Again Paul comes back to false teachers. There is no other class of people against which he hurls such scathing rebukes. They are "puffed up, knowing nothing, but doting about questionings and disputes of words, whereof cometh envy, strife, railings, evil surmisings, wranglings of men corrupted in mind and bereft of the truth, supposing that godliness is a way of gain" (6:4-5).

This last expression refers to temporal remuneration. These men were preaching primarily for the money they could get from it. But that is not the real profit from a godly life, even though "the laborer is worthy of his hire" (5:18). "But godliness with contentment is great gain" (6:6). We were born destitute and will die the same way. That which sustains life is all one can rightfully expect in this life. "For the love of money is a root of all kinds of evil" (6:10). The failure to understand that the rewards of the Christian life cannot be counted in material gain has been the source of great temptation, and the cause of much backsliding and resulting sorrow.

3. Personal Spirituality (6:11-16)

Paul's zeal for the success of the church was matched by an equal zeal for the quality of preachers whom he chose. He chose them carefully and taught them diligently. He was impatient with weakness of any kind. The gospel was deserving of the strongest and best. To Paul, Christ was not only the atoning Saviour but also the prime example of what Christian leadership should be. Notice His towering example when He stood before Pontius Pilate. Paul said to Timothy: Let that be your standard of attitude and conduct in the face of an evil world. Be morally sound. Be a Christian gentleman. Be all you have exhorted others to be, and avoid all the pitfalls you have become aware of. Practice as well as preach. The Christian life will be a fight and demand your strongest faith, but the reward is eternal life. As Christ is your Pattern, make yourself a pattern for others. God will see and will reward adequately; He is King of Kings and Lord of Lords. To Him "be honor and power eternal" (v. 16).

4. The Use of Wealth (6:17-19)

Here is an example of Paul's manner of writing. He has come to the end of what was in his mind to say and is ready for the benediction. But, like many another good preacher, he thinks of something more to say and proceeds to say it. It is a word of advice to rich people: "Charge them not to be haughty, nor to set their hopes on uncertain riches . . . They are to do good, to be rich in good deeds, liberal and generous" (vv. 17-18, R.S.V.). In this way they will build a good foundation for the riches of eternal life.

5. Closing Exhortation and Benediction (6:20-21)

Paul's closing entreaty to Timothy is full of personal feeling, and is a plea to avoid the theological speculations that have caused many to stray from the path of faith.

As if disliking to say farewell, Paul makes his benediction brief: "Grace be with you"—the shortest found in any of his Epistles.

TITUS

A. Introduction

This Epistle to Titus is next to the last of Paul's writings. It is less personal than II Timothy, while it has much of the emphasis already made in I Timothy. Written to one of Paul's most trusted workers, it breathes the air of trust and confidence. While Titus may not have been as gifted as Timothy, he was of a more even temperament and less given to discouragement. At the time Paul wrote to him, he was supervising the work on the island of Crete, an assignment which might have been comparable in its difficulties with that at Corinth.

B. Contents

I. Salutation (1:1-4)

Here Paul designates himself "a servant," literally a slave, of God, and "an apostle of Jesus Christ." As such he has been commissioned to lead "God's elect" into the faith and truth of the gospel. But his calling is not only one of labor; it is also one of hope—the hope of eternal life, which God had long since promised, but had now finally revealed in the gospel.

Thus Paul introduces his letter "to Titus, my true child after a common faith." To him he wishes "grace and peace from God the Father and Christ Jesus our Saviour."

II. Instructions (1:5—3:15)

1. Concerning Elders and Bishops (1:5-9)

Paul left Titus in Crete to perfect the organization of the churches there and to appoint elders and bishops over each congregation. The same officers are called both "elders" and "bishops," which perhaps signifies that the overseers should be men of maturity. Paul also instructs Titus what kind of men should be chosen. A bishop must be blameless in his family life, married only once and with children who are disciplined and morally upright (v. 6). He must be blameless in his personal life, self-disciplined and morally upright, always demonstrating that which is holy and good. In addition he must be sound in his doctrine, able to instruct others and to refute error.

2. *Against False Teachers* (1:10-16)

In appointing these bishops, Titus is to have in mind the forces which oppose the church. This opposition came principally from the Judaizers. These men were native Cretans who had accepted the heresy that salvation through faith in Christ must be preceded by the Jewish ceremonial rite of circumcision. Paul quotes a Cretan philosopher, Epimenides, who described his countrymen as "liars, evil beasts, idle gluttons" (v. 12). One can easily imagine the impact that these men had on the churches. They corrupted the truth because their minds and consciences were corrupted. Paul instructs Titus to "reprove them sharply," because "they profess that they know God; but by their works they deny him, being abominable, and disobedient, and unto every good work reprobate" (v. 16).

3. *Advice to Various Church Groups* (2:1-10)

In Paul's earlier Epistles he used the term "the faith" to designate the truth of the gospel. Here he uses the term "doctrine," and several times combines with it the descriptive adjective "sound" or "healthful." Sound doctrine must be the foundation of the preaching of Titus. To Paul doctrine is meaningless unless it issues in "sound" lives, and it is the task of Titus to bring soundness and health into the lives of the church members. Titus himself must always be a model of good works and a teacher of such soundness and integrity that his opponents will find nothing whereby they will be able to trip him up. Even the slaves who have been converted must be urged to be loyal to their masters—with no word concerning their possible freedom. They must by their lives uphold the truth of the gospel of Christ.

4. On Good Works (2:11—3:11)

This section contains two creedal statements of Paul, which Tenney terms "a fair digest of New Testament theology," and which he summarizes as follows:

1. The personality of God (2:11; 3:6).
2. The qualities of His love and grace (2:11; 3:4).
3. His title of Saviour (2:11; 3:4).
4. The saviourhood of Christ (2:13; 3:6).
5. The Holy Spirit (3:5).
6. The implication of the Triune Being of God (3:5-6).
7. The essential deity of Christ (2:13).
8. The vicarious atonement of Christ (2:14).
9. The universality of salvation (2:11).
10. Salvation by grace, not by works (3:5).
11. The incoming of the Holy Spirit (3:5).
12. Justification by faith (3:7).
13. Sanctification (purification) of His own people (2:14).
14. Separation from evil (2:12).
15. Inheritance of eternal life (3:7).
16. The return of Christ (2:13).[4]

These statements of Paul imply that the Christian Church had by this time become quite settled in its standard of doctrine, and that there was an accepted basis for life and conduct in the Church. Good works can result only from sound doctrine. The purpose of Christ's death was to "redeem us from all iniquity, and purify unto himself a people for his own possession, zealous of good works" (2:14). These things Titus is to proclaim with all authority.

Performing good works presupposes the absence of evil deeds. Disregard of authority, disobedience, evilspeaking, and the like, are to give way to obedience, kindness, gentleness, and brotherly love. If any man is found to continue in such evil practices after being admonished once or twice, Titus is to reject him from the fellowship of the church, because his conduct reveals his sinful character and condemns him.

[4] M. C. Tenney, *The New Testament*, p. 351.

5. Farewell Greetings and Benediction (3:12-15)

Paul had great faith in Titus. He was one of Paul's stalwarts. Most of Paul's admonition had been concerning the church and the relation of Titus to it. In closing, Paul reveals some of the duties imposed on Titus. Having been at Crete for some time, he is to meet Paul at Nicopolis, presumably to give a report, as soon as Artemus or Tychicus can be sent to take his place. Before leaving, Titus must supervise preparations for sending Zenas and Apollos on a journey, doubtless an evangelistic tour.

Paul has no time to exchange greetings among friends, as has been his custom in other Epistles, but merely says, "All that are with me salute thee" (v. 15). It is noticeable that this Epistle lacks the personal warmth found in those to Timothy. Even the benediction, "Grace be with you all," is addressed to the company with Titus rather than to Titus personally.

II TIMOTHY

A. INTRODUCTION

This Epistle is the last of Paul's writings which have been preserved. Indeed, it is doubtless the last Epistle he ever wrote. It is one of the more personal of Paul's Epistles, written while he was in prison awaiting martyrdom. It is "an intermingling of personal sentiment and of administrative policy, of reminiscence and of instruction, of sadness and of confidence."[5] Paul, the general superintendent, is about ready to lay down his gavel and turn over his duties to others. Timothy is one of his most trusted assistants, and although no one could or did take Paul's place, he seems to have meant for Timothy to be his successor.

A peculiarity of this Epistle which it shares with that to Titus is the reference to life in the salutation: "according to the promise of the life which is in Christ Jesus." As he nears the hour of death, he becomes increasingly conscious of life—the life he has lived for Christ, the life he is about to lay down, and the eternal life which awaits him. To Paul the past, the present, and the future were ablaze with life.

---

[5] M. C. Tenney, *The New Testament*, p. 353.

B. Contents

I. *Salutation* (1:1-2)

This salutation shows somewhat of the same formality found in I Timothy. Timothy is his "beloved child." Even though in prison he still signs himself "an apostle of Christ Jesus through the will of God." Paul does not here need to emphasize his apostolic authority to Timothy as he did in some of his other Epistles, but the expression reveals again the indomitable spirit of the aged apostle. He as much as says, "I may be down but I am not out." Note it again: not only an apostle still, but still in the will of God; in prison—through the will of God; with the executioner's ax above him—through the will of God; almost entirely forsaken—through the will of God. What a testimony! In all those things he was more than conqueror through Him who loved him.

II. *Pastoral Instructions* (1:3—3:17)

1. *Timothy's Heritage* (1:3-6)

Paul's primary reason for writing to Timothy a second time seems to have been the knowledge of troublous times for Timothy in the work of the church, which had brought him to tears (v. 4). How the younger man must have been heartened to have Paul say that he thanked God for him every time he prayed for him; to have him say that to be able to see him would be the apostle's greatest joy; to be reminded of the faith and confidence which his mother and his grandmother had in him; and to remember his experience when Paul had ordained him for the ministry by laying his hands upon him! Timothy was the possessor of a wonderful heritage. Paul tells him that timidity or a spirit of drawing back ought to have no place in him, for the spirit of the gospel is the spirit of power and of love and of self-discipline.

2. *Paul's Experience an Example* (1:8-18)

Timothy's greatest weakness at the moment seems to have been a certain type of forgetfulness—allowing the pressure of present difficulties to obliterate the consciousness of his many blessings. Both the difficulties and the blessings had come to him as the result of his being a minister of the gospel. He should therefore bear his share of sufferings and count his blessings, because in the last analysis God was responsible for the state he was in. It had ever been the same with Paul, but he could say: "I am not ashamed; for I know him whom I have believed, and I am persuaded that he is able to guard that which I have committed unto him against that day" (the final day of reckoning) (v. 12). Thus he urges Timothy to hold to substantial doctrine as Paul had taught him and be jealous for the truth through the help of the Holy Spirit, who dwells within him.

Paul further illustrates his own case by citing the fact that the churches in all Asia have turned against him. Only one man among them, Onesiphorus, could he name who had stood by him. This does not mean that all others had deserted him as Demas had (4:10). Crescens had gone to Galatia, Titus to Dalmatia, and Tychicus to Ephesus by Paul's orders. Luke was with him, and he requested Mark to come to see him. Paul's workers were true. But among the churches the people were either thoughtless or forgetful of Paul, or they had been turned against him. Onesiphorus of Ephesus had befriended him and had even visited him in his Roman prison. For this Paul was sincerely grateful.

3. Personal Encouragement (2:1-13)

"Thou therefore," in view of these things, be strong in Christ to pass on the truth to others in the same measure in which you have received it, and so the gospel will spread from person to person. Being a minister of the gospel is like being a soldier (vv. 3-4), an athlete (v. 5), and a farmer (v. 6). Paul exhorts Timothy to obey all the rules of his profession and to be the best workman possible. Hardships should not hinder him from doing his best.

Paul continues to say that, even though he is a prisoner for the sake of the gospel, the gospel itself offers the only true freedom to be found. For this reason he can endure everything in the light of the prospect of eternal life.

4. Public Relations (2:14-26)

Paul now comes to the consideration of Timothy's relationship with the members of his church. "Tell them as before God not to fight wordy battles" (v. 14, Phillips). It may not be necessary to think that the churches of Asia in Paul's time had more disputing members than churches of other days, but no other evil practice receives greater condemnation from

Paul. He makes an example of Hymenaeus and Philetus, who, by purposeless discussions, had been led into erroneous beliefs concerning the resurrection. Not only were they destroying the faith of some people, but they were removing themselves from the circle of the children of God and were growing careless in their own moral and spiritual lives.

Paul knew that it was more than could be expected to have a perfect church membership. Some members would be like gold and silver—dependable, lasting; others would be like wood and earthenware—fragile, easily ruined (v. 20; I Cor. 3:12-15). The ideal seldom if ever becomes the real. As Dr. J. B. Chapman used to say, "The church is not a museum; it is a workshop." Every pastor knows how much labor must go into the "perfecting of the saints."

Paul has been discussing some who were building characters of perishable materials—Hymenaeus and Philetus and their followers. He urges Timothy to have nothing to do with their practices, which, after all, spring from spiritual immaturity, but to "follow after righteousness, faith, love, peace, with them that call on the Lord out of a pure heart" (v. 22). Those who engage in controversies and quarrels have been trapped by the devil to do his will, and, perchance, through the efforts of godly people may one day repent and come again to the knowledge of the truth. But the servant of God (Timothy included) must live far above such a plane; he must be kind while he holds to the truth and seeks to lead others—even Hymenaeus and Philetus—into the truth.

5. *The Trend in the Future* (3:1-9)

Timothy may have experienced a measure of encouragement from Paul's statement that there would come a time when conditions would be worse than he was finding them among the professed followers of Christ. The term "the last days" seems obviously to refer to the consummation of the Christian era. In I Tim. 4:1, a more general period in the future was designated, but here the reference is more specific. There is evidence that the first-century Christians believed that Christ would return during their lifetime. If on that basis Paul could prophesy an increase of evil, how much more true are his words now that Christ has so long delayed His coming! Paul was true to Christ's parable of wheat and the tares when he taught that evil would increase as the end approaches.

"In the last days" people will be known for their unnatural and sinful affections, for self-centeredness, for willful, unrestrained perverseness, for "holding a form of godliness, but having denied the power thereof" (v. 5). They are likened to Jannes and Jambres, two magicians who are said in a Hebrew Targum to have opposed Moses. They will oppose the truth and follow their own corrupt imaginations. But their sin will become so obvious that their success will be small.

6. *The Source of Victory* (3:10-17)

Not only will conditions continue to grow worse and worse, but Paul has no hope to offer Timothy that his own situation will improve. "All that would live godly in Christ Jesus shall suffer persecution" (v. 12). There are two ways in which the balance between Timothy's situation and his ability to survive might have been gained—by lightening the load or by increasing his strength. But as Dr. R. T. Williams used to say, "God does not temper the wind to the shorn lamb; He grows more wool on the lamb's back." That is Paul's message to Timothy. Listing his own many persecutions and sufferings, he testifies: "And out of them all the Lord delivered me" (v. 11). Remember, Paul continues, your early training as a child and as a young minister, but above all take the Scriptures as your guide. They will teach you, reprove and correct you, and instruct you in righteousness. As a result you will be sufficiently equipped for every good work that will be required of you.

III. *Paul's Last Exhortation* (4:1-18)

1. *He Summarizes His Charge to Timothy* (4:1-6)

These verses have the ring of the final charge of a general superintendent at his last ordination service. There is the passion of the great heart of the Apostle Paul and his tender regard for his son Timothy. Before God and Jesus Christ, who will judge all men, he charges him to preach the Word of God with equal urgency when circumstances are favorable and when they are unfavorable. He must exercise direction over the lives of the church members, but always with great patience. The coming evil times will make it more difficult to preach because people will choose the lessons of fables rather than the truth of the gospel. But Timothy has just one major responsibility; he must with steady faithfulness and in spite of sufferings fulfill his call to the ministry and seek to convert people to Christ.

2. His Final Testimony (4:7-8)

How Timothy must have been stirred by this appeal, especially when Paul followed it with his testimony and the revelation that he expected to die soon!

Paul reviewed his life as having been a battle, a race, and a test of the truth of the gospel, and he had achieved victory in whatever way he considered it. He waited in momentary expectation the summons to death—death that was more than departure from this life; yea, a sacrifice poured out before God. In death he was sharing the sufferings of Christ on the cross. Death, to Paul, was a sacrament. It was a part of his total ministry for the cause of Christ and the spread of the gospel. For that reason he would triumph in death even as he had triumphed in life. The past with its many duties is completed; the present is secure in faith; the future is aglow with prospect. "Henceforth there is laid up for me the crown of righteousness, which the Lord, the righteous judge, shall give to me at that day" (v. 8).

3. His Loneliness and Desertion (4:9-18)

The imprisoned apostle longs for his friends. When he appeared before the Roman court, he had pleaded his case alone (v. 16). While some of his colaborers were absent on evangelistic missions, his friends at Rome had deserted him. Demas had left him for love of worldliness, and Alexander had labored maliciously against him. As he writes, Luke alone is with him, and he asks Timothy to bring Mark with him. He also asks for a cloak against the cold of the prison, and for some books. But in spite of his lonely state he testifies that the Lord stood by him and strengthened him to proclaim the gospel. God also delivered him from his enemies—not to longer life, but to residence in Christ's heavenly kingdom. To Him "be the glory for ever and ever. Amen."

IV. Closing Greetings and Benediction (4:19-22)

With greetings to some friends whom he knows he will never see again in this world, and with greetings of others to Timothy, he urges Timothy to come to him before winter. Again with reluctant haste he bids him farewell: "The Lord be with thy spirit. Grace be with you."

CHAPTER XIII

GOD'S LAST WORD TO MAN

(THE EPISTLE TO THE HEBREWS)

Like the majestic Matterhorn, the Epistle stands as a lonely mountain peak among the books of the New Testament. Its author unknown, it cannot be classified with the Epistles of Paul or the General Epistles. Hence we give it a chapter by itself.

A. INTRODUCTION

I. Authorship

This is one of the most debated questions in New Testament study. Much paper and ink, as well as brain energy, has been devoted to the discussion, but no final answer has ever been found. The earliest manuscripts of the Greek New Testament have for the heading simply "To the Hebrews." That is the accurate title. Actually the book is anonymous.

The facts of the case are that the authorship of this book was much debated in the Early Church. If the fathers of the second, third, and fourth centuries did not know who wrote the Epistle to the Hebrews, it ill behooves us to be dogmatic today about the matter. We shall notice what some of them have to say on this question.

Clement of Alexandria (*ca.* 195) was of the opinion that Paul wrote this Epistle originally in Hebrew (i.e., Aramaic) for the Jews and that Luke translated it into Greek for the Gentiles. But the objection to this theory is that the Epistle to the Hebrews, as we have it, is definitely not translation Greek. It is written in the nearest to classical Greek of any book of the New Testament. Origen (*ca.* 220) wrote: "Who wrote the Epistle, God only knows."

Meanwhile the Western Church either implicitly or explicitly denied the Pauline authorship of Hebrews. Clement of Rome (A.D. 95) quotes from it freely but never attributes it to Paul. Other writers in the West name only thirteen Epistles of Paul. Tertullian (A.D. 195), of North Africa, said that Barnabas wrote it.

Finally, however, Augustine was induced to accept the idea of Pauline authorship. Under his influence church councils finally decreed this as settled. But the Synod of Hippo (A.D. 393) listed "thirteen epistles of the apostle Paul, and one by the same to the Hebrews." This very awkward expression reflects the uncertainty about the matter. The fourth Synod of Carthage (A.D. 397) stated what has ever since been the Roman Catholic position: "fourteen epistles of the Apostle Paul."

The Protestant reformers were almost unanimous in their opinion that Paul did not write the Epistle to the Hebrews. In his commentary Calvin gives an excellent brief discussion of the matter. After mentioning the views held in the Early Church, both Eastern and Western, he states his own position as follows:

> I, indeed, can adduce no reason to shew that Paul was its author . . . the manner of teaching, and the style, sufficiently shew that Paul was not the author; and the writer himself confesses in the second chapter that he was one of the disciples of the Apostles, which is wholly different from the way in which Paul spoke of himself.[1]

Luther thought that Apollos wrote it. Certainly the description of Apollos in Acts 18:24 fits the nature of this Epistle. It exhibits the Alexandrian fondness for the allegorical interpretation of Scripture. It is "eloquent" in its lofty, oratorical, almost classical Greek style. And, thirdly, it is "mighty in the scriptures"; for no book of the New Testament is more thoroughly saturated with the Old Testament.

We must content ourselves with stating that the best conservative New Testament scholars today do not feel that Paul wrote the Epistle. The style is very different from that of the great apostle. Since the book itself does not name the author, we shall have to leave the question unsettled. It may be that Luke or someone else wrote it for Paul.

II. Date

The answer to this question is not quite as completely uncertain as that relating to authorship. Westcott, in the Introduction to his commentary on Hebrews, places the writing of

[1] John Calvin, *Commentaries on the Epistle of Paul the Apostle to the Hebrews* (Grand Rapids: Wm. B. Eerdmans Publishing Co., 1948), p. XXVII.

this Epistle just before the outbreak of the Jewish War in
A.D. 67. There are at least two reasons for dating Hebrews before the destruction of Jerusalem, A.D. 70. The first is that if
the event had already taken place it would seem that the author
would mention it as support for his argument. The second is
that the language of Heb. 8:4 and 10:1, 11 indicates that the
Temple sacrifices were still going on. This has not been true
since A.D. 70. So around A.D. 66 seems the most satisfactory
date.

III. Place of Writing

The only clue we have for an answer to this question is
found in 13:24—"They of Italy salute you." The Greek word
translated "of" is *apo*, which means "from." So the reference
could mean either that the writer was in Italy or that he was
sending greetings back to Italy from some Italians who were
with him. Recent scholars tend to favor the latter interpretation, while the former is that more traditionally held.

IV. Destination

The nature of the Epistle would seem to indicate definitely
that it was written to Christian Jews. It would also seem most
natural to hold that the Epistle to the Hebrews was written to
Christians in Jerusalem, or at least in Palestine. This was the
almost unanimous view of the Early Church and still commends itself strongly. Who would be more tempted than the
Jews of Palestine to return to Jewish ritual and ceremony?
With the splendors of the earthly Temple before their eyes
they would be the most susceptible to the arguments of the
Judaizers.

V. Purpose

The "why" of this Epistle seems clear. Its purpose was to
prevent the Christian Jews from going back to Judaism. Or, to
state it another way, the purpose was to show the superiority
of Christianity to Judaism, and thus to strengthen the courage
and faith of the Jewish Christians.

In concluding our discussion of these matters of introduction, where we have found so much uncertainty, we could
do no better than to quote appropriate words from Hayes:

> If the authorship of this epistle is uncertain, its inspiration
> is indisputable. If we do not know from what place it was
> written, we know that it brings us a message from heaven. If

we do not know to whom it was first addressed, we know that it addresses our own hearts, and speaks to our own needs.[2]

B. CONTENTS

The key word of this Epistle is "better." It occurs thirteen times in the thirteen chapters. Christ is shown as better than the angels (cc. 1—2), better than Moses (c. 3), better than Joshua (c. 4), better than Aaron (cc. 5—10). Christianity is declared to be a better covenant (c. 8). It offers a better rest, a better priesthood, a better altar, a better sacrifice. As already noted, the theme of the book is the superiority of Christianity to Judaism. In every way it is a better religion.

The meaning of the word "better" is suggested in 11:16, where it is defined as "heavenly." The Jews had an earthly Tabernacle, altar, sacrifices, priesthood. But we Christians, the writer asserts, have heavenly, spiritual counterparts which are actually the real as against the shadow. The material is simply the type of the spiritual, which is eternal.

I. The Superiority of Christianity (cc. 1—10)

1. The Better Messenger (cc. 1—2)

a. The Finality of Christianity (1:1-4). In the first two chapters of this Epistle, Christ is shown as better than the angels. Our word angel comes directly from the Greek word which means "messenger." Hence our caption, "The Better Messenger."

Three books of the Bible open with especially striking statements. Gen. 1:1 says: "In the beginning God created the heavens and the earth." John 1:1 declares: "In the beginning was the Word, and the Word was with God, and the Word was God." Hebrews begins with a similarly impressive piece of eloquent oratory.

The first two verses of this Epistle contain one of the most important declarations ever made to humanity—"God hath spoken." True religion is not man's futile groping after God but God's self-revelation to man. The climax of that revelation came in Christ.

The Old Testament is a record of how God spoke to the fathers through the prophets. This revelation covered a period of some one thousand years. It was given in various install-

[2] Hayes, *New Testament Epistles* (New York: Methodist Book Concern, 1921), p. 76 f.

ments ("divers portions") and by varying methods ("divers manners"). God spoke through dreams, visions, angels, miracles, events, as well as through His prophets.

But God's full and final revelation was "in his Son." An impersonal revelation of a person must necessarily be imperfect. So God sent His Son as the one perfect, personal revelation of the eternal, divine Person. In Christ we see God. Jesus said: "He that hath seen me hath seen the Father" (John 14:9).

Christianity succeeded Judaism. One might well ask, then, whether there will not perhaps be a new religion to supplant Christianity. In fact, that claim has been made by some sects.

The answer is that God has only one Son. Having sent Him, He has given to mankind the only full, final, perfect revelation of himself. The New Testament is the record of that revelation of God in Christ, as made clear to the writers by the inspiration of the Holy Spirit. In Hebrews we have "The Finality of Jesus Christ."

The language of verse 3 reminds us of Col. 1:15. Christ is the "effulgence" (radiance, shining forth) of God's glory, the "very image of his substance." The Greek word for "image" is *charakter* (our word character), found only here in the New Testament. It means a "stamp" or "impress." The statement of this passage, then, is that Christ is the manifestation of God's glory and the exact reproduction of His essence or nature.

J. Gregory Mantle has called attention to what he calls "Seven Alpine Peaks" of truth in verses 2 and 3. He notes that Christ is presented as: (1) the End of all history—"heir of all things"; (2) the Beginning of all history—"through whom also he made the worlds"; (3) the Sustainer of all things, or *throughout* all history—"upholding all things by the word of his power"; (4) the Manifestation of God—"effulgence of his glory"; (5) the Counterpart of God—"the very image of his substance"; (6) the Purifier of sins; (7) the Coregent with the Father—"sat down on the right hand of the Majesty on high."[3]

The fourth verse strikes the keynote of the rest of the chapter with its statement that Christ is "better than the an-

[3] J. Gregory Mantle, *Better Things* (3rd ed.; New York: Christian Alliance Publishing Co., 1921), pp. 36-42.

gels." The Israelites believed that their covenant was given by angels at Mount Sinai. Christianity did not have any such majestic beginning, they contended. The author of Hebrews begins by proving that Christ, the Messenger and Mediator of the new covenant, is better than angels.

b. *The Superiority of Christ to Angels* (1:5-14). Practically all of this paragraph consists of passages quoted from the Old Testament. In ten verses we have seven such quotations, one of them covering three verses. The Epistle to the Hebrews is literally saturated with the Old Testament.

Five or six of the seven quotations are from the Book of Psalms, showing the Messianic character of many of the praises of Israel. One is from Second Samuel and one possibly from Deuteronomy.[4] The Epistle to the Hebrews emphasizes the fact that the figure of Christ is prominent in the Old Testament as well as the New.

The purpose of this passage is to show that Christ is called God's Son, angels are commanded to worship Him, He is addressed as God, and He is invited to sit at God's right hand. In all these ways His vast superiority to angels is demonstrated.

The quotation in verses 10-12 reveals a striking fact. In Psalms 102, from which it is taken, Jehovah is mentioned eight times. But here Christ is equated with Jehovah. That is in line with the fact that the Septuagint normally uses *kyrios* (Lord) as the translation of the Hebrew "Jehovah" (or *Yahweh*). When the Christians applied the term *kyrios* to Christ, as is frequently done in the New Testament, it tended to identify Jesus with the Jehovah of the Old Testament. Thus there was in the very use of this term implicit affirmation of the deity of Jesus, which is made explicit in this passage in Hebrews.

c. *The Peril of Neglect* (2:1-4). One of the outstanding characteristics of the Epistle to the Hebrews is its alternating series of warnings and exhortations, what might be called its traffic lights. The green lights may be recognized by the phrase "Let us," with which many of the exhortations begin (e.g., 4:16; 6:1). They encourage us to draw near, to go forward.

[4] It is not clear whether the quotation in verse 6 is from Deut. 32:43 (LXX) or from Ps. 97:7.

But ever and anon as one drives on through the pages of this Epistle he is confronted with a red light of warning which flashes in his face. It warns of danger and death ahead and bids him beware.

The first of these red lights is found in 2:1. The King James reads: "lest at any time we should let them slip." But the Greek verb here means "flow past, glide by." Hence the better translation in the American Standard Version: "lest haply we drift away from them." The first warning, then, is against the danger of drifting. This is the most subtle and serious danger that confronts every Christian.

In verse 3 we have the unanswerable question: "How shall we escape, if we neglect so great a salvation?" It may not seem so terrible a thing to neglect as to reject God's wonderful salvation through Christ; but it is just as tragic, for ultimately both courses are fatal. For every one who deliberately rejects there are a hundred who neglect, and both are equally lost.

d. The Suffering Son of Man (2:5-18). In the eighth psalm, quoted in verses 6-8, "son of man" and "man" mean the same thing. The Psalmist is emphasizing the fact that man was made lord of all lower creation.

But here, as is frequently done in the New Testament, the older scripture is lifted to a higher level of interpretation and applied to Christ, as the ideal or representative Man. Now it is emphasized that "all things" are in subjection to Christ. He is the true Lord of all creation.

Yet He was made "for a little while" lower than the angels (v. 9). The purpose of His incarnation was that He might "taste death for every man" (v. 9). That is, He tasted the awful horrors of spiritual death when He took our place as a condemned criminal and was made a Sin Offering for us.

The tenth verse leads us into the depths of divine mystery. In what way was Christ made perfect through sufferings? Since the verb "make perfect" properly means to "bring to completion," this passage might be interpreted as meaning that His work of redemption could be brought to completion only through suffering. That is a minimum interpretation, but it probably does not exhaust the meaning of the passage.

The most important purpose of the Incarnation is stated in verse 14. While Jesus came to earth to show us God and to show us how we should live as sons of God, yet the great goal of His earthly ministry was His atoning death on the cross.

Perhaps no more comforting passage is to be found in this Epistle than we have in verses 17 and 18. Jesus shared our earthly life that He might be "a merciful and faithful high priest"—"merciful" because He knows our human frailties, "faithful" because He knows how desperately we need Him in the battle of life.

Jesus experienced childhood, youth, manhood; work, weariness, privation; suffering, temptation, sorrow, pain, and death. He knew the pinch of poverty. He had to associate with little, dull, stupid men. Yet He was victorious; and in Him we can conquer all things. His final triumph was His death (v. 14). It has been well said that death has never been the same since He died.

The high priest of Old Testament times bore the names of the twelve tribes of Israel on his breastplate, suggesting love and sympathy. He also bore them on his shoulders, symbolizing strength and succor. Likewise our High Priest bears each of our names in sympathetic love and strong support. J. Gregory Mantle has well summed up the meaning of verses 17 and 18 in these words: "The humanity of Jesus assures us of sympathy. His divinity assures us of succor."[5] He also has this beautiful statement: "Jesus sympathizes with His own so perfectly that every experience of sorrow that touches them throws its waves upon the shores of His heart."[6]

2. The Better Leader (c. 3)

There was no other man so highly venerated by the Jews as Moses. Some of the old rabbis said that there were fifty gates to wisdom and Moses held the keys to all but one. He was the great lawgiver of Israel. The five "Books of Moses" were held in higher esteem than any other part of the Old Testament Scriptures.

But the author of Hebrews boldly declares that Christ is greater than Moses. The latter was only a servant in God's house, while Christ is a Son over the house (vv. 5-6). The term "house" (used seven times in verses 2-6) probably re-

[5] Mantle, op. cit., p. 98.
[6] Ibid., p. 95.

fers to the people of God in both the Hebrew and Christian dispensations.

In verses 12 and 13 we have two more red lights. The readers are warned "lest" they have "an evil heart of unbelief in falling away from the living God." They are to beware lest any of them "be hardened by the deceitfulness of sin." There is nothing so deceiving as sin. Its glittering, glamorous neon signs mark the place of death.

Moses failed, as leader, to bring the Israelites into the Promised Land of rest. Christ is a better Leader because He will bring into rest all those who follow Him.

3. The Better Rest (c. 4)

The subject of "rest" is introduced in 3:11, 18. But in chapter 4 it is the dominant theme. Here Christ is presented as better than Joshua, who led the Israelites into Canaan but failed to give them a satisfactory rest.

Four kinds of rest are mentioned in this chapter:

a. *Creation Rest* (v. 4). In Gen. 2:2, quoted here, we are told that after six days of creation God rested on the seventh day. This was the foundation of the Sabbath day of rest commanded in the Mosaic law.

For Christians the Sabbath has been changed from the seventh day to the first day of the week. This is because we belong to the new creation which Christ began with His resurrection on the first day of the week. To continue to worship on the seventh day is to ignore the meaning of Easter. For every Sunday is in a very real sense a fresh commemoration of that first Easter morning.

b. *Sabbath Rest* (v. 9). The noun "rest" occurs seven times in this chapter and the cognate verb three times (vv. 4, 8, 10). Both the noun and verb come from the same root. It is a strong Greek compound, meaning a thorough ceasing; hence, "rest, repose."

But there is one interesting exception. In the ninth verse the word translated "rest" is *sabbatismos*. Literally it means "a keeping of sabbath."

How can one enjoy this "sabbath rest" in his soul? Mantle gives a fine answer: "When one life rules man—his own self-life having been hated, renounced and crucified—the true Sabbath begins."[7]

c. *Canaan Rest* (v. 8). The word "Jesus" here in the King James is the Greek equivalent of the Hebrew "Joshua." The context makes it clear that the Joshua of the Old Testament rather than the Jesus of the New Testament is meant.

The eighth verse can be understood only in the light of the seventh. The expression "in David" was evidently a popular way of referring to the Book of Psalms.

The quotation in the seventh verse is from Ps. 95:7-8. This psalm is also quoted twice in the third chapter, as well as three times in this chapter.

The point the writer is making is that if Joshua had really given the people rest in his day God would not still be talking about giving His people rest some centuries later when the psalms were written. The true Canaan rest awaits the believer who will accept Christ as his Sanctifier.

d. *Christian Rest* (vv. 1, 3, 10-11). This chapter begins with a warning against the danger of failing to enter into God's promised rest (v. 1). Then we are informed that the only means of entering into this rest is by faith (v. 3). The nature of it is described as ceasing from our own works (v. 10). It is resting in God's will rather than striving for our own way. It is trusting what Christ has done for us rather than struggling to earn salvation ourselves. Finally, the readers are exhorted to "give diligence to enter into that rest" (v. 11). Though we cannot enter by works into the Christian rest, yet we are diligently to seek it by faith. The highest rest comes only in the experience of entire sanctification.

Chapter 4 ends with a short paragraph (vv. 14-16) which is similar to the last two verses of chapter 2. It forms a transition to the subject of the high priesthood of Christ, which takes the central place beginning with chapter five.

As in the case of 2:17-18, these verses give a very comforting picture of the priestly ministry of Christ on behalf of the believer. There occurs here the beautiful, but unique, phrase, "Jesus the Son of God." In this are combined His humanity and His deity, both of which are essential to His being an adequate High Priest for us.

---

[7] *Ibid.*, p. 70.

We are told that we have a High Priest who can be "touched with the feeling of our infirmities." He was tempted in all points as we are, "yet without sin." This could mean either "apart from carnality," or "without sinning." Westcott, our best authority on Hebrews, prefers the former. But the latter was also true.

There is a twofold exhortation here: (1) to hold fast our confession; (2) to draw near. The Greek word for "help" (v. 16) suggests "running at the cry of." When we cry out in any time of need, our great High Priest comes quickly to help us "in the nick of time."

4. The Better High Priest (cc. 5—7)

The topic which is discussed at the greatest length in the Epistle to the Hebrews is that of Christ as High Priest. We have already found two brief but powerful passages on this at the end of the second and fourth chapters. The next six chapters (5—10) are saturated with the idea. It is especially dominant in the three chapters under present discussion.

a. The Humanity of Our High Priest (5:1-10). In the first four verses of this chapter we are given the qualifications and duties of a high priest under the Mosaic law. First (v. 1), he is to offer both "gifts" (meal offerings) and "sacrifices" (bloody offerings) for the sins of the people. Secondly, he must be one "who can bear gently with the ignorant and erring." The literal translation of the verb (participle) here is "being able to feel gently towards"—he must be a compassionate person.

Perhaps no other word more accurately keynotes the ministry of Jesus than the term compassion. Twelve times in the Synoptic Gospels we are told that He was moved with compassion or had compassion on the people. But since the verb is in the aorist tense in ten of the twelve instances, it may well be translated: "He was gripped with compassion." This was Jesus' instant reaction to human need whenever He found it. And we may be sure that He still reacts and responds in exactly the same way today. As our compassionate High Priest, He feels gently towards us in all our trials and tribulations.

Thirdly, the human high priest had to offer for his own sins as well as the sins of others (v. 3). This, of course, was not true of Jesus Christ, who had never sinned.

Fourthly, the high priest must be "called of God" (v. 4). This was definitely true of Jesus (vv. 5-6). God had appointed Him "a priest for ever after the order of Melchizedek."

In verses 7-9 we find another very striking passage about the humanity of Christ (cf. 2:10-18). It is interesting to note that this book which expresses in the strongest possible terms the deity of Jesus also states most startlingly the full extent of His humanity. Christ was no actor on the stage of life; He lived life in all its terrible, tragic reality.

One feels that he is treading on sacred ground when he reads about His "strong crying and tears" (v. 7). Here we get a glimpse of His agony in Gethsemane, which is described with great reserve in the Synoptic Gospels. But doubtless there were many other hours when He prayed thus. In fact, His whole life was a ritual of sacrifice. Not only on the cross, but throughout the days of His ministry, He "gave" himself for humanity.

In 2:10 we found the statement that Jesus was made perfect through sufferings. That amazing truth is reiterated here. The word "perfect" (v. 9) means "mature, ripe, fitted for His work."[8] Through His sufferings He was made our perfect High Priest.

We read that Christ's prayers were heard because of His "godly fear" (v. 7). A better translation might be "reverent submission" (Alford). The secret of having our prayers answered is complete submission to the will of God. And eternal salvation is for those who continually obey Him (present tense, v. 9).

b. Dull Listeners (5:11-14). Frequently the writer of Hebrews pauses to warn or exhort his readers. He evidently feels that they need a great deal of both. Here he chides them for being "dull of hearing." That is still a very common condition among professing Christians. Apparently the ones to whom this Epistle was addressed had been followers of Christ for a considerable time. The writer says they should by now be teachers (v. 12), but instead they need to be taught the very rudiments of scriptural truth. They need milk instead of solid food. They are still babes instead of mature persons. Just as physical growth is dependent on the proper digestion of food,

[8] W. H. Griffith Thomas, *Let Us Go On* (Grand Rapids: Zondervan Publishing House, 1944), p. 64.

so spiritual growth depends on the absorption of spiritual truth. Keen, careful listening to the Word of God is the primary requisite for growth in grace.

c. *The .Peril of Apostasy* (6:1-8). One of the great exhortations of Hebrews is to be found in 6:1—"Let us press on unto perfection." The verb "let us press on" is in the passive voice. Literally it means "let us be borne on to perfection." The significance of this is well pointed out by Westcott: "The thought is not primarily of personal effort . . . , but of personal surrender to an active influence."[9]

That is the main secret of being sanctified. So often seekers struggle at the altar of prayer, pleading earnestly with God to sanctify them wholly. We are never sanctified at the time of our greatest struggle but always at the moment of our complete surrender. No amount of pleading will substitute for the total abandonment of ourselves to the will of God. Unreserved submission to His will is the price of being sanctified. We cannot bargain with God. It is useless to attempt any compromise. His terms are always *unconditional surrender*. When we meet those terms we find perfect peace, and not until then. We cannot sanctify ourselves by our own efforts. But we can yield to the Spirit of God and let Him sanctify us wholly.

And then we must keep on yielding ourselves to Him throughout life, that by Him we may be "borne on to perfection" more and more in our daily living. For this verse certainly refers to the continuation as well as the crisis. It is a constant "call to perfection" as long as we live.

Verses 4-6 contain a much-discussed passage. The language clearly describes one who has become a Christian "and then fell away." The "if" of the King James Version is not supported by the Greek.

But having established the fact that this passage definitely teaches the possibility of falling away from God, we still face the greatest difficulty here: Can one who has fallen away be restored?

In reply to this we should note that the falling away is doubtless apostasy rather than backsliding. We must remember that the purpose of this Epistle is to warn Christian Jews against forsaking Christianity and returning to Judaism. In other words, the purpose of Hebrews is specifically to warn

<hr>

[9] Westcott, *op. cit.*, p. 143.

against the perils of apostasy. This passage should be fitted into the total pattern.

Then, again, a careful translation of the last part of verse 6 would eliminate the idea that one cannot be reclaimed from backsliding. It should be rendered "while they are crucifying again the Son of God." There is no salvation for a man while he is rejecting the sacrifice of Christ for his sins. This is exactly what one would do if he fell away from Christianity and went back to Judaism.

d. *Spiritual Sluggishness* (6:9-12). The writer is persuaded that his readers, because of their love, are not going to apostatize from the faith. But again he warns them (v. 12) of the subtle danger of being "sluggish." This evidently means the same thing essentially as "dull of hearing" in 5:11. Spiritual alertness and activity are the only safe prevention against sluggishness.

e. *The Divine Oath* (6:13-20). While urging his readers to remain steadfast, the writer is reminded of the example of Abraham. God made him a promise under oath, and kept the promise. The "two immutable things" (v. 18) are God's character and God's oath.

f. *The Order of Melchizedek* (c. 7). The phrase "after the order of Melchizedek" has already occurred three times in the book (5:6, 10; 6:20). Now it receives extended discussion.

Melchizedek is mentioned only twice in the Old Testament (Gen. 14:18; Ps. 110:4), but nine times in the Epistle to the Hebrews. He is described as "king of Salem" (Jerusalem) and "priest of God Most High." The language of verse 3 probably does not mean that he had no parents, birth, or death, but that he had no *recorded* genealogy. Some have held that he was simply a theophany (God appearing in human form). But it seems best to consider him an actual human being who played a unique role as priest of the true God. The idea emphasized here is that he stood alone, without predecessor or successor; his was an unchanging priesthood. Thus he became a type of Christ in His eternal priesthood.

In verses 4-9 the author uses what might seem to us a strange argument to prove the superiority of the priesthood of Melchizedek to that of Aaron. Since Abraham paid tithes to Melchizedek, thus acknowledging him as his superior, and since Levi was potentially "in the loins" of Abraham, therefore Melchizedek is above the order of Aaron.

A more powerful argument is made in verses 11-25. If the Aaronic priesthood had brought perfection, why was it prophesied in the Old Testament (Ps. 110:4) that a new priest should appear after the order of Melchizedek? The reason why the Levitical priesthood could never bring perfection, or completion, is that it was constantly changing in personnel (v. 23). But the priesthood of Christ is unchanging and eternal (v. 24). Because of this He is able to save "to the uttermost" those who come to God through Him. Some would tell us that this phrase means "to the end of time." But the only other occurrence in the New Testament of this Greek phrase (Luke 13:11) lends strong support to our contention that the expression is not to be taken in a temporal sense, but that it means "completely, wholly." It is thus a declaration of an uttermost salvation through Christ.

Another superiority of Christ's priesthood is stated in verses 26-28. The Levitical priests had to offer sacrifices daily for their own sins and for the sins of the people. Christ had no sins for which to offer sacrifice, and He made a "once for all" sacrifice of himself for the sins of the whole world. What a glorious truth! The chapter closes with the climactic declaration that Christ is eternally the perfect High Priest.

5. The Better Covenant (c. 8)

Often in Hebrews we find an anticipatory reference to a new topic before the main discussion occurs. So we find mention of "a better covenant" in 7:22, while the extended treatment of that subject is found in the eighth chapter.

The first verse of this chapter states "the chief point" of this Epistle—"We have such a high priest." The Jews were saying to these Christian converts: "You have no priest, altar, sanctuary, sacrifice. We have all these. You have nothing."

In answer to the Judaistic objection the writer declares that *we have* "such a high priest"; that is, the One whose superiority to Levitical priests has been demonstrated in the previous chapter.

But the main topic is the better covenant of which Christ is the Mediator (v. 6). The author quotes the outstanding passage in the Old Testament relating to a new covenant

(Jer. 31:31-34). In one of the darkest hours of Israel's history, when Jerusalem and its Temple were about to be destroyed, the prophet Jeremiah wrote eloquently of the new covenant which God would make with His people.

In the former covenant God's laws were written on tables of stone and perishable skins of animals. Under the new covenant God would write His laws in people's minds and on their hearts (v. 10).

This is a beautiful description of the experience of entire sanctification. When we voluntarily surrender completely to His will He crucifies the old self-will so that we desire with all our hearts to do God's will. That is what it means to have His laws written on our hearts.

6. The Better Sacrifice (cc. 9—10)

a. The Day of Atonement (9:1-10). Chapter 9 begins with a description of the ancient Tabernacle and its worship. The outer room of the Tabernacle proper was called the holy place. It was thirty feet long by fifteen feet wide and held the seven-branched lampstand and the table of the bread of the Presence. In this room the priests ministered daily. But into the holy of holies beyond, containing the ark and the mercy seat, only the high priest could go and that only once a year. This was on the great Day of Atonement, when he took the blood of the sin offering and sprinkled it on the mercy seat to make atonement for the sins of the whole congregation of Israel. It was the most important day in the life of the nation.

b. Eternal Redemption (9:11-28). In contrast to all of this is the sacrifice which Christ made once for all, and which was accepted by the Father as a sufficient atonement for the sins of the whole human race. His sacrifice was perfect and therefore fully adequate.

The word "obtained" in verse 12 is literally "found." Through His earthly ministry, His agonies in Gethsemane, and His death on Calvary, Christ sought and "found eternal redemption." When He cried on the cross, "It is finished," He thereby declared that He had secured salvation for us.

The logic of verses 13-14 was a powerful answer to the claims of the Judaizers. If the blood of bulls and goats could purify, how much more the blood of Christ, the sinless Son of God! Verse 22 states an important truth: "Apart from shedding of blood there is no remission."

c. *The One Perfect Sacrifice* (10:1-18). If the sacrifices of the Levitical system had been perfect, they would not need to have been repeated (v. 1). But Christ—and He alone—perfectly fulfilled the will of God (v. 7). Therefore His sacrifice was acceptable.

The writer quotes from Ps. 40:6-8 to show that even the Old Testament declared the inadequacy of animal sacrifices and meal offerings. But Christ was to come in a human body,[10] fully doing the will of God.

d. *A Threefold Exhortation* (10:19-25). In this brief paragraph we have three closely connected exhortations, all introduced by the phrase "let us." The first is, "Let us draw near." Christ has opened the "new and living way" for us into the very presence of God. With His blood sprinkled on us we can with boldness and confidence draw near to God.

The second exhortation is, "Let us hold fast." Since we know that God is faithful to His promises we should not waver but "hold fast the confession of our hope."

The third exhortation is very striking: "Let us consider one another to provoke unto love and good works." Too often we consider one another to provoke to anger or impatience. If all Christians carried out this exhortation there would be a great deal more of happiness in our homes.

The paragraph closes with an admonition not to forsake our assembling together. The early Christians had no beautiful church sanctuaries with comfortable pews and sweet organ music. Often they met together at the risk of their lives. We read in the second century of their gathering during the early morning for their services of worship and then dispersing before daylight to avoid detection. A few hours in such places as the catacombs at Rome or the underground chapel in the house of Ananias near Straight Street in Damascus would make many American Christians ashamed of their carelessness about church attendance.

e. *A Solemn Warning* (10:26-31). Verse 26 has caused some people great concern for fear they had committed "the

---

[10] The quotation in verse 5, "a body didst thou prepare for me," is from the Septuagint, not the Hebrew.

unpardonable sin" in deliberately sinning after they were saved. But it should be noted that "sin" here is a present participle, indicating continuous, repeated, or customary action. The thought is that if we consciously, deliberately, willfully keep on sinning, the blood of Christ no longer atones for our sins. There is no denial here of the fact which human experience has demonstrated over and over again; namely, that no matter how deeply into sin a person has gone (even after conversion), if he repents and asks God's forgiveness there is a full pardon awaiting him. But many never repent because they become hardened in their sins, and so are lost.

The language of verse 29 does not describe the one who has weakly fallen into temptation and sinned. It applies more particularly to the apostate, as in 6:6 (where the language is very similar). But willful continuance in a backslidden state could lead one into the condition here described.

` f. A Note of Encouragement (10:32-39). In chapter 6 the sharp warning against apostasy was followed by a gentle word of confidence. And so it is here. The writer reminds his readers of the sufferings they had already endured for Christ. They had even rejoiced in the loss of property (v. 34), knowing that they had an eternal possession in heaven.

So he exhorts them not to cast away their confidence (v. 35). They need "patience," or endurance, that after having done God's will they may finally receive the promise. He believes that his readers will press faithfully on, as he does, and thus be saved eternally.

II. The Christian Way of Life (cc. 11—13)

1. The Better Country (c. 11)

Hebrews 11 is the great "Faith Chapter" of the New Testament. It has been called the Westminster Abbey of the Bible, for here are enshrined the names of the great heroes of the past.

The chapter begins with a definition of faith. It may be translated: "Now faith is a *confidence* concerning things hoped for, a *conviction* of the reality of the unseen." Only faith can give this. The writer of Hebrews says, "By faith we understand." Beyond experimentation and reasoning lies the realm of faith. The most important things in life can be known only by faith.

Three antediluvians are cited as examples of faith. In Abel we have the worship of faith, in Enoch the walk of faith, and in Noah the work of faith. This suggests a striking trilogy of the Christian life. By faith we worship, walk, and work.

The expression "by faith" occurs eighteen times in this chapter. It is the keynote of the Christian life. The writer is showing that long before there was any material Tabernacle or altar, men walked by faith and pleased God. Faith has always been the basis of man's relation to God and always will be.

Abraham is the one who receives the longest treatment in this chapter (vv. 8-19). He is the great example of the *obedience* of faith. Actually faith and obedience cannot be separated. A person cannot have one without the other. Faith includes obedience, and obedience proves faith.

At four great crises in his life Abraham believed and obeyed: (1) he left his own country; (2) he sojourned in the promised land; (3) he received Isaac in his old age; (4) he offered up Isaac. Here we have faith separating, sojourning, receiving seed, and sacrificing.

The real meaning of "better" is suggested in verse 16— "But now they desire a better country, that is, a heavenly." Without faith one is tied to the material, a slave of the earthly. Faith frees one to live "in heavenly places" (cf. Ephesians). The life of faith is the larger life.

The writer goes on to name the patriarchs as heroes of faith. He mentions Isaac, Jacob, and Joseph. In spite of their human frailties, which show up so prominently in the Old Testament account, these were men of faith.

Moses is the second most prominent character in this chapter. Abraham was the father of the Israelitish nation but Moses was its founder. Both were outstanding giants of faith. In Moses we have faith refusing (v. 24), faith choosing (v. 25), faith evaluating (v. 26), and faith enduring (v. 27). Again we see the close connection between faith and obedience. One cannot believe unless he obeys, and one does not obey unless he believes. This is the winning combination in life.

Joshua is not named, but is clearly implied in the conquest of Jericho. Rahab, an insignificant character, is named as an example of faith. God still has His heroes of faith among the lowliest laymen. In fact, they sometimes put great leaders to shame with their simple, sincere trust in God.

Lacking time to cover the rest of the Old Testament catalogue of great men of faith, the writer simply lists a few more names in verse 32. Since he had stopped with the Book of Joshua, he cites four outstanding characters from the Book of Judges, picks up Samuel and David, and then sums up the rest under the one term "prophets." Thus he would say that all the great men and women of the Old Testament were great because of their faith. It was faith, not ritual or ceremonial, that made them acceptable with God.

2. The Better Life (cc. 12—13)

a. *The Christian Race* (12:1-17). With the grandstand filled with "so great a cloud of witnesses"—the heroes of chapter 11—we are admonished to "lay aside every weight, and the sin which doth so easily beset us," and to "run with patience the race that is set before us."

One does not run a race encumbered with an overcoat or with weights attached to his feet—unless it is a handicap race. So the Christian must lay aside everything that would hold him back. The "sin which doth so easily beset us" is better translated "sin which clings so closely" (R.S.V.)—an excellent description of the carnal nature. If we are going to win this Christian race we must not only get rid of all excess baggage of worldliness, selfishness, and undue absorption with material things, but also of carnality. The old nature of sin within is the greatest single hindrance to successful Christian living.

The word for "patience" is better translated "endurance." The Christian life is not a hundred-yard dash; it is a cross-country race. It is an endurance contest. Not a fast spurt at the beginning but the steady holding on is what counts. And everyone who gets to the end wins this race. Jesus said: "He that endureth to the end, the same shall be saved" (Matt. 10:22).

But the most important secret of success in winning this race is "looking unto Jesus." A thousand things would distract our attention and turn us aside. Only by keeping our eyes on Him can we win.

The most prominent word in verses 5-11 is "chasten" or "chastening," occurring eight times in seven verses. The Greek terms refer to "child-training." So perhaps the best English translation is "discipline," which serves both as noun and verb. There is no progress in the Christian life without discipline.

Heb. 12:14 is one of the great holiness texts of the New Testament. But it is perhaps quoted incorrectly more often than correctly. One often hears this reference cited as saying: "Without holiness no man shall see the Lord." That truth is contained in the verse, but that is not its main emphasis. Rather, it consists of a twofold command: "Follow peace" and "Follow holiness."

The word "follow" here literally means "pursue." It is used by Greek writers of a hunter pursuing his prey. Furthermore, it is in the present imperative. So the meaning of the verse is, "Keep on pursuing peace with all people, and keep on pursuing holiness; without this you will never see the Lord." It emphasizes the need of right relationships to both our fellow man and God. And holiness must be a lifelong pursuit, not just a crisis experience. It is tied in here with the picture of a cross-country race.

b. *A Final Warning* (12:18-29). The writer cannot close his book without another word of warning. So he reminds us that if terrible judgment overtook the Israelites for refusing to listen to Moses we may expect a far worse fate if we close our ears to Christ.

c. *Closing Exhortations* (c. 13). The final chapter of the book is filled with exhortations to: love (v. 1); hospitality (v. 2); kindness (v. 3); purity (v. 4); freedom from love of money (v. 5); submission to authority (v. 7); steadfastness in doctrine (v. 9); separation to Christ (v. 13); and prayer (v. 18).

Heb. 13:12 is another great holiness text—"Wherefore Jesus also, that he might sanctify the people through his own blood, suffered without the gate." Not only did He suffer to save us, but He also suffered to sanctify us. In the light of this truth no one has a right to treat the experience of entire sanctification as a "take it or leave it" proposition. The Christian is just as much obligated to consecrate himself completely to Christ to be sanctified wholly as the sinner is to repent and be saved. The sufferings of Christ on Calvary constitute the great call to holiness.

For the Jewish readers verse 13 meant separation from the camp of Judaism. For us it means separation from the world and all halfway Christianity.

The Epistle to the Hebrews begins by showing the superiority of Christ to angels and all earthly leaders. It ends by calling on us to live the life of faith and follow this Christ fully.

CHAPTER XIV
PERSECUTED AND PURIFIED
(THE GENERAL EPISTLES)

The General Epistles are designated thus because they were not written to any particular churches or individuals, as were Paul's, but to the Church as a whole. This group includes, in the order of our English Bible: James, I and II Peter, I, II, and III John, and Jude—seven in all. But since the Epistles of John are treated in a separate chapter we shall here discuss only the four non-Johannine General Epistles.

As we have already noted (in Chapter III), the General Epistles follow Acts in the oldest Greek manuscripts. But we are more familiar with their position in our Bibles today, namely, after Hebrews and just before Revelation.

JAMES

A. INTRODUCTION

I. *Authorship*

The Epistle begins with the words: "James, a servant of God and of the Lord Jesus Christ." But what James was this? Four men by that name are mentioned in the New Testament.

The tradition of the Early Church is that this Epistle was written by James the brother of Jesus, who became head of the church in Jerusalem. Eusebius quotes Clement of Alexandria as saying: "Peter, and James, and John, after the ascension of our Saviour, though they had been preferred by our Lord, did not contend for the honour, but chose James the Just as bishop of Jerusalem."[1]

This James is mentioned only twice in the Gospels (Matt. 13:55; Mark 6:3). In both of these places he is listed as one of the brothers of Jesus. Some prefer to take the term "brother" as meaning stepbrother (son of Joseph but not of Mary) or cousin, in the loose sense of Oriental usage. But it seems best to take the word in its most natural sense of full brother.

In the apostolic age James came into prominence. When Peter was released from prison, he said to his praying friends:

---

[1] Eusebius, *Church History*, II, 1.

"Tell these things unto James, and to the brethren" (Acts 12:17). This suggests clearly that James was acting as main pastor of the Jerusalem church. Similar language is used in Acts 21:18—"And the day following Paul went in with us unto James; and all the elders were present."

But even more significant is the language of the fifteenth chapter of Acts, which describes the first church council at Jerusalem. When various speeches had been made by Peter, Barnabas, and Paul, we read: "And after they had held their peace, James answered . . . my judgment is" (vv. 13, 19). Clearly James was acting as moderator of this conference. Paul also mentions him as a leader at Jerusalem, in Gal. 1:19; 2:9, 12.

We read in the Gospels (John 7:5) that the brothers of Jesus did not believe in Him. But in Acts 1:14 they are mentioned as among the 120 in the Upper Room waiting for Pentecost. It would seem that the resurrection of Jesus had changed their attitude, so that they now believed fully in Him.

Perhaps his relation to Christ was one of the reasons why James was chosen for this place of honor and responsibility. Another reason would be his reputation for piety. Clement of Alexandria, in the quotation given above, calls him "James the Just." This tradition is reflected in other early writers. It is especially interesting to note what Josephus, who was not a Christian, has to say about him. Writing in the first century, he tells us that Ananus, the high priest, brought before the Sanhedrin "the brother of Jesus, who was called Christ, whose name was James."[2] The result was that James was delivered to be stoned. But the Jews, who had great respect for James, raised an outcry and Ananus was deposed.

Apparently James was a logical link between the Jews and the Christians in those early days in Jerusalem. He had the respect of both groups, and so was a valuable leader.

II. Destination

The Epistle is addressed to "the twelve tribes which are of the Dispersion." This could mean the spiritual Israel, the Church of Jesus Christ. Or it could mean Christian Jews everywhere.

[2] Josephus, *Ant.*, XX.9.1.

III. Date

The date of the Epistle of James is rather uncertain. Many conservatives feel that it was written about A.D. 45, and so is the oldest book of the New Testament. There is much to be said in favor of this view. The strongly Jewish character of the Epistle argues for an early date, before the separation between Jews and Christians became so pronounced as it did later.

Other conservatives hold a date in the early sixties. If James was martyred in A.D. 63, as tradition seems to indicate, then the Epistle was written not later than that year.

IV. Character

The Epistle of James is the most Jewish book in the New Testament. This is shown in many ways. One of the most striking items is the reference to a local congregation as a "synagogue" (2:2, K.J.V.—"assembly"). This is the only place in the New Testament where the Jewish term "synagogue" is applied to a Christian church. It is in striking contrast to the phrase "synogague of Satan" (Rev. 2:9), written after years of persecution of the Christians by the Jews.

The main emphasis of James is ethical, rather than theological. It is closely akin to the Wisdom Books of the Old Testament and to the Sermon on the Mount in the New Testament. Anyone who reads the Sermon on the Mount and then reads the Epistle of James will be struck by the similarity of teaching.

V. Relation to the Epistles of Paul

The main emphasis of Paul is on faith; the main emphasis of James is on works. This led Martin Luther to speak disparagingly of James as an "epistle of straw." He felt that James almost contradicted Paul's teaching on justification by faith.

But Luther was unduly biased at that point. The Epistle of James is a very wonderful, worth-while supplement to the Pauline letters, not a contradiction of them. Paul himself often emphasizes the need of good works.

B. CONTENTS

I. Salutation (1:1)

We have already discussed the author and destination of this Epistle, as indicated in this verse. There remains only the last word—"greeting." The Greek is *chairein*, the usual word of greeting at the beginning of Greek letters of that day, as found in the papyri. (Paul uses a slightly different form, *charis*.) It is of interest to note that this term *chairein* is used in Acts 15:23, at the beginning of a brief letter written by this same James. None of the other writers of Epistles in the New Testament uses this form.

II. The Value of Temptation (1:2-18)

How can one "count it all joy" when he falls into "manifold temptations" (v. 2)? Only by believing that "the proving of your faith worketh patience." In other words, temptation is of value in strengthening our Christian experience.

Martin Luther is said to have been asked: "What is the first qualification for the ministry?" He answered, "Temptation." The second? "Temptation." The third? "Temptation." Only a tested worker can be trusted.

In verses 5-8 the author urges his readers to pray in faith. Doubting in praying brings only disappointment.

In verses 9-11 we are warned not to trust in riches. Our faith is to be in God, not in material possessions. The latter have too often proved to be a hindrance to faith.

In verses 12-18 the writer returns to his discussion of temptation. He emphasizes the fact that God never tempts anyone, although He does test us. Evil does not come from God, but "every good gift and every perfect gift" does. That is, God is the source of all good.

III. Hearers and Doers of God's Word (1:19-27)

Typical of the wisdom teaching of James is verse 19—"Let every man be swift to hear, slow to speak, slow to wrath." That is good advice for all of us.

But we are to be doers of the Word, as well as hearers (v. 22). Otherwise we shall be like a man who looks in a mirror and sees that he needs to wash his face, but then gets busy and neglects to do it. This is similar to Jesus' closing illustration in the Sermon on the Mount.

Verse 27 gives James's definition of true religion: "Pure religion and undefiled before our God and Father is this, to visit the fatherless and widows in their affliction, and to keep oneself unspotted from the world." Champions of the social gospel emphasize the first part and forget the last. But perhaps we are just as guilty when we give all our attention to the last clause and fail to carry out the first admonition.

IV. *Warning Against Partiality* (2:1-13)

Jesus championed the cause of the poor, and so does James. The latter teaches us that it is an unchristian attitude to show partiality to the rich. He reminds his readers that it is the rich who oppress them (v. 6). Also the rich are often irreligious (v. 7). It is then both morally and logically wrong to show partiality to them.

What Jesus specified as the second greatest commandment —"Thou shalt love thy neighbor as thyself"—is here called "the royal law" (v. 8). That interesting phrase suggests that it is a law which carries divine authority. But it also suggests that it refers to conduct becoming a king. We sometimes sing that we are children of the King. But do we act like it?

V. *Faith and Works* (2:14-26)

James's treatment of faith and works in this paragraph has caused a great deal of discussion. On the surface it looks as though his teaching is in flat contradiction to that of Paul, and that is exactly what Luther contended. Especially difficult is his statement that Abraham was "justified by works" (v. 21). For Paul tells us emphatically in the fourth chapter of Romans that Abraham was not justified by works but by faith. How are we to harmonize these two?

D. A. Hayes has an excellent treatment of this problem. He suggests that Paul and James are using the terms "faith," "works," and "justification" in two different senses.

By "faith" James meant an intellectual assent to the doctrines of the Church, which can be just dead orthodoxy. On the other hand, Paul was talking about a vital attitude of accepting Christ and His salvation into one's heart and life.

When we come to "works," the reverse is true. Paul was referring to the works of dead legalism, done simply with a sense of duty. James had in mind the works that inevitably issue from a heart filled with the love of God.

As for "justification," Paul was speaking of the entrance into the Christian life. This is always by faith, never by works. But James was thinking of our final salvation, which is dependent on our living a life of good works as the fruit of our faith. That is, real faith will always produce good works.

VI. *The Unruly Tongue* (c. 3)

This chapter begins with a warning against too many wanting to be teachers. James reminds his readers that the one who desires to be a teacher of God's Word takes upon himself a tremendous responsibility. For the teacher must be an example of what he teaches. If he fails, his condemnation is greater.

The treatment of the tongue is one of the greatest passages on the subject in all literature. James uses strong language: "So the tongue also is a little member, and boasteth great things. Behold, how much wood is kindled by how small a fire! And the tongue is a fire: the world of iniquity among our members is the tongue, which defileth the whole body, and setteth on fire the wheel of nature, and is set on fire of hell" (vv. 5-6). Every kind of beast, bird, and reptile has been tamed; "but the tongue can no man tame; it is a restless evil, it is full of deadly poison" (v. 8).

There is nothing that gives us more trouble or gets us into more difficulty than our tongues. One brief remark, made thoughtlessly, can start a train of tragedy that runs on for years, causing untold sorrow and suffering.

One of the worst forms of antinomianism is the idea that, because our hearts have been sanctified wholly, therefore whatever we say is holy. When one excuses his critical, unkind, cutting remarks that hurt others and hinder the work of God, by saying, "God knows my heart is pure," we have one of the greatest travesties on religion. It is our responsibility by the help of the Holy Spirit so to control our tongues that more and more we speak always as Christ would speak.

The last paragraph of the chapter (vv. 13-18) underscores the fact that true wisdom is always accompanied by meekness. The beautiful phrase "meekness of wisdom" (v. 13) reminds us of the words of the all-wise Master: "I am meek and lowly in heart" (Matt. 11:29). Meekness is one of the surest signs of Christlikeness.

The seventeenth verse of this chapter is the greatest gem in the Epistle—"But the wisdom that is from above is first pure, then peaceable, gentle, easy to be entreated, full of mercy and good fruits, without variance, without hypocrisy." This ranks beside 1:27 as a definition of true religion.

Any religion that is not basically and fundamentally and primarily pure is not Christian. But what are we to say of those who boast that they are pure in heart, yet are not "peaceable, gentle, easy to be entreated"?

VII. Warnings Against Pleasure and Pride (c. 4)

James warns that selfish pleasure is the cause of much of our trouble. It produces strife and discord (v. 1) and hinders our prayers from being answered (v. 3). Selfishness is the real cause of human woe.

The Epistle of James has many strong statements. One of them is found here in the fourth verse: "Ye adulteresses, know ye not that the friendship of the world is enmity with God? Whosoever therefore would be a friend of the world maketh himself an enemy of God."

Pride is one of the greatest sins in God's sight. We see that clearly in the life and teaching of Jesus. Here the truth is emphasized again. God pushes away the proud, but gives grace to the humble (v. 6). Throughout almost the entire New Testament humility is stressed as one of the most important Christian virtues.

Pride leads us to judge others and so causes division. But who are we to be judging our neighbor (vv. 11-12)?

VIII. Closing Injunctions (c. 5)

The Epistle of James breathes the spirit of the Old Testament prophets. As one reads the words of the first paragraph here (vv. 1-6) he can easily imagine that he is listening to Amos or Micah. Like them, James is forceful in his denunciation of the greedy selfishness of the rich.

The church of James's days was undergoing persecution. An oft-recurring theme in these General Epistles is patience under suffering. That is the topic of vv. 7-11.

Verse 12 is almost a quotation from Jesus' command in Matt. 5:34—"Swear not at all." This is one of the many reflections in this Epistle of the Sermon on the Mount.

Nowhere else in the New Testament do we find more careful directions for praying with the sick (vv. 13-18). In case of illness James says that one should call the elders of the church, who are to pray and anoint with oil. He declares that the prayer of faith will result in the healing of the sick person. But all of this must be accompanied by humility and the confession of our faults. People are very reluctant to meet this last condition.

But erring from the truth (v. 19) is more serious than physical illness. So James closes his Epistle with an admonition to help restore those who have wandered from the right path.

The Epistle of James is insistently and persistently practical. It warns us against a contentment with rejoicing in our great salvation while we fail to put into daily practice the essential principles of Christianity. Many Christians find comfort in the promises of God, but pay too little attention to the precepts of the Word. The Epistle of James has a message for us all with its strenuous insistence on good works as the indispensable proof of an inward faith.

FIRST PETER

A. Introduction

I. Authorship

The Early Church was unanimous in ascribing this Epistle to Peter, the apostle of Christ. While Irenaeus (ca. 180) is the first known writer to state definitely that Peter was the author, yet the evidence is abundant from then on, and no other writer is suggested by the church fathers.

Not only is the external evidence strong for Petrine authorship, but the internal evidence lends strong support. The Epistle has considerable to say about Christians being "living stones" (2:5) built on the "chief corner stone," Christ (2:6). We are reminded that the writer's name, Peter, means "a stone." There are a number of incidental references to Peter's contact with Jesus (e.g., 5:1-2, 5). Also he calls Mark his son (5:13), and the Early Church is unanimous in connecting Mark with Peter. There is every reason to accept the opening words of the Epistle: "Peter, an apostle of Jesus Christ."

II. Destination

The First Epistle of Peter is addressed "to the elect who are sojourners of the Dispersion in Pontus, Galatia, Cappadocia, Asia, and Bithynia." The term "Dispersion" (or Diaspora) is most commonly applied to the scattering of the Jews throughout the world in the last few centuries before Christ. But the reference here could be to the dispersing of the early

Christians from Jerusalem because of persecution (Acts 11:19).

The destination of the Epistle is definitely stated as Asia Minor. We have no record of Peter having preached there, but it is not at all impossible that he did so. At any rate he wrote this letter to the Christians of that area.

III. Date

There is considerable reference in I Peter to suffering for the faith. Evidently, then, the Epistle was written at some time of persecution. If, as we hold, Peter wrote this letter, then it must have been during the persecution under Nero, A.D. 64. For there is very strong early tradition to the effect that Peter was put to death by Nero, who died in A.D. 68.

IV. Place of Writing

In 5:13 we read: "She that is in Babylon, elect together with you, saluteth you." It seems best to take the word "Babylon" as referring allegorically to Rome, as in the Book of Revelation. There is strong Early Church tradition that Peter and Mark—mentioned in 5:13 as with Peter—worked together in Rome. More than this, Clement of Alexandria, Papias, Eusebius, and Jerome all testify that this Epistle was written in Rome.

V. Purpose

The purpose of the Epistle was to comfort the readers in the persecutions they were enduring and to encourage and strengthen their faith. The writer is also concerned that they shall be established in holy living.

B. CONTENTS

I. The Privileges and Duties of the Christian (cc. 1—3)

1. Salutation (1:1-2)

As usual in letters of that period, the Epistle begins with the name of the writer and then indicates to whom it is written. Peter also combines "grace" and "peace" in his salutation, as Paul regularly does in his greetings.

2. The Blessing of the Christian (1:3—2:10)

a. The Trial of Faith (1:3-12). The main keynote of First Peter is hope. This appears immediately in the first verse (v. 3) of the body of the Epistle. The resurrection of Jesus Christ has given us a living hope of our inheritance in heaven.

In verse 4 we have a reserved inheritance; in verse 5 we have a preserved inheritor. God is just as able to guard us down here as to protect our inheritance in heaven. This is our hope.

The trials which the readers were undergoing were a test of their faith (v. 7). If they remained true they would come out as pure gold, just as Job testified (Job 23:10).

There is an interesting comment here (vv. 10-12) on the inspiration of the Old Testament. It is stated that the prophets did not realize the full import of their prophecies concerning the sufferings and glory of Christ. But though they did not understand, they recorded what the Spirit directed them to write. The only hint they had was that they were writing for future generations.

b. *Practical Holiness* (1:13-25). The hope of the Christian is bound up with the second coming of Christ (v. 13). This is what enables him to endure suffering and hardship.

A second keynote of this Epistle is *holiness.* "As he who called you is holy, be yourselves also holy in all manner of living; because it is written, Ye shall be holy; for I am holy" (vv. 15-16). Obviously the emphasis here is on practical holiness. While Paul deals with the doctrine of sanctification, Peter is more concerned with the ethical emphasis.

The command to be holy is based on the character of God. It is not the arbitrary dictum of an Oriental despot, but the inevitable demand of the divine nature. Since God is holy we must be holy if we would have fellowship with Him. In the Old Testament the ceremonial aspect is emphasized. A holy God is unapproachable except through sacrifice. But in the New Testament the ethical concept of holiness, which shines through very definitely in the prophets, becomes dominant. If we would fellowship with a holy God, now and throughout eternity, we must both be made holy in heart and be careful to live a holy life. We realize that we cannot live a holy life without a holy heart; but we should not rest in the assurance of a holy heart and fail to be zealous in living a holy life. An inward holiness which does not manifest itself outwardly will stand the test of neither God nor man.

One of the great New Testament passages on redemption occurs here—"knowing that ye were redeemed, not with corruptible things, with silver or gold . . . , but with precious blood, as of a lamb without blemish and without spot, even the blood of Christ" (vv. 18-19). This is the basis of our call to holiness. If Christ paid the awful price of His life's blood that we might be redeemed and made holy, then we can do no less than surrender ourselves to be forgiven and cleansed. Rejection of Christ's atonement or refusal to let Him cleanse us by His blood is ingratitude of the worst sort.

c. *Stones and the Stone* (2:1-10). As noted in the Introduction the name "Peter" means "a stone." So the figure he uses here is appropriate. The house of God is built with "living stones." But Jesus Christ is the "chief corner stone" (v. 6). There is nothing here about Peter being the cornerstone, or of his being the foundation on which the Church is built. He would be the first to say that he was simply one of the living stones with which the house of God is being built throughout this age.

The Israelites prided themselves on being the chosen people. But in this age it is the Church of Jesus Christ, composed of both Jews and Gentiles, which constitutes "the people of God" (v. 10). What Israel was supposed to be but failed to become, the true Church is—"an elect race, a royal priesthood, a holy nation, a people for God's own possession" (v. 9).

The archaic translation of that last phrase—"a peculiar people"—has given support and direction to all kinds of foolish fanaticism. Our modern sense of "peculiar" has nothing at all to do with the original meaning of this passage. The Greek here means "one's private possession." Our English word "precious" would fit much more accurately here than "peculiar."

3. *The Duties of the Christian* (2:11—3:22)

a. *As a Pilgrim* (2:11-12). Peter uses another figure for the Christian life, that of a pilgrimage—"Beloved, I beseech you as sojourners and pilgrims, to abstain from fleshly lusts, which war against the soul" (v. 11). At the longest, our time here is very short. In comparison with eternity it is but the flicker of an eyelash. We need to cultivate our ties with eternity and keep somewhat detached from time. In the last analysis only that can be timely which is timeless.

b. *As a Citizen* (2:13-17). Peter admonishes his hearers to "be subject to every ordinance of man for the Lord's sake." One is reminded of the incident of Jesus instructing Peter to pay the required tax, though he had to fish for the money (Matt. 17:24-27).

c. As a Servant (2:18-25). Servants are told to submit to their masters. Even if they are punished unjustly they are to take it patiently. For this they have the great example of Christ, "who did no sin" (v. 22), and yet was condemned and crucified as a criminal. The Spirit of Christ alone can make us Christlike.

d. As a Wife (3:1-6). Wives are admonished to be in subjection to their husbands, in keeping with the customs of the times. To do otherwise would have resulted in criticism of the Christians and reproach on the name of Christ.

Verses 3 and 4 constitute one of the two outstanding passages in the New Testament on dress, as quoted in the *Manual* of the Church of the Nazarene. The other is I Tim. 2:9-10.

It should be noted that the wearing of gold is not forbidden here, any more than the wearing of clothes ("putting on apparel"). In both cases it is the motive of *adornment* that is condemned. When one wears either gold or clothes purely for adornment rather than for utility, modesty, or neat appearance, then this scripture applies, and only then.

But sometimes we forget the positive side. It is "a meek and quiet spirit"—not a dogmatic, contentious one—that really adorns Christianity. This is incumbent not only on the women but on everyone (v. 8).

e. As a Husband (3:7). Husbands are to remember that they are "joint-heirs" with their wives and treat them with tenderness. A sincere attitude of unselfish love is the essential thing for both husbands and wives.

f. As Everyone (3:8-12). The Christian duties for everyone are summed up in verse 8. They are co-operation, compassion, love, tenderness, humility. These are the virtues which grace the life of the true follower of Christ.

g. As One Under Persecution (3:13-22). The background of persecution comes into view again in verses 13-17. Once more the readers are admonished to remember the example of Christ (v. 18).

The interpretation of verse 19 is difficult. The "spirits" mentioned here may be human beings or angelic beings, or both. Perhaps the preaching was in the nature of a proclamation that redemption had now been purchased.

II. Suffering and Humility (cc. 4—5)

1. The Trials of the Christian (c. 4)

a. *Suffering with Christ* (4:1-6). Since Christ suffered while in the human body, we should expect the same. When accepted with the right attitude, suffering becomes a means of spiritual grace.

b. *The Brevity of Time* (4:7-11). Since "the end of all things is at hand, we should be watchful and prayerful." Above all things "we are to have real love toward one another" (v. 8).

For those who preach or plan to preach, verse 11 has a tremendous challenge. Goodspeed renders it most effectively: "If one preaches, let him do it like one who utters the words of God." That is a high concept of the Christian ministry.

c. *Fiery Persecution* (4:12-19). The churches of northern Asia Minor were apparently having their baptism of suffering. But they are to rejoice because they are sharers in Christ's sufferings. However, Peter admonishes them to be sure that it is for righteousness' sake that they are being persecuted (v. 15).

2. Closing Admonitions (5:1-11)

This paragraph is filled with miscellaneous exhortations. The elders of the Church are to tend the flock as faithful shepherds (v. 2), not "lording it over the charge" allotted them (v. 3). Rather, they are to be examples to the flock.

Once more the frequent note of humility is sounded (vv. 5-6). Perhaps when Peter wrote the words, "All of you gird yourselves with humility, to serve one another," he was remembering that scene in the upper room when Jesus girded himself with a towel and washed the feet of His disciples.

After further admonitions to trust (v. 7) and watchfulness (v. 8), the writer gives a beautiful promise for these persecuted Christians : "And the God of all grace, who called you unto his eternal glory in Christ, after that ye have suffered a little while, shall himself perfect, establish, strengthen you" (v. 10).

3. Conclusion (5:12-14)

Silvanus, or Silas, was apparently the scribe who wrote this letter at Peter's dictation. As we have noted, "Babylon" probably means Rome. Mark, "my son," was with Peter.

The Epistle concludes with a brief, but beautiful, benediction: "Peace be unto you all that are in Christ."

SECOND PETER

A. INTRODUCTION

I. Authorship

While the tradition of the Early Church is strong for the Petrine authorship of I Peter, the same cannot be said for II Peter. The main cause is the very marked difference in style between I and II Peter. The First Epistle is written in good, smooth Greek. The second is written in clumsy, broken Greek. How are we to harmonize these facts under one authorship?

Jerome suggests the answer. If Peter employed a different scribe for the First Epistle and this scribe used considerable freedom in composition, then the difficulty is resolved.

When we examine the Epistle we find that Silas is named as the amanuensis for I Peter (5:12). But no scribe is mentioned in the Second Epistle. If Peter had to write the second one himself in prison shortly before his death—when no scribe would be available—then the differences can easily be explained.

Incidentally, this takes care of another point. Some scholars have objected to the Petrine authorship of I Peter because it is written in such excellent, nearly classical Greek. But Silas may well have been proficient in the use of this language. Second Peter is written in exactly the kind of rough Greek that we should expect from the pen of a rugged Galilean fisherman.

II. Destination

The Epistle is addressed "to them that have obtained a like precious faith with us." It is then in the widest sense a general Epistle, addressed to all Christians everywhere.

III. Date

Obviously the question of date is wrapped up with that of authorship. If Peter wrote this Epistle it must be dated not later than A.D. 68, when Nero died. For, as we have noted, the early tradition is definite that Peter was put to death by Nero. Perhaps a date around A.D. 67 would fit best.

B. CONTENTS

I. Growth in Grace (c. 1)

1. Salutation (1:1-2)

The writer calls himself "Simon Peter, a servant and apostle of Jesus Christ." Simon was Peter's original, Jewish name. "Peter" is Greek, and was given to him by Jesus.

2. The Secret of Safety (1:3-11)

One of the greatest problems afflicting the Church is that of backsliding. In this paragraph Peter gives us the secret of security against this. He says that we are to supplement our faith with virtue, knowledge, self-control, steadfastness, godliness, brotherly affection, and love (vv. 5-7). If these things abound in us, our Christian experience will not be unfruitful.

He then goes on to say: "Wherefore, brethren, give the more diligence to make your calling and election sure: for if ye do these things ye shall never stumble." One is constrained to ask why we have to give diligence to make our calling and election sure if all believers, as soon as they are saved, are eternally secure. It might be objected that the writer here is speaking simply of the danger that we might "stumble." But the King James and the Revised Standard Versions both have "fall." And Thayer states that the reference here is to "the loss of salvation."[3]

On the other hand, there is no need for backsliding. We are told that if we give diligence to incorporating these Christian virtues in our daily living we shall never stumble or fall.

3. The Certainty of the Christian Revelation (1:12-21)

Because the writer knows that "the putting off of my tabernacle cometh swiftly" (v. 14), he is anxious to strengthen the foundations of the Church. So he points out what these foundations are—not "cunningly devised fables," but firsthand experience: "We were eyewitnesses of his majesty"

---

[3] J. H. Thayer, *A Greek-English Lexicon of the New Testament* (New York: American Book Co., 1889), p. 556.

(v. 16). Peter was right there to see and hear: "This voice we ourselves heard borne out of heaven, when we were with him in the holy mount" (v. 18).

One of the most important passages in the New Testament on the subject of inspiration is found in verses 20 and 21: "Knowing this first, that no prophecy of scripture is of private interpretation. For no prophecy ever came by the will of man: but men spake from God, being moved by the Holy Spirit." In the light of verse 21 probably the matter of "private interpretation" in verse 20 should be referred to the writers, rather than readers, of prophecy. That is, the prophets were not expressing their own opinions, but were speaking "from God" as they were "moved" (literally, "being borne along") by the Holy Spirit. They were lifted out of themselves and beyond themselves in their understanding of eternal truth. What they wrote they had received by revelation from God.

II. Dangers of the End Time (cc. 2—3)

1. False Teachers (c. 2)

The second chapter of this Epistle is a closely knit unit, describing the nature, work, and fate of false teachers. Evidently Peter felt that the danger from heresy within the Church was becoming a more serious threat than that from persecution without.

He says that these false teachers will deny the Master (v. 1). That is the crowning heresy of any so-called Christianity. Christianity without a divine Christ is no Christianity at all.

The false teachers are also described as lascivious (v. 2) and covetous (v. 3). Heterodoxy soon leads to "heteropraxy."

Then the writer cites three examples of God's judgment: (1) the fallen angels, who are reserved in Tartarus; (2) the antediluvians who perished in the Flood; (3) Sodom and Gomorrah. The deduction he makes from this is that "the Lord knoweth how to deliver the godly out of temptation, and to keep the unrighteous under punishment unto the day of judgment" (v. 9).

A further characterization of the false teachers is given in verses 10-22. They are daring, self-willed, blasphemous (v. 10); "creatures without reason, born mere animals" (v. 12); full of adultery and covetousness (v. 14); followers of the way of Balaam (v. 15); "springs without water, and mists driven by a storm" (v. 18). It is a black picture indeed which the apostle paints of these heretics.

The chapter closes with a very vivid picture of the nature of backsliding. Those who forsake the way of truth to follow these false teachers are likened to "the dog turning to his own vomit, and the sow that had washed to wallowing in the mire." Perhaps if a person would contemplate this twofold picture before yielding to temptation he might be deterred from backsliding!

2. The Last Days (3:1-13)

In the first verse the author indicates that this is the second Epistle he has written to the same group. This is the only suggestion we have as to a definite destination.

We find in this chapter one of the most graphic descriptions of "the last days" (v. 3) to be found in the New Testament. We are told that mockers will appear, ridiculing the idea of the second coming of Christ (v. 4). They claim that everything has continued unchanged since creation. But they forget the Flood, when almost all mankind and animals perished. They are like the evolutionists of our day who hold to a steady development, forgetting that cataclysms and catastrophies have played a major part in the history of humanity.

The apocalyptic language of vv. 10-12 has often been considered ridiculously exaggerated. But to us who live in the day of atom bombs and H-bombs the statements here do not seem extravagant. We now know how terribly and tragically literal the fulfillment of these predictions could be.

But current conditions do not leave us pessimistic and despairing. For, "according to his promise, we look for new heavens and a new earth, wherein dwelleth righteousness" (v. 13). The Christian's eternal hope is never blacked out by the catastrophes of time.

3. Conclusion (3:14-18)

The Bible is everlastingly practical. The vivid hues of apocalyptic imagery simply form the background for an exhortation to holiness. If everything material is going to perish, then we should be concerned primarily about the spiritual. As in Jesus' Olivet discourse, the main emphasis is on being ready to meet Christ at His coming (v. 14).

The closing admonition is to "grow in the grace and knowledge of our Lord and Saviour Jesus Christ." That is our lifelong assignment.

JUDE

A. Introduction

I. Authorship

The author identifies himself as "Jude, a servant of Jesus Christ and brother of James." There are a number of men in the New Testament named (James or) Jude. But the most logical deduction is that James the brother of Jesus and head of the Jerusalem church is the James mentioned here. That would make Jude likewise a brother of Jesus and so the one mentioned in Matt. 13:55 and Mark 6:3.

II. Destination

The Epistle is addressed "to them that are called, beloved in God the Father, and kept for Jesus Christ." Evidently, then, this was intended as a general Epistle for the whole Church.

III. Date

The only clue we have as to date is that most scholars today feel that Jude was written before II Peter. The Epistle is closely parallel to the second chapter of II Peter. But the language of the former seems rather more fresh and original. If we hold to the priority of Jude, then a date around A.D. 65 would be most likely.

IV. Purpose

We are given no clue whatsoever as to where this Epistle was written. But the purpose is definitely stated in verse 3— "I was constrained to write unto you exhorting you to contend earnestly for the faith which was once for all delivered unto the saints." As in the case of II Peter, Jude was written at a time when the Church was seriously threatened with heresy.

B. Contents

This Epistle, like Paul's letter to Philemon, is only one chapter in length. It was written to score one point—the need of defending the faith—and it does that effectively.

I. Salutation (vv. 1-2)

Jude has his own trilogy of greeting: "Mercy unto you and peace and love be multiplied." Peter in both of his Epistles follows the Pauline pattern—"grace and peace"—which is found in all of Paul's Epistles except the two to Timothy, where "mercy" is added. These are all great words with rich meanings for the Christian life.

II. Defense of the Faith (vv. 3-4)

This is the purpose of the Epistle. The statement in verse 4 is almost exactly the same as in II Pet. 2:1. Heresy, rather than persecution, is the main concern of these two Epistles.

One of our duties is to learn how to contend for the faith without being contentious about it. Some have overemphasized the word "contend." The Greek term is one that was used for athletic contests. And one of the basic requirements for such events was that participants obey the rules and observe fair play.

III. The Doom of the Ungodly (vv. 5-16)

As in the case of II Peter, the author cites three examples of God's judgments in the past: (1) the Israelites in the wilderness; (2) the fallen angels; (3) Sodom and Gomorrah. Peter substitutes the antediluvians for the Israelites.

The story of Michael contending with the devil about the body of Moses is taken from the *Assumption of Moses,* a Jewish apocalyptic work probably written in Palestine soon after the birth of Christ. The reference here would indicate that this book was being read in Christian circles.

Three interesting expressions occur in verse 11: "the way of Cain," "the error of Balaam," "the gainsaying of Korah." The first was the path of selfish disobedience; apparently Cain did not bring the sacrifice which God required. The second was the way of covetousness, of commercializing the prophetic gift for the sake of money, of seducing to immorality. The third was rebellion against divine authority.

The superior vividness of Jude's language shows up most markedly in verses 12 and 13. Here we find several very striking expressions used to characterize the false teachers: "hidden rocks in your love-feasts; . . . clouds without water, carried along by winds; autumn trees without fruit, twice dead, plucked up by the roots; wild waves of the sea, foaming out their own shame; wandering stars, for whom the blackness of darkness hath been reserved for ever."

The only clear example in the New Testament of a quotation from an apocryphal book occurs in verses 14-15. Here we find a rather long sentence quoted from the Jewish Book of Enoch. This book was known to Justin Martyr, Irenaeus, Clement of Alexandria, and Origen and must have been rather widely read in the Early Church. Tertullian spoke very favorably of it.

IV. Building Up in the Faith (vv. 17-23)

The best way to defend the faith is to build oneself up in the faith. This we do by praying in the Holy Spirit (v. 20). Jude continues: "Keep yourselves in the love of God, looking for the mercy of our Lord Jesus Christ unto eternal life" (v. 21).

V. Benediction (vv. 24-25)

One of the most beautiful benedictions in the New Testament is that found here. Jude glorifies the God who is able to guard us from stumbling and to present us faultless before the presence of His glory.

CHAPTER XV

PURITY AND PERFECT LOVE
(THE JOHANNINE EPISTLES)

THE FIRST EPISTLE OF JOHN

A. INTRODUCTION

I. The Epistle and the Gospel

The First Epistle of John is a companion book to the Gospel of John. The two are closely related in subject matter, language, and emphasis. The Gospel was written "that ye may believe that Jesus is the Christ, the Son of God; and that believing ye may have life in his name" (20:31). The purpose of the Epistle is given in such expressions as: "that ye may know that ye have eternal life" (5:13); "that ye may not sin" (2:1); "that our joy may be made full" (1:4); and "because your sins are forgiven you for his name's sake" (2:12). Thus we may say that the Gospel was written in order that people may have life, and the Epistle was written as a treatise on that life.

Christ is the center of both books. He is the source of life to the believer (John 1:4), and He is the Advocate of the believer (I John 2:1). The Gospel was written to prove that the man Jesus was the Christ, the anointed of God. The Epistle was written to show that the Christ, the anointed of God, was incarnate in the man Jesus. In both, John writes of Christ from the point of view of His having already died and having been resurrected and having returned to the Father.

The Christ he knows is not only the Babe of Bethlehem (in fact he does not mention His birth), nor just the Man of Galilee and the Christ of the Cross, but also the resurrected Lord who had returned to heaven and sent the promised Holy Spirit. John alone, of all the Gospels, presents Christ as the eternal Logos—word, reason—of God.

II. The Purpose of the Epistle

In addition to, or perhaps included in, the purpose as noted above, John wrote his Epistle to combat errors, while, at the same time, he sought to establish believers in the faith. The first century of the Christian Church was an age of excessive idol worship and saw the flowering of an intellectualism which militated against the Christian faith. This latter, known as Gnosticism, was a mixture of Oriental mysticism and Greek philosophy. One of its chief principles was a dualism between spirit and matter. God, spirit, goodness, reality were good and forever opposed to the observable world, which was evil. The world was not made by God, but by a lesser being, one of a series of emanations from God, who was in a sense the enemy of God. The result of this thinking was that spirit (good) and matter (evil) could never unite; therefore, the incarnation of Christ was an impossibility. From this arose Docetism, which claimed that the body of Christ was not real—it was only an appearance. The two main principles of Gnosticism were the superiority of knowledge and the evil quality of matter, which, in turn, led to asceticism on the one hand or to antinomianism on the other.

This was the heresy which had infiltrated, and even risen within, the Church of John's day. He sought to meet it with a true knowledge of a Saviour and a salvation which could forgive us our sins and cleanse us from all unrighteousness (1:9). He met error with truth.

III. Characteristics

There are a number of key words in this Epistle—know, love, life, light, and believe. They are pertinent both in combating error and in establishing the Christians in the truth. The name God is used repeatedly—some sixty times in all—but the reference is to God in Christ—God the Son incarnate in the flesh. The term Father is always used to distinguish between God the Father and God the Son. John understands the Godhead to be a trinity—Father, Son, and Spirit.

While it is not easy to outline this Epistle, John's purpose is clear, and his thoughts are orderly. He moves quite logically from one topic to another, but his method gives the impression of a series of concentric circles, or perhaps interlocking circles, rather than a straight line. He returns to a topic again and again, making new approaches and bringing in new material.

The author does not say to whom the Epistle is written. According to 2:19 it might be to a single church, a closely knit group of which John was a member. Whether that be so or not, his message was to the Church of his day, with which he was very familiar. He knew the people intimately and addressed them as children. He used the familiar "you" and "we" repeatedly, thus associating himself with his hearers and with his own message. But it does not follow that John shared in all of the experiences of his readers at the time of the writing. If he had, he was no better than the most sinful to whom he wrote. Rather, he used what we call the "editorial we." He identified himself with them as a member of the race of men who were lost without Christ, and to whom salvation was offered, as if to say (to paraphrase 1:9 as an example): "If anyone will confess his sins, God is faithful and just to forgive him his sins and to cleanse him from all unrighteousness." John wrote as a preacher might preach, letting the definite pronoun "we" stand for the indefinite pronoun "anyone."

This is an Epistle of love: "Love not the world" (2:15); "We know that we have passed out of death into life, because we love the brethren" (3:14); "Let us not love in word, neither with the tongue; but in deed and truth" (3:18); "Let us love one another: for love is of God" (4:7); "God is love" (4:8). The mark of the Christian is love for God and love for others. His love is grounded in the love of God, who gave Christ as the Saviour of the world, and is the evidence of true fellowship with God. This is an Epistle of fellowship, and fellowship might well be considered its key thought. John seeks to bring the believers into the same fellowship with God which he himself enjoys and thereby create a fellowship of the saints. It is more than friendship and more than companionship. It is a communion of identical spirits, bound together with cords of love and faith.

It is an Epistle of holiness. The blood of Jesus Christ will cleanse from all sin (1:7). The anointing of the Holy Spirit is the portion of the children of God (2:20). These two truths are basic. Furthermore, John exhorts his readers to lives of love and purity, warning them against worldliness and false teaching.

It is the Epistle of the victorious life. While John does allow for the possibility of Christians' inadvertantly com-

mitting sin (2:1), in the same breath he also says that one
purpose for his writing is that they may not sin, and points the
way out of sin through Christ. To John there is no twilight
zone, no middle ground, in the Christian life. There are, in
the final analysis, just two groups of people: those who have
the spirit of Christ and those who have the spirit of the antichrist; those who walk in darkness and those who walk in
the light; those who have not confessed their sins and those
who have confessed; those who have not been cleansed and
those who are cleansed. John holds out before his readers
the life of victory over all sin through the benefits of the
atoning death of Jesus Christ. He makes no allowance for
known sin in the Christian because ample provision has been
made to take care of it. The Christian has received eternal
life through Christ, and is thereby clearly distinguished. "He
that hath the Son hath the life; he that hath not the Son of
God hath not the life" (5:12).

B. Contents

I. Introduction (1:1-4)

This Epistle represents the mature thinking of the aged
John on the gospel of Christ. He had associated with Him
during His earthly ministry, had preached the gospel for long
years and thought deeply upon it. The experience of the years
had served only to confirm his faith in the Christ he served.
This Epistle represents the condensation of that life, its experiences and its meditations. It represents John's last major
effort in defense of the gospel and for the edification of the
Church.

In answer to those who disbelieved the doctrine of the
Incarnation, John says that He who was the Son of God (John
20:31) was also a real Man: he himself had seen and touched
and heard Him. The Christ of the Christian gospel was both
divine and human—both God and Man. John preaches that
it is possible to have fellowship with this God-Man.

II. God Is Light (1:5—2:29)

This beautiful metaphor is the core of the first two chapters of the Epistle. God is Light. Light stands for moral goodness and purity as against the nonmoral or immoral qualities
of evil. It is a term for the imagination perhaps more than

for the mind; it is more easily grasped than explained. It is the quality of the life which Christ manifested.

1. Walking in the Light (1: 5-10)

The Church preached the glad message that men need not walk in the darkness of sin, but can walk in the light of truth. Walking in the light will bring one into a fellowship with God and fellow Christians, into an experience of heart cleansing through the blood of Christ (v. 7). To say that God cannot cleanse the heart from all sin in this life is to deny this clear statement.

To some this was not a joyful message because they denied being in sin. But John says that the man who claims to have no sin (v. 8),[1] or to have committed no sin (v. 10), makes both himself and God liars. The fact is that Christ has revealed sin and made provision for its removal. "If we [anyone] confess our sins, he is faithful and righteous to forgive us our sins, and to cleanse us from all unrighteousness" (v. 9).

2. That Ye Sin Not (2: 1-6)

An experience of salvation from sin has moral and practical aspects. Initial forgiveness must be followed by continual obedience. An obedient heart is one's assurance that he is walking in fellowship with Christ. Continued obedience causes one's love for God to increase, to mature, to be perfected—unmixed with any competing allegiances. The exhortation not to sin is based upon the exhortation to love God supremely. To John it is wholly incompatible to love God wholeheartedly and, at the same time, sin against Him.

John also recognized the weakness of human nature and the possibility of one sinning through negligence. This, to John, is the exception, not the rule. But if this should occur, Christ is the Advocate who can and will forgive. He can do this because by His death He has atoned for the sins of all men, and through Him one may be restored. But this is not normative Christianity for John. His ideal, made gloriously possible through Christ, is that everyone shall walk in the light and increase in love.

[1] This does not apply to the sanctified Christian, whose heart has been cleansed from all sin (v. 7). It is a general truth that all men have sin until that sin is removed by the cleansing Blood.

3. *The Commandment—Old and New* (2: 7-11)

The life of a Christian is a life of obedience to Christ. That is the only way to know Him. That is what John means by walking in the light.

The commandment, or word of which John speaks, is the pre-eminent commandment of Jesus: "A new commandment I give unto you, that ye love one another; even as I have loved you, that ye also love one another. By this shall all men know that ye are my disciples, if ye have love one to another" (John 13: 34-35). "If ye keep my commandments, ye shall abide in my love; even as I have kept my Father's commandments, and abide in his love. . . . This is my commandment, that ye love one another, even as I have loved you. Greater love hath no man than this, that a man lay down his life for his friends. Ye are my friends, if ye do the things which I command you" (John 15: 10-14). The commandment is the commandment of love. It is old because God is Love, and it is new because Jesus made it real. It is old because it was enshrined in the old covenant, and it is new because it is revealed in the new covenant. It is old because it was written in the letter of the law, and it is new because it is lived in the spirit of the law. It is old because it has always been in existence, and it is new because it can never grow old. Walking in the light is walking in love.

4. *My Little Children* (2: 12-14)

John writes as an elderly man who thinks of everybody as his children. The "children," "fathers," and "young men" are perhaps best interpreted as terms of endearment representing the whole church group. To the children he says, "Because your sins are forgiven for his name's sake," and, "Because ye know the Father." These two thoughts are parallel. One comes to know the Father by having his sins forgiven. To the fathers he says, "Because ye know him who is from the beginning," repeating these words a second time. To the young men he says, "Because ye have overcome the evil one," adding the second time, "Because ye are strong, and the word of God abideth in you."

5. *Do Not Love the World* (2: 15-17)

The term "world" has several meanings as used by John. In "God so loved the world . . . " (John 3: 16) it refers to the human race, as also in "the whole world" (v. 2). In "the world was made through him" (John 1:10) it means the universe. In "the prophet that cometh into the world" (John 6:14) it means the habitable earth. In the present paragraph it is used to denote that way of life among sinful men which is alienated from God and opposed to God. That is the world the children of God are not to love, while at the same time they love all men for whom Christ died. They are not to love it, because it is sinful and will soon pass away. Moreover, the desire for it will also disappear. In contrast to this, the children of God have the promise of eternal life.

This godless world system is made up of "the lust of the flesh," the desire for sensuous enjoyments; "the lust of the eyes," the desire to see unwholesome or impure sights; and "the vainglory of life," the boastful display of that which one possesses.

6. Antichrist (2:18-29)

From the thought of worldliness John turns to that of antichrist—and to him there is a very close connection between the two. The spirit of worldliness is the spirit of antichrist.

John allows for the appearance of a personal Antichrist in the future, but his concern is with the spirit of antichrist already present. It is the spirit of opposition to Christ, denying that Jesus is the Christ and denying the Father-Son relationship. It is more than failure to believe: it is deliberate, reasoned rebellion. It is represented by the Gnostics, of whom we spoke earlier. Some church members had been deceived by this error and had left the church.

Over against this spirit by which those of the "world" had been imbued, there was an anointing by Christ for His obedient followers. By it they could know the truth through divine illumination. By it they could distinguish between false and true teachings. By it they could meet Christ confidently at His second coming. The world has the spirit of antichrist; the Christian has the Spirit of Christ.

III. God Is Love (3:1—5:17)

This is the second main emphasis of the Epistle. John has moved gradually in his discourse from revelation, "God is light," to experience, "God is love." However, the two—light and love—have never been separate in his thinking. One of the results of walking in the light is love for the brethren (2:7-11). One of the marks of the child of God is this same love (3:10-18). In this section love is seen as a gift of God. One may know much about God, knowing that God is Light, without really knowing God, for God is also Love. "He that loveth not knoweth not God; for God is love" (4:8). God revealed himself as Love by sending Christ into the world. A man comes to know God as Love only when he accepts Christ and His salvation. God's love for man becomes the inspiration and source of man's love for his fellow man. That love in the heart and life is the evidence of one's fellowship with God.

1. The Children of God and the Children of the Devil (3:1-10)

In this way John has made a sharp distinction between the Christian and the worldling. He openly states that those who have received the experience of the new birth (3:10) are the children of God, and those who have not received it are the children of the devil. God's children are strangers to "the world." The devil's children are strangers to God. No one is a child of God in this sense by his own right or by his own efforts. God's love, manifested in Christ through His incarnation and atoning death, makes it possible for every man to become a child of God if he will.

The children of God love one another. They live righteous lives. They do not sin. In fact, John goes so far as to say that they cannot sin because they have been born of God (3:9). This is a moral impossibility—not a natural one—in the same sense that it is impossible for a mother to murder her child whom she loves supremely. This impossibility is based upon the law of love which rules the heart and life. The children of God also have the prospect of seeing Christ someday, and of then being like Him. There is no promise that Christ's coming, as such, will have any transforming power over the lives of men. Rather, they will be like Him then because they have been made like Him now—transformed by the power of the new birth.

2. Love and Hate (3:11-24)

Coming again to the subject of brotherly love, John draws a strong contrast between love and hate. Christ, who died for man's sins, is the Example of love. Cain, the first murderer, is the example of hate. Love is of the substance of life—hate is of the substance of death. Love, and life, and truth, and obedience, and faith in Christ, and abiding in Christ are similar in meaning. They are not synonymous expressions, but represent the various sides of the experience of the child of God. They are in Christ, and He is in them by the indwelling of the Spirit. Hate is of the world, and the world hates the Christian. But the Christian can stand before God with perfect confidence, provided his own heart is free from condemnation. He obeys God because he loves Him; he believes in Jesus Christ and loves the brethren. God, in turn, loves him and answers his prayers.

3. *Try the Spirits* (4:1-6)

The exhortation to love is followed by the equally important exhortation to test the spirits. John has the Gnostics in mind, for he says that the test of whether one is true or not is his attitude toward the incarnation of Christ. To John, Christology is the fundamental doctrine. By this the Christian can determine who is of the world and who is of God. And he can overcome this spirit of antichrist, "because greater is he that is in you than he that is in the world" (v. 4). In the face of the easy tolerance found in the Church of our day, one must admire the boldness and clear-sightedness of John. To be uncertain is to be lost. To know the truth is to be free. John's is an "either-or" religion.

4. *Love Perfected* (4:7-21)

It is not surprising that man should love God, but the greatest demonstration of love was on God's part when He gave His Son to atone for man's sin. By responding to this love one may become a child of God, and God will dwell within him by His Spirit. Not only can the believer know God in this way, but he may also have his love for God and man perfected or made complete. The converse of love is fear—fear of punishment for wrongdoing. But "perfect love casteth out fear" (4:18). There are four classes of people in the world: those with neither fear nor love, who have willfully rejected the revelation of God in Christ; those who have fear but no love; those who have both fear and love; and those who have no fear, but are filled with perfect love. This standard of perfect love is normative for the Christian life to which John seeks to lead his readers. It is an ideal standard, to be sure; nevertheless, it is also an attainable standard. The presence of the Holy Spirit in the heart is the evidence of this experience of perfect love (4:13).

5. Victory Through Christ (5:1-12)

To believe that Jesus is the Christ is to be a child of God. Yet John adds that to be a child of God means also to love the children of God, to love God, and to keep His commandments. This faith in Christ makes the believer an overcomer of the world. Christ, then, is not only the Foundation of doctrine, but He is also the Fountain of life—the guarantee of victorious living in a world of sin.

John here digresses somewhat to proclaim the witness which had been borne to Christ. He first lists two: Christ "came by water and blood" (v. 6). The water refers to His baptism by John the Baptist, at which event the Spirit descended as a dove upon Him, and the voice from heaven said, "This is my beloved Son . . . " (Matt. 3:17). The Blood refers to Christ's sacrificial death on the cross. Both the water and the Blood are joined to proclaim positive witness that Christ is the Son of God come in the flesh. Added to these, the Holy Spirit bears witness that Jesus is the Christ. In the face of this threefold witness, which was not of man but of God, the man who refuses to believe in Christ makes God a liar.

6. The Sin unto Death (5:13-17)

John now completes his concept of sin. He has said, "If we say that we have no sin, we deceive ourselves" (1:8). "If we say that we have not sinned, we make him a liar" (1:10). All men have at one time been sinners, both in principle and in deed. Sin is very real to John. "Sin is lawlessness" (3:4)— the transgression of the law of love. The sinner stands opposed to Christ. The greatest sin is Christ-rejection. But there are forgiveness and cleansing for the sinner through faith in the blood of Christ (1:7-9). There is also restoration for the one who may fall from the love of God into a life of sin (2:1). But one of John's major emphases is that the child of God need not sin.

In this section John adds the thought that the sinner may destroy himself by his sin—"There is a sin unto death" (5:16), or there is a sinning which is unto death. There is also a sinning which is not unto death. Nevertheless "all unrighteousness is sin" (5:17).

In this, our author is warning against sin of all kinds. One may not know when a man is sinning the sin unto death. But Christians should pray for sinners. Prayers for one individual will avail, while prayers for another may fail; the determining factor lies in the attitude of the sinner. He may respond to the gospel message and be saved, but he may also resist until there is no longer any saving value to his friend's prayers. The awful truth is that a man may place himself outside the scope of the gospel.

IV. Conclusion (5:18-21)

John's spiral of discussion has been the beautiful journey of a man going up a familiar, winding path. He closes his Epistle with a reaffirmation of certainty. All the antichrists in the world cannot rob him of the things he has learned. Listen to them. He who is born of God does not commit sin. He is kept from sin by Christ, the only begotten Son of God. The Christian knows that he belongs to God, even though the world around him is under the dominion of the evil one. Jesus became incarnate, and has given His followers insight into discerning the truth concerning Him. As His children, they abide in Him. And, finally, "This is the true God, and eternal life. My little children, guard yourselves from idols." Thus closes the Epistle of the incarnate, resurrected, everliving Christ.

THE SECOND EPISTLE OF JOHN

Unlike the first Epistle, this second Epistle has the characteristics of a personal letter—greetings from the writer with a promise of a visit, followed by a concluding message from other friends.

The author is undoubtedly John, the author of the first Epistle. The "elect lady," while thought by some writers to be an individual, should more probably be interpreted as a church; the "children" would then be the members. This opinion is borne out in the Epistle, where the singular pronoun of verse 5 becomes plural in verse 8. First, the church is spoken of as a unit and then as composed of individual members.

The first emphasis of the writer is upon love for one another and obedience to the commandments (vv. 4-6). This emphasis has been covered in the treatment of the first Epistle. John does not add anything new at this point.

In verses 7 to 11 he warns against those who have gone out of the church, who do not believe in the second coming of Christ—the same group spoken of in I John 2:18-19. Thus John adds this further deceitful error to the doctrine of the antichrist. They reject both the incarnation and the second coming of Christ. Concerning these people John says that they are not of God. In other words they are not Christians, nor partakers of the love of God. The church is warned against receiving them into its fellowship or even being cordial to them. A friendly attitude is a sign of acceptance, and must not be tolerated.

If this attitude of John's seems to be one of unwarranted intolerance, one should note the seriousness of the error and the deadening effect that its acceptance would have upon the church. Christ is the foundation of the Christian faith, and if faith in Him be destroyed there is no further ground for salvation.

Refraining from saying more because he hopes to visit the church and deal with matters on a personal basis, the author closes with, "The children of thine elect sister salute thee."

THE THIRD EPISTLE OF JOHN

This short Epistle is likewise by John and is addressed to Gaius, his close friend, and a member of the church involved.

If tradition is correct, John had appointed bishops over the churches under his charge and had appointed Diotrephes over this one. But Diotrephes resented John's authority and ignored some of his letters of instruction. What was more, he talked falsely against John; and he refused to accept some traveling missionaries whom John had sent, putting them out of the church and not allowing the members to entertain them. So John wrote Gaius, a trustworthy member and perhaps a man of some influence in the church. Without accusing Diotrephes of heresy, he accuses him of obstructing the work of the Lord on the six counts listed above. Furthermore, he promises to visit the church and take up the matter personally.

These traveling missionaries, sanctioned if not sent out by John, were a profitable adjunct to the work of the local churches and were dependent upon them for support. John stresses the obligation of the church to take care of them and share in their labors. Demetrius seems to have been the one whom Diotrephes at this time had turned away, and John recommends him as a man well thought of by everyone, and as a preacher of the truth.

Again our author closes with the promise of a visit, when he can consider problems in a person-to-person manner, and with greetings to all the friends. "Peace be unto thee. The friends salute thee. Salute the friends by name."

CHAPTER XVI

TRIBULATION AND FINAL TRIUMPH
(REVELATION)

A. INTRODUCTION

I. The Place of Revelation

The Bible would be quite incomplete without the Apocalypse of John—like a story without an ending, a drama without a climax, a task not finished. The Bible is God's revelation to man recorded in many different types of literature, and covers the whole span from "the beginning" to "the end." That revelation introduces us to the creation of the heavens and the earth and the corruption of human society and concludes with John's vision of a new heaven and a new earth wherein dwelleth righteousness. It starts with the formation of the sun, moon, and stars, and ends in a place where there will be no need of the sun. It begins with the man who first fell into sin and ends with the Man who redeemed the race from sin. It opens with the promise of redemption and closes with redemption completed. It commences with Satan loose in the Garden of Eden and culminates with him bound in the bottomless pit. It first reveals God as sovereign Creator and finally pictures Him as sovereign Ruler.

History, poetry, drama, and prophecy reveal to us God's dealings with man and man's response through the period of Israel's history. Gospels and Epistles give God's message during the first century of the Christian era. But this long period of special revelation came to an end with the death of the last of the apostles. Subsequent history has borne this out since the Church has recognized its canon of scripture as closed with the chosen list of these writings. Since this is the case, God's recorded message to man would not be complete without some message concerning the course of history for the future and its final consummation. And this the Revelation of John purports to give. It is a philosophy of history describing in symbolic form the continued struggle between good and evil so long as the world shall stand, with the guarantee that, though evil shall continue to increase, God and His people will triumph in the end.

This does not mean that the rest of Scripture has no message beyond its own day—far from it. Truth is eternal. Neither does it mean that the Old Testament prophets did not look far into the future. But the prophets differ from the apocalyptist in that they seek to reform the wayward, promising doom and punishment and destruction to the disobedient with the hope that they will repent. The prophets were all evangelists. The Apocalypse is not evangelistic. It describes the destruction of the wicked and God's triumph over them.

There is perhaps no book of the entire Bible that has been avoided as much as this one. Many have been ready to say that it is a concealment rather than a revelation. Still, it is a revelation, one which can be understood even though some of its imagery and symbolism are hard to fit into a consistent pattern. The Apocalypse has its own peculiar difficulties; while we do not propose to solve all of its problems, we do hope to put it in its proper setting and find that it does reveal God's truth.

This is a Christian Apocalypse, and carries throughout its length a distinctly Christian character, which is lacking in the Jewish apocalypses. Nevertheless it does arise out of the Jewish apocalyptic type of literature to which it is indebted for much of its symbolism; the Books of Daniel and Zechariah, for example, as well as Ezekiel. In times of great national crisis Israel always had a revival of Messianic hope; and when the nation was beneath the heel of a foreign power, the apocalyptic literature served as encouragement and promise of complete triumph over its enemies. Ezekiel was one of the first of such writers. Writing during the siege and final downfall of the Southern Kingdom, a contemporary of Jeremiah, he preached the overthrow and restoration of Jerusalem. But his manner of receiving messages through visions (c. 1) and his description of the battle of Gog and Magog (c. 38) class him with the apocalyptists.

The apocalypse, which means a revelation, is a distinct type of literature; yet the imagery and symbols constitute more than just a literary form. They stand for objective reality behind the imagery. Ezekiel saw the four-faced creature with the wings and the concentric wheels having eyes, but therein he saw the majesty and omnipresence and omniscience of God. In similar manner, John describes things and events which were revealed to him.

II. Authorship and Date

This book declares itself to be a revelation given to John, a servant of God. Much primitive testimony from as early as the second century can be found to support the claim that this was John the Apostle. While there are difficulties connected with the traditional view, it is equally difficult to identify a John who fits the case better than the apostle.

The weight of evidence places the writing of the Revelation at about A.D. 95, during the persecution under the Roman Emperor Domitian. The author was an exile on the Island of Patmos, off the coast of Asia Minor not far from Ephesus, the apparent victim of an organized persecution of Christians.

III. Summary of Contents

The outline of this book is brief and simple. It has a prologue (1:1-3); the letters to seven churches in Asia (1:4—3:22); the body of the book containing the apocalypse proper (4:1—22:5); and an epilogue (22:6-21). The letters to the seven churches do not constitute a part of the main apocalypse, although they are related to it. They are what John saw in a book and wrote in response to "a great voice, as of a trumpet" (1:10). The apocalypse proper is the record of what he saw and heard as he beheld a door open in heaven, to which he was taken in the Spirit. It consists of a number of distinct visions: the vision of heaven as the setting for the subsequent visions (cc. 4—5); the opening of the seven seals (6:1—8:5); the seven trumpets (8:6—11:19); the sevenfold vision of the last days (cc. 12—14); the seven last plagues (cc. 15—16); the fall of Babylon the Great (cc. 17—19); the millennium (20:1-10); the end of the world and the judgment (20:11-15); the holy city (c. 21); and a vision of everlasting life (22:1-5).

IV. Purpose

The first thing necessary to a meaningful interpretation of this great book is to find the purpose for its writing and the end which the author sought to achieve. Much of the imagery is difficult to explain, and some of it will always remain a mystery. But explaining the symbols and finding the message they convey are entirely different. The latter is without doubt of primary importance.

In general, the Apocalypse describes the age-old struggle between right and wrong. God, Christ, the Spirit, Satan, angels, men, and nations are all involved. They are arrayed on the two sides of the conflict. The many symbols stand for these combatants and for the various phases of this battle to the death. It is Christ and His followers arrayed against Satan and his followers. The battle is waged both on earth and in the heavens. Christ becomes the Conqueror because of His atoning death and subsequent resurrection. He is the Lamb slain from the foundation of the world, the Alpha and the Omega, having the keys of death and Hades, and the Rider on the white horse, crowned with many crowns.

V. Method of Interpretation

The history of the interpretation of the Apocalypse through the centuries reveals a large number of methods which may be classified as the *preterist*, the *historical*, the *futurist*, and the *spiritual*. There are variations of these theories, and none is entirely exclusive of the others. Briefly stated, the preterist method holds that the book refers almost exclusively to the past. It was written to meet the circumstances of that day, and the age of the author saw the fulfillment of his visions. The historical method holds that it covers the history of the world during the entire Church age. Thus the various visions are identified with the outstanding events in history. The futurist method says that the book—after chapter three— depicts events which will come to pass at or following the time of Christ's second coming. The spiritual method denies any literal interpretation of this book. Each vision and symbol is to be interpreted allegorically to teach whatever spiritual lesson one may find.

Each method has its merit and produces truth that leads to a better understanding of this great book. To limit oneself to one of these theories of interpretation is to limit the message that John doubtless meant to convey. But there are a few basic principles inherent in the book itself which are necessary to a sound interpretation. They may be briefly stated as follows: (1) the Apocalypse claims to be a special revelation to John from God; (2) it has its background in a period of great tribulation for the Church; (3) in essence it reveals the final triumph of righteousness over unrighteousness; (4) it is best interpreted when considered as a unit; (5) as with the messages of the Old Testament prophets, local conditions are met with principles of response and action which have their application in every similar age of history; (6) the book claims to deal with conditions reaching down to the end of time and the culmination of human history on this earth; (7) it speaks of things and personalities and events in terms of symbols which cannot always be taken literally; (8) it speaks of beings and conditions in the spirit world which must always defy one's complete understanding of them; (9) because of this fact and the references to events yet future, much of the book must remain a mystery as long as we are on this earth.

B. CONTENTS

I. The Prologue (1:1-3)

"The revelation of Jesus Christ." John is saying that his is a revelation given by Jesus. Thus Jesus becomes central in both the process and the substance of this revelation to John. The Revelation was given by God to Jesus Christ, which He in turn showed to John by an angel messenger. Christ is thus the Mediator of this revelation and at the same time the prime Participant upon the stage of action. No wonder, then, that blessings are pronounced upon all who hear and obey. To these things which were shown him, John bears witness.

II. Letters to the Seven Churches (1:4—3:22)

The introduction (1:4-20) to these letters is of two parts. First, John pronounces upon the churches a blessing from the eternal God, from the complete retinue of His attending servants, and from Jesus Christ. Christ overshadows the other divine beings in John's vision by the multiplicity of descriptive names by which He is known. Christ is "the faithful witness, the firstborn of the dead, and the ruler of the kings of the earth" (v. 5). John describes Christ's work of redemption: He "loveth us, and loosed us from our sins by his blood; and he made us to be a kingdom, to be priests unto his God and Father; to him be the glory and the dominion for ever and ever" (vv. 5-6). He will one day come in the clouds. He is the Alpha and Omega, the Almighty (vv. 7-8).

Secondly, John describes how his vision came to him. Having suffered as other Christians for the cause of Christ, he had been exiled to the Island of Patmos. On "the Lord's day" he found himself in the Spirit, an experience perhaps similar to that of Ezekiel in Babylon. Hearing a great voice, he turned and saw seven gold lampstands, in the midst of which was the form of One whose figure and clothing were of the highest brightness, in whose hand were seven stars, and in whose mouth was a two-edged sword. Called by John "a son of man," this was a symbolic representation of Christ in His purity and commanding authority and judgment—Christ in the midst of His Church. As John fell prostrate before Him, he was told that the lampstands were the seven churches and the stars were the pastors of the churches. He was again commanded to write what he saw.

The seven churches were all actual churches, possibly some of those to which John had ministered. It is thought that he had lived for some time in Ephesus, perhaps superintending the work in Asia Minor. The characteristics of each of these churches are most aptly described in the seven letters. Since there were many more churches than these seven, these were chosen because seven is considered to be a perfect number, and thus they represent all the churches of John's day.

These letters have shared in the great variety of interpretations given the entire book. We must recognize that they had their primary application to the churches to which they were written. Then there may be some truth to the interpretation which makes each church represent a certain period of church history. Those who do so, describe our own day as the Laodicean age. But these letters find their richest application of truth when they are regarded as God's message to the Church of every age, given as an admonition to the Church universal, before He proceeded to reveal the great struggle with the forces of evil through which the Church must go. The conditions found in the seven churches are such as may be found in the Church of almost any age. And the criticisms leveled against them, together with the warnings and exhortations, are sufficient to cover the emergencies arising in the Church which is still militant and not yet triumphant.

Each letter is prefaced with a description of Him who sends the message, a description admirably significant to the church addressed. Each is also concluded with a warning or exhortation equally appropriate.

1. To the Church at Ephesus (2:1-7)

Ephesus was situated in Asia Minor at the mouth of the river Cayster. It was located at one of few outlets to the sea through the surrounding hills, and consequently became a great trading center. It was on the main route from Rome to the East. About a mile northeast of the Greek city was the temple sacred to Artemis (Acts 19:35). Paul spent about three years at Ephesus on his third missionary journey, and before he left suffered a great deal of opposition (Acts 19; I Cor. 15:32; 16:8). He had visited the city briefly at the close of his second missionary journey (Acts 18:19-21). On his second visit he witnessed the Ephesian Pentecost (Acts 19:2-7).

John had much good to say of this church. He commended the members for their faithful toil and endurance in the midst of hardship, for their ability to spy out false teachers, and for their opposition to the Nicolaitans. Whether a distinct sect or not, this last reference seems to be to certain persons of an antinomian tendency, who stressed the liberties of the gospel above its requirements. Yet for all their faithfulness, there was one serious difficulty with these Ephesians: they had left their first love. They had been so diligently working for the cause of Christ and fighting so strenuously against the inroads of error that they had lost the love which at first had motivated them. They had been drawn away from the true spirit of Christ. The exhortation to them was to return to their initial experience of grace where love was primary; if not, God would remove their lampstand (church) from its place—either from its place of leadership and influence or from being a church altogether. This message comes from Him who is among the lampstands and who holds the seven stars (v. 1)—He who has the authority to do as He has said.

2. To the Church at Smyrna (2:8-11)

The city of Smyrna is located on the Aegean Sea just north of Ephesus. It was a maritime city and boasted two ports on the gulf.

The letter to this church comes from Him "who was dead and lived again." The tone of the letter is the kindest of all seven. Recognition is made of the members' tribulation, their poverty, the slanderous abuse which they suffer, the expectation of further tribulation, and the evident fact that there will be no relief. But just as Christ found His greatest triumph in death and resurrection, they too would receive a crown of life—eternal life—as a reward of faithfulness.

3. To the Church at Pergamum (2:12-17)

The city of Pergamum was located due north of Smyrna, about fifteen miles from the coast of the Aegean Sea. It stood on a huge rocky hill which dominated the broad plain below. It was the capital of the Roman province of Asia from 133 B.C. until after these seven letters were written, and it was one of the provincial centers of the Imperial cult of emperor worship. It thus exercised a goodly degree of authority, both officially and religiously. There is no other reference to this city in the New Testament beside this one.

The message to Pergamum comes from Him "that hath the sharp, two-edged sword." The message is one of authority and judgment. The church in the city has remained faithful to the name of Christ even in the face of the martyrdom of one of its leaders. This is praiseworthy because here also was "Satan's throne." Satan is doubtless used symbolically for the entrenched imperial power of Rome, which was by that time officially arrayed against the Christians. However, in spite of their faithfulness, the Lord still had a few things against them. There were those in the church who held to the teachings of Balaam and of the Nicolaitans. This is the same error as found at Ephesus. This minority was using its liberty as Christians to maintain its social standing with the heathen, counting heathen practices as insignificant. The result was eating meats offered to idols and practicing outright immorality. It was a compromise with evil. The charge against them was a serious one. They must repent. If not, Christ himself, He who stood in higher authority even than Rome, would come and make war upon them to their destruction. But the fruits of obedience are also great (v. 17). In contrast to the sinful practice of eating meats offered to idols, the obedient will be given to eat of hidden manna—the assurance that God will supply all their needs. The white stone speaks of endurance and purity, and the new name is the "name which is above every name," Christ's own new name (Rev. 3:12)—

the passport to the blessings of the new heaven and new earth (21:1).

4. To the Church at Thyatira (2:18-29)

Thyatira is located east of Pergamum in a valley through which runs the highway from Constantinople to Smyrna. It was founded about 300 B.C. as a garrison city, although the valley was probably inhabited long before that. It was closely associated with Pergamum. In Roman times it was a trading center.

The letter to this church resembles that to the church at Pergamum. The message comes from "the Son of God, who hath his eyes like a flame of fire, and his feet like unto burnished brass." The church is commended for its works, love, faith, and patience. While Jezebel is here used to symbolize the sin which the church tolerated among some of its members, the evil is much the same as that found at Pergamum: immorality and the use of meat offered to idols. The rewards for this evil are symbolized by descriptions that might well depict the ravages of war when a city is sacked by the enemy, even as Thyatira had suffered in her many wars. But to the faithful in the church are promised all the victories of the conqueror. And the promise is the more significant because the city was very unpretentious in its location and fortifications, being mostly a buffer city before advancing armies. The victories of God's faithful will be just as noteworthy—far beyond what would normally be expected of them. This letter foreshadows the great victory of the Church of Christ so evident throughout the Apocalypse.

5. To the Church in Sardis (3:1-6)

The city of Sardis was located between Smyrna and Thyatira. It was founded about 1200 B.C. on a plateau 1,500 feet above the valley of the Hermus River. It was inaccessible except from the south. It made a natural stronghold and was one of the greatest cities of ancient times. During the days of the Roman Empire the city had spread to lower levels on the north and west, and the old city on the high plateau was virtually uninhabited. The city was living on its past glory.

The letter to the church at Sardis has some elements in common with that to the Ephesian church. It is introduced with the words of Him who has "the seven Spirits of God, and the seven stars."

This church is in worse condition than any of the others. It is dead—yet with some remaining signs of life because of a few faithful members. Its glory is all in the past. If it will, it can repent and be restored. If not, Christ will come like a thief in the night and destroy it. But a promise still remains for the faithful few—they shall be clothed in garments of white and walk in purity of life, and their names will remain in the book of life. Christ will also acknowledge them as His own before the Father and angels.

6. To the Church at Philadelphia (3:7-13)

The city of Philadelphia was located twenty-eight miles east of Sardis in the valley of the Cogamis River, a tributary of the Hermus.

The letter to this church is similar to that to Smyrna. Among other things, both churches are praised more than condemned. Blessings are promised for the entire church, not just for a segment of faithful members, as at Thyatira and Sardis. And in both churches the Jews are a hindrance and are called a "synagogue of Satan."

In this letter Christ is called "he that is holy, he that is true, he that hath the key of David, he that openeth and none shall shut, and that shutteth and none openeth." This is in keeping with this church, which had been faithful to its opportunities. An open door for the spread of the gospel had been placed before it, and, though small and weak, it had been faithful in the midst of severe trials. As a reward it is promised the humiliation of the "synagogue of Satan" and protection for itself in the midst of trials; and the promise of Christ's return is given. Its final reward is sure if it continues steadfast in the faith. Added to this is the promise of permanent dwelling in the temple of God, and of a new name, which is imperishable because it is the name of the new city Jerusalem and of Christ and the Father.

7. To the Church at Laodicea (3:14-22)

The city of Laodicea was situated about fifty miles east of Ephesus in the valley of the Lycus River. Its history goes back to the third century B.C. It was a manufacturing and trading center and the seat of a medical school. The city was a center of the Imperial religion of Rome and had a large Jewish population.

In the letter to this church Christ is described as "the Amen, the faithful and true witness, the beginning of the creation of God." The condemnation leveled at this church is more severe than that against any of the others. He has no good thing to say except to imply that it is not as bad as it might be. Its spiritual state is one of compromise—neither hot nor cold. The life of its members is marked by secularity —they are satisfied with worldly riches and are ignorant of their spiritual poverty. But Christ still loves them and chastens them for their benefit. The strongest evangelistic note of all the letters is struck here: "Behold, I stand at the door and knock . . . " And the promise is equally strong: "He that overcometh, I will give to him to sit down with me in my throne, as I also overcame, and sat down with my Father in his throne."

The foregoing discussion has endeavored to show that the subject matter of the letters was appropriate to the churches to which they were written. Doubtless they were also written to fortify the Church of Christ against the woes and tribulations described in the remainder of the Apocalypse, which are sure to come as the battle is waged continually between right and wrong. When all is done and the books are opened for judgment, the Church may be triumphant through "him that loved us, and loosed us from our sins by his blood" (1:5). "He that hath an ear, let him hear what the Spirit saith to the churches" (3:22).

III. The Apocalypse Proper (4:1—22:5)

1. The Vision in Heaven (cc. 4—5)

There is a break at the close of chapter three. The second phase of the revelation to John begins with chapter four. He is transported in his vision through an open door in heaven into the presence of God, who is seated on a throne. John attempts a description of what he saw, and one cannot but note the singular likeness to Ezekiel's description of what he saw by the river Chebar in Babylon (Ezekiel 1). Ezekiel is much more elaborate in his writing than John, who is inclined here as elsewhere to conservatism. Both describe the throne with

One seated on it, the creatures with wings—each having the face of a lion, an ox, an eagle, and a man—the many eyes looking in all directions, and the scroll. In addition to this John sees twenty-four elders and seven spirits of God, while the elders and the four creatures sing and give glory and honor to God upon His throne.

There follows a full-dress drama among this group. In the right hand of God is a book covered with writing, sealed with seven seals. A great angel calls for someone to open the book, but no one in all the expanses of the universe is found worthy to do it. While John weeps for sorrow, One appears in the group whom an elder introduces as the Lamb, the Lion of the tribe of Judah, the Root of David. He will open the book because He has conquered and is therefore worthy. He is called the Lamb twenty-eight times in Revelation. He has conquered by the atonement on Calvary and by virtue of that sacrifice becomes the center of the activities. This is not now the Christ depicted in Hebrews, sitting at the right hand of God in intercession, but the Christ of conquest, standing ready for battle in behalf of God and His Church.

As He takes the book, which in some way holds the answers to the prayers of the saints (5:8), there follows a time of rejoicing by those assembled. They are joined by thousands of thousands of angels who take up the refrain: "Worthy is the Lamb that hath been slain to receive the power, and riches, and wisdom, and might, and honor, and glory, and blessing" (5:12). And then all living creatures in the universe join in the chorus: "Unto him that sitteth on the throne, and unto the Lamb, be the blessing, and the honor, and the glory, and the dominion, for ever and ever" (5:13). What a transport of ecstasy for John! What a picture of the Christ for Christians of every age! The Lamb who was the Victim has triumphed and won the right to become the Lamb who leads the forces of righteousness to victory. It is from this vantage point that John sees his subsequent visions. While they are not to be taken chronologically as signifying certain specific events in world history, they do follow a developing pattern as the conflict between the Lamb and His followers progresses against the entrenched forces of evil. From this point of view, too, we should view our part in the struggle and our resources as God's children today.

2. *The Seven Seals* (6:1—8:5)

There follows the opening of the seals by the Lamb, one by one. By their opening there will be revealed in the book the answers to the prayers of the saints. Six of the seals are broken in quick succession. The first reveals a rider on a white horse going forth to conquer. This signifies victory. The second reveals a rider on a red horse who takes peace from the earth. This signifies war. The third reveals a rider on a black horse with a balance in his hand. This stands for famine. The fourth reveals death riding on a pale horse, followed by Hades, and they are given power to kill with war, famine, pestilence, and wild beasts. This stands for judgment upon sin. The fifth reveals the souls of murdered saints beneath the altar of God, who are given white robes and told to wait awhile until vengeance should be meted out upon their slayers. This stands for martyrdom. The sixth reveals a great convulsion of the earth and heavens, and the men of earth, great and small, hiding from the wrath of God and the Lamb.

An interlude in the breaking of the seals occurs in chapter seven, in which four angels hold back the destructive forces of nature while a fifth angel puts the seal of God upon the foreheads of His saints. This is reminiscent of the miter which Aaron, the high priest, wore upon his forehead, on which was inscribed, "Holiness unto the Lord" (Exod. 28:36). The numbers, totaling 12,000 from each of the twelve tribes of Israel, have no special significance because the twelve tribes as such have no place in the gospel dispensation. This is a Jewish manner of expressing the inclusion of the Jews in God's plan of redemption. In addition to the 144,000[1] there was a countless multitude from all peoples of the earth, clothed in white, waving palms, and praising God and the Lamb. The only difference between the two groups is that the first is described in its consecrated state after the fashion that would be meaningful to the Jews, the second in terms understandable by people in general. The significance of this interlude would seem to be that "the Lord knoweth them that are his" (II Tim. 2:19). As a shepherd knows his sheep, as a parent knows his children, so God knows those who are praying to Him out of the struggle to the death with the powers of evil.

[1] In Jewish use of numbers 144,000 would suggest completeness.

At the beginning of chapter eight the seventh seal is opened. A period of silence follows, and then there appear eight angels before God, seven with trumpets and another who mixes incense with the prayers of the saints and pours the mixture on the altar. The smoke of this offering rises before God. Then the angel pours fire from the altar upon the earth, which responds with thunders and lightnings and earthquakes. This evidently means that the prayers of the saints have been heard by God, who gives evidence of His awareness of the need and of His power to help, by the forces of nature. Every peal of thunder and every flash of lightning is crying out that God hears and answers prayer.

From the book which the Lamb has now opened by the breaking of the seals, John has seen a great heavenly drama. God's people are crying for help. God answers by witnessing to them of their acceptance with Him and by portraying the struggle they must fight with evil on this earth. There will be war and martyrdom, yet victory and justice at last. Judgment rests in the hands of God, who demonstrates His wrath against the wicked and His power to save the righteous. It is significant to notice that the convulsions of nature in 6:12-17 are to the wicked evidence of the wrath of God, while those in 8:5, which are in essence the same, are to the saints evidence of the love of God.

3. The Seven Trumpets (8:6—11:19)

The scenes which appear at the blowing of the seven trumpets are inherent in and proceed from the vision of the seventh seal. It might even be said that they constitute a commentary upon the seventh seal, especially the last part of it.

The first trumpet is blown, and destruction falls upon a third part of the earth's vegetation. The second trumpet is blown, and destruction falls upon the sea and its inhabitants. The third trumpet is blown, and destruction is loosed upon the inland watercourses of the earth. An indication of the meaning of these destructive forces may be gained from the name of the star, Wormwood (v. 11), which means great calamity and sorrow. The fourth trumpet is blown, and the heavenly bodies—sun, moon, and stars—are darkened.

The woes and destruction are getting worse, and an angel comes forth to warn of the increasing fury ahead. The fifth trumpet is blown, and there follows a scene of woe, the description of which exceeds any other such scene in the whole Revelation. The torments this time come from beneath, from the bottomless pit. Described as scorpions and locusts like horses, the forces of evil are turned against the wicked on the earth. Evil is in conflict with itself. The king of the nether regions, Destroyer by name, leads his forces against the wicked in this world. Sin brings its own judgment. The evil world system is tormented and tortured by the very evil which rules it.

The sixth trumpet is blown, and four angels are released to destroy—probably the same four angels mentioned in 7:13, who were then holding back the powers of destruction until the people of God would be sealed. Now they are loosed to kill. But they are soon lost sight of in the multitude of horses —two hundred million strong—which destroy with fire, smoke, and sulphur issuing from their mouths. Their tails also bite like serpents. This scene is an extension of that under the fifth trumpet and is a powerful description of the destructive forces of wind (see 7:1): hurricanes, tornadoes, and the like.

John remarks that those who were left did not repent, but continued in their idol worship and immorality. Not that he expected repentance. He sees only the wickedness of evil men who are doomed to everlasting punishment.

Corresponding to chapter seven, chapters ten and eleven constitute an interlude between the blowing of the sixth and seventh trumpets. They constitute two visions of a consoling nature, no doubt appreciated by John after all he had just seen.

Another great angel appears with a small book in his hand. At the sound of his voice seven thunders speak. John is not allowed to write what the thunders say, nor what is in the little book. He is made to eat the book, which becomes bitter in his stomach. Apparently certain things are withheld from John for the time being. But he will be shown the great purpose toward which God has been working when the seventh trumpet is blown.

The scene changes in chapter eleven. John is told to measure the temple, but not the outside court. In other words, the Church is to be preserved. It has been suffering, but God will still allow his two witnesses to testify. They are described as olive trees and lampstands—the one the oil givers, the other the light givers (Zech. 4:2-3). Their further description (v. 6) seems to refer to Elijah and Moses, and if so the two witnesses are the prophets and the law (Matt. 17:1-8). They will be killed in Jerusalem (the seat of the Temple and thus the Church), but will rise again, and they will ascend to heaven. The encouragement to John here is the permanency of the law and the prophets in the face of all the destruction he has been witnessing. The two witnesses may also represent the permanent testimony of the Church.

Then the seventh trumpet sounds, and God's great plan of the ages is seen to be consummated. "The kingdom of the world is become the kingdom of our Lord, and of his Christ: and he shall reign for ever and ever" (11:15).

4. Another Sevenfold Vision (cc. 12—14)

The end of the visions, however, has not come, for John is next confronted with another vision of sevenfold character. Earth is embroiled in the conflict, but none of the participants are of earth. Therefore we judge that this sevenfold vision has to do primarily with struggles in the spirit realm. These are struggles fought on behalf of man and his salvation.

In the first vision (c. 12) the dragon, Satan, the perfection of the powers of evil, sets himself to destroy the newborn man child, who is saved by being caught up to the throne of God. Then Satan makes war in heaven against the angel Michael, but is defeated and cast out. Doubtless this has reference to the coming of Christ as Saviour of the world and Satan's many attempts to thwart His purposes, because a voice is heard to say: "Now is come the salvation, and the power, and the kingdom of our God, and the authority of his Christ" (v. 10). Satan is defeated in heaven, and his final overthrow assured. "Rejoice then, O heaven and you that dwell therein! But woe to you, O earth and sea, for the devil has come down to you in great wrath, because he knows that his time is short" (v. 12, R.S.V.).

Then Satan pursues the mother of the male child, perhaps God's chosen people, Israel; but, being frustrated in his efforts, he turns to the rest of her offspring, doubtless meaning the Church, those "that keep the commandments of God, and hold the testimony of Jesus" (v. 17).

The twofold vision of the beasts in chapter thirteen is reminiscent of Daniel's vision, chapter seven. There the various beasts are said to represent various kings or rulers, and the same may be said for the two beasts here. No attempt is made here to list a succession of kings. The beasts are placed after the defeat of Satan as described above, and they are followed in the visions by mention of the judgment and the angel reapers; thus we may well suppose that this vision has reference to conditions existing toward the close of the dispensation. They are described as exercising absolute authority over the lives of men and fulfilling all the requirements of the man of sin of whom Paul writes in II Thess. 2:3 ff. (The second beast is elsewhere called the false prophet—16:13; 19:20; 20:10). It is commonly held that the first beast represents civil authority and the second beast religious authority.

There is a series of visions in chapter fourteen, which are in direct contrast to those in the previous chapter. Christ, the Lamb, stands on Mount Zion with a great host of His ransomed saints. There swell the strains of great music—a song that only the redeemed know how to sing. An angel appears with the gospel for every people and nation of earth. At the time when the earth is being ruled by godless dictators, the gospel is spread abroad throughout the whole earth. Another angel announces the fall of Babylon the great, the seat of apostasy (17:1—19:21). Still another angel announces that he who follows the beast shall drink the cup of the wrath of God. It is a time to test the endurance of the saints.

Next John sees a vision of two reapers: one for the righteous, the other for the evil. The evil ones are put into the wine press of God's wrath. So great is this wrath, and so many are the wicked, that John describes the scene as blood flowing for two hundred miles, deep enough to reach a horse's bridle. This is judgment upon the wicked. "The wages of sin is death" (Rom. 6:23). "The soul that sinneth, it shall die" (Ezek. 18:20).

5. The Seven Plagues (cc. 15—16)

Here, as in 11:19 and 14:20 and perhaps 8:5, John has reached the culmination of the triumph of God over the wicked. The purpose of continued emphasis upon this theme must be that John is observing it in greater detail and writing it down as it comes to him. It is even as a man catches the view of a landscape; the details follow upon the first panoramic view. John also himself begins to understand what these visions mean, because he now calls them signs (12:1; 15:1).

These seven plagues follow the reign of the beast on the earth, and those who had been victorious over him are seen standing with harps in their hands, singing the song of Moses and the Lamb. As Moses had delivered the children of Israel from the bondage of Pharaoh, so now the Lamb has delivered these saints out of the bondage of the beast. Seven angels appear out of the temple in heaven and pour out upon the earth seven bowls of the wrath of God, resulting in a plague upon man and upon nature. In some instances these plagues are similar to those brought on the Egyptians by Moses. Notice that there are no righteous people left on the earth.

The first bowl of wrath brings sores upon men. The second turns the waters of the sea into blood, and all living creatures therein die. The third turns the rivers and fountains of drinking water into blood. The fourth affects the sun until it burns men with its heat. The fifth has the opposite effect to the fourth—there is no light, and men suffer without the benefits of the sun. The sixth dries up the waters of the river Euphrates, preparing the way for the kings of the earth to be drawn by evil spirits to prepare for a great battle at Armageddon. The seventh again announces the end. Great convulsions in nature result, followed by a deluge of hailstones. Men curse God because of them, and the great city Babylon (see next section) is challenged to vent her wrath against God.

6. The Fall of Babylon (cc. 17—19)

In the great struggle up to this point, the powers of evil have been led by the dragon (Satan) and have become centralized on earth in the great beast (13:1) and the false prophet (13:11 ff.). In this present vision, which is associated with the seventh plague above, John is shown the power of evil on earth, centralized in the great city Babylon, described as a harlot. It is not necessary to determine what city this is; however, in the day when John wrote, the organized power of evil which fought against the Church was Rome, and Rome has been in existence ever since. In Daniel's interpretation of Nebuchadnezzar's dream (Daniel 2) the fourth part of the image, the legs of iron, represents the Roman Empire. The final portion, the feet and toes of iron and clay, represents in part an extension of the Roman Empire. It might be well to observe that not only is Rome still a city, but Rome has given of herself to the world in two great respects: secularly, the jurisprudence of the free world today stems largely from ancient Roman law; and religiously, the Roman Catholic church is one of the most potent ingredients in the life of the world of our day. In our present passage, the seven heads of the beast on which the harlot rides are seven hills, and Rome, the city of the seven hills, is the beast. While not endeavoring to state just how Rome becomes the Babylon of the Apocalypse, we feel that this treatment of the subject does justice to the material in hand and to Daniel's own method of interpretation (2:36 ff.).

In chapter fourteen the Lamb did not do battle with the beast and the false prophet, because their leader, the dragon, had already been defeated in the spiritual realm. But now organized evil on the earth—Babylon and her followers—makes war on the Lamb during one brief period when unbridled power is given to them by God. At that time the Lamb is victorious. The kings who follow the harlot turn against her and destroy her. God uses them to accomplish His purpose (17:15-17).

There follows rejoicing in heaven and consternation on earth (c. 18). Kings and merchants who depended upon the great city for their power and wealth mourn her passing. But the scene shifts again very quickly to heaven, and an angel throws a great stone into the sea as a symbol of Babylon's fall.

In chapter nineteen all heaven breaks loose in great anthems of praise: "Hallelujah, Salvation, and glory, and power, belong to our God" (19:1); "Hallelujah: for the Lord our God, the Almighty reigneth" (19:6). The marriage supper of the Lamb is in preparation, because the Lamb's bride has been made ready, perhaps referred to previously in 14:1-5. John seems to observe this scene from a distance, and then he sees heaven open and One, who is called Faithful and True and the Word of God, comes forth riding on a white horse. He is followed by the armies of heaven, clothed in white and on white horses. He wears many crowns and is bespattered with blood. This is the Lamb, the Lion of the tribe of Judah, the Root of

David, who is now King of Kings and Lord of Lords. He comes forth on the white horse of His purity to receive the acclaim due Him, for He has conquered the dragon and the beasts and the harlot and has destroyed His enemies. Thus is pictured the great host of the faithful, represented as a vast army with Christ at the head; an army, because the Christian life has been a warfare; victorious, because Christ has led them; clothed in white, because they have "washed their robes, and made them white in the blood of the Lamb" (7:14); riding white horses, because they are victors in a holy warfare.

The birds are called together by an angel to eat the flesh of kings and of mighty men, the beast and the false prophet have been cast into the lake of fire, and their followers slain with the sword which issued from the mouth of the Lamb on the white horse.

The answer to the prayers of the saints has been revealed from the book which the Lamb opened (5:5). And there remains only the final disposition of both the victors and the vanquished.

7. The Millennium (20:1-10)

As John's vision continues, the dragon, Satan, is cast into a bottomless pit by an unnamed angel, where he remains a thousand years. He is made to suffer the horrors of the pit from which such great torments had come upon the wicked of earth at the blowing of the fifth trumpet (c. 9). During this time Christ reigns with His saints. While the account says that He reigns with those who had been beheaded for His sake, who had also been resurrected, it may well be supposed that all the righteous are to be included. In the same manner of inference, it may be that the reference to the rest of the dead, who are not resurrected until the close of the thousand years, is to the unrighteous dead.

At the end of this time Satan is loosed and goes out to deceive the nations, Gog and Magog, who are located in the far reaches of the earth. As the result of this deception they march against God's saints on earth and surround them and "the beloved city," but they are quickly destroyed by fire coming down from heaven. Satan is cast into the lake of fire with the beast and the false prophet to be tormented together forever.

8. The White Throne Judgment (20:11-15)

There follows the judgment of the dead. The judge who sits on his white throne is not identified, but is presumably the Lamb. He judges those who stand before Him on the basis of what they had done as found written in the book. These dead being judged apparently include all those who have died, both righteous and unrighteous. Those whose names are not found in the book of life are thrown into the lake of fire with the beast and the false prophet and the devil. This to them is the second death.

Summary Statement

It is appropriate here to pause long enough to review in general the writer's method of interpreting the Apocalypse and to throw some light on the millennium and the white throne judgment. John wrote what he had seen in a vision or a series of visions. His representations of beings and events were symbolic. In chapter one the seven lampstands are said to represent churches; and the seven stars, the angels (messengers or pastors) of those churches. Christ appears in many forms and bears various names. He is called the Lamb, the Lion of the tribe of Judah, the Root of David, the King of Kings and Lord of Lords. He is said to have a sword coming out of His mouth, ruling the nations in great anger with a rod of iron. This is a picture of Christ in His role as Leader of His conquering Church. The seals, the trumpets, the four living creatures, the different colored horses, the dragon, the beast, the false prophet, the multitude, the two witnesses, the woman, the man child, the harlot, the frequent use of seven, and many other expressions, stand for certain things in this great drama of the ages. In some cases we are told what they represent, as, for instance, the dragon standing for the devil (see 17:9-12). In some cases they are identified in part, as the harlot standing for a great city with the mysterious name, Babylon. In some instances we are able to make a fair estimate, such as the two witnesses representing the law and the prophets, or perhaps the law and the gospel, and the number seven representing universality or completeness. In many other cases it is impossible to know with certainty what is meant. But the point to note is that this book is a great symbolic representation in which John observes the interplay of forces—good and evil, both temporal and spiritual, pertaining to both earth and heaven—in a panoramic display which comes to him in a wide variety of imagery.

Therefore, to take any specific event or image and literalize it in a dogmatic manner would result in the loss of the unity of the book and violate its basic principle of presenting truth. "The imagery is suggestive rather than dogmatic."[2] The prophets of Israel spoke to their day by sermon, parable, and illustration, meeting conditions with principles of action which have application to other days besides their own. In much the same way the writer of the Apocalypse, who wrote more as a prophet than as an apostle, met conditions of his day with a message given through imagery of various kinds. He, too, dealt in principles which apply to other and future occasions. To limit the symbols to certain specific events, or to become dogmatic concerning their meaning, may close the door to further light which the passing of time may throw upon the truth. We may well say that prophecy is always in the process of a more complete fulfillment.

At this point John has come, in a real sense, to a climax in his visions. The issue has been clearly drawn, the struggle has been carried to its final end, and the victory has been won. The lesson John has sought to teach is clear. He has seen in vision the final defeat of Satan and his forces and the final triumph of Christ and His people. This great truth was revealed to John through symbols, many of which are difficult, or even impossible, to understand. But the central truth is not hard to come by: "The kingdom of the world is become the kingdom of our Lord, and of his Christ; and he shall reign for ever and ever" (11:15).

9. The Rewards of Righteousness (21:1—22:5)

In John's vision nothing essential remains at this point but to describe the rewards of the righteous. The unrighteous have been cast into the lake of fire and are not spoken of again except in contrast with the righteous. They have already received their penalty.

The rewards of righteousness are summed up in the concept of the new Jerusalem, where God will dwell with His people (21:3), and where all traces of earth's sorrows will

---

[2] *Expositor's Greek Testament*, V, 301.

be erased (21:4). The pledge of fulfillment is given to John by the One seated on the throne who calls himself the Alpha and Omega (v. 6) and promises to "make all things new" (v. 5).

The new heaven and new earth of verse one are not described, but seem to find their counterpart in the new Jerusalem. When the angel takes John up into the mountain to see the Lamb's bride, it is the holy city which he sees (vv. 9-10). The city thus stands for both God's people and the place of their eternal abode with God. Or we might say it stands for both the redeemed universe and the redeemed people. It has upon it the names of the twelve tribes of Israel and of the twelve apostles, which reminds one of Paul's description of the Church "built upon the foundation of the apostles and prophets, Christ Jesus himself being the chief corner stone" (Eph. 2:20).

This city is made ready as a bride adorned for her wedding (21:2), having the glory of God upon it (21:11). Its foundations, walls, gates, and streets are of the most costly and beautiful materials (21:15-21). No temple is in this city because God and the Lamb are there, and thus there is no need of any mediation in worship (v. 22). The Lamb is the lamp, and the glory of God is its light (v. 23). All the glories of earth will be added to it, and the darkness of night will never be known in it (vv. 24-26). Only that which is pure will be allowed (v. 27). Through the center of the city flows the river of life nourishing the tree of life, which provides food and healing for the nations (22:1-2).

IV. Epilogue (22:6-21)

At this point the angel who had been showing John these things and the Alpha and Omega, who was seated on the throne, both speak to John. John records their words with some comments of his own. It is somewhat difficult to know what is said by each, but what follows confirms the truth of John's unusual experience and assures him of Christ's return to earth. Blessings and cursings are promised the readers of this book according to one's attitude toward it. Those who have washed their robes will be allowed to enter the city and have access to the tree of life.

The angel fades from the scene, and Christ himself speaks to John. He is not called by any of the symbolic names as previously, but introduces himself with the words: "I Jesus have sent mine angel to testify unto you these things for the churches. I am the root and the offspring of David, the bright, the morning star" (v. 16). And He continues with a great evangelistic appeal, a most fitting climax to this last book of the Bible. "And the Spirit and the bride say, Come. And he that heareth, let him say, Come. And he that is athirst, let him come: he that will, let him take the water of life freely" (v. 17). And John adds: "He who testifieth these things saith, Yea: I come quickly. Amen: come, Lord Jesus. The grace of the Lord Jesus be with the saints. Amen" (vv. 20-21).

APPENDIX I
CHRONOLOGICAL CHART OF NEW TESTAMENT HISTORY

(Note—Most of these dates are only tentative. For Pauline chronology see Olaf Moe, *The Apostle Paul* [Minneapolis: Augsburg Publishing House, 1950], pp. 14-19.

5 B.C.—Birth of Jesus
4 B.C.—Death of Herod the Great
4 B.C.—A.D. 6—Archelaus king of Judea
4 B.C.—A.D. 33—Philip tetrarch of Ituraea and Trachonitis
4 B.C.—A.D. 39—Herod Antipas tetrarch of Galilee and Perea
A.D. 26-36—Pontius Pilate procurator of Judea
ca. 34—Conversion of Saul
A.D. 41-44—Herod Agrippa I king of Judea and Samaria
ca. 46-48—Paul's first missionary journey
ca. 48—Council of Jerusalem (Acts 15)
ca. 49-51—Second missionary journey
ca. 52-56—Third missionary journey
52-ca. 58—Felix procurator of Judea
ca. 56-58—Paul in prison at Caesarea
ca. 58-62—Festus procurator of Judea
59-61—Paul in prison at Rome
62-67—Further travels of Paul
67 or 68—Death of Paul (and Peter?)
66-70—Jewish War
70—Destruction of Jerusalem
ca. 95—Exile of John on Patmos

APPENDIX II

THE ROMAN EMPERORS UNTIL A.D. 96

27 B.C.—A.D. 14, Augustus   Luke 2:1
Octavian, in practical control from the Battle of Actium in 31 B.C., became emperor with name Augustus in 27 B.C. Constructive measures and peace characterize his administration. In Judea, Herod the Great was king of the Jews until 4 B.C. Then Antipas, Philip, and Archelaus were in control of Palestine (under Rome). Archelaus was deposed in A.D. 6 and Judea came under the procurators. Most significant event of his reign: birth of Jesus ca. 6 B.C. (cf. Luke 2:1).

A.D. 14-37, Tiberius   Cf. Luke 3:1
Wise and skillful as a ruler, but domestic troubles and a conspiracy made him morose and suspicious. During his regime Pilate was one of the procurators. The ministry and death of the Baptist and Jesus took place during his reign, which also witnessed the first Christian Pentecost, the birth of the Church, and the conversion of Saul.

37-41, Caius Caligula
Popular because of lavish expenditures and reduced taxes, he then resorted to tyranny to replenish treasury and was assassinated. His mad attempt to have his statue erected in the Temple is perhaps reflected in Mark 13:14 and II Thess. 2:1-12.

41-54, Claudius   Acts 11:28; 18:2
A man of mediocre ability, he was generally tolerant of religions and humane in attitude toward slaves. Because of a Jewish riot "at the instigation of one Chrestus" (Suetonius' *Life of Claudius*, XXV) the Jews were expelled from Rome (Acts 18:2). Paul's first missionary travels and the first of our New Testament literature during his reign.

54-68, Nero   Acts 25:10-12; 27:24
Adopted son of Claudius. At first ruled wisely under guidance of Stoic philosopher Seneca. However, plots and intrigue led him to banish Seneca and later order him to kill himself. Then Nero killed his wife and had her mother assassinated. Extravagance and ineptness at administration led Nero to use violent means to replenish the treasury. Hence, when a fire broke out the rumor that Nero had set it was

given a wide audience. In order to escape blame Nero accused the Christians. At this time many Christians were tortured to death. Among his victims were Peter and Paul. The Jewish Revolt began in 66.

68-69, Galba, Otho, Vitellius

The reign of each of these rulers was too brief to have any significance.

69-79, Vespasian

During his reign Jerusalem was destroyed by his son, Titus, who was later associated with Vespasian as coregent.

79-81, Titus

A popular and benevolent ruler.

81-96, Domitian

Brother of Titus. Demanded divine honors. In the province of Asia, at least, Christians experienced severe persecution. The Book of Revelation reflects this situation. The Johannine literature is usually placed in his reign.

BIBLIOGRAPHY

This very brief bibliography is presented as an aid to further study. It is not an exhaustive list for advanced students.

A word should be said about the commentaries listed. In almost all cases the best commentaries on the several books of the New Testament are based on the Greek text. Since this study is prepared for lower division college students, who cannot be assumed to be familiar with that language, no commentaries on the Greek text are cited, except one on the Pastoral Epistles. The reason for that exception is that there is no satisfactory one on the English text for those books.

General

FARRAR, F. W. *The Messages of the Books.* New York: Macmillan Co., 1927.

MANLEY, G. T. (ed.). *The New Bible Handbook.* London: Intervarsity Fellowship, 1947.

TENNEY, MERRILL C. *The New Testament.* Grand Rapids: Wm. B. Eerdmans Publishing Co., 1953.

VOLLMER, PHILIP. *The Writings of the New Testament.* New York: Fleming H. Revell Co., 1924.

Archaeology

CAIGER, STEPHEN L. *Archaeology and the New Testament.* London: Cassell and Co., 1939.

COBERN, CAMDEN M. *The New Archaeological Discoveries.* Sixth Edition; New York: Funk and Wagnalls, 1922.

FINEGAN, JACK. *Light from the Ancient Past.* Princeton: Princeton University Press, 1946.

FREE, JOSEPH P. *Archaeology and Bible History.* Wheaton: Van Kampen Press, 1950.

Commentaries

Cambridge Bible for Schools and Colleges. Edited by J. J. S. Perowne. Cambridge: University Press, 1886.

CLARKE, ADAM. *The New Testament of Our Lord and Saviour Jesus Christ.* 2 vols. New York: Methodist Book Concern, n.d.

DUMMELOW, J. R. (ed.). *A Commentary on the Holy Bible.* London: Macmillan Co., 1909.

ELLICOTT, CHARLES J. (ed.). *Commentary on the Whole Bible.* 8 vols. Grand Rapids: Zondervan Publishing House, n.d.

Interpreter's Bible. Edited by G. A. Buttrick, *et al.* 12 vols. New York: Abingdon-Cokesbury Press, 1951. Liberal.

JAMIESON, ROBERT, FAUSSET, A. R., AND BROWN, DAVID. *A Commentary on the Old and New Testament.* 6 vols. Grand Rapids: Wm. B. Eerdmans Publishing Co., 1948.

LANGE, JOHN PETER (ed.). *Commentary on the Holy Scriptures.* 24 vols. Translated from the German, and edited, with additions, by Philip Schaff. Grand Rapids: Zondervan Publishing House, n.d.

New Bible Commentary. Edited by F. Davidson, *et al.* Grand Rapids: Wm. B. Eerdmans Publishing Co., 1953. The latest and best one-volume commentary on the Bible.

Pulpit Commentary. Edited by H. D. M. Spence. 23 vols. Grand Rapids: Wm. B. Eerdmans Publishing Co., 1950.

Geography

ADAMS, J. McKEE. *Biblical Backgrounds.* Nashville: Broadman Press, 1934.

DALMAN, GUSTAF. *Sacred Sites and Ways.* Translated by Paul P. Levertoff. London: Society for Promoting of Christian Knowledge, 1935.

SMITH, GEORGE ADAM. *The Historical Geography of the Holy Land.* Twentieth Edition; London: Hodder and Stoughton, n.d.

WRIGHT, G. ERNEST, AND FILSON, FLOYD V. *The Westminster Historical Atlas to the Bible.* Philadelphia: Westminster Press, 1945.

Introduction

CARTLEDGE, SAMUEL A. *A Conservative Introduction to the New Testament.* Grand Rapids: Zondervan Publishing House, 1938.

CLOGG, FRANK B. *An Introduction to the New Testament.* New York: Charles Scribner's Sons, 1937.

GOODSPEED, EDGAR J. *An Introduction to the New Testament.* Chicago: University of Chicago Press, 1937.

MILLER, ADAM W. *An Introduction to the New Testament.* Anderson, Indiana: Gospel Trumpet Co., 1943.

THIESSEN, HENRY C. *Introduction to the New Testament.* Grand Rapids: Wm. B. Eerdmans Publishing Co., 1943.

Chapter I. Why Study the New Testament?

DANA, H. E. *Searching the Scriptures.* Kansas City: Central Seminary Press, 1946.

HUNTER, ARCHIBALD M. *The Message of the New Testament.* Philadelphia: The Westminster Press, 1944.

Chapter II. The World into Which the New Testament Came

ANGUS, S. *The Environment of Early Christianity.* New York: Charles Scribner's Sons, 1920.

BOOTH, HENRY K. *The World of Jesus.* New York: Charles Scribner's Sons, 1933.

DANA, H. E. *The New Testament World.* Nashville: Broadman Press, 1937.

JOSEPHUS, FLAVIUS, *The Works of.* Translated by William Whiston. Philadelphia: Henry T. Coates and Co., n.d.

MATTHEWS, SHAILER. *New Testament Times in Palestine.* New and Revised Edition; New York: Macmillan Co., 1933.

SCHURER, EMIL. *A History of the Jewish People in the Time of Jesus Christ.* Authorized English Translation. 2 vols. Edinburgh: T. & T. Clark, 1890.

Chapter III. The New Testament Transmitted and Translated

GOODSPEED, EDGAR J. *The Making of the English New Testament.* Chicago: University of Chicago Press, 1925.

GOODSPEED, EDGAR J. *New Chapters in New Testament Study.* New York: Macmillan Co., 1937.

GREGORY, CASPAR R. *Canon and Text of the New Testament.* New York: Charles Scribner's Sons, n.d.

MAY, GEORGE GORDON. *Our English Bible in the Making.* Philadelphia: Westminster Press, 1952.

SOUTER, ALEXANDER. *The Text and Canon of the New Testament.* New York: Charles Scribner's Sons, n.d.

WEIGLE, LUTHER A. *The English New Testament.* New York: Abingdon-Cokesbury Press, 1949.

Chapter IV. The Messiah-King

BROADUS, JOHN A. *Commentary on the Gospel of Matthew* in *An American Commentary on the New Testament.* Edited by Alvah Hovey. Philadelphia: American Baptist Publication Society, 1886.

DODD, C. H. *The Parables of the Kingdom.* London: Nisbet and Co., 1936.

FILSON, FLOYD V. *Origins of the Gospels.* New York: Abingdon Press, 1938.

HAYES, D. A. *The Synoptic Gospels and Acts.* New York: Methodist Book Concern, 1919. The best introduction to these four books of the New Testament.

HUNTER, A. M. *A Pattern for Life.* Philadelphia: Westminster Press, 1953.

MORGAN, G. CAMPBELL. *The Parables of the Kingdom.* New York: Fleming H. Revell Co., 1907.

MORISON, JAMES. *A Practical Commentary on the Gospel According to St. Matthew.* London: Hodder and Stoughton, n.d.

PLUMMER, ALFRED. *An Exegetical Commentary on the Gospel According to St. Matthew.* London: Elliot Stock, n.d.

Chapter V. The Conqueror-Servant

BRANSCOMB, B. HARVIE. *The Gospel of Mark* in *The Moffatt New Testament Commentary.* Edited by James Moffatt. New York: Harper & Brothers, n.d.

MORISON, JAMES. *A Practical Commentary on the Gospel According to St. Mark.* London: Hodder and Stoughton, n.d.

Chapter VI. The Son of Man

GELDENBUYS, NORVAL. *Commentary on the Gospel of Luke* in *The New International Commentaray on the New Testament.* Edited by Ned B. Stonehouse. Grand Rapids: Wm. B. Eerdmans Publishing Co., 1951. Best recent commentary on Luke.

GODET, F. *A Commentary on the Gospel of St. Luke.* 2 vols. Translated from the second French edition, by Shalders. Edinburgh: T. & T. Clark, n.d.

MORGAN, G. CAMPBELL. *The Gospel According to Luke.* New York: Fleming H. Revell Co., 1931.

ROBERTSON, A. T. *Luke the Historian in the Light of Research.* New York: Charles Scribner's Sons, 1920.

Chapter VII. The Son of God

Addresses on the Gospel of St. John. Providence, R.I.: St. John Conference Committee, 1905.

HAYES, D. A. *John and His Writings.* New York: Methodist Book· Concern, 1917. Excellent introduction to John's writings.

HENDRIKSEN, WILLIAM. *New Testament Commentary: Exposition of the Gospel According to John.* 2 vols. Grand Rapids: Baker House, 1953-54. Excellent new commentary.

HOWARD, W. F. *Christianity According to St. John.* Philadelphia: Westminster Press, 1946.

LINN, OTTO F. *The Gospel of John.* Anderson, Ind.: Gospel Trumpet Co., 1942.

MORGAN, G. CAMPBELL. *The Gospel According to St. John.* New York: Fleming H. Revell Co., n.d.

TENNEY, MERRILL C. *John: The Gospel of Belief.* Grand Rapids: Wm. B. Eerdmans Publishing Co., 1948.

WESTCOTT, B. F. *The Gospel According to St. John.* Grand Rapids: Wm. B. Eerdmans Publishing Co., 1950.

Chapter VIII. Pentecost and Missions

BRUCE, F. F. *Commentary on the Book of the Acts* in *The New International Commentary on the New Testament.* Grand Rapids: Wm. B. Eerdmans Publishing Co., 1954. Best recent commentary on Acts.

HACKETT, HORATIO B. *A Commentary on the Acts of the Apostles* in *The Complete Commentary on the New Testament.* Edited by Alvah Hovey. Philadelphia: American Baptist Publication Society, 1882.

MORGAN, G. CAMPBELL. *The Acts of the Apostles.* New York: Fleming H. Revell Co., 1924.

RACKHAM, RICHARD B. *The Acts of the Apostles in Westminster Commentaries,* edited by Walter Lock. Eighth edition. London: Methuen & Co., 1919.

Chapter IX. Problems of the Primitive Church

GROSHEIDE, F. W. *Commentary on the First Epistle to the Corinthians* in *The New International Commentary on the New Testament.* Grand Rapids: Wm. B. Eerdmans Publishing Co., 1953.

HAYES, D. A. *Paul and His Epistles.* New York: Methodist Book Concern, 1915. Excellent.

MORGAN, G. CAMPBELL. *The Corinthian Letters of Paul.* New York: Fleming H. Revell Co., 1946.

PHILLIPS, J. B. *Letters to Young Churches: A Translation of the New Testament Epistles.* New York: Macmillan Co., 1947. Makes many passages come alive with new meaning.

Chapter X. The Meaning of Redemption

FINDLAY, G. G. *The Epistle to the Galatians* in *The Expositor's Bible.* Edited by W. R. Nicoll. New York: A. C. Armstrong and Son, 1893.

MOULE, H. C. G. *The Epistle of St. Paul to the Romans* in *The Expositor's Bible.* Edited by W. R. Nicoll. New York: A. C. Armstrong and Son, n.d.

RIDDERBOS, HERMAN N. *The Epistle of Paul to the Churches of Galatia* in *The New International Commentary on the New Testament.* Grand Rapids: Wm. B. Eerdmans Publishing Co., 1953.

TENNEY, MERRILL C. *Galatians: The Charter of Christian Liberty.* Grand Rapids: Wm. B. Eerdmans Publishing Co., 1951.

THOMAS, W. H. GRIFFITH. *St. Paul's Epistle to the Romans.* Grand Rapids: Wm. B. Eerdmans Publishing Co., 1946.

Chapter XI. Preaching from Prison

FINDLAY, G. G. *The Epistle to the Ephesians* in *The Expositor's Bible.* New York: A. C. Armstrong and Son, 1897.

JOWETT, J. H. *The High Calling: Meditations on St. Paul's Letter to the Philippians.* New York: Fleming H. Revell Co., 1909.

MILLER, H. S. *The Book of Ephesians.* Houghton, N.Y. Word-Bearer Press, 1931.

MOULE, H. C. G. *Colossian Studies.* New York: George H. Doran Co., n.d. Also in *Cambridge Bible.*

―――. *Ephesian Studies.* London: Hodder and Stoughton, 1900.

―――. *Philippian Studies.* London: Hodder and Stoughton, 1904. Also in *Cambridge Bible.*

ROBERTSON, A. T. *St. Paul and the Intellectuals.* New York: Doubleday, Doran and Co., 1928. On Colossians.

SIMPSON, A. B. *All in All, or Christ in Colossians.* New York: Christian Alliance Publishing Co., n.d.

THOMAS, W. H. GRIFFITH. *Christ Pre-eminent.* Chicago: Bible Institute Colportage Ass., 1923.

WUEST, KENNETH. *Philippians in the Greek New Testament.* Grand Rapids: Wm. B. Eerdmans Publishing Co., 1942.

Chapter XII. Pastor and People

MOULE, H. C. G. *The Second Epistle to Timothy.* Grand Rapids: Baker Book House, 1952.

SIMPSON, E. K. *The Pastoral Epistles.* Grand Rapids: Wm. B. Eerdmans Publishing Co., 1954. This commentary on the Greek text is the only up-to-date, scholarly, conservative one on these Epistles.

Chapter XIII. God's Last Word to Man

HAYES, D. A. *The New Testament Epistles.* New York: Methodist Book Concern, 1921. Good introduction to Hebrews, James, I & II Peter, and Jude. Does not accept the Petrine authorship of II Peter.

MACAULAY, J. C. *Devotional Studies in the Epistle to the Hebrews.* Grand Rapids: Wm. B. Eerdmans Publishing Co., 1948.

MANTLE, J. GREGORY. *Better Things.* New York: Christian Alliance Publishing Co., 1921. Brief, but very helpful.

MURRAY, ANDREW. *The Holiest of All.* New York: Fleming H. Revell Co., n.d.

THOMAS, W. H. GRIFFITH. *Let Us Go On.* Grand Rapids Zondervan Publishing House, 1944.

Chapter XIV. Persecuted and Purified

GLOAG, PATON J. *Introduction to the Catholic Epistles.* Edinburgh: T. & T. Clark, 1887.

ROBERTSON, A. T. *Studies in the Epistle of James.* New York: George H. Doran Co., 1915.

THOMAS, W. H. GRIFFITH. *The Apostle Peter.* Grand Rapids: Wm. B. Eerdmans Publishing Co., 1946.

Chapter XV. Purity and Perfect Love

CANDLISH, ROBERT S. *The First Epistle of John.* Grand Rapids: Zondervan Publishing House, n.d.

GORE, CHARLES. *The Epistle of St. John.* New York: Charles Scribner's Sons, 1920.

ROSS, ALEXANDER. *The Epistles of James and John* in *The New International Commentary on the New Testament.* Grand Rapids: Wm. B. Eerdmans Publishing Co., 1954.

Chapter XVI. Tribulation and Final Triumph

McDOWELL, EDWARD A. *The Meaning and Message of the Book of Revelation.* Nashville: Broadman Press, 1951.

NEWELL, WILLIAM R. *The Book of Revelation.* Chicago: Grace Publications, 1935.

RAMSAY, WILLIAM. *The Letters to the Seven Churches of Asia.* New York: A. C. Armstrong & Son, 1904.

SEISS, J. A. *Lectures on the Apocalypse.* Tenth edition. Grand Rapids: Zondervan Publishing House, 1951. Older standard premillennial work.

TRENCH, RICHARD C. *Commentary on the Epistles to the Seven Churches in Asia.* New York: Charles Scribner's Sons, 1862.

INDEX